The Horse of Pride

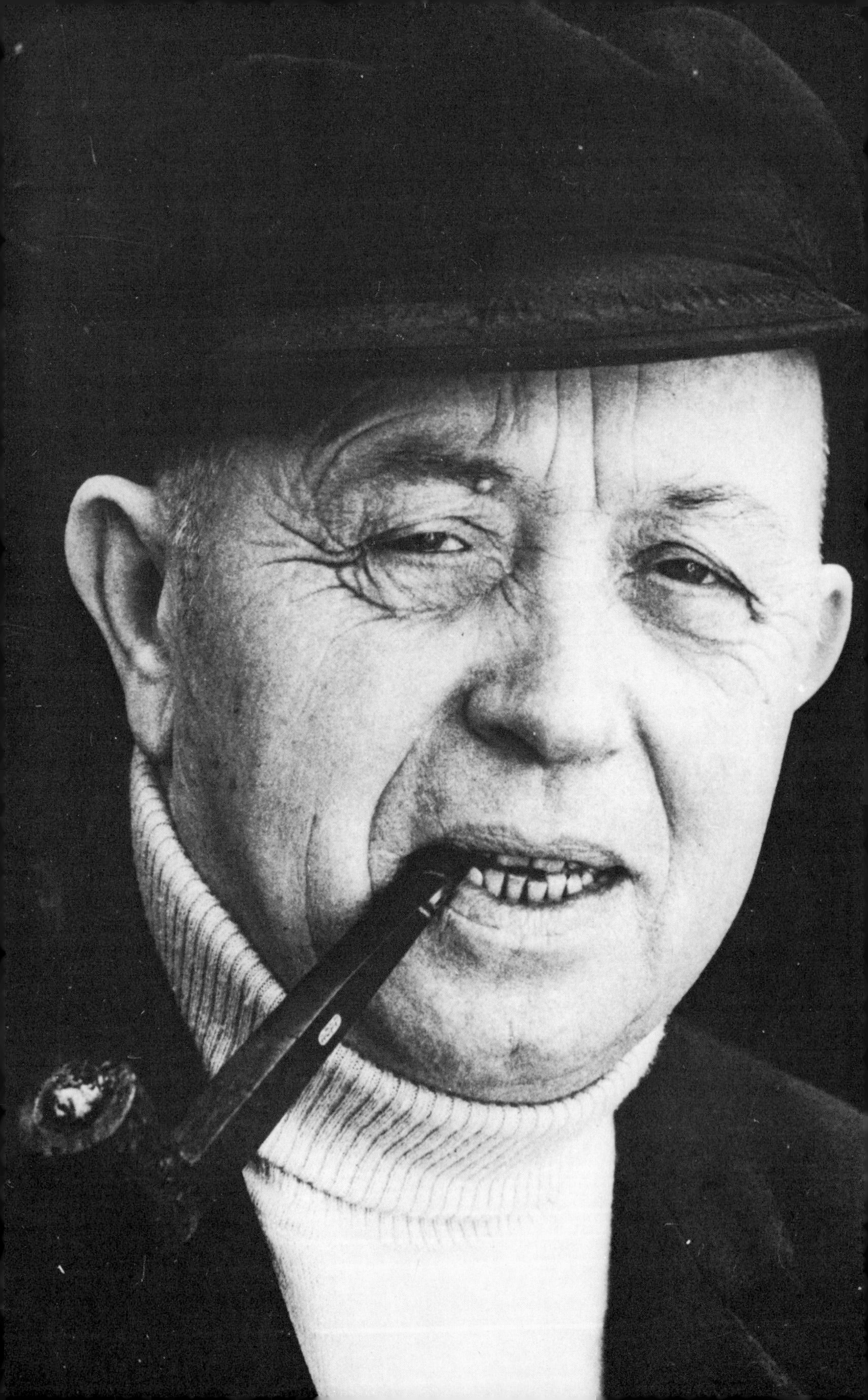

The Horse of Pride

Life in a Breton Village

Pierre-Jakez Hélias

Translated and Abridged by June Guicharnaud

Foreword by Laurence Wylie

New Haven and London
Yale University Press

Pierre-Jakez Hélias

Published with assistance from the
Kingsley Trust Association Publication Fund
established by the Scroll and Key Society of Yale College.

The Horse of Pride has been translated
from *Le Cheval d'Orgueil,* © 1975 by
Librairie Plon, Paris.

Second printing, 1978.

Designed by Sally Harris
and set in VIP Garamond type.
Printed in the United States of America by
The Murray Printing Company, Westford, Massachusetts.

Published in Great Britain, Europe, Africa, and
Asia (except Japan) by Yale University Press,
Ltd., London. Distributed in Australia and
New Zealand by Book & Film Services, Artarmon,
N.S.W., Australia; and in Japan by Harper & Row,
Publishers, Tokyo Office.

Library of Congress Cataloging in Publication Data

Hélias, Pierre-Jakez.
The horse of pride.

Translation of Le cheval d'orgueil.
1. Hélias, Pierre-Jakez. 2. Brittany—Social life and customs.
3. Brittany—Biography.
I. Guicharnaud, June. II. Title.
DC611.B9173H4413 944'.11 78-6929
ISBN 0-300-02036-8

*Since I am too poor to buy any other horse,
at least the Horse of Pride will always have
a stall in my stable.*

Alain Le Goff the Elder

Contents

Illustrations

Foreword

Pierre-Jakez Hélias's grandfather was so poor that he could not afford a horse. Still, he said, he would always have a horse in his stable—the Horse of Pride.

Le Cheval d'Orgueil is an epic, an epic of peasant life in Brittany during the first half of this century. It is also an ethnographic description of a culture that has all but disappeared. It is an intimate social history of the Third Republic. It is a case study in the quarrel over ethnicity. It is an account of a childhood. Above all, it is a gripping tale. Pierre-Jakez not only absorbed the lore of the three people who brought him up; he learned from them the art of storytelling, and he has spent his adult life talking about his native *pays bigouden*, the area of Pont l'Abbé, southwest of Quimper.

Hélias writes to arouse not pity but respect for the Breton peasant culture he knew. He vaunts the will of his people to accept their *condition humaine* and, thanks to the Cheval d'Orgueil, to lead a dignified existence. His *sabotier* grandfather told him:

> Whenever you hear a cry for help and there's no one anywhere around, it's your own unhappiness that's howling inside you. Or else it's the World Bitch, which has just jumped on somebody you know. Whenever that happened to me, I grabbed hold of my spade and started turning up the ground as if I were about to kill.

Hélias adds:

> He was a placid and gentle man, that grandfather of mine. And such types are often the most dangerous. That damned slut, the World Bitch, must have known it. [p. 18]

Wealth has little meaning in life. The basic virtue, which overcomes poverty and disaster, is a sense of human dignity, the cardinal virtue of the *livres de morale* of the Third Republic. The joys of life are found in honest labor, in adaptation to nature, and in the warmth of human relations: evenings before the fire when grandfathers tell stories, the simple (though extravagant for peasants) celebration of rites of passage and religious fêtes, the home leaves and eventual return of the father from the front, the ins and outs of neighbor and kin relationships, the struggle for and pride in school success. In later years during the tourist season there was always the fun of watching *les kodakeurs*, the exotic tourists, gaping at and trying to photograph the Bretons. Or rather the Bigoudens, for Hélias's country is the *pays bigouden,* the most picturesque of Breton *pays* because of the tall, slender coiffes of the women.

Professor of Celtic at the University of Rennes, Hélias has also written novels and poetry. For years he wrote for newspapers and directed radio and television programs. It comes as no surprise that his French is simple, popular, at once poetic and direct. But it is a surprise to learn that French is not his native language. Hélias writes his books in Breton and then translates them into French.

He gives a fascinating account of how he was forced to learn French when he was sent off to school. This process helps us understand what life was like for millions of children under the Third Republic, when the inexorable drive toward centralization destroyed provincial identity. In all parts of France, and even in the colonies, non-French-speaking children were required to speak only French. Each day at school the first child who uttered a word in his own language or dialect was given an object to wear around his neck—a stone, a trinket, anything. In Brittany this was called a *vache*, since "cow" was slang for a stupid person. The child had the right to rid himself of the *vache* only by passing it on to the next child who blundered into not speaking French. The *vache* passed from one child to another all day, and at the end of the day the child who was still wearing it was punished for the sins of all the culprits. Africans and Indochinese have told me they were involved in the same system in French schools they attended.

This little mechanism was a small detail among the vast array of inducements that forged unity among the infinitely varied elements that made up the French Empire. Any child who would learn French could become civilized and thus, to a degree, French. In this way the benefits of civilization, which the French equated with their own culture, were available to all. An ambitious family that wanted its bright child to succeed in life was willing to sacrifice its own cultural identity and, along with the government, exert its influence in socializing the child so as to merit a share in French civilization. This was the price of success in French society.

Hélias's career beautifully illustrates this ideal. His family spoke Breton and knew little French. One grandfather was a farmhand, the other a part-time *sabot*-maker. His father and mother both had to work away from home as well as farm the best they could the bit of land at their disposal. Their house was a dark cottage with a floor of clay—*toadmud*, they called it. They managed to eat decently, but cash was always short. There were few material possessions. A cheap watch was a family treasure. When Pierre-Jakez succeeded in the local school and won the right to go on with his education in Quimper they could not scrape up the money to fit him out properly. But the family sacrificed what it could for him and gave him moral support in his struggle to learn French. Eventually he succeeded through the educational system, just as the lay moralists of the Third Republic said he might.

This is not the only book on the *pays bigouden.* By coincidence it is the most thoroughly studied and analyzed *pays* of France. In 1960 the *Délégation générale à la recherche scientifique et technique* decided to organize an exhaustive study of a single French commune. They designated Plozévet, the birthplace of Hélias's father, only seven kilometers from Pouldreuzic, a contiguous commune and the home of his mother, where he himself was raised. Since Hélias takes for his subject the whole *pays bigouden*, his book includes both communes. The study of Plozévet began in 1962 and for five years was carried on intensively by interdisciplinary teams of hundreds of social scientists: anthropologists, medical researchers, psychologists, sociologists, demographers, ethnologists, geographers, historians. Indeed, research still continues, and social scientists from other countries have joined.

Naturally, there has been an avalanche of reports. Many have been published in articles and books; thousands of pages still lie in manuscript. Hours of film have been produced by ethnographic cinematographers. Two books in particular have been successful: Edgar Morin's *Commune de France: la Métamorphose de Plodémet*[1] and André Burguière's *Bretons de Plozévet.*[2] Although Hélias has a few good words to say about certain aspects of the project, he is on the whole skeptical, at times disdainful, about anthropological studies made by outsiders.

> The newcomers did some good work, it is certain, but they have had to admit that their assigned task was immense and delicate, even for multidisciplinary teams. Part of what was human, essential, always escaped them, slipped through the meshes of the tight nets thrown out by those fishermen whose functions ended in *-logue*. This was a source of amusement for an old man in Plozévet: "We've been eaten by the mice," he said. A wink and then: "They didn't get away with everything!"[3]

In this book Hélias gives us "what they didn't get away with," what some would call the "soul" of the society, the essence of the *pays bigouden* that escapes teams of social scientists. Both approaches are valid and indeed the two are complementary. The social science studies contain much information that enables us to compare the structure of Plozévet with that of communities elsewhere. This does not interest Hélias. His account contains fascinating, intimate details and analysis of values missed by the others.

Chronologically there is little overlap. The studies sponsored by the *Délégation à la recherche scientifique* emphasize Plozévet

1. Paris: Fayard, 1967. I do not know why Morin changed the name from Plozévet to Plodémet. A translation of this book has been published in the United States as *The Red and the White* (New York: Pantheon, 1970).
2. Paris: Flammarion, 1975.
3. *Le Cheval d'Orgueil* (Paris: Plon, 1975), p. 543.

since the Second World War. *Le Cheval d'Orgueil* is concerned mostly with the early years of the century. It is based on information that Hélias absorbed from his grandfathers and his mother, who together dominated this period of his life. (One wonders about his father; he is rarely mentioned, although he was around except during the First World War.) He gives us so intimate a glimpse of his family life before he was born that, as in the case of Tristram Shandy, we have the impression that he was witness as well as actor in his conception and birth. Since he is primarily preoccupied with his childhood experience, which he recounts admirably, his subject matter is limited to life in the *pays bigouden* before the Second World War.

This time difference is emphasized in the last chapter, entitled "The New Testament." Here he deals with Brittany in the last decades and describes in a few pages what life was like for him when he left home to carry on his education. The *pays bigouden* is left behind and Hélias's main concern moves to larger, more abstract questions. What does he mean by peasant civilization? What is the relationship of Breton peasantry to others? What brought about the decline of the civilization? What is the future of the Breton autonomy movement? He deals with these problems in concrete terms, however, so that his style is maintained. He says, "Comme dit à peu près Monsieur de Montaigne, je n'enseigne pas, je raconte," and even before I read this sentence I had been reminded of Montaigne's commonsense style and wisdom.

This book is a monument, a monument to a dead culture, for Hélias painfully but inescapably recognizes that Breton peasant culture is dead. It is ludicrous, even lugubrious, to think that a culture can be revived with such pitiful efforts as attaching a BZH plaque to the license plate of a car! The essential character of traditional Brittany depended on conditions that have disappeared or evolved: the isolation of the peninsula; the pervasive power of the Church in everyday life; the predominant use of the Breton language; the material, technical, and moral bases of the peasant condition. The centralizing force characterizing French history has done its work. Universal military service, public education, and mass culture have helped homogenize France.

In peasant cultures everywhere an individual's sense of identity is essentially associated with the countryside he has experienced personally. The people of the *pays bigouden* identified with *le pays*, not with the region or the province. Indeed they differentiated themselves from Bretons of other *pays*, ridiculing the cultural variations they encountered. They felt less in common with people from *pays* speaking other Breton dialects than with Bigoudens who had migrated to Paris. The larger Breton identity is an invention of the modern autonomy movement. By the time it was invented the combined experiences of the Third Republic had already forged the strongest patriotism of all, a patriotism of France. "J'ai deux amours, mon pays et Paris," the song goes, not "ma province et Paris." The shoulder-to-shoulder contact of Breton men with men from other parts of France during the First World War created a tie that transcended regions. No institution that does not develop from roots in the past can live, says Hélias.

He consoles himself for the death of his culture with a quasi-mystical conception of reincarnation. The essential virtues of *bigouden* peasant civilization live on, he says, through their fusion into the greater entity of French culture. This is the only way that Brittany may make a unique and substantial contribution that will benefit all French people. Hélias has written his account in order to describe this contribution explicitly; its warmth and intrinsic interest have brought understanding and pleasure to thousands of French readers.

When I first read the book I was saddened by the thought that it could not be made available to English readers. The task of translation seemed impossible. The style is colloquial. There are many Breton expressions, and sometimes even the French translation sounds strained because Hélias wishes to convey a flavor of Breton, the language in which he obviously *feels*. Furthermore, since much of the book is concerned with precise, practical aspects of everyday life there are technical terms for which equivalents do not exist in other languages. This homely sentence, for instance, from a description of how his mother made cakes: "Alors, ma mère lâche le *rozell* pour attraper une longue râclette de bois, la *spanell*, avec laquelle elle détache la galette de la tuile en commençant par les bords." Even more awkward to translate are implicit social distinctions. For most of us, a farmer is a farmer, but when one describes peasant France one must be precise about social and professional nuances among different kinds of farmers—*fermiers, métayers, maîtres, valets, laboureurs, ouvriers agricoles,* etc. The problem is complicated by the fact that the technical meanings may evolve over decades and vary from region to region; besides, one peasant may play two or three of the roles at once. What confuses the matter even more is that Hélias himself is not too precise.

June Guicharnaud has accomplished a miracle in this translation. To the degree that it is possible she has been precise, but at the same time she has expressed in English the earthiness of the text. So far as I can tell, we now have in English a translation that rivals Hélias's own French translation of his Breton text.

Laurence Wylie

A Breton storyteller fifty years ago

1 Like Father and Mother

> The un-named rank and file . . . miss their share of credit, as they must do, until they can write the despatches.
>
> T. E. Lawrence
> *The Seven Pillars of Wisdom*

When Pierre-Alain, my father, married Marie-Jeanne Le Goff, he had only one league to travel from the Kerveillant farm in Plozévet to reach the town of Pouldreuzic, where, from then on, he was to live with his wife. He went there on foot, holding his back straight as could be, because on his head he was carrying a pile of twenty-four hemp shirts, which constituted the bulk of his possessions. Indeed, those shirts were about all that his mother, Katrina Gouret, had been able to provide for his wedding. The hemp had been harvested, retted, and hackled at Kerveillant, and then spun on a wheel by Katrina herself. As usual. Once the thread was ready, it was twisted into two large skeins and brought to the weaver. The first skein, of pure hemp, was to be used for making potato bags. The threads of the second were a blend of hemp and wool, which made for a softer cloth. That one was to provide shirts for the entire household. Afterward, the shirts and the bags would invariably meet on people's backs, the shirt bearing the weight of the bag. Both would be liberally patched up when, because of wear and tear, the skin of a man or of a potato showed through. In addition, empty bags would be doubled up, one corner tucked into the other, and then serve as hoods and cloaks during the periods of heavy rain, since the poor devils at that time were unacquainted with any other type of outer garment. After my father had fought in the First World War, from beginning to end, the army allowed him to keep his last artilleryman's coat, which he had had cut into his first overcoat. It lasted him ten years.

The men and boys, however, did have linen shirts for Sundays. One, sometimes two. But they never enjoyed wearing them; for those shirts didn't cling to the body; they'd slip around on it. Also, they were too thin and made you feel naked. Luckily, you also had double-breasted waistcoats which came right up to your neck and generously covered your hips, so that you were sure to be protected on holidays, whatever the season. But nothing was better than hemp shirts for daily work. They virtually drank up your sweat, but never made you feel cold. They served as coats of mail for the poverty-stricken knights of the soil. Since they were worn both day and night, they had the same grayish hue at the end of the week as at the beginning. A blessing, I assure you. But you had to have a lot of them, because the laundry was done only twice a year, in the spring and in the fall. When the shirt you were wearing was completely stiffened by soil and sweat, you'd strip it off and throw it on top of a pile in some chest or in a corner of the shed. There it would await the big wash in April or September. And the whole cycle would begin all over again.

For the women, the big wash was a chore of great importance. Like all the really serious jobs, it lasted for three days, which corresponded to Purgatory, Hell, and Paradise, in that order. On the first day, the laundry was crammed into huge wooden buckets covered over with a *linsel skloagerez,* a kind of hemp cloth that was very loosely woven and therefore porous. A thick layer of carefully sifted ashes was spread on top of the shroud. In large caldrons, water was heated to the boiling point and then thrown over the ashes, which took the place of a detergent, for soap and other such products were unknown at the time or too expensive. Once the water was laden with ashes, it dripped through the coarse cloth, permeating and soaking into the laundry. The women then let chemistry do its work during the night. On the following day the whole pile was loaded into a wagon and brought to the public *lavoir,* or wash-trough.

There the women from the village and the surrounding countryside, armed with paddles, came to help on condition that they would be helped in turn. From dawn to four in the afternoon they would beat the laundry, not having eaten anything other than the broth they had gulped down before leaving. But their tongues never stopped wagging. After each piece was scoured clean in the first wash-trough, it was thrown into an adjoining one that was smaller and cleaner. When the last piece had been washed, one of the women would strip off all her lower garments and step down into the trough, her skirts tucked up all the way to her hips, to collect the laundry and hand it to the others, who would wring it out. More than one of them caught their deaths for having ventured into the cold water while in a sweat.

Then the laundry was spread out on some meadow or neighboring moor or, preferably, hung on clumps of dwarf gorse—a better way to dry and bleach it than having it lie flat on the grass. It was then, and only then, that the women would go off and eat. The next day one or two of them would spend all their time keeping an eye on the laundry and turning it over. Occasionally, ashes that hadn't been properly sifted had left spots, despite all the paddling. And those spots had to be removed or the laundresses might well have lost their reputations.

Every village had its own wash-trough, and often a double one, as I mentioned above. There were also several scattered around the town, each of which belonged to a "group"* that had its own customs and was in charge of keeping it in good repair. Moreover, there was no lack of streams. In April you could hear the paddles echoing all through the valleys. When children would ask for an explanation of the noises and blasts that woke them up early in the morning, they were told that it was the Horseman of Springtime riding in to open the flowers, cause the buds to burst, help the plants to rise out of the ground, and perform a thousand other tasks—the effects of which they would see if only they knew how

*See below, chap. 6. (Trans.)

to use their eyes. They might perhaps even see the Horseman himself if they got up before sunrise and held a certain seed in their hands—although no one ever explained precisely which kind. In September the same racket, but more muffled, would start up again. The Horseman of Springtime was departing; the good season was over until the next call of the cuckoo. And that was that.

My father's twenty-four hemp shirts never became acquainted with his body. My mother simply cut them up into dishrags without ever daring to tell Katrina Gouret, who would have been vexed. That was in 1913, when hemp was already becoming obsolete. One was able to get coarse linen shirts (*rochedou briz*) at fairs and at open markets or from peddlers who would wander through the countryside on foot. Only the old men remained faithful to hemp right to the end, along with the village show-offs and the strong men who were still proving themselves in Breton wrestling: the hemp shirt was an essential part of their athletic gear. Unlike bourgeois cloth, you could really grab onto it without any danger of it tearing. But those honorable men the weavers finally disappeared, one after another, for lack of work. And today many Bretons can no longer find out what professions lay behind their family names (*gwiaders*), which are carried on by their descendants. Time flies by.

My father was the eldest son of a poor couple who managed, with great difficulty, to make do by renting a small part of a house and a few fields of the large outlying Kerveillant farm. After him, to complete the brood, came six brothers and a little sister. They all lived in one single room which they entered by the gable. A mud floor, a large fireplace, a small barred window. It gave me the only opportunity I ever had to see, and to experiment with, a double-decker box-bed that slept four. A layer of broom took the place of a mattress, and the quilts were stuffed with bales of oats. Above the room was an attic which you reached by climbing a ladder and which was used for everything, sleeping included.

Also at their disposal was a manger large enough for two or three cows and about as many pigs, often less, but never more. In that house the fat itself was lean. My grandparents broke their backs working three pieces of land. In addition, they worked by the day on the large neighboring farms to earn a few extra sous or simply to pay off, with their own sweat, the loan of a horse or a wagon. They never stopped. When my grandmother Katrina had finished with her fields, her animals, her housework, and her children, she would immediately start spinning on her wheel. My grandfather Alain carved wooden shoes, which he would go out and sell in order to make ends meet. He was never called anything but "the sabot-maker," except when he was asked to tell his tales, sitting round the fire. Then he was "Jean the Wonder-Man" (*Yann ar Burzudou*). But that's another story.

My father was nevertheless able to attend elementary school until the age of twelve. The sabot-maker would have liked all of his children to be educated. He himself read passages out of books, and that was quite rare at the time for a man of his station. He could read both Breton and French, preferably aloud. Someone told me that he had once heard him, with book in hand, declaiming out in his field as a form of recreation. I myself saw him handling my schoolbooks as a priest would the Gospels. A man like that naturally had ambitions for his children's education.

At Kerveillant the school was nearby. Not even three-quarters of a league of sunken, muddy roads to wade through, then the potholes of the main road, and you were right in town, despite the winds and the rains. During the winter the children would leave at night and return at night. "We were resin-candle children," said my father. At noon the luckiest of them would eat a hunk of bread or some soup in the house of a friend or relative, while the others ate in the corner of a doorway, and that was that. Since my father was the eldest, my grandmother would entrust him with a few sous in order to see to it that the four others were as well fed as possible. But sometimes they couldn't resist the lure of a candy shop, for even the poor feel the need to live it up from time to time, and in such cases they had to last out, with empty stomachs, until they got their evening potato soup or gruel. An empty stomach and wet, worn clothing against the human hide. But no matter! They were tough and hard to kill. As for the cold, they took no notice of it. The talk of the town was a frail woman—an innkeeper and a baker—who would pull a pot of embers out of her oven to warm herself. She would then place the brazier on the floor, stand squarely over it, let her heavy skirts balloon out, and feel the heat rise along her legs toward whatever happened to be up there.

The most formidable trial for the little ones was crossing a frightening place called Pont-Ebeul in the dark or at dawn, if it was murky. The road sloped down into a narrow valley before passing through a stone archway over a stream. All sorts of wonders took place there. The most common was to see the water suddenly brighten into green, while, right in front of you, an altar would surge up, covered with a cloth and bearing two lighted candles. The altar blocked the bridge. It was useless to try and slip through to the right or to the left of it, for you were in danger of falling into the water or the mud, as a few people had learned at their expense. The best thing to do was to move straight ahead, unafraid. As you walked forward, the altar would gradually retreat. Finally, when it reached the level of a mill that rose up at the entrance to the town, it would disappear. One day, at the Ti-Lonk Inn, someone said that all you had to do was to turn around and take three steps backward. When you reached the bridge again, nothing was there anymore.

That altar, it appears, never harmed a soul. When a night owl once fell into the mud hole at exactly that spot, he was naturally accused of having had too much to drink. The green glimmerings were merely the reflection in the water of glow-worms that crawled about under the archway by the dozens. But when my father was a farmhand at Kergivig, one of his jobs was to help the women of the house cross through Pont-Ebeul on their way to six o'clock Mass on Sunday mornings. He would take that opportunity to climb down under the bridge and pick up a handful of glow-worms to convince the women that they had nothing to fear. But they never quite believed him.

The important thing on your way there was not to come upon the Man with Carrot Fingers, who had a preference for such places. He was described to me as a very tall character, wrapped in a large cloak, his head covered by a hat which hid his face and had a brim that fell way down over his shoulders. Sometimes he merely played a dirty trick on you—pushing you into the water, for example, with a good kick precisely where your back takes on a new name. At other times he would stop a carrier going to the fair and jump in next to him on the wagon seat. It was then that one could see his hands. They had very long and tapered fingers, similar to the white carrots fed to cows, with red hair on them instead of radicles. A few minutes later the wagon's tarpaulin would fly off, although there wasn't the slightest breeze. The carrier would get out, swearing hell fire and damnation, catch his tarpaulin, and then secure it firmly with four of those knots that only a man from Plozévet knows how to tie. After the wagon moved on about a hundred yards, the tarpaulin would fall straight to the ground. The miserable driver would pick it up again, double his knots, and tighten them with all his strength. Wasted effort. For a few minutes later the tarpaulin would gently slip off. And the poor man had to start over. And once he finally had climbed back into his seat, no one was there anymore.

Tricks like that were one thing. But if you were out walking, it might be that you'd hear the sound of steps behind you. Almost before you had the time to turn around, the Man with Carrot Fingers had caught up to you. He'd walk with you for a moment and then draw all the wisdom out of you, if you see what I mean, making you into a simpleton for the rest of your life. A man my father knew well had had much the same experience. Another one managed to do better. He was let off with his neck wrung and a crooked mouth, like someone who'd been caught in a strong wind at harvest time. But he never recovered.

Now around 1910 there were two vicars in Plozévet who were thought to indulge in "magical tricks." It was said that they were in possession of a book of magic that was perhaps an Agrippa, one of those tomes of wizardry that has to be tied down with a chain and whipped with all your might to keep it from moving. One of them especially, Monsieur C, had considerable influence on the population, including the free-thinkers, of whom there was never any lack out there. Indeed, people went so far as to insinuate, in undertones, that he might have been the Man with Carrot Fingers. Here's the story that really established his reputation. One day he went to lunch at the Rector of Lababan's, at least one league from Plozévet. Upon leaving the town, he passed in front of a forge. The blacksmith and his helper were doing everything humanly possible to hold down a horse that wouldn't stand still. "You're having a lot of trouble with that animal," said Monsieur C politely, as he walked by. The blacksmith, who was in a bad mood and who had no particular respect for the clergy on weekdays, muttered between his nose and his chin: "I'll be able to shoe him a hundred times before you've finished stuffing your belly at your crony's in Lababan, you old bag of grub!" Monsieur C, whose ears were very acute, heard him. "I'll bet," he said, "that on my return, this poor horse will still be barefoot." He then continued on his way to Lababan. "Go to the devil," screamed the blacksmith, sweating with anger and irritation.

Believe it or not, he went on exhausting himself the entire afternoon trying to control an unwilling animal. Although he knew the beast well, it had proved to be so nervous and cunning that he risked his life every time he even tried to take hold of its hoof. All afternoon an unremitting battle was waged between the blacksmith, dripping with perspiration, and the horse, whose hide steamed in the sun like laundry. Stubborn as only a Bigouden can be when he puts his mind to it, the man persisted, using every means possible, in trying to subdue the horse, by now a wild animal whinnying for all it was worth, tossing its head—its mane absolutely bristling—kicking its four horseshoes, minus one, and swinging around its rein like a flash of lightning. A horse straight out of the Apocalypse.

When the sun began to sink into the sea, Monsieur C passed by the forge again.

"Well, smithy, I told you so."

"You went and cast a spell over me," shouted the smith, at the end of his wits.

"A spell? What's that? Instead of blurting out idiocies, my friend, you'd do well to be patient for a while. Go on working that horse. When the evening Angelus rings, he'll calm down all by himself."

And it turned out just as he'd said.

Occasionally, my Uncle Alain hadn't managed to learn his catechism lesson, especially during the winter. How could he have? Every minute of the day was devoted to the school he went to, which was three-quarters of a league away, and he had to take mud roads to get there. He would leave at night with his brothers and would return at night, as I said before, to sort of scribble out his homework by the light of a resin candle. And on days when there was no school, he had thousands of unfinished jobs to do both outside and in, not counting the cows. So it wasn't a bit surprising that his catechism booklet had rarely left his briefcase.

One December day, in the early 1900s, the vicar of Plozévet who happened to be in charge of the catechism was so furious at Alain's ignorance that he put him in a corner of the church and then deliberately forgot him. Poor Alain, standing with his hands behind his back under the statue of Saint Isidore, stayed there a long time meditating on his unworthiness—which shows that though he failed to learn his catechism by heart, he was putting its doctrine into practice. Night had fallen by the time the vicar reappeared to oust the penitent, no matter how determined he was to beat his breast in that holy place until dawn. Alain set out for his Kerveillant farmhouse (*penn-ti*), somewhat worried at the thought of the reception he would get, and knowing full well that Saint Isidore could be of no help.

The night was dark, just barely lighted toward the west by that faint glimmer of Purgatory which always hovers over the sea when it's enraged and never fails to upset the boldest of nocturnal walkers. Probably in order to drive it out of his mind by removing it from his sight, the little boy left the road and took the first shortcut he could find. From then on, protected by high slopes and familiar copses, he moved ahead rapidly, at times almost running; for he was consumed by hunger, which had grown more acute as he'd stood at the feet of Saint Isidore. Suddenly, at the turning in a path and just a few feet in front of him, he noticed an odd character blowing on a low fire made of brambles and gorse. Indeed, he was blowing so hard that Alain could actually hear him, yet the fire refused to blaze. The boy stopped so that he could stand and watch with increasing astonishment: Lighting a fire at night in the middle of a country road? What a strange idea! And to begin with, who was the man? All he could see of him was a large back covered by an old, tattered cloak (*chupenn*) and a huge hat with a brim that fell over his shoulders and concealed his face. But little Alain was well acquainted with all the backs, all the old, torn clothing, and all the hats from Kerveillant to Plozévet. He didn't have to see the front of the man to be able to swear he wasn't from that region. Besides, what, if you please, does a Bigouden child do when he encounters a stranger at night on his own territory? He takes to his heels and rushes to inform his father. Alain turned and was about to flee when all at once everything surrounding him was in flames. The stranger had disappeared, leaving a diabolical laugh behind him. The fire spread to the slopes along the road. The gorse was crackling; the brambles were sputtering. Everything around the panicstricken boy was buckling into blazing red. It was as though the flames were alive and trying to lick him, like monstrous tongues. So he let out a piercing wail and, with his eyes closed, charged straight into hell.

He never knew how he'd got back to Kerveillant. But he was so frantic and in such a pitiful state that his father the sabot-maker (*my* grandfather) must have believed half his story, even though the boy couldn't show him one singed hair. The two of them, hand in hand, returned to the place where the miraculous phenomenon had occurred. Alain was sniffling a bit, but his father was of the opinion that one mustn't allow a child to remain in a state of fear, any more than one would an animal. And there were no traces of fire on that hell-infested road.

"You were the victim of a goblin," said the sabot-maker.

"That's not true. I was wide awake. I saw the whole thing with my living eyes. It was blazing all around and in front and in back, I swear."

"Hmm! And tell me why you were so late getting home!"

The child had to explain all about how he hadn't known his catechism, how the priest had been displeased—very displeased—how he'd been punished by having to stand under the feet of Saint Isidore, and about the glimmer of Purgatory over the sea.

"It was Monsieur L who taught you the catechism, wasn't it?" asked the sabot-maker.

"Yes."

"Then he played a magic trick on you, my son. Monsieur L knows how to do them. He has the Book. And you have no excuse. He wanted to punish you for your ignorance. It serves you right."

Whenever my father happened to talk about his years in elementary school, he would always recall the trouble he'd had with a teacher who, according to him, was an excellent educator but extremely brutal and known for being unfair. Still, it was unfortunate that my father had been forced to give up his studies before he could receive his elementary-school diploma, which was, you might say, the doctorate of poor devils such as he. The principal, who had few illusions, came to seek out the sabot-maker of Kerveillant.

"Let me have your son for one more year. Just one year."

"I can't, sir. One year is too long for a man as poor as I. He's my eldest. There are six others, not counting my little girl. I need him to help me feed them. If I had any alternative . . ."

The eldest son was first hired at Kerfildro, the farm my mother came from. There, on the job, he completed his training. The following year he was a farmhand at Lestrougi. Then he spent four years at Kervinou and two at Kergivig, where he was the foreman; in other words, he had reached the height of his career. Those four farms were very near to one another and to Kerveillant as well, which was considered the cradle. If my father kept going from place to place, it was not because he was dissatisfied or unstable. It was so that he might move up in the hierarchy of farmhands and obtain higher salaries as he made his reputation. Also, he sometimes changed places so that he could work for an employer who knew his business better than the others. The big farmers* were well aware of the value of the laborers in the vicinity and even in the adjacent counties. They were able to judge them either from big jobs, when everyone worked together, whether clearing the land or threshing, or by how they maintained their own fields and in what condition they kept the animals that had been entrusted to them. And there were even more subtle criteria, such as a laborer's repertoire of Breton or French songs; his ability to dance the gavotte; his strength and skill when it came to public games, which were in fact tests; his devotion to his duties; and the number

*The term as used throughout is ambiguous. For a precise definition, see below, pp. 225–26. (Trans.)

of times he frequented inns. Everything counted when it came to evaluating a man or a woman. Each one of them could expect to be constantly "on other people's tongues," as they say in Breton, favorably or unfavorably. And people's tongues never stopped praising you to the skies or helping to bring about your undoing. All you needed was a somewhat pronounced trait of character or mode of behavior to receive a nickname that stuck to your skin for the rest of your life. In consideration of which, everybody knew precisely with whom he was dealing and would never think of buying a pig in a poke.

That was how the sabot-maker's eldest son gradually became well known as a "magnificent worker" (*labourer kaer*). From contract to contract, his wages increased perceptibly. During the first years it was his father who went to fetch them. They somewhat improved the family's circumstances and were extremely welcome. But the other children were nevertheless obliged to leave the nest very early on and to seek their fortunes elsewhere. That accounts for the names given them by the family: Corentin de la Marne, Alain de la Somme, Jacques de Lorient, Michel de Rezé, Guillaume de Rennes, and Henri de Paris. Only their little sister, Marie-Jeanne, was married in Plozévet and lives there still, in the house the sabot-maker had had built at the edge of a pinewood, in the last years of his life.

Even more important than wages were food and esteem, which always went together. In those days, country children often lived with a partially empty gut. To them all the plants that were remotely edible and didn't give you the runs—from wild sorrel to primroses, all the berries that grow along the roads, all the fruits in the orchards, and all the vegetables in the open fields—were things to be coveted. When they stole, it was more out of need than gluttony. The October chestnuts, in particular, provided the best evening meals. The children would go out "chestnuting" for the whole family. But the trees were strictly guarded by certain landowners who kept a jealous watch over their property. My father told us how he was once caught by the neighborhood miller just as he was snitching chestnut shucks in the woods around the mill. He happened to be high up in the branches of the tree when the owner arrived unexpectedly and began throwing rocks at him, as one would at a squirrel. The child had to slide down to the ground, where the demon grabbed him by the collar and dragged him to the channel that supplied the millwheel. In a state of rage, the man called him every offensive name he could think of and threatened to drop him on the wheel, which might have broken all his bones. He would indeed have done just that, had it not been for his wife, who was a good person. She warned him that if he were responsible for anything serious happening to the child, the sabot-maker from Kerveillant would come and call him to account for his behavior with an ax. My father got off with a bad fright and the loss of his bag, which was a great misfortune for a poor little boy.

In his station as foreman, the harder he worked, the better he was fed. That was more or less the general practice. The amount each laborer received depended not on his appetite but on the work he had accomplished. Even the size of the soup bowl was proportionate to each one's output. Sometimes the big farmer's bowl was smaller than his foreman's, if the one had sweated more copiously than the other. On the other hand, the largest bowl on the table would sometimes belong to the horse, which was being fattened up for the mid-April fair. Don't misunderstand me: the horse didn't come to eat at table. The soup was poured into its trough once the bread had been properly soaked through. But the very presence of that equine soup-tureen showed how important the horse was as an asset.

Moreover, in certain places the foreman's preeminence was due to the fact that he was responsible for the horse or horses, and capable of getting the best out of them, while at the same time keeping them in good condition. He was required, most especially, to know how to whistle in such a way that they would pee at a specific time—or "pour themselves out," as the saying goes. It was no small matter. Some farmhands never managed to do it. The foreman was also the one who not only rode the finest of the animals on the farm when there were races or shows, but who got them into the sea, into the Bay of Audierne, for their yearly ritual bath.

In short, the foreman represented the farm to which he was contracted almost as much as the big farmer or his tenant. In the outside world he had to do honor to his superiors on every occasion. That explains why he would always try to be the best on those big jobs when everybody worked together, especially during the harvesting and the land-clearing.

At that time the moors and the coppices were still being cleared in order to make fields that would bring in some income. But the main job was to restore plots of land that had not been worked for several years. Very hard on the arms. Stiff and overabundant ground-cover, with roots that had got entangled with dwarf gorse, had to be dug up. That was done with the help of a large hoe, called a *marre.* Everyone had his own, which he would keep in as good condition as possible by means of his very own devices. Each time, before the start of that exhausting chore, the hoe had to be heated in the fire at the forge and beaten on the anvil. The iron, which had been specially hardened, sometimes broke but never bent.

On the appointed day, at the crack of dawn, the men would gather at one end of the field that was to be cleared. Each farm had delegated either the big farmer himself or the foreman, and sometimes both. The owners would line everybody up, taking care to skillfully single out the strongest and most courageous of them to lead the others. When the signal *eom de'i!* ("Off you go!") was given, they'd launch into their work and not stop—except to eat, drink, or pee—until they had come face to face with the slope across the way. The best of them did everything in their power to stay out in front, while the others made it a point of honor to follow as well as they could. A cloud of dust covered all those chaps wielding their hoes. Few words were exchanged. Suddenly, some boss or some foreman who felt that he had to prove himself would forge ahead with all his might and take the lead. There was always someone else who just couldn't bear that challenge and would give all he had in order to overtake him. The rest of the group, shouting and screaming, would cheer on the competitors. But the game never lasted very long. After all, the men had to save their strength in order to see the day through. Besides, going fast wasn't everything. A far better idea was to plow deep down and to pick up the roots carefully, putting them to one side as you moved along. Afterward they would be piled up in the farmyard and serve as fuel to heat the animals' food. Firewood was rare and expensive. Nothing was allowed to go to waste.

Meanwhile, at the house, the women were bustling about preparing crêpes for all those laborers. And, believe me, they had to make over a dozen of them for every hoe functioning out there. When lunchtime came round, each one had to wait his turn to fill his belly. The older men ate first and then left the benches to the young men. Among the *crêpières* there were always a few girls with good figures. They had been chosen by the mistress of the house to please the boys, who never failed to joke with them and give them a hug. Then, in order to shake themselves free, the girls would smack them in the face with one of the rags they used to grease the griddle. That mark of interest (or perhaps of affection, who knows?) sent the boys who received it into transports of joy. They'd return to the fields very proud of themselves and blacker than coal miners. Not for all the gold or money in the world would they have washed their faces before evening.

The poor people who worked for others during the day would group together and figure out ways to clear their own uncultivated land at night, by the light of the moon. They had already broken their backs from sunrise to sunset. But none of them ever balked at having to sacrifice their time of rest if it meant helping someone of the same station as themselves. Occasionally the big farmers would go to bed, but the foremen were always on the site, whether by command or out of good will. It has even been said that those night land-clearings were in fact parties, because everyone who participated was among his equals.

I shall have the opportunity to return, time and again, to that civilization of the soil to which we all belonged. At this point, I am merely repeating what my father told me personally about a time before I was born. In those days a strange Doctor N used to be seen capering about the county astride a spirited, formidable horse. Whenever he had notified someone of a death sentence or helped a child come into this world, he would always go on singing or whistling the same tune. People used to say that he was a "nutty scientist" (*eun droch desket*). He would speak to his horse using words he himself had invented, and his horse would answer him in the same language.

Meanwhile, the time for military service was drawing near. My father was sent to the 35th Artillery Division in Vannes, and to the stables, as was only fitting for a foreman. From that period of his life he kept a thick notebook filled with Breton and French songs which he had had copied and illustrated by a noncommissioned officer, to whom he gave the few sous he earned. When he returned to Plozévet, all he needed was to find himself a wife. He met Marie-Jeanne Le Goff.

Thus spake my father.

The lives of poor people rather often resemble those novels or plays which self-satisfied bourgeois critics, in comfortable circumstances, call bad melodrama. My mother had been obliged to assume responsibility for her family when she was only eleven. Her own mother had just died at the age of thirty-eight, having been struck down at the wash-trough, where she had gone to work too soon after her last delivery. She left eight children to be cared for, my mother being the eldest of the girls. My Aunt Lisette, who was then three months old, was still in the cradle. My grandmother, who for three weeks had been running a high fever, called my mother to her bedside on the eve of her death and gave over the household to her, weeping for the last time. The little girl, in spite of her grief, took careful note of the instructions she received. When his wife breathed her last, my grandfather Alain Le Goff fainted on the bench attached to the box-bed. He was the best man I have ever had the opportunity to know in this world, here below. He was to faint again when the body was put into the coffin and yet again when it was lowered into the grave. It is no exaggeration, nor is it by any means literature, to say that he had lost his one and only. During the years that followed—despite circumstances that could hardly have been more uncertain, and his large family of children—he was proposed to on behalf of a woman in the vicinity whom everyone considered a good match. He refused that honor as an act unworthy of him. He never wanted to remarry. Besides, all his children and their families were grateful and affectionate to him right to the end. Indeed, that man discouraged ingratitude. I don't know exactly what stuff he was made of, but he was so serene in his rectitude that you would have sworn it was effortless. I was just about twenty when he died and was going to a school of so-called higher learning. But no philosopher ever impressed me as much as he. When I'm sorely tempted to admire someone, I see Alain Le Goff's face before me again and am sure not to lose my head. Don't, please, speak to me of heroes.

From that time on, my mother saw to everything. She began straightaway. While the dead woman was still on her bed, the little girl was receiving people on behalf of her father, who was overwhelmed by sorrow. She attended to all the provisions necessary for the vigil. On the day of the burial, in accordance with the custom, she had to feed the whole family, which arrived from the four corners of the county. She gave up the convent school, where she had shown great promise of receiving a diploma. During the weeks that followed, neighboring women came to inquire after little Lisette in her cradle—a skinny child who often threatened to bid them all farewell. One or another of the women, who was then nursing her own offspring, would remove the pins from her undershirt and give her breast generously to the motherless child. In the end Lisette chose to live. And, for the most part, the visits stopped. What could you expect? All those people, or almost all, were struggling night and day to earn a living. Besides, there were other misfortunes that had to be dealt with elsewhere. Alain Le Goff's mother-in-law stayed on only a few days after her daughter's death. Instead of helping, she never ceased complaining, though she had a hearty appetite. She was a constant annoyance to my mother, who had enough on her hands caring for the five little ones. Luckily, she went home very soon, pleading deadly fatigue. Her son-in-law and her grandchildren didn't see her again for several years. When she was too old to fend for herself, she wanted to come and live with them. That good man my grandfather would have welcomed her willingly, but my mother firmly opposed it. Not out of spite, but because at that point, her family didn't go back any further than her father. And there was nothing more to say about it.

Then began an unremitting struggle against the "World Bitch."

Early in the century, in the Bigouden region, many people were still poverty-stricken. It was a disaster, like so many others, and one you couldn't do much about. The slightest blow of fate was enough to bring down those who were already victims of the Devil, yet didn't have him "living in their purses," nor were they "pulling him by the tail," as they say in French; in other words, their purses weren't empty, they weren't hard up. Yet a shipwreck, some infirmity, a disease that afflicted men or animals, a stable fire, a bad harvest, an overly harsh employer, or merely the seven daily misfortunes would force you out onto the roads for a time, begging from door to door, a prayer between your teeth, and your eyes shut to block out the humiliation. Sometimes the men chose to hang themselves, and there was always a rope in the shed which was there for the asking. The women preferred to drown themselves, and there was always a well in the farmyard or a wash-trough at the bottom of the field. Indeed, poverty was so obsessive that people expected to encounter it, at any turn in the road, in the form of a raw-boned, shaggy bitch, its chops curled back, showing yellow teeth: the World Bitch. It was mute and sly, so that nothing ever warned you of its arrival: that was the tragedy.

Beware of the World Bitch
Which jumps on you and never barks.

For a long time, my grandfather Alain Le Goff dreaded the World Bitch, but he always managed to protect himself from it. He told me several times how, when he happened to be alone in the middle of the fields, he didn't dare stop working because the World Bitch always crept in the very moment there was a pause. He also said: "Whenever you hear a cry for help and there's no one anywhere around, it's your own unhappiness that's howling inside you. Or else it's the World Bitch, which has just jumped on somebody you know. Whenever that happened to me, I grabbed hold of my spade and started turning up the ground as if I were about to kill." He was a placid and gentle man, that grandfather of mine. And such types are often the most dangerous. That damned slut, the World Bitch, must have known it.

Alain Le Goff went right on making every effort to feed his family. Indeed, he did so well that none of his children ever knew what it was to go hungry. As for himself, he contrived to pick up his own food as best he could outside the house, yet without ever wronging a soul. Most of the time, when he got home, he'd claim that he had already eaten. And when a ten-pound loaf of bread was almost down to the heel, he would casually announce that he had absolutely no appetite. The children never asked questions.

He was born one league from there, in the parish of Landudec, of poor day-laborers who lived in a hamlet called "Poull ar Markiez." Orphaned at a very early age, he was taken in by his godfather, a sort of gamekeeper at the large manor house in Guilguiffin and who, in addition, had kept a small farm not far from the parish church, where he was the verger. My grandfather had several sisters, all of whom were scattered here and there at their godfathers' or godmothers', as was the custom in those days whenever parents were lacking. After two or three years at school, he worked on his guardian's farm and did many of the latter's other tasks as well. He would go from the cows to the plough and from the plough to the church bells. Then he left to do his stint of military service, which gave him the opportunity of becoming acquainted with Africa and, especially, the holy city of Kairouan, which he regularly recalled to mind—why, I never knew, since he said nothing about it. When he returned home, he took a wife from the Kerdaniel farm, an annex of the Guilguiffin manor house. And soon the chestnut cradle was filled with one child after another.

After a few years he came to live in the county of Pouldreuzic, having gotten a small job there as an assistant district road-repairman. But his contract was such that for several years he had to work outside the county, at Peumerit and Treguennec. He would leave at night once he had swallowed some soup, and, wearing his wooden shoes, would walk three to nine kilometers in the dark, and over bad roads, in order to get to the site by sunrise. He would then return at night, having gone a roundabout way in order to make a stop at some familiar woodland or farm. In his bag he often brought back vegetables, fruits, chestnuts, medlars, pine cones, and dead wood. He had asked for them and received them, because the owner was a true friend of the family, for grandfather would never have wanted to take even a handful of wild sloe without asking the owner's permission.

In the summer my mother would get up at dawn, and in the winter, well before. She'd begin by carefully putting on her coiffe, or headdress—a complicated procedure which she had learned to do properly by the age of six. She would then make the pig's slop, milk the cows, prepare breakfast for the children, get them up, send them off to school, lead the cow to the field a half-league away, knit on her way back, do the housework, wash the clothes, get the midday meal ready, crochet as she returned to the field, work the land with as much strength as she could muster, come back pulling the cow by its rope and with a load of hay on her back or a heavy basket in her hand, find her children at home, make them behave and do their homework, mend the worn clothing, rage and fume or laugh heartily, depending on the circumstances, cram some more food down the pig, milk the cow a second time, cook the gruel or the potatoes, do the dishes, put the whole brood to bed, tidy up, return to her crocheting or her sewing by the light of a small, portable kerosene lamp, wait for her father, and not get to bed until he had.

That was her life from the time she was eleven until she was twenty, with no respite whatever. On Saturdays she would rub down the furniture with all her might and polish the brass nails, one by one. Every three months, provided with a proxy, she would go to Plonéour to cash her father's money order. She had only to walk nine kilometers each way, and it was no waste of time. As she trotted along, she would crochet lace, which brought her a few silver coins to buy handkerchiefs and aprons, if she had managed to make ends meet. Occasionally, on feast days, she'd find the time to strut around the town square with the other girls, once she had pinned onto the ribbon of her coiffe, at the level of her ear, a large red rosette called "the Pompadour"—a name that's synonymous with pride.

The most dazzling event of her life, at age fifteen, was the wedding of one Marie-Louise Le Rest, which revolutionized the whole town and attracted all the well-to-do people in the county. Nine hundred attended the wedding feast. The embroiderer Baptiste Alanou and his brother Sylvestre had spent months making up the gala Bigouden costumes, all of them embroidered in green and yellow. Never again did anyone see six dozen of them at the same time. The very poor girls were absolutely wide-eyed, trying in vain to take in the whole spectacle. When Marie-Jeanne Le Goff went home, she discovered, alas, that a thief had gone through the house, knowing it was empty, as were all the others on the occasion of that first-class wedding. He had taken half the bread, half the butter, and an alarm clock which was the family's pride. Panic-stricken, she ran off to find her father, who was in charge of pouring the wine at the feast because of his reputation as a sober man. Alain Le Goff wasn't particularly upset when he heard about the disaster.

"Well!" he said, smiling. "Now one more person has a full stomach. And I'm glad to know that he still has something of a conscience, since he left us a bite to eat for tomorrow."

"But father, the alarm clock?"

"Yes, of course, the alarm clock. But you've got to admit that he couldn't have taken just half of it."

Later on, they learned that the thief, a man from a neighboring county, had tried to sell the alarm clock to farmers in Laraon, with no success, as it turned out. By the time he was arrested, the clock had disappeared. My grandfather took it upon himself to save enough money, at the expense of his stomach, to buy a hanging clock for his daughter. Eighteen months later he had the necessary twenty francs. The clock was screwed onto the kitchen cupboard. It is still there.

Marie-Jeanne Le Goff's main place of work was the house in which she lived all her life. The family had barely moved in when their mother died. Before that, they had had pitifully inadequate lodgings, which they shared with the animals, in a tradesman's courtyard. In Pouldreuzic many other honorable people were just as badly housed; but it's understandable that when Alain Le Goff first rented our present house, the entire family had felt they were being transported to a palace. And that palace became their very own property a few months later. I must say that, for once, luck had been on Grandfather's side. In those days everything that was for sale inevitably fell into the hands of a few families of notables who already owned a good half of the town, having been unable to buy anything in the country, where the farms were either annexes of the nobility's manor houses or belonged to bourgeois from Quimper. Property in the sun was then considered preferable to wealth in the form of money. People would always buy, and they would sell only if they were somehow forced or driven to do so.

Selling land was thought to be a premonitory sign of one's downfall. The notary public would be informed the moment word got about that the merest shack or the most indifferent moor was in danger of changing hands.

As it happened, my grandfather was the first to know that the owners of our house were in such reduced circumstances that they had to part with it immediately, if they were to avoid living out their last days in hunger. He didn't have a sou to his name, but because of his good reputation he found willing lenders, and the deal was concluded before the news had leaked out. When one of the most important notables, who was sick in bed at the time, learned about it, he made his children a frightful scene, accusing them of wanting to bankrupt him by missing out on a transaction he would have made, had his fever not clogged his ears. Now it was too late. But Alain Le Goff had piled up debts amounting to 1,500 francs—in other words, a fortune for a man of his station. For years he was unable to sleep in peace. Then Jean, his eldest son, joined the army to fight in Indochina. He handed over his entire enlistment bounty to his father. The postman brought it in a sackcloth bag brimming over with five-sou coins. All the riches of Golconda trickled onto the table. The next day the balance of his debt was paid off, and from then on, Alain Le Goff indulged in a packet of tobacco a week, or almost.

Separate from the house was a manger for the animals. There was a farmyard in the back, large enough for a pile of straw and a shed for the rabbits, the tools, and "the conveniences." Inside, there were two real rooms on either side of the hallway, and a large fireplace in the one to the east. There was a loft for the corn, buckwheat, kidney beans, and potatoes. There was even another stone fireplace in that loft, around which they could perhaps build a room later on, once they had enough money. The Le Goffs were more than delighted.

Of course, there was still a lodger in the room to the west—a weaver by the name of Hénaff, whose loom would bang away all through the day and sometimes at night, when he had a rush job. But he was an honest, peaceable man. On the other hand, the few sous he paid as rent were such a necessity and so anxiously awaited that the family kept an eye out for his customers when they came to pay for the finished product. I might add that the weaver never failed to settle his accounts as soon as he could. Whenever he placed the money on the table, my mother would heave a sigh of relief, for, like as not, she had just spent her very last coin. She would open a bottle of wine as a treat for the old boy. It was always the only bottle of wine in the house. The family drank water, their one extravagance being a cask of *piquette,* a kind of tart substitute for wine which Marie-Jeanne, in her free time, would make out of a bowl of molasses or barley, colored with chicory.

Everyone was truly distressed when they had to ask the weaver to leave. But after all! The children were growing up, and the girls simply had to have a room to themselves. Now, as it happened, half of the house next door was for rent. So the loom was dismantled part by part, all put together again just twenty meters away, and that's all there was to it. But the wretched weaver could never get used to his new dwelling. You figure it out. Shortly afterward, he came to see his former lodgings again. As he was leaving, he said to my mother: "Marie-Jeanne, I really can't live over there." The next day he was found hanging directly above his table. He had put on his best suit and had carefully shined his shoes for the journey, like the respectable Christian he was. It is well known that no Breton can be held responsible for his despair, which must be attributed to his "star." And everyone hoped that, although he had taken his own life, the honest artisan would be allowed to sit at the right hand of the Father. Amen!

Unfortunately, my family's expenses turned out to be more than they had figured on and they could not make do without the rent from the room to the west. Shortly after the girls had moved in, they had, somehow or other, to fix up the end of the loft around the stone chimney. They found a lodger for that cubicle at once, but he was not cut from the same cloth as the weaver. A jack-of-all-trades, he would sort of find something to do at the baker's on the square when the work was easy and when he had made up his mind to work, but those two conditions rarely coincided. In other words, it was difficult to see the color of his money—a problem compounded by the fact that he preferred to invest it in strong drink. When he was in a normal condition, he was bearable, although no one quite knew how to take him. But when he had alcohol in his blood, he'd become violent. My first years of life were poisoned by the fears he would arouse in me and in which he took malicious pleasure. I am bringing up the subject straightaway so as not to have to return to that unpleasant character.

Once in a while I would be alone in the house when he'd return unexpectedly. At such times I'd squat down under the mantel. I would hear him drag his sabots in the hall, muttering to himself. He'd strike the wooden partition savagely with his stick out of sheer spite, because he knew I was there trembling in a corner of the hearth, all crouched down against the stones darkened by soot. As he walked past my door, he'd put his thumb on the catch and rattle it several times as if he were about to come in. But he never did. He would lumber up the steps, rubbing his shoulder against the partition. I'd wait until he had opened his door upstairs before I would painfully make my way out on shaky legs and take refuge in the field across the way until my parents returned. But the old brute had more than one warped trick up his sleeve. I once heard a noise in his lock and thought he was closed into his hovel. After a few minutes I opened my door to escape. Then I saw him squatting at the turn in the stairway and looking at me with terrifying eyes. He had moved his key around in the lock, but instead of going in, he had come down again to frighten me. I was then about six years old. If I didn't drop dead that day, it was only because my heart is firmly jammed between my ribs. With a wad of tobacco in his mouth and saliva dribbling down his chin, he said sneeringly from the top of the stairs: "You're gonna tell your father, aren't you, you little snot!" At the sight of my giant of a father, he became gentle as a lamb. I said nothing about it to the head of the family so as not to be accused of lacking pride. But from then on, whenever he'd arrive unexpectedly, I would slip out through the window.

In point of fact, that old man covered us with shame. He would urinate into an old pot, which he emptied out of his garret window onto the road. It made a blackish streak on the slate of the roof. Our house was thus disgraced in the eyes of the passersby. Of course, my grandfather's mild admonishments had absolutely no effect. Finally, old age got the better of that lazy lout. He became bed-ridden, was taken to the poorhouse in Pont-l'Abbé, and died there shortly afterward. Alain Le Goff shed a few tears for him, but he would have wept for Judas himself. As soon as the lodger was gone for good, the first thing my father did was to place a ladder against the front of the house and clean the roof. Once the garret was scrubbed down with *eau de Javel*, a form of chlorine, we breathed more freely. The field across the way began to smell good again. And much later on, the garret became my room.

Everything considered, the Le Goffs' financial situation continued to improve over the ten years that followed my grandmother's death. The eldest boy—at first a soldier in Indochina, where he had been made an officer, and who had returned only to be killed at the front during World War I—allotted a large share of his pay to his father. The second was employed by a pork butcher in Quimper and was soon in a position to provide for the family out of his salary, which he never failed to do. The two others joined the Navy. At the time, two of the girls, Marguerite and Marie, were already employed as maids in good houses. Given the kind of culture we were born into, it was honorable work. When my mother reached the age of twenty, she had only one little sister to look after. Sometimes she even had the time to fold her hands and do nothing, knowing full well that no one in the house, except perhaps her father, had ever gone hungry while she'd been in charge. For a short while, there had apparently even been a gold coin, bearing the head of Napoleon III, stashed away in the cupboard. The family hadn't been able to keep it, of course, but all of them had held it in their hands.

My mother had already been proposed to more than once when my father came to ask for her hand. Obviously, she hadn't the slightest dowry, nor any hopes of one. A dowry was fine for the bourgeoisie, landowners or not. But a poor girl was judged by her work and her bearing. In that respect, there wasn't a thing anybody could teach Marie-Jeanne Le Goff, which was clear in a parish where everyone kept an eye on everyone else. So it was pointless for any of them to try to talk black into white. Besides, she was free to make her own decisions. Her father always liked to say: "Since she's the mistress of the house, it is only fair that she be her own mistress." At that time, going to a matchmaker (*kouriter*) was still the custom, even though that official go-between had given up his broom stick (*baz-valan*), to which he owed one of his names. But my mother had no need to resort to his good offices. She and her husband had met and chosen one another without any intermediary. Moreover, to use the phrasing of French classified ads, the circumstances of husband and wife were such that they made a perfect match.

They married in 1913, and it was a poor man's wedding. There were only about 120 guests, each of whom paid five francs for two whole days of feasting, interrupted by local gavottes called *jibidis* and *jabadaos*. According to the custom, the caterer invited the family on the third day to eat the leftovers. On the evening of the first day there was a pitched battle between the young men of Pouldreuzic, my mother's home, and those from Plozévet, my father's. The latter had been invited to the ball by the groom. And since the girls from Pouldreuzic found them to be better dancers than the boys from their own parish, they apparently made too great a show of their preference for the Plozévetians, which led to bitter words, challenges, a few isolated fights, and an exchange of the type of insult that can only be washed out with blood. They called each other, reciprocally, sticks, louts, loony simpletons, short-range pissers, and, as a finishing touch, yellow-assed dogs. They even accused each other of fouling their breeches. Eventually, the young men from Pouldreuzic, who were in the majority, threw rocks at them and sent the Plozévetians running toward their place of origin. They didn't give up the chase until they were a half-league from the town, and they wouldn't have stopped there had the alarm not been given in Plozévet at the beginning of that storm of abuse, bringing out a company of Boy Scouts to support their side for a counterattack in the Vallée des Moulins. The whole time, my father was in agony. He would very much have liked to join in the fight, but he had to stay beside his young wife. Anyway, how could he have chosen sides? He had either to take up the cudgels for his home town and offend his wife's family, or go to the rescue of Pouldreuzic and be considered a Judas. He opted for playing the role of Pontius Pilate. Sticking his thumbs into the armholes of his vest, he kept count of the blows. All the same, it was a fine wedding.

Custom still required that the newlyweds not be left to themselves until the evening of the third day. The first night was dedicated to the Virgin; the second, to Saint Joseph. And then came the "milk soup" ceremony, which was both symbolic and rather spicy. The recipe for that soup varied from one region to another and depended on the young people's imaginations, but it always included a string of garlic cloves. The milk in the soup proclaimed that the couple's life together would be pleasant; the garlic warned them to expect many disappointments. The younger guests would generally bring it to husband and wife at the banquet table, heartily singing the song of their ancestors—a sad ballad that was meant to make any bride of good stock weep with one eye and laugh with the other. Then the oboists* and bagpipers would strike up another milk-soup tune that was livelier and well known for its tendency to "dry away the tears," prompting all the people at the tables to loudly rejoice.

Actually, that was merely an official and public formality with which one complied because of what remained of a superstition that was meant, in some strange way, to prevent the soup from "turning sour" in future—in other words, to prevent any discord from spoiling the marriage. It was, in effect, the height of the feast and corresponded to the solemn exchange of rings at the church. However, on the evening of the third day the couple's best friends would often wait until they were in bed together to bring them that celebrated milk soup, seasoned with the most unexpected ingredients, and accompanied by a barrage of the most off-color jokes concerning the third member of the Trinity. In anticipation of which, traditionally, the newlyweds would get into their box-bed fully dressed and lie in wait for the arrival of the soup gang, led by the best man. My parents claim that they escaped that part of the pagan rite. Marie-Jeanne Le Goff never missed an opportunity to laugh on condition that it was open and above-board. But her dignity, tinged with suspicion and strengthened by twelve years of daily struggles to ensure that her family be esteemed by the others, had given her such a reputation, or so one must believe, that not even the sharpest cock of the village would have dared to make plans for offering her that type of soup. And as for

*The Breton oboe, or *bombarde,* has a range of only one octave. (Trans.)

my father, he was a foreigner, so to speak, since he was born in the shadow of the neighboring steeple and was therefore a rival. Besides, even in those days the old tradition had turned into such a circus that many newlyweds firmly rejected it. And yet, much later on, I myself attended a celebration of the ritual. To be absolutely frank, I held up my end of it without feeling ashamed.

At any rate, on Thursday the carpenter brought the cupboard that my grandmother Katrina Gouret had had made in Plozévet so that her eldest son could pile up his hemp shirts next to the trousseau her daughter-in-law had made with her own hands. It arrived at Pouldreuzic in a wagon that had just been washed for the occasion, and drawn by a freshly groomed horse, with a braided tail and a rosette pinned to its headstall. And it was the carpenter himself who drove that grandiose horse and carriage. He had got dressed up in his best suit and had put on his best hat. When he was in full view of the square, where the young people were waiting, he shouted out joyfully and was answered with a tremendous uproar. All the able-bodied people were standing in their doorways. The wagon was driven straight up to the bride's house, followed by a gesticulating escort bawling out a song that had been specially composed by someone who knew how to put pen to paper. When the cupboard was taken out, there was a merry scuffle, each person considering himself honor bound to touch the piece of furniture on its feast day. It was carried into the house and set up in a spot from which it has never been moved. Alain Le Goff offered a generous amount of drink to all those friends of good will, as well as to his closest neighbors. After which, the young men led the good-natured carpenter, who was respectably tight, all the way to the last houses in town and left him to the discretion of his horse. It was then that, for the very first time, my father spent the night in his new house. The cupboard had cost ninety francs.

Thus spake my parents.

2 Early Childhood

I spent a long time living in rural regions with the peasants, and was deeply moved when I discovered how much they knew. They had a wealth of knowledge. In comparison, I was no match for them.

Mao Tse-tung

In that particular year, the fourteenth of this century, the first days of August were hot enough to deaden the cows in the fields. The men had lost so much water sweating that they couldn't spit as far as their sabots. On their slopes the gorse was so dry it was the color of dust, and the patches of land in between were so many troughs in which the muggy air, grown stale, had a consistency so like oakum it could have been piled up on pitchforks. The white sky at noon was like a slack sea at daybreak. If any birds were flying, they were silent as fish. No doubt the sea still dwelled in the Bay of Audierne, but it was too weak to swell into waves and too colorless to look alive, blended as it was with the sandy shore. You would have had to climb on its back to be sure it was really there. But how could one set sail without a breath of wind? Things weren't calm, they were stupefied. No storm was in the air, but a kind of muffled apprehension caused the living to tighten their shoulders. Nothing moved anywhere except the poor peasants, who had no choice but to harvest if they were to have bread. It was then that everyone learned what the world was about to beget: war. I was then six months old.

My mother and father were toiling in the Méot field, cutting the wheat with sickles. And it was time. For the seeds were about to fall from the overripe heads. No one was to blame for that but the "Government Boys," who had given the order that my father be sent to Vannes, in the artillery, for his twenty-eight days of military service, just after haying time. Ever since he'd returned, looking gloomy, the poor man had been doing his best to catch up with his work, knowing that from then on his days were numbered. His hemp shirt, heavier than lead, stuck to his spine. The crunching of his sickle as he laid waste armfuls of cracklingly dry straw deafened his ears and, luckily, numbed his mind. Every once in a while the harvester would straighten his back and take time off to sharpen his and my mother's sickles, for my mother was cutting away behind him but unable to work at the same pace. The couple stopped for a moment to catch their breath, one beside the other, not saying a word. And what was there to say? They could see their whole destiny out there before them: the field from which they had to extract their daily bread. One quarter of a league from there, in the direction of the sea, was their parish steeple, their only capital; in the shadow of the steeple was a small whitewashed house in which a six-month-old child, with no one to care for him, was awaiting his mother's milk: that, if I may say so, was me. And the frightful heat, the dreadful calm, portended a misfortune that had to be borne, since nothing could be done about it. A winged insect rose ponderously out of the straw, buzzing like a thresher. (My mother told me all this; I'm not making it up.) It was painfully dragging beneath it a huge, black, hairy abdomen, uglier than the seven deadly sins. When she saw it, my mother turned her head away on the pretext of having to straighten a pin in her coiffe. She did it perhaps only because of the ominous insect. Swiftly, with the back of his hand, my father slapped it down and crushed it under the heel of his sabot.

At five in the afternoon the bells of the parish church were set to ringing in a mode that made one think the sexton had lost his head. Actually, the poor devil was signaling a fire that was to last for over four years throughout the world. How could he have found the right tone? He was going from one bell to another, striking them with the awkwardness of despair. But everyone clearly understood his extraordinary language.

My father picked up his sickle and wielded it a few times, but more and more slowly. Then he bent one knee to the ground and lowered his head. Suddenly he stood straight up, threw his tool far into the distance, and started to walk toward the town through the fields, without ever once unclenching his jaws. My mother sat on the ground and wept into her apron.

But come now! Someone had to finish cutting down the wheat, which is precisely what she did before going back to the house, but not before she had found her husband's sickle out under the hazel trees on the slope. When my father went off to war, it was that sickle which she herself was to use. Being a man's tool, it helped her to get the work done faster. It was often sharpened on a stone moistened with tears, which made for a better cutting-edge. We were to have twenty sous a day, my mother and I, to keep ourselves alive.

When my father returned from the battlefield, he let his wife keep the sickle. For he thought he was no longer its master, that mother had truly earned it. And she was to reap many a harvest afterward. In the end, its blade wasn't much bigger than that of a pocket knife. I rather think that tears are more effective than stone for wearing down a sickle.

When I was born, a doctor had to be called in. One expense my parents could well have done without, not to mention the fact that it was somewhat humiliating for my mother, who felt she ought to have been able to give birth without the help of anyone but the "old missus" who acted as a midwife. When my sister came into the world a few years later, there was no need for all that fuss. Marie-Jeanne Le Goff, around eleven in the morning, merely left the wash-trough where she had scoured a mountain of laundry, found the strength to heat up the noonday meal, and only then had a neighbor call in the "old missus" Marie-Jeanne Le Rest, who delivered her around three o'clock. After which, she was so anxious about her laundry that she would very likely have gone off to get it herself had she been left alone. She would not agree to relax until somebody had got hold of the wheelbarrow and had hustled off to carry home everything that was still on the wash-trough; for all that laundry lying around on the stone might have ruined her reputation as a housewife: one does not leave off in the middle of work that's half-done.

But for *my* arrival into the world, since I was a first child, the circumstances were so unfavorable that the midwife was worried. She suggested that someone go and fetch the doctor in Plogastel, the county seat, which was seven kilometers away. So my father borrowed a bicycle with solid tires and rode off into the night without any light at all. He returned with the doctor, who was also on a bicycle, but his had a carbide light attached to the handlebars. And I made my appearance, almost without having to be asked twice, and apparently full of beans but altogether devoid of nails. "He won't be mean," said Alain Le Goff.

On the following morning the midwife showed her spectacled face again. She was quite willing to admit that the doctor had done a decent job for such a young man. But she practically ignored his advice on the way I was to be attired. So I was tightly swaddled, especially the lower parts of my body, in order that my legs and back would be strengthened. Everyone dreaded lameness, which was thought to be congenital in the Bigouden region. Even my arms were so tightly bound to my hips that I looked like a miniature mummy or, more precisely, like the baby in La Tour's painting of the Nativity, which is in the Rennes museum. Since mummies and La Tour were completely unknown in the region, people compared the packaged baby to "a trimmed bale of straw." At the time, such bales, perfectly lined up on a layer of broom, were used in the place of springs on a box-bed. I can at least guarantee (having often been asked the question) that the old missus Franseza did not remodel my head with her hands, which, if one is to believe certain tales, was standard procedure at the end of the nineteenth century. That aesthetic modus operandi had been renounced long before. Marie-Jeanne Le Rest didn't remember ever having seen it practiced. "That's the sort of thing bone-setters do," she said, pursing her lips. "Bone-setters or witches. Those kinds of people have nothing to do with newborn children." Having thus had her say, Marie-Jeanne, to show her contempt, made such a face that her steel-rimmed spectacles almost fell off her nose. And, to her, spectacles were worth all the diplomas in the world.

Thanks to the presence of a real doctor at his daughter-in-law's bedside, my grandfather the sabot-maker used to delight, later on, in calling me "the Son of the King of Hibernia" and in predicting that my future would be filled with glory and honors. For the time being, my other grandfather, Alain Le Goff, had Piton the carpenter build me a new cradle out of high-quality chestnut, properly studded with brass nails, which my Aunt Lisette waxed and shined with all her might even before I came to occupy it. That cradle (which at the time of this writing is my grandson's) is an exact replica of the cradle in which my mother, uncles, and aunts had slept, each in turn, and which was one of a kind. The whole time it was in use, you could actually see your face reflected in the wood. Then Alain Le Goff lent it to a neighbor, Jean-Marie P, who hadn't enough money to buy one for his children. Jean-Marie kept it for years—that is, long enough to accommodate his whole brood. About two months after I was born, Grandfather went to get it back. The borrower, having no further need of it, had relegated it to his hen house. The cradle was in very sad shape, I can tell you, after having been used as a nest and a roost for the fowls. Alain Le Goff didn't want to take it back. "I will not allow my grandson," he said, "to be brought up on hen droppings." So he counted out his sous and went straight off to see Piton the carpenter.

Two days later came the baptism ceremony. Three or four talkative women were bustling around, decking me out in lace dresses, and on my head they placed the white bonnet without which there can be no valid atonement for original sin. My mother had crocheted me a white blanket, a scaled-down version of those that embellished all the beds in the house, and which later on would take its place on my cradle. At that point, it was meant to cover me completely while I was in the arms of the woman who had given me her milk until my mother's came in. She had put on her best clothes and her most beautiful coiffe, as had my Aunt Marie, my mother's sister, who was to be my godmother. My godfather was my Uncle Jakez, my father's brother, who, behind his blond moustache, was a bit nervous at the idea of the responsibilities he was about to take on.

Standing as godmother or godfather was neither an empty nor a gratuitous honor. In case of need, Jakez Hélias was obliged to give me refuge and food; and, God knows, in our family as in others, that need arose so often that there were countless orphans in our parish who had been taken in, at least for a while, by their godfathers or, lacking one, their godmothers. On the other hand, baptism creates a link of spiritual kinship between a godfather and his goddaughter or a godmother and her godson—a kinship so strong that they are not allowed to marry. Godfathers and godmothers must be Catholic Christians. It is also essential that one of them have taken his or her first communion and that the other have reached the age of reason. All that was repeated in full to my Uncle Jakez and my Aunt Marie, who knew it perfectly well.

The procession of some ten people thus took off for the parish church, Saint-Faron et Saint-Fiacre. At the head of it was the woman who had given me her milk and was preparing to do so again before the baptism in order to calm me down. She moved ahead with all the majesty she could muster, from head to toe, carrying me cautiously on her right arm, since the left is more likely to encourage the endeavors of Satan. On either side my godfather and godmother were trying to keep in step with her. Jakez Hélias had stuck his thumbs into the armholes of his vest, which is a sign of dignity. With his right hand deep down in his pocket, he was fingering the money intended for the priest, the verger, and the altar boys. He had more small coins in another pocket for future purposes. Marie Le Goff, in all her finery, and with her long gold chain round her neck, was worrying about the dragées and candies carried by my Aunt Lisette, who was directly behind her. My father followed them unpretentiously, along with a few members of the family. As the procession passed by, people rushed to their doorsteps and children ran from one house to another to spread the news.

At the church everything went off perfectly. My godfather at my left and my godmother at my right answered the priest's questions very well indeed. The priest himself breathed on my little face to rid me of the Evil Spirit; repeated the sign of the cross; performed the laying on of hands; blessed the salt before putting it on my lips; placed his stole on the package (me); had me taken to the baptistery; moistened my eyes, ears, and nostrils with his saliva; anointed me with the oil of the catechumens; put on a white stole in place of his violet one; sprinkled me with baptismal water; traced the sign of the cross on my head; and gave a lighted candle to my godfather. All that accompanied by murmurings partly in Latin and partly in Breton. Amen. Then everyone went to the vestry to sign their names.

When we left, all the bells were set to ringing. Outside, a group of children were waiting, shoving each other around to get a good place out in front. My godfather and godmother threw handfuls of candy and dragées in every direction, and the children fought over them tooth and nail, right on the ground in front of the cemetery. The crowning display of those fireworks were the twelve coins my godfather took out of his vest pocket and deftly threw in the air to end the game or, more precisely, the battle. (A few years later I myself was among the fighters.) In the meanwhile, my godmother was distributing the few candies and the few sous she had kept for the smaller and weaker children, knowing well that the strongest and cleverest of the bunch had appropriated three-quarters of the baptismal shower.

All that remained to be done was to have the newborn child receive a civil blessing at a few desks in the registry office before returning to the house, where the traditional lavish meal for great occasions had been prepared. And I, together with the rest of the party, made the rounds of the small taverns, which did me no harm whatever. I know at least one person who was forgotten by the woman carrying him during that compulsory pilgrimage, so that the whole group had to retrace their steps to recuperate the baby. My own party was not too interested in strong or sweet drinks. They went to the taverns merely out of respect for custom. While the others were sipping away, my "milk mother," who was seated on a bench, turned slightly toward the wall, undid her bodice, and gave me her breast to alleviate the bite of the salt.

A few days later it was my mother's turn to go to church. She made her way there for the first time since my birth expressly for the churching ceremony. The missal clearly specifies that the point of the ritual is to thank God and to ask for his mercy and his blessing, not to beg for pardon or purification, since the marriage sacrament has already given a woman the right to be a mother. Mothers were therefore advised to rejoice. And yet, due to a vague feeling of guilt, to certain taboos that hark back to time immemorial, and to the fixed feast of Candlemas itself, women, in spite of themselves, had a sense of being in a state of disgrace until that "return to the church" and that new blessing, which regained them their place among the faithful and allowed them to appear in public again. They might well have found it a terrible ordeal had it not been made easier by the participation of the whole community.

This is how it worked. The woman who had "had something new" would dress "in between her Sunday best and her everyday clothes"—in other words, respectably but not ostentatiously. Then she would put on her mourning cloak, a heavy cloth cape with silver clasps and a hood, which she'd pull up over her coiffe to hide her face. Before leaving home, she would stand in the doorway for a moment or so to give people time to turn their heads away. Of course everyone knew, by word of mouth, that she was to be blessed at three o'clock.

And indeed there she is, going off to church, walking very close to the houses. All the women have gone home, and not even the most curious of them dares to do more than peek out from behind her curtain. As for the men, those who happen to be on the road at the time always pretend to be busy with something so as not to see her. The woman enters the cemetery by climbing over the low wall, not through the main gateway. She walks round the church and stands in front of the baptistery porch. The priest, who had been notified of her arrival beforehand, is there awaiting her in a surplice and a white stole. He gives her a lighted candle before blessing her with the aspergillum. "Adjutorium nostrum in nomine Deum." After saying a verse or two from an antiphon in Latin, he puts one end of his stole into the mother's hand and leads her into the church. It is like a second baptism. The woman kneels in front of the altar and gives thanks to God, as the priest goes on uttering his verses. Then he sprinkles her with holy water in the sign of the cross. "Pax et benedictio Dei omnipotentis . . ." Amen. It is over.

The woman stands up, lowers her hood, unfastens the silver clasps, and leaves the church, carrying her head high. She takes off her cloak and folds it over her arm. In accordance with the custom, she goes and meditates for a few minutes at the family tomb, now that she has put herself right with the living and the dead. She leaves the cemetery through the large gate. As if by chance, all those who didn't want to see her before just happen to be out on the road she has taken so that they may speak to her amiably about one thing and another, but certainly not about the reason that had brought her to church on a weekday, all alone, and wearing her funeral cape when the knell hadn't tolled for anyone. Just before leaving her, each person, looking off into space, asks: "How is your family?" And she replies: "Very well. Couldn't be better." No need for any further questions. All the women in town know in detail about every event that might be called a milestone in the lives of both mother and child during the past few days. Not to mention the specifics of the baptismal meal. The neighboring women, who have had the run of the house, couldn't wait to tell all.

Before returning home, the mother does her marketing at her usual shops. She apologizes:

"I just haven't had a chance to get out these days. And I've had so many visitors there's almost nothing left in the house."

"Of course, of course," says the baker.

"Such things happen," says the grocer.

"So I've heard," mutters the butcher, with a smile.

In short, her shopping bag is full by the time the woman rushes through the door to nurse her baby, whom an obliging knitter has been keeping an eye on.

In a few days a stream of women will arrive and go into raptures over the newborn child, while they enjoy bowl after bowl of the mother's coffee. Unless times are so hard and the pocketbook so empty that they have to wait several weeks or several months before paying their respects. But they will do so, you can count on it.

In my brand-new chestnut cradle I was learning to use my voice. The cradle had been placed on the bench attached to my parents' bed so that my mother could stretch out an arm and rock me during the night if I got into a temper. But all day long, for hours at a time, I was there by myself, despite hasty visits from one or two neighborhood children who had been asked to look in and see how I was doing. My mother was out in the fields, my grandfather on the roads crushing stones, and my father felling trees or working as a pit sawyer, having given up his job as a farm foreman, which was hardly suitable for a married man. He had to earn a few sous one way or another. Soon war broke out; the men were away for four years or more; and the job of working the land was shouldered by women and old men. In the morning my mother would leave for the Méot field with the cow, after having gorged me with her milk. When the Angelus rang at noon, she'd return for a quick meal, change my diaper, nurse me again, and go off to plough up the ground until four or five o'clock.

Then I'd be suckled again, after which she would tend to the cow and the pig (we had only one, but were in hopes of having two some day, once my father returned). At nightfall Grandfather would be there. He'd take me in his arms for a while and my mother would laugh. I have the impression that I heard her laugh without stop ever since I was born. Indeed, she laughed all her life—at least every time it was possible to give way to laughter without hurting anyone or wasting time. Although absolutely exhausted and burdened with worries, she was always resilient enough to choke with joy at the slightest opportunity, and to such an extent that she often had to sit down to catch her breath. A wonderful mother.

When she knitted or crocheted, she would sing a song called *Labousig ar hoad* ("The Little Bird of the Woods") in a clear and somewhat quivering voice that was perfection. And that song was just the thing for getting rid of my quite normal miseries. When my teeth really plagued me, my mother would grab one of the handles of my cradle beside the bed and rock me—or, rather, shake me—as fast as she could, chanting as often as necessary the following words, which were supposedly conducive to patience:

Wine wine wine
He'll turn out just fine.
Wup wup wup
He will soon stand up.

According to her, it was a rather superior cure for toothaches. If all was well, she would place the cradle on the mud floor and, to help me fall asleep, would rock me with her foot to the accompaniment of a *rimodell* (a doggerel) about animals, which was slower than the "Wine wine wine, Wup wup wup." It was called "Singing Didedoup." I found it irresistible.

Didedoup dibidin
Here's the dog coming in.
Didedoup dibedack
With the cat on its back.
Didedoup dibedowse
And, between them, the mouse.

Finally, when she saw I was asleep, she'd take her foot off the cradle and just murmur a hymn that would lead me to *Kerhun,* or Dreamland, the land without a moon. Why without a moon? You know perfectly well. If you keep your mouth open and the moon shines into your throat, you'll be plain silly for the rest of your life. In *Kerhun* there's no danger of that.

When my sister came into the world some years later, I would hear my mother murmur the same doggerels and sing her the same songs, along with a few others she had learned in the meantime, some of which were in French, if you please. She was particularly fond of those because she was trying to get used to the language so that she'd be able to converse with her sisters-in-law, who didn't know a word of Breton. Also, the sounds of French delighted Marie-Jeanne Le Goff, who liked to use certain words just to hear them coming out of her mouth or ringing in her ears. Besides, she wished to prepare her daughter to come to terms with a world in which the language spoken by the city bourgeoisie would one day take over the countryside. But she did not intend to renounce Breton for all that. Indeed, Breton will never be renounced.

When I myself used to come back from school, the very first thing I did was to rock my sister to sleep with the ancient lullabies. They didn't always have the desired effect. "That's because she's a girl," said my grandfather to console me. I wanted nothing more than to believe it.

Marie-Jeanne Le Goff began holding me up when I was three months old. But I really spoiled the family rotten, walking all by myself before the age of ten months. That was thanks to my Aunt Lisette, who would steer me about in secret when we were alone in the house. As soon as my back was strong enough, she put her hands under my arms from behind, picked me up, placed my tiny feet on her wooden shoes, and began to take very small steps, holding me upright. And my feet got better and better at following her sabots. A few weeks later I had progressed to the point of dragging a "walkers' toy" behind me. It was a pine cone at the end of a string. In Breton we called it a "pine pig," and to me it really was an animal. Before that, my favorite toy had been a discarded wooden spoon, on which I also cut my teeth.

My mother nursed me until I was eighteen months old. She then closed her shirt and her bodice once and for all. My feelings were somewhat hurt, but everyone explained to me that if I wanted to become a man, it had to stop then and there. Well, all right. But life certainly wasn't easy! A short while back, I had been made to eat my gruel all by myself; in other words, my mother had stopped putting the warm spoon into her mouth before giving it to me. Everyone knows that a mother's saliva helps her child to digest wheat gruel. And indeed, not only did I burn my mouth rather often, but I also found that since I had been left to my own devices I had far more trouble digesting. I was the victim of the traditional methods of child care, which no one ever dared to question under penalty of ending up on the high road with a beggar's knapsack strapped to one's back.

As for traveling, I had started that a long time before. First, on my mother's arm, going to church, for she took me to Mass just as soon as she could, out of pride, which the Lord God will forgive her as He forgives others. It was also on her arm that I visited all the houses of her acquaintances in the parish. The moment I was able to hold onto her neck, she put me on her back to go and see my grandparents in Kerveillant, which meant walking two leagues both ways. And, wretch of a child that I was, I pulled on the ties of her coiffe to undo the knot. When the weather was fine, I would go to the field on her back, and if it was raining when we returned, she'd wrap me up in her apron. She knew that in the cities there were little carriages for taking children on walks. It was even said that one had been ordered in the region by some big shot. We, however, hoped that once my father came home from the war, and perhaps even sooner, we would get a wheelbarrow.

In the meantime, when my grandfather was free, I sometimes went to Pont-Gwennou, the small field, or to Méot, the large field, riding piggyback. I really felt good way up there. Alain Le Goff had a nice smell about him—a mixture of soil, dust, and sweat. He would walk at his own pace, never stop, and ask me what I saw from there, high above the slopes. And I'd tell him. From time to time he'd break into a slow trot to shake me up a bit and make me laugh. Or else I would cover his eyes with both hands, and he'd whirl around on the nails of his sabots. Besides, we'd meet all sorts of people:

"What have you got there on your back, Alain Le Goff?"

"A bag of something, I'm not sure what."

"I'm not a bag. I'm Grandfather's grandson."

"Come now, this is the first time I've ever heard a bag talk," said the other man. And he held out his hand to shake mine. I was still too shy to utter the words "Hello, Uncle," but that would come in time.

"Why did you say I was a bag, Grandfather?"

"Because he wasn't polite. He should have addressed you first."

I quite agreed. With the back of my hand, I wiped my runny nose and then looked about me sternly. "You mustn't hold it against him," said Grandfather. "He spoke without thinking, but he's a good man." Right, so he was a good man.

Another way of getting to the field was in a two-handled basket. Inside it there was a bag, folded in four, on which I sat. My mother would take hold of one handle, my grandfather the other, and off we'd go, with me clinging to the wicker rim. "Hold on tight, boy!" And as the two carriers walked along, they'd swing me higher and higher until I got dizzy. I was delighted. Sometimes, especially on the way back, when I had worn myself out playing in the field, I would fall asleep in the basket.

It so happens that the very first strong emotion I ever felt in my life was aroused in the Méot field. For it was there, at the age of three, that I was whirled about on the horns of Grandfather's red cow. And neither the cow nor I was to blame. While I was picking buttercups in the grass where it was grazing, at one point it came up so close to me that one of its horns got entangled in the sleeve of my little dress, which was gathered in by an elastic. The animal tried to extricate itself and began tossing its head wildly. At the same time, I began to scream, terrifying the poor beast, which lifted me up in the air and broke into the fastest gallop it could manage. My mother and grandfather, who were digging in the soil nearby, came running. Once they detached me, they found that I wasn't hurt, but I was so upset I wet my dress. And not for the first time. Grandfather didn't hold it against his cow; he was incapable of holding a grudge against anyone, much less an animal. But my mother, in a state of rage, impulsively whipped it on its spine with the rope. Then she wept and moaned: "What would his father say if he had been crippled!" My father was then leading his horses down the paths of war, with a cannon directly behind him.

After that little incident, I continued to roam about on the backs of my mother, grandfather, aunts, and uncles, when they were passing through the region in their military blue or their sailor collars. I visited all the members of the family, who were scattered about from Plozévet to Landudec and all the way to Pouldergat. I went to every "pardon," or religious festival, in the area, during which one prayed the Lord God to put an end to the war. As time went by, I was carried less and less, and tried to take the longest walks possible on my own legs. I yearned for the day when, all by myself, I'd be able to go and see my grandfather the sabot-maker and my grandmother Katrina Gouret in Kerveillant. That was to be a long time coming. Yet I was a big boy. It seemed a century ago that I had left my cradle, which had become too short, and taken my place in Alain Le Goff's box-bed, separated from him by a kind of thick bolster filled with a bale of oats. Behind that rampart I was able to romp about as I liked, while Grandfather, on the other side, would lie majestically on his back, motionless, like the stone knight Troïlus de Mondragon, whom I later encountered in the Quimper museum.

One day I was playing with my little friends in front of the house of Guillaume Le Corre, the shoemaker, some forty yards away from home. And suddenly, in the street, we heard shouting, windows opening, the sound of sabots hurrying along, and whispers interspersed with strange silences. We knew what it was: a soldier back on leave who hadn't told anyone the day of his arrival and had not come from the railroad station. At the station there was always a group of women and children who stood around waiting just in case. When a soldier stepped off the train, a flock of little messengers would scatter throughout the region shouting: So and so's father is back! But sometimes the man on leave would come from Quimper on foot. He hadn't had the patience to wait for the train that could have brought him home, taking the long way round by Pont l'Abbé. What are five or six leagues to a peasant-soldier! At other times he might happen to find a horse-charabanc which would depart from its usual route just to take him near his destination. That was why the "boys from the front" would appear when one least expected them.

This one had appeared in the middle of the square. He was standing there very stiffly in his big blue coat with shiny buttons, his cap set straight on his head, and his two haversacks slung crosswise over his shoulders. The women had surrounded him and were questioning him in low voices, trying to find out if he had seen their husbands and when. One of them whispered something into the ear of a kid about ten years old who rushed toward me at a wild gallop: "Little Pierre, hurry up and tell your mother! Your father's here." I knew I had a father at the front. He often came up in conversation, and there was talk of what we ought to do when he returned. In my prayers he and my uncles came before any of the others. But I didn't remember him at all. And there he was, there he was walking up the street. God, he was tall! But why hadn't he brought his horses? True, we had no stable. His coat was hanging heavily over his long leather gaiters. I'd never grow that tall. As he drew near, the women pointed me out to him with their fingers. So I fled toward the house, dashed into the kitchen, where my mother was preparing pig slop, and shouted: "Mother, there's a man coming!"

I met him the following day. My mother was dressed almost, but not quite, in her Sunday best, and we went out to pay our respects to the head of the paternal branch of the family, my grandfather the sabot-maker. Then, along with grandfather, we visited a few other of our Plozévet relatives. As we passed through the streets, my father talked to the families of his army pals, giving them the news. And almost the whole time we walked, I was sitting firmly up on his shoulders. Down below I could see my mother's coiffe moving as she walked alongside us, with her new umbrella under her arm. I got a little dizzy, perched up that high. When the time came to leave, night had fallen and I was worn out. I awoke the next day in the box-bed at Kerveillant. My grandmother gave me two sous, even though I had completely tangled her thread while playing with the spinning wheel. My grandfather lifted me onto his back and got me home by noon. There I found my father, who had just then returned from the Méot field in his peasant clothes, with his large spade on his shoulder. Only a few days more and he was off again, having ploughed up the ground wherever it was needed, and having repaired everything that wasn't working. He had even trapped a rat which, for some time, had been performing a diabolical saraband between the manger and the loft, exacting his tithe and spoiling our supplies, the filthy beast. The rat got caught in a wire trap baited with salt pork. A big fire was lit in the hearth and the animal was roasted in its snare. That was the only way to get rid of others of the same species if ever they felt inclined to take its place; for while it was burning, it gave out such horrible shrieks that never more, as they say, would a rat stick its neck out either in our house or anywhere around it. The same method was used for vipers.

Now that the rat had been captured, my mother no longer dreaded going up to the loft. No matter how strong-minded a woman may be, those sly noises that disclose the presence of an invisible rodent are enough to make her, or anyone, feel uneasy. Besides, those thieves make their mess in the grain that's spread out up there. Whenever my mother thought of the mill-hand coming to take the grain away to grind and perhaps noticing that it wasn't as clean as it ought to have been in a well-kept house, she was so ashamed that the blood rushed to her face.

I was not to see my father again until the end of the war. There was too much work to be done at the front for him to get away. The "front"! What a strange word! It bore no resemblance to any of the others we knew. It was a *French* word, one of those words you learn only in school. Well, we would now know at least one of them when the time came for us to go.

After every High Mass the verger would climb up on the cemetery wall to proclaim the news and the rules and regulations. Gentlemen in bowler hats would ride by in traps on their way to the town hall. It was said that the mayor had a lot of work to do, poor man. We watched the weeks and months go by. The war, the front lines, the dead. Where was all that happening? And why? We were fighting against hateful people called "krauts." Sworn enemies. There were pictures of them wearing pointed helmets. I saw one of them glued onto the back of the tobacconist's window. People said there were others in the school downtown. Those "krauts" must have had tough hides to hold out against our fathers. Or perhaps there were so many of them that the strongest woodcutters had grown weary striking them down. Then we learned more words—the French for trenches, shells, and a seventy-five. There were no Breton words to convey their meanings.

The older I got, the more I found that people's clothes were beginning to look shabby. Even on Sundays the men's striped trousers were patched at the knee. The women had ripped off the velvet stitched onto their skirts and had sewn it onto their bodices. It made them look neater. And the grocer didn't have much left in his shop. "Go and ask Uncle Daniel if there's any sugar!" my mother told me. I went. Uncle Daniel, the grocer, had no sugar. Uncle Guillaume Le Corre didn't even have any leather to reinforce sabots; in fact, he didn't have any nails either. Apparently, there was a blacksmith near Plovan who forged them himself and sold them by the half-dozen.

At the house we had a hollowed-out table, with a movable top, which contained our supply of flour. It was the table my mother used for kneading the dough for buckwheat bread—the kind that's most filling and the best for keeping hunger at bay. When the dough was ready, my grandfather would put it into a white coarse hemp bag and take it to the baker's. When the round loaf came back, cooked and hot, we had a feast day. But sometimes a few other ingredients, which had once been meant only for animals, had to be mixed in.

And money was scarce. Now that I was a big boy, I was given a five-sou coin to go to Uncle Daniel's and fetch a kind of brown molasses which was spread on the bread. One helping cost three sous. "Don't forget," Mother told me, "you'll get change—a reddish-brown coin." And sure enough, Uncle Daniel gave me the change and closed my fingers tightly over it, advising me not to lose it.

One day a revolution broke out in our town. Everybody gathered in the square. Screams, wild laughter, tears, and all the inns filled. The country people rushed into town, whipping their horses like madmen. The bells, as if for some gigantic baptism, rang out loud enough to shatter the steeple. Then we learned yet another French word, even stranger than the others and which echoed from mouth to mouth like applause: *armistice*.

The soldiers and sailors returned one after another. They had been allowed to keep their uniforms for the very good reason that they had nothing else to wear. Not all of them returned. I'm not speaking of the dead, of course, nor of those who were seriously disabled and lying about in hospitals with only one leg, one arm, or one eye, but of the tough guys all in one piece and in good health who, on their way home, had found work that suited them. Although four years of war hadn't estranged them from their region or their families, those years had broadened their worlds for them and given them the opportunity to make plans for the future. Even before they left for the front, many of them had been condemned to exile. Now, in their birthplace, even the space left by the dead had been filled; and land was almost as scarce as before, as were the means of earning a living. So the bachelors stayed on wherever they had found jobs, occasionally lured there by some chum from the trenches who had spoken highly of his own region. And besides, marriageable girls with some resources weren't all that rare in other parts of the country.

My father returned in fairly good shape. Of that whole adventure, what stayed with him was his satisfaction at having conquered those notorious "krauts"; his utter disgust, which never diminished over the years, at the thought of the three horses that had been killed right out from under him; and the miseries the others had gone through. "It's pitiful," he used to say, "to see animals made to suffer like that." As for his own miseries, he didn't mention them until much later, when he began to grow old. He never spoke of the Marne, Verdun, or the Chemin des Dames except with the men who, like him, had been there. And even then, not within earshot of anyone indiscreet. The reminiscence of the war we heard about most often was a memorable stop during which his company spent their time gorging themselves with champagne in the deserted cellars of Epernay. The irony of it was that Father didn't at all care for that sort of drink.

The men were reintegrated into family life both in the house and in the fields, though they were somewhat surprised at the changes that had taken place here and there. Somewhat annoyed, too, at having to once again obey their fathers, who had continued to run the farms in their absence. Soon those fathers would have to let them take over. Since they had spoken to lots of people of their own station during the war years, the soldiers had picked up some new ideas. It wasn't that they had any great plans as yet, but they were ready to make them. Those whose wives had been in charge of everything for four years had more trouble getting back to their previous routine. But the women had acquired such habits and had labored so hard night and day that they found it difficult to give up their prerogatives. A few heroes covered with medals never did manage to take command again. True, our women are strong-minded; that's well known.

So the veterans enjoyed their glory in public and among themselves. For years, on November 11, Armistice Day, they were the masters of the town, both respectful and proud at the services, but wildly unrestrained at the inns. And woe to the "slackers" who failed to hug the walls on that particular day! At school the teachers glorified all the sacrifices made by the soldiers—the very last soldiers: of that there was no doubt. They had settled everything for a thousand years and for the three words: Liberty,

Equality, Fraternity (in French). Soon monuments were built in memory of the dead. Statues. Not of the big shots, not those bronze generals displayed in city squares. But of the privates, yes. In those melodramatic poses popularized by the newspapers during the war. The veterans thought that was how it ought to be. It was their right. They had been just like that, in body and soul—no different. The plaques on the pedestals were inscribed with dozens and dozens of names. One hundred and eight in all.

My father now had a blue cotton suit, its single-breasted jacket buttoned up to the neck, and a peaked cap for everyday. He talked about taking the test for getting a driver's license. And I was soon to proudly watch him at the wheel of a Packard truck filled with building planks. The day after he returned, he had put his service record, various papers and dispatches, and a *Croix de guerre* into the cupboard. Thoughtfully, he had turned the cross over and over in his hand and shyly looked at my mother, as if to apologize:

"I don't think it's worth anything at the baker's," he said.

"What we're going to do is buy a frame for it," my mother replied. "As for the baker, we'll manage just as we used to."

And shortly afterward, they decided to begin their new life together by redoing the floor of the house, which had such deep holes in it that you sprained your ankles. It was a mud floor. I knew it from one end to the other. I had fallen on it rather often when I was beginning to walk, precisely because of those damn holes. But you never hurt yourself badly on mud. It's cold, of course, when you sit on it with a bare behind, but it's so easy to keep in good shape, it's so easy to live with! No need to clean your sabots before coming in. The wet mud on your soles doesn't dirty anything at all. Either it blends in with the rest or, once it's dry, it is swept out with a branch of broom. You never feel uneasy about throwing bones on the floor or even scraps to the dog, if you happen to have one. The cat can knock over its milk without provoking the housewife's thundering rage. One basin of water is enough to wash the whole thing down, and the mud floor feels all the better for it. You have to give it enough to drink, after all! It even remembers, to my slight embarrassment, that when I was very young, I provided it with a few splashes of piddle from my own self, which a handful of sawdust and a strong sweep of the broom got rid of, with no harm done to the "toad-clay."

For that hardened mud, on which people used to walk every day of their lives in all the houses of my acquaintance, was called toad-clay, I'm not sure why. Was it because of its grayish color, or its flinty warts, or because the animal in question likes to live in soil and darkness, whereas frogs have a preference for water and sun? At any rate, it is a mixture of sand, clay, and ordinary soil, with, on occasion, some ashes thrown in. Every householder had his own recipe for preparing his floor, just as every housewife has her own recipe for making stew. Once in a while, some man or other would botch the job, and his floor turned to dust or wouldn't dry. A well-kept house was known for its flat, smooth floor, all neat and trim, with a slight shine to it. Often it was a bit uneven in places—under the legs of the benches and chairs or under the buckets, the stew pots, and the churn. In other words, it wore out like any piece of clothing or any tool, depending on the stress that was put on it. When necessary, it was patched up with a handful of the same substance, which soon took on the color of the whole. But you couldn't always find exactly the same clay or the same sand, and as a result, the floor would come to resemble a mysterious map of the world, with black, gray, or yellow continents that recalled no region on earth. That's why my father decided to tackle the job of completely redoing our floor.

Now that he was back, there were two men at table during mealtimes. Alain Le Goff would sit at the head, which was to the right, near the window, and on the bench with a back. It was the master's seat, and he was still the master. Indeed, he remained so until his death. Across from him was my father, who sat on the bench attached to the box-bed. The foot of the table belonged to my mother, who practically never sat down. There she would place her milk jug, her bowls, and her various pots and pans—everything she needed for cooking. That was also where she dressed her hair early in the morning. As for me, I would curl up near my grandfather, who was in charge of my basic education.

The great event in my life at that point was my promotion to the rank of a little man. A few months earlier, I had been promised that I could wear trousers, and I must admit that I found it was taking too long a time, so that I never stopped insisting, occasionally in tears. Ever since the age of five, I had considered myself too big to tolerate skirts. Some of my little friends were already sporting plush trousers which they had sometimes inherited from an older brother who had outgrown them. And they didn't hesitate to make me swallow some bitter pills. The same type that some of my schoolmates were made to swallow later on—those who were to wear short pants until they got into senior high.

All boys wore skirts from the time they were born until they were five or six. It was very convenient when we had to relieve ourselves, more especially since we never wore underclothes to cover our behinds. Still, if we remained in skirts for too long, people were apt to think we weren't tidy enough to make do with trousers, which was embarrassing. It was generally mothers who delayed the "trouser-ceremony," perhaps because they saw it as an indication that they were losing their sons to the world of men. All that's very fine, but we were rigged up like girls, and yet we knew—given a certain distinctive feature between our thighs—that we were not. We had a peg at the place where they had a scar. When it came to clothing, the only thing that distinguished us from them was the glass-beaded tassel that adorned the back of our three-cornered caps, whereas little girls had a rosette in the same place, with two long ribbons hanging down their backs. It plainly wasn't enough. And after all, girls continued to wear skirts all their lives; they didn't have to get accustomed to anything else. We, on the other hand, had to undergo a rite of passage that couldn't help but make us somewhat uneasy. How would we manage with those buttons and suspenders? And it would have been out of the question to turn to our mothers for help once our skirts were back in the cupboard, along with our lace collars and tasseled caps. I counted on Grandfather to help me out, and not breathe a word of it to anyone. In any case, since I would have to take that test, surely it was best to get it over with as soon as possible!

My mother finally agreed to it. One day we apprehensively climbed into the motorcar of Alain Le Reste, my father's boss. It was a De Dion Bouton, the second automobile in the region. Not all that long ago, women had crossed themselves when they saw it pass by. The cows in the fields, terrified by the noise, had ripped out their stakes and run for miles. Alain Le Reste was driving, wrapped up in an animal skin, and wearing mica goggles on his nose. There were only two seats. I was next to him, on my mother's lap, holding onto the handle of the water can on the running board, which was to supply the machine with drink. It went faster than a horse-charabanc, but all the jolting over the ruts and the potholes was really a trial. "Don't watch the road, little Pierre," said Alain Le Reste. "You'll get dizzy and you might fall out." I decided to close my eyes.

In Quimper we hesitated between "Charles Leduc Dresses You Well and Inexpensively" and "Saint-Rémy Dresses You Better and Less Expensively." In the end, I was provided with a lower-middle-class garment of brown cloth, which had been chosen a few sizes too big for me because I was still a growing boy. Since the war, little Bretons were no longer dressed in scaled-down versions of their fathers' clothes.

The last stage of the ceremony consisted in inviting our close relatives to the trouser-feast. There were ten or twelve around the table, and they had already dug into the roast when my Aunt Lisette, who had carefully dressed me in the other room, led me to them in all my glory, smiling bravely in spite of a twisted suspender. Exclamations and compliments—an interminable outburst of them. I was called a young man. Then somebody said: "Now he'll be able to go to school."

So there I was, feeling both proud and uneasy.

At least I would not have to face my teacher with an empty head. My grandfather had begun my education just as soon as I was out of my cradle. As a matter of fact, it used to be the duty of grandfathers to attend to their grandsons. Because of their age, they were excused from such arduous and steady work as running the house, which was uniquely the father's and mother's concern. They were restricted to giving advice, and only when they were asked for it. I knew some who were still in charge, but they weren't real grandfathers. Since the chores were numerous, they spent all their time exercising their authority. Thus they found it hard to find enough free time to educate their grandchildren. A real grandfather was a person who no longer had any responsibilities, which made him a natural ally of children, who hadn't any as yet. A young child and an elderly man were accomplices. The parents would agree to let them be together for a few years, until the father deemed that the time had come to take his son in hand. And that put an end to the green-garden paradise.

It was on Alain Le Goff's lap that I had my first rhythmical rides, as he bumped the mud floor with the heels of his sabots, marking time to a kind of nursery rhyme which I shall never forget as long as I live because I still hear it repeated to other children:

> Gee up to Pont-Croix, gee up to Quimper
> To Pont l'Abbé we have got to repair
> So we can find flour for the lady.
> The lady of the fields is of the same ilk
> As people who do not like soup made of milk.
> And the gentleman, though he did go to school,
> Fell right on his ass in the deep of the pool.

At the end of that mouthful of galloping words, Grandfather would spread his knees; I'd fall between his legs; but he would hold onto my arms to keep me from plunging into the pool like the lady's gentleman. And did I laugh! And we'd go on again and again until I was done in.

He would also pinch my five fingers, one after another, beginning with the thumb, and teach me the French equivalent of "This little piggie went to market." That's how I gradually got to know my fingers: the one that measures (the thumb), which is also called *morzolig al laou* (the lice-hammer);* the gruel (or index) finger; the long (or middle) finger; the heart (or ring) finger; and the dancing (or little) finger. Grandfather didn't stop there: he began teaching me numbers by relating them to my own body. He would ask the questions and give the answers, but it was up to me to explain those answers by pointing out which parts of the body each referred to and by holding up the required number of fingers:

> "What makes one?" —"Just me myself."
> "What makes two?" —"The old man's ears."
> "What makes three?"—"My eyes and nose."

*See below, chap. 4. (Trans.)

"What makes four?" —"My knees and elbows."
"What makes five?" —"The fingers on one hand."
"What makes six?" —"My nostrils, legs, and arms."
"What makes seven?"—"The holes in my head."

When I asked why we never went beyond seven, Grandfather told me that seven was the number of days in a week and that the seventh day was a day of rest. In that way he taught me those days of the week, all of which, in Breton, begin with "di." That was odd: "dilun, dimeurz, dimerher, diriaou, digwener, disadorn, disul." I was amazed that, with all that knowledge in his head, it didn't explode.

What pleased me about my grandfather was that the words in *his* mouth played leapfrog; they also knocked against each other like marbles, and some of them even made exactly the same noise at regular intervals. There are very few people I know who speak like that. Is it perhaps because they don't know how? Or because they didn't have a grandfather like Alain Le Goff?

"Where did you learn those things, Grandfather?"

"In Poull-ar-Markiz. From a blacksmith who rarely opened his mouth, but when he did, he always spoke exactly like that."

Grandfather himself preferred to listen to others, even when the others would have liked to hear him speak. But he always replied with great courtesy when questioned about something he knew, unless his answer might have proved to be harmful to someone. In that case he would dodge the question by saying: "I'm too old." I then thought I was his best friend, just as his other grandchildren did when their turns came and when I had become too big a boy to be his accomplice in every respect. As he told me, "Now you must listen to your schoolmasters, who are much more learned than I am." Of that, I have never been convinced.

But for the time being, I kept an ear out for his most trifling words and tried not to forget them, which was possible because he often repeated the same ones over and over again. He did it intentionally, of course. For example, when he'd take the bucket over to Marie-Jeanne's wells at Kerveillant, he would always say:

Let's go and draw out seven pails
To fill our tank before it wails.

Then he'd go on to something else:

> *Karr uz men* (Cart wears out stone)
> *Men uz karr* (Stone wears out cart)

That one's hard, isn't it? Slowly, he explained it to me. The very next time I saw a wagon bumping along the road, I watched it move from one rut into another, in order to verify that phenomenon.

I wasn't so stupid as not to realize that Grandfather's way of speaking avoided small talk and provided capsules of wisdom when you took the time to digest their contents and, at the very start, to pronounce the words correctly, separating them one from the other. What I didn't know at the time, and what he was to tell me long afterward, was that his sets of words were meant to prepare our mouths to speak properly. Children are apt to mumble. The noises they make are no more than approximations of sounds. How come that our illiterate ancestors invented those exercises to teach their children to speak? One is tempted to think they knew more about pedagogy than the professional pedagogues.

The day I could emit, flawlessly and without hesitation, the very ancient mouthful concerning six monks pursuing six girls riding six horses—*c'hweh merh gwerh war c'hweh marh kalloh ha c'hweh manah war o lerh*—I would clearly be able to express anything, not only with my lips but also with the very bottom of my throat. Whether the girls were virgins, or the six horses stallions, or the six monks lascivious by choice was not my problem at the time. But surely man's language was a diabolical invention!

Alain Le Goff knew how to read very well, but he never did. It was my mother who deciphered all the letters from uncles and aunts out loud, and it was she who answered them, but he knew how. He also knew how to do arithmetic very fast in Breton, but all in his head; he couldn't do it nearly so fast with a pencil and paper. When he was still working out on the road, I had seen the other repairmen come and ask him to work out their accounts. I had seen him practice drawing letters and numbers in the soil with his stick. Indeed, it was he who prepared me for school, teaching me how some of them sounded and how they were depicted, shaping them with a movement of his hand.

How could I help but grow in strength and in wisdom with a grandfather who worked on you like that! When I was old enough to go to school, Alain Le Goff changed his methods and his means. However, there were still nights when—I don't know why—it was hard to get me to go to bed. Despite the fact that my mother would open the box-bed doors and put an earthenware bed-warmer under the cover when it was cold, I noticed nothing and wanted no part of it. After a while, my parents would show signs of getting angry. At that point, grandfather would empty out his pipe, knocking it against his sabot, and begin to laugh to himself. To laugh softly, shaking his head as if he were rejoicing over something he alone knew. I found it irresistible. One night I asked the usual question:

"What is it, Grandfather?"

"You'll never believe me," he said. "There's no point in starting to tell you about it. You might even go and call me a liar. I'd find that very unpleasant."

I protested vigorously. I was almost on the verge of tears at the idea that Grandfather could believe I was capable of considering him a liar. To me a liar was someone who was out to harm you or who concealed the harm he had done. I knew what Grandfather's lies were: he had seen things that no one else would ever see, especially not me if I persisted in not going to bed.

"Tell me, Grandfather. And before you're even finished, I'll be under the comforter."

"It's the best place to digest what I'm going to talk to you about—something one doesn't see every day. I saw . . ."

That was it! I had guessed as much. We were going to play "I saw." Our pleasure would last all through the week and even longer if we went about it the right way.

"I saw," said Grandfather, "on my way to the Méot field this morning, a young white hen from Kerzouron who was walking so prettily down the road that I asked: 'Young lady, where would you be going in a white dress?' 'To be married,' she said, 'to a rooster from Laraon, the handsomest of them all.' " And off we went!

"I saw" naturally pleased me more than riddles. But riddles were meant, not to put me to sleep, but rather to keep me awake. Of course, Grandfather generally ended by giving me the answer, and he also helped me in all sorts of ways—especially with gestures and mimicry, manipulating objects, looking at a particular spot which indicated the solution to the problem, or suggesting two different riddles with the same solution. For example: "What is the laziest creature in the world, which always goes to work moving backward?" Since I couldn't find the answer, he merely went on. He took off his sabot and looked at it thoughtfully: "What is it that always travels on its head?" Now that one was easy: a nail, of course. Or else, when we had gone to the small Pont-Gwennou field and Alain Le Goff was busy putting his plants into the soil: "What grows bigger and bigger the more you withdraw something out of it?" Hmm. But just by observing, I got that answer: a hole. Still, there were painful moments, when no gestures were possible and there was nothing around to guide me. "What do you have which is yours and isn't useful to you, but which is useful to me and to others?" I was on the verge of tears when Grandfather helped me out: "It's your name!"

Even though I could ask my little friends his riddles and enjoy watching their embarrassment, I preferred Alain Le Goff's moral lessons, which seemed to me more serious now that I felt I was a little man. One day, Grandfather, in order to light his pipe, stopped in the shelter of a slope topped with gorse. "Be like gorse," he said. "It's happy from one end of the year to the next, with its flowers that show its strength and its health. It's covered with spines, which protect it from those who come up too close without having asked permission. Its skin and its pith are hard—good for feeding a horse. For gorse is just like a man, exactly. It's not like broom. Broom was made in the image of woman, always affected, and bowing to the first passerby if there's the slightest breath of wind. Broom doesn't flower for long; it lacks strength. It's good for making brooms to clean the house with. And who uses those brooms, son, I ask you? Women."

In the same earnest and steady voice, I once heard him tell my little sister: "Be like broom, my girl—like courteous and decorous broom, which curtsies to everyone who comes by. Broom is beautiful to the eye, elegant, trim and gentle, with delicate flowers. Broom is just like what a woman ought to be. That's why it's made into brooms for cleaning the house, and it doesn't scratch the toad-clay. Could anyone sweep with a clump of gorse? Half the dust would be left behind. Bad work. Gorse is uncouth, like a wild boy, and so spiny that it has to be ground up before it can be given to horses. And horses are a man's business, aren't they?"

My little sister agreed. And I agreed as well. When we got angry with each other, I would call her finicky-broom and she'd call me prickly-gorse. And each of us was determined to be worthy of our symbol. When the two mix, something has gone awry in the world.

The month of November was the month for tales. As it got dark very early, my grandfather would bring his cow home before six o'clock. It took an hour to attend to the household chores by the light of a rootstock fire, and then the kerosene lamp was lit so that we could bolt down what passed for supper. Directly afterward began our evening round the fire. My mother would lower the wick as far as possible. Kerosene was too expensive.

The flames in the hearth struggled courageously against the darkness. All around us the brass nails on the cupboards and the box-bed shone like glow-worms on the night roads. You could hear the sound of my father's sabots coming and going on the mud floor. Silent as usual, he'd be getting his tools together to whittle out stakes or to splice old reins. And he'd sort out willow twigs to be used for weaving round baskets. My mother had already settled down in her low chair in front of the fire, her apron filled with worn-out clothes. I myself would be awaiting my grandfather, who always lingered too long over his horse in the manger. But there he was—finally! The old man would climb up on the hearthstone and sit on his bench, resting one shoulder against the black wall.

As carefully as he did even the very slightest things, he would choose a half-burnt-out firebrand and use it to separate the ashes from the glowing embers, with the help of his sabots, thus building up a huge kind of hill which looked exactly like those volcanic mountains of Auvergne that you see in geography books. Then he'd make a hollow in the hill, in the shape of a crater. (See how learned I used to be!) And that crater took the place of a spittoon, for Grandfather was rather a meticulous and clean man. Clean above his station. You'd never see him splurting saliva all over the place like so many others. No, never!

Once he had finished, the old man would rub his hands vigorously, with a laugh of satisfaction. And he'd draw out his pipe—a fat briar pipe with a copper band, his pride of the year. Late in December he would always receive a new pipe from Paris, where two of his sons lived. Each time the package arrived in the mail, Grandfather would open it with trembling hands and never fail to rave about it, saying: "Now there's a pipe for you! There isn't another like it in the county."

Grandfather would slowly fill his pipe, very attentively, as is only proper for a procedure of such importance, and light it with a firebrand that had rolled out of the crater onto the hearth. As the thin smoke swirled around his kindly face, the old man would clear his throat and spit into the ashes. Whereupon I'd leap up close to him on the bench. He belonged to me. I would forget the eighteen nails and seven buttons (four made of horn and three of mottled glass, what a disaster!) which I had lost playing marbles with big Goyat, that cheater. I'd no longer dread my teacher's reproving eyes, or his steel ruler, which might well be slammed down on my knuckles the next day if I hadn't learned to conjugate my verbs. But to hell with all that! Grandfather would begin to talk; Grandfather was saddling his smoke-horse and giving me a blue colt to follow him on his search for a strange country where I knew everybody. And gee up!

> Gee up to Pont-Croix, gee up to Quimper!
> To Pont l'Abbé we have got to repair
> So we can find flour for the lady.

Grandfather would open his bag and his puppets would begin to live on his tongue. The first was himself; the second, me; and the others, people from the neighborhood. Every night we'd go from one adventure to another, and how they'd turn out nobody knew, not even the storyteller. At least no one alive, except perhaps the main character, Yves Mensonge, and a mysterious power which Grandfather called "the Office," though I swear he had never read the works of Kafka. Yves Mensonge would drag us along in his wake and fling us, blissful as we were, straight into the midst of danger, so tightly bound to him that we couldn't tear ourselves away. And then suddenly there'd be no more Yves and no more Mensonge, or Lie. We had to go and find the Office to untangle a situation that was taking a turn for the worse. But that was for the following night. We were incorrigible players, with no memory whatever and no ill feelings. Yves Mensonge knew that only too well.

Sometimes the most difficult part was to get Grandfather going when his mind was clouded with worry, which I had to respect. He'd smile weakly, and his pipe would usually sulk when he'd try to light it. I understood. Butter that week had been scarce. I hadn't seen "fresh meat" on the table for some time. The pitcher plants, a species of Nepenthes, were being smothered by crabgrass. Grandfather put his ear up close to the wall. Behind that wall was the manger:

"Listen to that! Isn't it the cow coughing?"

"Yes, I think so."

"She's rarely sick. I'm going in to see!"

Often I didn't really hear a thing, but I shared his concern. Poor as we were, the cow was easily our most valuable possession.

Once he had come out, Grandfather would sigh. Actually, some nights were very difficult to get through. The yield from our peas hadn't been enough to pay the rent for our fields, and we'd have to buy a bag of superphosphate to feed the depleted soil. But buy it with what? And there he was, walking about at the age of seventy, carrying in his hands a spade that grew heavier from year to year. Grandfather was heartbroken thinking about his old age. He would have liked to go on working right to the end, until the day he died one springtime, when from his window he could see thousands of green sprouts quivering in the field across the way—a field of hard and soft wheat which was enough to bring tears to the eyes of the most unfeeling peasant. But before then, he would have to unharness the bag of bones he was soon to become; no doubt of that. Like all the other old men, he would walk his cow at the end of a rope along the grassy ditches, keeping an eye out for the gendarmes at every turn in the road, since grazing is forbidden on common property.

Still, that black cow! That swarthy old dear, that silken girl, that rich master's cow which had won first prize at the county agricultural fair! Grandfather throbbed with emotion as he thought of his happy fate on this earth. It's really something to own a black cow!

All cheered up, with a clear mind, it wouldn't have taken much to convince him that he was shamefully lucky. The potatoes looked promising. They'd be easy to sell. Part of his pension that was in arrears was due to come in and would be more than enough to pay for the superphosphate. Besides, he could perhaps rent a field closer to town, which wouldn't tire his poor legs all that much. He knew just the one. And he also knew that he'd manage by himself. After all, he still had a few years left. And a few years were eternity, so to speak. All was well.

His nose in the sky, Grandfather rubbed his hands. "Those mischievous stars," he said, "aren't they making encouraging signs to me?" He winked at them in return. His daughter was right when she took him for an elderly child. OK, so he was an elderly child! The good man returned to the house and climbed up on the hearthstone beside his grandson to concoct some story out of the experiences of a long life—the life of a creature who had never stopped gazing at the world with a pure eye and who would have quite naturally thought himself a poet had he known what that was.

Yves Mensonge had climbed up on the hearth along with Grandfather. He wasn't even a shadow, yet a place was kept for him every night right next to me. I wasn't at all comfortable, I can tell you. But he was there; I knew it. Sometimes the bench cracked right under him. Besides, Grandfather was making conversation with him, looking him straight in the eye, and asking him this or that. The only answers I heard were from the old man's lips, for he repeated them to me so that he could call me to witness. I personally didn't dare to contradict Yves; I was too close to him. He might have seized me by the scruff of the neck with his hooked arm, and then what would have become of me, hanging from an invisible hand! I would have heard the pitiless laugh of "the Other Horned Demon."

The Other Horned Demon was the name we gave to our devil. A rather special devil—not the usual one, which was depicted on the painted tablets that Father Barnabé hung on a rope across the chancel, during the retreats, to explain the Last Judgment. You know the one I mean! A kind of red beast with a long tail, who's eager to sting the hides of the shrieking damned. No. Ours was a very human devil. He looked just like a good Breton from Lower Brittany who had run through his money and his possessions—a wandering Jew who roamed about aimlessly and indulged in noble works: arranging marriages, spreading joy at wedding feasts and vigils, salting the pork. Sometimes I felt like making friends with him in spite of his burning eyes. "Stop right there, son," said Grandfather. "That one's the Bad Spirit, a master of villainy! Mind you don't give in to him!" I sighed. Well, that was that! But there were so many things one could learn from the Other Horned Demon! For he was at the same time Grandfather and Yves Mensonge.

As for Yves Mensonge, what tricks was he about to pull now? And what was the Other Horned Demon doing here with that striking a resemblance to my teacher? What was he up to? My head began to nod, gently, gently. Oh, how I felt like going off to sleep! But it so happened that I couldn't because of a pair of glowing eyes—the eyes of the Bad Spirit. However much the Bretons are said to be close cousins of the Devil, it was best, all the same, to keep awake, for that cousin had got himself a bad reputation. Grandfather's pipe was still smoking. He was talking without stop, and it wasn't for me, but for the others. And the others, if I understood rightly, were answering him. At any rate, under the mantel there was an indistinct murmur, swelling and swelling . . .

I awoke with a start. Someone was knocking loudly against the partition. It was my mother, who had gone to bed long before, calling us to order: "Father, it's time to put the child to bed. How will he ever get up in the morning to go to school? You're no more sensible than he is. I may just have to make up a bed for him in the loft."

Every night it was the same thing. A day would come when the family council would surely separate us. So the two accomplices, terrified, made it over to their box-bed in a corner of the kitchen. Grandfather helped me to undress. The last two embers had gone out. We climbed into bed, making as much noise as possible to show our good will. I was already falling asleep when Grandfather's thumb struck me on the shoulder. I half-opened one eye.

"There's something new up there," whispered Alain Le Goff.

"Where?"

"Astride the top of the bed. Look at him, playing with my belt!"

"I see him. But who is he?"

"Who? The Other Horned Demon!"

I pulled the cover up over my head so that I could laugh my heart out. (Shh! I had to beware of my mother, who was lying in wait for us.) When I stopped, I could still hear Grandfather, who had turned his body right up against the partition, choking with joy.

One day Alain Le Goff asked me: "Before tonight, would you be able to find me two sticks, each with only one end? I need them badly and haven't the time to look for them myself. I'll give you a two-sou coin for your trouble."

I didn't answer right off. Ever since I'd got to be six years old, I would first consult myself. I knew that Grandfather wasn't talking just to make noise with his tongue. And whoever failed to pay attention to his words was in danger of feeling like a simpleton shortly afterward. I also knew that he had been entrusted with my early education and that he'd do his utmost so that I wouldn't make the family blush the day I confronted the schoolteacher who was soon to teach me French. Schoolteachers, I was told, took great pleasure in setting traps for you. Alain Le Goff wanted to get me accustomed to their tricks so that I'd be on my guard. He himself had been trained the same way by an uncle-guardian, and that's why he was so wise, with no thanks to any school. But with those two one-ended sticks, he had caught me so unprepared I was about to invent some excuse on the spur of the moment. If I didn't, it was only because I dreaded seeing Grandfather's blue eyes turn the other way, and hearing him, with a sigh, say something like: "Well, I'll just have to give my two sous to somebody else."

No, not on your life! I didn't care a hoot about the two sous, but I couldn't bear the idea of that somebody else. So let's see, thought I. The next month of April, with its April Fool's Day, was still far away because the last one wasn't far behind.

"Well," said Alain Le Goff, drawing on his pipe, "then I can't count on you?"

"Two one-ended sticks are hard to find. But maybe, if you'd be satisfied with one . . ."

"They always come in twos, that's all I know. When you take one of them in your hand, you're actually holding them both."

"And most of them are in which direction?"

"They're in all directions," said Alain Le Goff.

"But how can you tell that a stick has only one end?"

"How? Don't you know? It's when the other end isn't there."

He had said his last word on the subject. He merely took off for the fields without looking back, for he knew that I was about to set out on my search. I began by closely examining the gruel stick, which was standing in the chimney corner. It had a tail to hold onto and a head (an end) for stirring the paste. Could that be it? But Grandfather could simply have taken that one. And besides, there was only one of them. How could it have been easier to find two? I went into the shed. There I found spades, shovels, rakes, pitchforks, and pickaxes, all with handles. A handle has only one end, since the other has some iron and a tool attached to it. But could a handle be considered a stick? I took it upon myself to answer no. Ten minutes later I was climbing the path that ran along the Rector's Field* and then went down into the meadows. On every slope there were dozens of branches just waiting to become sticks. And right over there were two that looked like brother and sister. In my mind I could see them cut down, but between the two of them they had four ends.

So I went back toward the house to see how things were going. I let the sun pull the day behind it. Surely I was as courageous as anyone else. Indeed, I was ready to exceed all the limitations of my six and a half years to get my hands on those one-ended sticks. But I could sense, even then, that if I hadn't found them before nightfall, Grandfather would have found them himself. And I experienced an odd pleasure as I savored my defeat, anticipating my surprise when the old man would bring me the "key to the castle." That's what he called the solution to the muddles that beset us from all sides the entire time we have our eyes open. He himself never failed to find that key.

*See below, chap. 3. (Trans.)

In fact, there he was, returning from the Méot field, walking at his own pace, as usual, with his hat pulled down over his eyebrows because the sunset that evening was glowing red, too red for those blue eyes of his. He was wielding a stick that he used from time to time to assist a left leg which had become sluggish from overaction. Only one stick, not two, otherwise I would have sworn that he had found what he needed. For that stick was not the one he'd gone off with. When it came to walking sticks, Grandfather had over seven of them which he had made himself, not counting his Sunday cane for going to Mass, which he had bought in a store, if you please. The cane was kept in the wardrobe, stretched out over his fine striped trousers, whereas the sticks were hung on the beams of the manger, being given new life by the animals' breath. First of all, there was a *penn-baz*, a club-shaped stick with a leather shoelace attached to its grip so that a man could tie it to his wrist; for not so very long ago it had served as a weapon in case of attack. It had never been used by peaceable Alain Le Goff, who had nonetheless learned to manipulate it very well indeed. Then there was a stick made of holly, for outings of four leagues and even longer. Straight as an arrow, that one came right up to the shoulder of a tall man; in fact, it had to, for you needed it to jump from one slope to another, over the mud roads. There was also the "whistle-stick," so named because if you whistled through a hole in its grip, it made the noise of a reptile, one of which had been sculpted on the twists of the stick itself. And there was the "surveyor-stick," with notches that marked off inches, feet, ells, and all the other various measures Grandfather made use of. Finally, there were the "excuse-sticks." Much thinner than the previous ones, they were absolutely unfit for driving the road from under your feet—mere switches that could just about knock the heads off thistles or scratch your back when it itched. It was one of those that Alain Le Goff had taken with him in the morning. And there he was, coming back with a masterpiece of a stick which had a red top and a gray bottom, whereas the middle was tightly sheathed in heavy waxed thread that must have come straight from Guillaume the shoemaker.

"Well, now! How about those two sticks, each with only one end? Where are they?"

"I haven't seen hide nor hair of them, Grandfather."

"It's my fault," he said with a smile. "You would have needed a knife and you're still too young. But the day you're seven years old, you'll have one. I give you my word."

"But you needed those sticks before tonight!"

"Here they are. Look carefully."

He gave a sharp pull on a kind of waxed-thread ring, which he held in one hand, and as he turned the stick with the other, the thread began to unwind. I saw half the stick fall—the red half, which, under the thread, was cut at an angle. "It's chestnut," said Alain Le Goff. And when the gray half was completely uncovered, you saw that it too was cut at an angle. "Now it's oak." I was looking at it so hard that I had trouble keeping my eyes from popping out.

"A few minutes ago I had two sticks in one. When I held the oak in my hand, it was the chestnut that touched the ground. Each was a separate stick, you see! The most difficult part was finding two branches of the same thickness and of different kinds of wood so that no one would go and claim that it was the same stick. You know how people are: they never want to believe anything until they've seen it and touched it. Once you have the two sticks, you cut each one at an angle, and each with a notch, so that they fit perfectly, one on top of the other; then you bind them along the angular cuts with a thread that's strong enough to bite deeply into the bark and hold it all together securely. As I'm doing."

And with those words, Grandfather began to reconstitute the red and gray stick, and, in the end, only two of the four ends were left. Once he had finished, the good man laid the object on my knees: "It's for you. Bring it up close to your ear and you will hear the 'key to the castle' turning."

"There's nothing more beautiful than a tree," Alain Le Goff liked to say. The poor man had never had a tree of his own, but all those he could see with his eyes were his accomplices in the great game of Creation. He liked some of them better than others—not the most triumphant, but those that toiled to survive in the brutal wind. He would go to see them during the winter, when they were bare.

"Look how they're working," he'd say.

"And what are they doing?"

"They're linking the earth to the sky. That's very difficult, son. The sky is so lightweight that it's always at the point of taking off. If there were no trees, it would bid us farewell. Then there'd be nothing left for us but to die. May God preserve us."

"But there are countries where no trees grow at all. I learned that in school. They're called deserts."

"That's just the point, son. There are no men in those parts. The sky slipped away."

I pretended that I hadn't understood. As for him, he lit his pipe, smiling. No one has ever smiled like Alain Le Goff, and that's why men are so unhappy on this earth. He struck the gnarled trunk with his open hand:

"You can see that the trunk of a tree is a thick rope. Sometimes there are even knots inside. The strands of the rope work themselves loose at each end so that they can fasten onto the sky and the earth. At the top they're called branches, and at the bottom, roots. But it comes to the same thing. The roots try and find a way down through the ground just as the branches make their way into the sky."

"But it's harder to get into the ground than into the sky."

"Well, no! If that were true, the branches would be straight. And look how twisted they are on this apple tree right here! I tell you they must try and find their way. They grow; the sky resists; they change direction as often as necessary. They have a lot of trouble, you know. Maybe even more trouble than the roots at the bottom."

"And what gives them so much trouble, Grandfather?"

"It's the wind, the rotten wind. The wind would like to separate the sky and the earth. It thrusts its tongue between the two of them. And behind it, there's the sea, just waiting to cover everything. But there are the trees, which stand fast against them both. The blessed sun helps the branches, while the rain comforts the roots. A holy battle, my son. The fighting never stops in this world."

"But what about us? What should we do?"

"Have confidence in the trees withstanding the wind."

Alain Le Goff's smile was so serene, I found it difficult to believe that the world was at stake in that bitter struggle between the elements. I was living in safety on a level with tree trunks, while the birds kept a close watch over the heavenly roots and while all sorts of mute little bugs were bustling about in the dark around the branches underground. But more than once, when a southwester would come howling over my countryside, I did go out and keep an eye on the tall elm trees that edged the Rector's Field. I was afraid of seeing the sky slip away under the tongue of the wind and of remaining stark naked on an earth that had been stripped bare. Thanks to the trees, I avoided that apocalypse until the day I lost my childish wisdom, yet found no other explanation of the world.

Progressing from doggerels to obscure tales and from proverbs to riddles, time flew by. I tackled the scholarship examination and was admitted to the lycée, which meant seven years at boarding school, with drums marking off the hours. When I had to go to Rennes to take the oral exam for the *baccalauréat*, Alain Le Goff came along with me and had got all dressed up: leather shoes, striped trousers—dull-and-shiny—a velvet waistcoat buttoned up to the neck, a hat with ribbons, and a watch chain. I don't know which of us was more miserable. Grandfather awaited the verdict at the home of his youngest daughter, Aunt Lisette, who had married Uncle Guillaume, my father's brother. He closed himself into a bedroom, where he ate himself up with anxiety, while I was to suffer in a classroom at the Faculté des Arts. But he had first given me a hint as to how to keep from trembling in front of my judges. It's apparently as old as the hills: "If you're afraid of the gentleman standing before you, son, try to imagine him naked. A highbrow frog is, after all, just a frog."

I passed the exam. There was rejoicing in the humble abode on the rue Bara. Grandfather took a large bill out of his old wallet. "I don't know much about champagne," he told Aunt Lisette, "but rush out and get us a bottle. We're going to act like the big shots."

And Alain Le Goff, whom no one had ever seen at a bar, drank a full glass of that beverage, of which he later said that were it injected into the backside of a dog, the poor beast would run around the world yelping with pain. As we walked down the street to the railroad station on our way back to the train, Grandfather stuck out his chest like a county councillor campaigning for office. I understood that my own *baccalauréat* was his as well, since he was the only true master I ever had.

From time to time, at unexpected hours and on unexpected days, a tall devil of a man would appear on the town square, having just arrived from Plozévet. His clothes, which once had been blue, were worn out and bleached from wear and tear. On his head was a faded hat without any ribbon on it, but which was proudly tilted back, touching the nape of his neck. On his feet were large beech sabots, and their straw pads, which came up to his ankles, were twice as thick as anyone else's. In his hand he carried a stick which he twirled every six steps he took. The man had gray sideburns like the three Jules—Grévy, Ferry, and Simon—and the very same nose as the Bourbon kings of France. Walking like a king who was having trouble with his left leg, his brow held high and his shoulders swinging loose, he'd climb up toward our house, using his stick right and left to salute all his acquaintances, who were watching him from the windows and doors of their houses. He was my other grandfather—the one who had priority, being my father's father—the sabot-maker of Kerveillant. One day, between Meros and Kervinou, I had heard him called "Jean the Wonder-Man."

When I'd be out playing on the road, I would walk down to meet him, for I never failed to see him arrive, nor indeed did any of the other children. I don't know how he managed to attract every eye to him as soon as he'd appear. The moment he saw me, he'd wave his stick way up in the air and begin to laugh. Without bending down at all, he'd put his hand on my shoulder: "Why you've grown taller; you're a good boy, little Pierre." Then he'd take me by the hand, lift a prophetic finger, and utter one of those sayings that were his very own and which would send me into a state of rapture because I felt they were a kind of sesame by which we would become reacquainted after a few weeks:

> I don't know why and know nothing about
> How Jakez Perros's teeth all fell out.

I'd drag him behind me all the way to the house. And we would both go in, but not before he had proclaimed from the doorway: "Here we are, the two most beautiful animals in the world!" When Alain Le Goff was there, he would rise to greet his old comrade. The two men were very different from one another. But as it happened, there was a complicity between them, so that from time to time they needed to agree on fundamental things, which had no relation to people's daily behavior. The sabot-maker spoke and Alain Le Goff listened, but the sabot-maker knew perfectly well what Grandfather would say had he wished to speak, so he spoke for the two of them. To my ears that was something both new and familiar. I was tempted to think that it took precisely those two grandfathers to produce a grandson of good stock. When I sat down in my usual place next to Alain Le Goff, he said: "Go on now and sit next to your chief grandfather!" I didn't argue, but walked to the other end of the table. The sabot-maker put an arm around me: "Would you like to come to Kerveillant and spend a day or two or even more? Your grandmother hasn't seen you for a long time."

"Of course he'll go," replied Alain Le Goff. The sabot-maker explained that the Meill-Douget Mill carrier would come by in the evening with his wagon empty and would take both of us in it like lords. Another wagon would bring me back at some later date. My chief grandfather knew all the wagon drivers in the world. He swore that I wouldn't be bored, and I knew he was telling the truth. He went on to talk about his bees.

At that point my mother returned and, having expressed her surprise, took the glasses and bottles out of the cupboard, put some coffee on to boil, and covered the table with food, before getting a few of my things together. Perhaps I'd come back in three days, or perhaps a week, nobody knew, especially not the sabot-maker, but she would get news of me from all the journeymen who roamed about the region. If need be, she could always walk over and fetch me. Two leagues is nothing. Perhaps I could even make it back by myself.

The sabot-maker took out his knife and raised his glass:

> Good health to all the creatures dear!
> This drink's about to disappear.

He took a sip, set his glass down on the table, and wiped his mouth with the back of his hand:

> Here's to Paradise for all our dead!
> This drink's now done for and gone to my head.

Night had fallen by the time the mill carrier arrived and had a drink himself before taking us off in his floury wagon. We couldn't wait for my father, who returned too late. But ever since he'd been driving a truck, he had quite a few opportunities to stop and visit at Kerveillant. So off we went, bumping along the road, as I, very proud of myself, sat between the driver's knees and held the reins. When I grew up, if I were strong enough, I'd be a mill carrier and never stop whistling from dawn to dusk.

At Kerveillant my grandmother Katrina Gouret was awaiting us. She was a small woman and very plump in her thick petticoats and beneath a coiffe that was much lower than my mother's because of her age. She had bright red cheeks, which were a pleasure to see, and a kindly smile that almost never left her face despite a life of hard work and ordeals. She had prepared some coffee soup for me in a bowl covered with a plate and had put it near the fire to keep hot. There was a much larger bowl of potato soup for the sabot-maker. After the soup came an omelet, but that was too much: I fell asleep over it. So I was undressed and carried over to the box-bed.

That box-bed was the only one of its kind I have ever known. It was a double-decker crate in which my father and his brothers—all four of them—had slept until they left home. But during family reunions I myself had slept in it with three others. With my godfather Jakez and my Uncles Guillaume and Henri, or perhaps Corentin, I don't recall. What I do recall is that the enormous crate would creak all over every time anyone turned in it. You'd also hear the straw crackling and the bales of oats rustling. And it was full of all the laughter and jokes of the brothers while they'd been in it together. One time the two uncles on top deliberately rammed their backs against the straw mattresses, threatening to make the whole top collapse onto the two occupants below (one of whom happened to be me), who in turn banged their fists up against the boards to make them keep still. I was a bit frightened when it creaked too much, but the crate was strong, so on we'd go!

The day after my arrival, when I opened the box-bed doors and got up, Grandfather was already carving his sabots in front of the house, under the trees. Quick, then!—my trousers, my stockings, my slippers—and I appeared in the doorway. Grandfather stuck his knife into the huge chopping block he used as a workbench. He took off his blue Phrygian cap ("a Republican cap, son!") to wipe his forehead. "From where I stand, I can hear your stomach growling," he said. "Go and eat your soup. Empty bags never stand upright." My grandmother was somewhere in the fields, but my bowl of hot soup was waiting for me next to the low fire. It was nine o'clock. The sabot-maker came back into the house to have a snack. He had been working since dawn. At the head of the table there was a kind of large, flat wicker basket (a *koloenn*), in the middle of which was a rope attached to a pulley on the ceiling. Grandfather pulled on the rope and the *koloenn* rose, uncovering a round loaf of bread. After knotting the rope to a nail in the wall, he took a *plên*, a two-handled knife, which he used to slice the bread very evenly, straight across the loaf. Once we'd had our fill, the rope was detached from its nail, and the *koloenn* descended, covering the bread again.

I spent the morning watching Grandfather make sabots out of chunks of beech, and kept wondering how he managed to work with such large and heavy tools. Of course, his sabots were not meant for young ladies: they were too bulky and had one end that looked like a pig's snout—fine for laborers and suitable for tramping about in the mud. Ah, those beech shavings smelled so good!

"Will you teach me how to make sabots, Grandfather?"

"No, son. You'd never have really enough to eat. A shoemaker, why not? But it would be far better to learn to read, write, and speak French. Then you'll have bread and meat every day. And you'll walk on leather soles. During my seven years of military service I walked from Châteauroux to Belfort on leather and felt that I actually had wings. The city boys who were in the same regiment didn't even know how to use their legs. But they knew everything else, or so they said. I myself never went to school. But

I learned to read so well in the army that I now manage to make out parts of *The Lives of the Saints*. Your grandmother, though, spent three months with the nuns. Unfortunately, it was too expensive. She was forced to leave the convent school. So she continued her education later on, at the same time as her children were learning. While they were sleeping, she'd look into their books and notebooks. But I don't have her kind of mind. I only remember things that are absolutely useless. Or else things that are very useful but which wouldn't please your mother if she heard me telling you about them.

"Tell me anyway, Grandfather. She isn't here."

Grandfather put his paring knife to one side. He looked around suspiciously.

"Well, here goes! Every time you need to relieve yourself, remember this. When it's a question of shitting, turn your nose toward the wind so that the bad smell will be blown behind you. When it's merely a question of peeing, turn your ass toward the wind so that the urine will be blown in front of you. If you don't pay attention to that, you may well get a noseful of bad smell and your trousers full of urine."

Agreed. I never breathed a word of that lesson to my mother, but it was to serve me well, believe me. Just as another of his suggestions was to serve me well—a suggestion he went on making until the day he died: "When it comes to food, kowtow to people as much as you have to in order to eke out a living for yourself and your household, but never a whit more, do you understand, never a whit more, even if you're ordered to by the most powerful big shot in the world."

Alain Le Goff said the same thing, but he had no trouble living peacefully since he was never tempted by anything that might have made him dependent on others—even for a few moments. As for my chief grandfather, he had a worm that kept worrying his mind, and the only way he managed to silence it was by throwing himself completely into his work. From time to time that worm would lead the sabot-maker into a life of adventure. He had always felt like gadding about to see what was happening in the world, and associating with all sorts of people, and learning new things, even when those new things proved to boggle the mind. On his way back, he'd be unable to resist the pleasure of sharing the two cents worth of wisdom he had stored up at his own expense and the few francs worth of madness he had inherited; indeed, he went so far as to invent certain tales that made him famous in the county and which people were still talking about some forty years later.

As soon as he had finished his work in the fields or on his chopping block, he would try to escape into new realms in order to deaden the worm. All he had to do was to fill a hemp bag with dough for buckwheat bread, place it on his head, and take it to an oven in Lababan to be baked, for a number of roads to open up at random, the most perilous of which was the road home. At such times, well after night had fallen, there would still be no sign of the sabot-maker. He was probably telling wondrous tales somewhere under a fireplace mantel. Or else he was tramping about on sunken roads on his way to a place where a gathering of honest folk would be awaiting him—people who needed him to keep them in high spirits.

Once a nocturnal adventure almost turned out disastrously. One winter morning his son Guillaume was walking to his school in Plozévet. It had snowed a good deal during the night. As he was passing the Kergivig farm, the young boy noticed a pile of snow at the edge of the road which resembled a newly made grave. He drew near and realized that it was a man stretched out, stiff as a corpse; and the man was his father. At a gallop, he made his way back to Kerveillant to inform the owners, the Le Guellecs, who went out to fetch the sabot-maker and brought him back to his *penn-ti* in a handcart. My grandmother Katrina, who didn't get unduly excited, lit a hellish fire in the hearth and then had her husband laid on the fireplace bench. It was nine o'clock. A half hour later, the sabot-maker had thawed out and recovered consciousness with a great sigh. Once he had revived, he got into his box-bed and slept until noon. After which, he ate what there was to eat and began to work, as if nothing had happened. People were to say that if he hadn't been such a "night cat," he would have lived to be 120 years old, given his constitution.

But such unexpected escapades were rare. Grandfather had other means for appeasing his cankerworm. Indeed, his reputation for knowing so many tales was such that at the end of harvest time, he was sought out in his Kerveillant *penn-ti* in order that he might transform a gathering of peasants in a farmhouse into so many knights and ladies of the Round Table who, as if by some miracle, would be speaking Plozévet Breton at a king's court. For the sabot-maker needed no more than one person to listen to him—a person who could be interested in something other than the land, or any sort of possessions, or the price of suckling pigs, or daily bread, or Sunday meat soup, or similar stuff and nonsense—for him to start speaking aloud, building up a whole structure of wonders. So it's not at all surprising that children were his best audience. And the most privileged of the children at that point was me, his eldest grandchild. Clearly, whenever I visited Kerveillant, I was constantly at his heels.

A quarter of a century after Grandfather's death, when I myself was a voice on the radio every week for half an hour, or when I would speak in person in the town and villages, the old men of my county would tell me time after time: "You're not so bad, but you're still not up to the sabot-maker." Nothing could be truer. For if ever he was at a loss, he'd contrive to bring forth stories out of nothingness. And he made them sound so believable that he was capable of causing an uproar in an entire parish. Over and again he would invent anecdotes out of whole cloth, which he'd then expand to include memorable events, and he did it in the very presence of the characters he was portraying. In fact, he was so precise about place, time, and personalities that the heroes, in spite of themselves, ended up believing that it had all really happened to them. At least once, the sabot-maker, inventing tales in the most whimsical manner, called Alain Le Goff as a witness to what he was saying. Since it happened that Alain Le Goff had actually been there, he was flabbergasted. Sometimes the supposed protagonist of the story would go around telling about his adventure to anyone who cared to listen. He would even tell the sabot-maker himself, who made believe he didn't know about it, keeping a perfectly straight face and pretending that he found it incredulous.

The following, if you like, is an example of my chief grandfather's humor: He was once clearing a moor that belonged to the Brenizenec Mill and was working like a slave to transform it into a potato field. The moor in question happened to border on a road. All the passersby would stop to ask Grandfather what he was doing. Ten or twenty times a day he'd patiently answer: "I'm felling trees; I'm digging out stumps; I'm cleaning the ground; I'm breaking up the soil," etc. Then one day he got fed up, and when he was approached by an old woman who was well known for not being able to hold her tongue, even under penalty of death, he whispered in her ear: "I've been entrusted by the Mayor of Plozévet to prepare a special cemetery for the one-eyed veterans of the First World War. Keep it a secret, please!" Straightaway the old hen rushed off and cackled about the news everywhere she went. As soon as the one-eyed veterans heard about it, and since—alas—there was a good handful of them, they went to the town hall to vent their indignation. Indeed, they went to see Monsieur Le Bail himself, who immediately sent for the sabot-maker:

"Yet another of your tall tales! What ever possessed you to invent that stupid story?"

"Is it my fault, Monsieur Le Bail? All the people who take that road, all those peasants, like me, know perfectly well what I'm doing, since they see me doing it. They wouldn't need more than half an eye to know it all. Instead of that, they ask me a stupid question. So I gave them the stupidest answer I could think of."

Henceforth the small field in question has been called the "Cemetery for One-Eyed Veterans." God only knows how scholars in the future will explain that name.

Between every two of such fantastic tales, my chief grandfather taught me lots of things that were calculated to make my life easier. One in particular was that in our region, at least in all the well-kept houses, the women always managed to control the entire household, even when they pretended to obey the head of the family, though only in public. Knowing that, I shall forever live in peace in my own home and be happy in my own shoes. Do as I do if you prefer not to raise your voice or roll up your sleeves for a dubious battle.

I was twelve or thirteen when, one Easter, I went to visit my Plozévet grandparents and took my sister Lisette with me, who was much younger. Grandmother Katrina gave us eggs, according to the custom. She put them in a colored handkerchief, which she delicately knotted. "Lisette," she said, "this handkerchief will be yours for good once the eggs have been eaten, but only on condition that you don't break any of them on your way home." (The eggs, by the way, were hard-boiled.)

And that's how one brought up little girls.

Grandfather opened his cupboard and took out a small pile of bronze coins bearing the head of the Emperor Napoleon III. He gave me twelve sous, but gave only eight to my sister. "He has more than I do," wailed Lisette, on the verge of tears. "That's because he'll soon have hair under his nose," replied Grandfather. "Would you like to have hair under your nose, my girl?" Lisette didn't dare breathe another word. She forgot to sulk on our way home, trailing well behind me so that she wouldn't break a single egg. The next evening and during the days that followed, she never stopped whining and claiming that it wasn't fair to reward someone beforehand for a moustache that might never exist. Finally, just to have some peace, I gave her two sous, and she promised to find me a few warm pigeon-droppings to help the hair grow more quickly under my nose. The best part of it was that she kept her promise.

The next time we went to see our grandparents, the sabot-maker drew me aside:

"What did you do with the sous I gave you, Perig?"

"First of all, I gave two of them to Lisette. That way we each had ten."

"You did the wrong thing, son. And what use did you make of your own ten sous?"

"I bought some licorice sticks and some jam cakes."

"And what about Lisette's?"

"That girl's a miser already. She keeps them with her, under her pillow, knotted in a corner of Grandmother's handkerchief."

Grandfather made no comment. But when we were about to leave, he presented Lisette with fifteen sous, and me, with only a five-sou coin, as he murmured into my ear: "I think I did better this time, given what the world's coming to. But, in the name of God, don't ever hand this coin over to your sister, even if she scrapes her knees on the ground, begging you to."

And that's how one brought up little boys.

The author, aged about five, in a mourning skirt and apron. This was before he graduated to long pants.

The author and his mother, aged eighty, in front of Alain Le Goff's house

3 Our Father Which Art in Heaven

> The language a man speaks is a veritable world in which he lives and acts; it is a more profound and a more essential part of him than the land and those things he calls his country.
>
> Romano Guardini

The Saint-Fiacre fountain was set up right in the middle of a meadow at the low end of town. Fiacre was an Irishman who, along with Faron, is the patron saint of our parish. Faron had been a bishop whose seat was in Meaux, and Fiacre merely a hermit under his protection. That he might have a garden, Faron had offered him as much land as he could enclose within a ditch that he was to dig in one day. Fiacre took his spade, dragged it behind him, and the land opened up of itself as he moved ahead. And it was because of his garden—one almost as beautiful as the Garden of Eden—that the godly Fiacre became the patron saint of gardeners. Now it happened that in addition to all his other virtues, Fiacre possessed healing powers. He had merely to stretch his hand out over the heads of the ailing and, whatever their disease, they became healthy forthwith. Thus—between two catechism lessons—spake Monsieur Pelleter, the rector of our parish. He didn't mention the fact that Saint Fiacre was best known for his curing of hemorrhoids.

At the bottom of the granite alcove that curves around the fountain, which is like a large font mirroring the clouds, there is still an oak log, strangely cracked and protected from looters by part of a rust-eaten rosary. That log is an effigy of Saint Fiacre, whose features were gradually obliterated over the centuries. But it's still there, you can be sure. And if you look down through the clear water of the fountain, you can see shining shards of colored faience—a kaleidoscope that used to fascinate the children. From time to time they would get the impression that other shards had settled over those that covered the bottom. Where did they come from? No one seemed to know. And why were there shards in the Saint-Fiacre fountain in the first place? When we used to question our parents about it, they'd look surprised. And if we persisted, we knew that a slap was in the offing.

If I remember correctly, it was Yann Audeyer who one day told me the secret of it all. A road-repairman by trade, Yann Audeyer was one of Alain Le Goff's two best friends, the other being Joz Scuiller. Grandfather called them his brothers. Whenever the roller came past our house to macadamize the road, Yann would spend the night with us, for he lived very far away, in Meill-Bondeleg, in the direction of Plogastel. At such times I'd learn things from him that my teacher didn't even know. One night, when I happened to be alone with him, I spoke to him of the Saint-Fiacre fountain. He smiled.

"I really shouldn't tell you this, but I think you know how to hold your tongue. Of course, the blessed Saint Fiacre is not the patron of my parish; ours is Saint Germain. But people say that the women come to your fountain on the sly and throw in the pieces of a plate or of a bowl they'd broken while doing the dishes. Then they kneel down and say a prayer. Maybe it's to ask the saint to keep their hands from being so clumsy or to appease their husbands' righteous anger. You'd better not ask your mother about it or you might get a wet rag thrown in your face."

"But how do you know that, Uncle Yann?"

"I know it because when the men from around here are in a good mood, they freely admit that the prayer to Saint Fiacre is the one and only secret that women are able to keep."

Sometimes the children would go and kneel on the stone edge of the fountain and spend a long time looking at the multicolored puzzle. Not that they were trying to understand their mothers or their sisters; they did it because among the bits of faience were a few bronze coins bearing the head of Napoleon III, which they were trying to spot. All they had to do if they wanted to be two or four sous richer was to roll up one sleeve. But the grim horror of Hell would tie their innards up in knots. Stealing from Saint Fiacre meant losing one's immortal soul. Then all of a sudden one of them would put his hand in the water and, with a flick of his wrist, splash it all over the others, before fleeing at a wild gallop. The others would take off after him, shouting vulgar insults and threatening him with certain subtle forms of torture. But the virtue of Saint Fiacre's water, dripping down their skin under their shirts, eventually transformed them into little angels, and the chase would degenerate into a game of leapfrog.

It is said that coins were thrown into the fountain by a few very old women who remembered that the godly hermit had been known in the past for possessing some obscure power. But the current generations have forgotten. Everything dies away. There is no longer a cult of Saint Fiacre. And yet the father of a man named Kel ar Zaout, who is still alive, stuck a pin into the statue's eye one day to see if it would suffer. Shortly afterward, the sacrilegious man developed leucoma in one of his eyes. The saint had paid him back in kind.

At least that's what they say.

I have also heard tell that before the First World War, people, though they were by no means any better, had more faith than they do today. I can bear witness to that, based on what I've heard from my own family. Just listen to this!

When my maternal grandmother, Alain Le Goff's wife, fell sick, she promised that if she were cured, she would go to Rumengol and light a candle that cost four reals to the statue of the Virgin of Cure-Alls. She died. She was thus meant to die. Alain Le Goff had my mother go on the pilgrimage in her place and fulfill the vow even though she hadn't been cured. One doesn't play games with vows. It cost a great deal of money. My mother brought back a picture of the All-Powerful Lady—an oval picture under glass, which was placed on the kitchen cupboard. It is still there.

When my mother was young, she was subject to headaches and went several times to the Chapelle de Saint-Germain-en-Plogastel to make her devotions and to drink the fountain water. Three or four leagues wasn't much of a walk. And since her headaches did go away, she would take me along with her later on, during the First World War. Then there was the youngest of my Le Goff aunts, Lisette, who, at about age twelve, had scabs all over her scalp. After a treatment that consisted of an old wives' remedy, a sort of ointment, she went almost blind for a few days. My grandfather sent her directly to the Chapelle de la Clarté in Combrit to drink the fountain water. She took the "carrot-train"* as far as Pont l'Abbé and went the rest of the way on foot, praying and in a state of recollection. The scabs disappeared and she regained her sight.

One of my uncles had trouble speaking. He chopped up his words, as they say in French. So he went on a pilgrimage to the chapel in Tréminou, near Pont l'Abbé—a place you took children who were late talkers or who were unable to pronounce words correctly. If you weren't cured in Tréminou because your sins weighed too heavily upon you, you had no choice but to take a horse-charabanc to the church in Comfort, where there was a carillon with a rotating cylinder at the entrance to the chancel. The mute child would shake the carillon and make it ring a hundred times louder than the jingling of small change. There's the story of one boy who had never uttered a word in his life, but who, when he heard the noise of the bells, suddenly cried out: "Sell ta! Pegemend a drouz!" or "Heavens! What a lot of noise that makes!" Miracle of miracles!

As I mentioned before, the disease we dreaded above all in the Bigouden region was a weakness of the legs which caused many men, and even more women, to limp. An inherited disease, perhaps, but one that we could have well done without. And after all, we had a number of saintly figures in our province who were said to protect you from that misfortune. In Plogastel, the county seat, at a place called "Le Pont du Voleur," there is a fountain dedicated to Saint Peter in which you bathed children who had weak backs or who were late walkers. And there's another fountain with the same healing virtues on the Tréguennec marsh, near

*See below, chap. 4. (Trans.)

La Chapelle de Saint Vio. On the day of the pardon,* around 1925, I saw a group of Bigouden mamas, each awaiting her turn to splash her baby, who was naked from the waist down, with the "nice healing water." Even in 1969 a few grandmothers were rubbing their grandchildren with that water—the last grandmothers who trembled a bit at the thought of those bygone apprehensions and who somewhat indulged that bygone hope.

In the cemetery at Lababan, the mother-parish of Pouldreuzic, we had a kind of small ditch or, rather, a hole, which was the last recourse for children who limped. True, Lord Paban, the protector of that *lan* (a sacred place), was a more powerful figure than either Faron or Fiacre. Isn't he said to have once been the Pope at Rome? He's called Pabu in the region of Léon, which is ample proof that his saintliness is known far and wide! At any rate, the little cripples would sit barefoot on the edge of the hole and their legs were rubbed with the soil from the bottom.

In that same parish of Lababan, to the north of the large road that goes from Pouldreuzic to Plozévet, there is a fountain called "la Fontaine des Maux Poignants," or "the Fountain for Agonizing Ailments." Also, on the rock face of a nearby grotto, a primitive alcove had been built for the Virgin. The water from that grotto was said to be the ultimate for intestinal diseases. Women went there to wash their babies' diapers if they happened to be suffering from distended bellies or diarrhea. Indeed, my own diapers had once soaked in that water; for it would appear that stomach trouble was one of the maladies that most affected the Bigouden children. Everyone dreaded the possibility of it turning into a "raging bellyache," because then they would have to call in a doctor and hear, from his own lips, one of those terms that smacks of extreme unction. But the Virgin of Tronoen also healed such diseases in her chapel on the marsh, which was rather far from town but not too far for those penitents who knew how to walk, in all confidence, on their own leathery soles. Actually, all good Christians, even healthy ones, had to make a pilgrimage to that chapel at Tronoen, which was set up in the wilderness facing the ocean. For it is there that the whole story of the Lord Jesus is told

*A Breton religious festival, described below. (Trans.)

in stone images on the two levels of a granite calvary so worn down by the centuries that the holy figures have no faces anymore. In the chapel itself, part of the floor was made of mud, and, using just a bit of that mud, people could make plasters to cure their ulcers. But, above all, when diluted in water, it brought a sense of calm to one's body. Joz Sciuller once tried the treatment and felt all the better for it.

As for me, the only water I ever drank, and only while I was still in skirts, was from the Chapelle de Lavern in Plonéour, which also cured intestinal diseases. We knew, of course, that big shots from the cities—people as rich as the sea—traveled a very long way, and at great expense, to drink beneficial water or to sprinkle themselves with it in various ways. Waters of that sort are even bottled and then sold to those frail people who can't make do with cider or red wine. Vichy, Vittel—that's what they're called. They, too, come up from the ground, but ours tasted better in the throat. And they didn't cost a cent. As for the fountains of the saints, there was no reason to doubt their healing powers, since those particular saints used to be displayed in all our churches and chapels. The Virgin, Madame Marie, devotes herself to everyone; that's only fair. Therefore she's everywhere. Apparently, there is one place she's especially fond of. It's in the south, beyond the Dordogne, a kind of Holy Land called Lourdes. We would have been happy to go there; in fact, we thought we might even get there one day if we could afford it; and we would bring back water from that region. But for the time being, Notre-Dame de Penhors, rising high over the sea that bathes our parish, was perfectly capable of caring for us. She never moved from her chapel. She knew us. We could ask her for all the blessings we lacked and, above all, to protect our brothers the fishermen, who were constantly venturing out into the Bay of Audierne.

Besides, our very own saints knew all about the woes that plague peasants. We had qualms, however, about going too often to beg favors of them. That the women went on the sly to the Chapelle de Kergoat in Quéméneven when they had so-called "woman's trouble" was understandable; what else could they do? But daily life brought each of us his share of minor wounds and temporary ailments, and we had to cure them by our own devices. Calling in a doctor for anything so unimportant was considered almost a disgrace, a sign of weakness and cowardice that showed you were a sissy. What's more, people inevitably thought you were at death's door. Not to mention the expense, which, for most of us, wasn't within our means. Of course, we were very pleased to have a doctor in the county seat. A capable man, it appeared. Whenever you'd go to the fair at Quimper, it set you up to be able to brag to the peasants from the north or the east: "We have a doctor . . . ," never specifying exactly where. Isn't it true that a district without a doctor is always inhabited by a bunch of poor devils? Grandfather sometimes talked to me about "the doctor from up there," Monsieur Neiz, a horseman who would arrive riding hell-bent-for-leather and begin by asking the patient: "Do you sleep well? Do you eat well? Do you shit well?" When the answer to all three questions was yes, Monsieur Neiz would look at the entire household with terrifying eyes and explode: "Then why in the world are you bothering me?"

Thanks to our fathers' experience, we inherited a certain number of remedies to help us make do on our own. The children all knew that if they stepped on a nail when running barefoot down the road, they first had to make the wound bleed and then pee on it. In such cases, cupping your hand was very useful if, in the dry mud of a dirt road, you couldn't find the deep imprint of a cow's hoof to fill with the urine needed to bathe the wound. After that, you'd look for a slug or a snail. Their slime served as a collodion. It was also good for getting a speck out of your eye. But you had to beware! In 1972 my friend Youenn Broustal told me that there was an old man in his town who used to sleep by the fireside. Once, as a joke, his friends rubbed his eyes with that slime. When the old man awoke, he found it impossible to unglue his eyelids. They had to be washed with very hot water for a very long time before he was able to move them again. It was probably that property of slug's slime which convinced me to use it myself, when I was in elementary school, to remove some warts from my hands which had persisted in spite of the purple ink that everyone said did wonders. And as a matter of fact, they did disappear. The slime made a very hard coating which smothered the excrescence in a few days. But I forgot one part of the remedy, which consisted in piercing the slug through with a stick that you planted in the ground. When the slug had dried out, the wart was gone. Or so they said. But I personally couldn't swear to it.

For small sores you used pennywort, which we call "*Krampouez-mouzig*" and which grows in the cracks of old walls. Before putting it on the painful spot, you had to carefully remove the tiny transparent film that covers it. For deeper or infected sores, it was advisable to use a lily petal, but not until it had been steeped for some time in the first liquid that comes out of a still. If you had a felon, you took one or several lily leaves, placed them on top of it, wrapped them in a piece of clean cloth bound tightly with a thread, and waited. Would you like to hear of an even more subtle remedy? Place a bottle over a small pear that's just barely attached to its tree. Fasten the bottle properly, turn it away from the hottest rays of the sun, and protect it further by covering it with a straw case. When the pear has grown in the bottle, unfasten the whole contraption, fill the bottle with *lambig* (distilled cider), and cork it tightly. That will provide you with an invigorating and delicious smelling drink; but also—if someone in the family has an unbearably painful felon on his finger—you can break the bottle, after having decanted the precious liquid, of course. The patient then sticks his finger into the flesh of the pear bursting with *lambig*. How could any sore resist—if not the pear—at least that cider brandy, which is the best "worm-killer" in the world? As for the apothecary, let him keep his jars!

Lambig was used for almost everything. To cure toothaches, for example. All you had to do was to soak a crust of bread in it, place the crust on the painful tooth, and bite down hard. That worked for grandfather, who never drank brandy. In any case, it was far preferable to walnut-leaf poultices, which you applied to your cheek and which sometimes ate away your skin if they were boiling hot; indeed, the burn was often so bad that your beard would never grow on the spot.

Another ailment we often suffered from was the type of earache that doctors call "otitis." It wasn't at all surprising, since most of the people worked throughout the day, whatever the weather, in open fields and exposed to every sort of inclemency you can think of, but especially the seven winds of the mariner's compass, which would never stop changing direction. One very old remedy for otitis consisted in finding a woman who was nursing her baby and would agree to give you a bit of her milk, which was then poured into your ear. I have never seen it done, but the sabot-maker had, ten times. Although I don't mean to run down mother's milk, everyone knew that a houseleek plant got better results. When the juice of that plant was poured into your ear, it hurt, but the otitis was cured.

A few old men were still using "chou-cochon" (yellow dock, of the genus Rumex) as a purgative once a year and felt very well after it. They would have the root boiled and then swallow the liquid. Whooping cough was treated with carrot juice, unless the cough was so hard to get rid of that one's only recourse was the milk from a white mare. As for the "swollen head" disease, the mumps, I can still see myself with a napkin tied around my face, complete with a bow on top, which made me look exactly like an Easter egg just made for the city bourgeoisie. But my grandfather the sabot-maker brought me some orange honey from his beehives. And that was that.

Indeed, Alain Le Goff claimed that cures for every bodily ailment could be found all around us, within our reach, in herbs which, in the Breton language, bear the precise names of the diseases they cure or the names of the saints who protect us from them. The problem is that we don't always know how to go about using them. We often make mistakes. And what then? We have to try something else. After all, the "paper-diploma doctors" themselves aren't infallible. And when nothing you try gives results, you have to get rid of the disease by your own powers. Just as fish do. Isn't a person who's in good shape from top to bottom, who is vigorous and flourishing, said, in Brittany, to be a "healthy fish"?

Not only bodily ailments were provided for by those saintly figures who protect us on all sides; there was also the saving of souls—eternal salvation—which could not be achieved if one's life were not regulated by the precepts of the Church. That was why our first teachers were priests and nuns. They were there to keep watch over potential sinners (which all of us are at every moment), to be strict about teaching us the catechism, and to lead us, without ever weakening, onto the strait way, at the end of which lies the matchless reward of Paradise, where we shall find, as living people, all the saints of the fountains and the great motionless images of our spiritual family, who presided at church services a thousand times more solemnly than the portraits of our real family, set up on the kitchen cupboard, presided over our meals. That was why we were taught, very early on, that the community of our town could be perfectly unified only in church, where all antagonisms were resolved. And we were also taught that the most respectable figure, before whom all the big shots bowed down, was the rector of our parish, "*an aotru person,*" "the lord priest."

Indeed, directly between the high and the low ends of town stood the parish church of Saint-Faron et Saint-Fiacre, right in the middle of the cemetery. But since our church was not on the square, which lay slightly to the north of it, one section of a street between the two was sometimes called the center of town in order to indicate that it didn't belong either to one end or to the other. It was a kind of neutral territory.

The little scamps from the high end of town made the square their headquarters, whereas the headquarters of the "dogs from the low end" was the land around the church. Those who lived between the two chose one group or the other, depending on the circumstances. Though the pitched battles between the two factions took place in the countryside, the challenges were often made in the center of town, each group accusing the other of having overstepped the boundaries. At such times they would taunt each other, questioning certain distinct anatomical features. One of the leaders, for example, once taunted his opposite number with: "I saw you relieve yourself the other day behind the slope. Your ass is the color of a turnip." Behind him, his own special chorus sneered or clapped. Then came the reply: "There are too many mice in your house. One of them got into your trousers and ate up your flesh peg. Now you can't even pee standing up." So open war was declared. There were always some adults who kept their ears open for such objectionable remarks—respectable or religious people who were concerned about our good reputation in this world and our salvation in the next. Monsieur the rector, his vicar, and Sister Bazilize would be informed of our rhetorical profligacy. And the next catechism session was sure to be stormy.

I can't say why we who lived at the high end of town had the humiliating impression that the church belonged to those at the low end, who managed to rub it in at every opportunity. Was it because the largest houses and the richest families lived around the church? Was it because, in that particular church, the people who lived at the low end or in the middle of town didn't enter by the same door as those who lived at the high end? Or because more of them sat in the Gothic high-backed chairs of the chancel, as did the important farm owners, who lived neither at the high nor at the low end? Was it because of that imposing and mysterious presbytery, which was walled in and turned its back on the high end of town, on the north side? At any rate, such was the case. And besides, we had the reputation—deserved or not—of having a far richer repertoire of objectionable words at our command than the "dogs from the low end." Although that linguistic superiority helped us considerably during our clashes, it did not help matters when it came to the heavenly host. Apparently, we made the little girls in the convent school hide their faces somewhat too often.

While it had no church and no presbytery, the high end of town did have the Rector's Field—a large pasture surrounded by slopes planted with elm trees, between cascades of gorse and brambles. It was a meeting point for the seven winds of the mariner's compass, but there was always a slope that was sheltered from their games. Against that slope a few women could generally be found knitting or embroidering while they kept an eye on laundry that had been laid out to dry. At the first threat of rain, they would shriek out to their housewife friends who were busy elsewhere and who would come running to pick up their laundry. The spectacle was very like a ballet, with coiffes and skirts rapidly crossing the square meadow. In my youth, whenever the women weren't there, the Rector's Field was ours. And somehow we knew that it was a privileged place. Even the worst of us never felt brave enough to think up any foolish pranks while we were there. Was it the trinity of elms under which we regularly consulted that turned our minds to serious things? At any rate, parents were free from worry, or almost, when they knew that their children were going the rounds among the four slopes which separated them from the world of temptation. Nothing bad ever happened in that field. Indeed, it led one to believe that the air was filled with guardian angels. Little girls were left in peace to embroider bales of chiffon with their colored threads, free from boys pulling their hair and thus somehow getting their revenge on them for Eve's sin. And when a bird's-nester would fall out of a tree, he'd clasp the ground without breaking an arm or a leg or even a magpie's egg. Yes, it's a pity that children didn't play often enough in the Rector's Field. A few new saints might have been added to our grandchildren's calendars. But wisdom weighed heavily upon them; some devil would lure them out in search of adventure onto the rocky moors, where there were said to be more wild boars than men, although none of us ever saw any sign of them, not even a head. When children would resign themselves to spending their time in the peaceful field, it meant they were hiding some sin, trying to neutralize some feeling of remorse, or piling up indulgences with an eye to the Last Judgment.

It was there that the black habit of Sister Bazilize would make its appearance from time to time, her white wimple setting off her stern features and making them even harsher. Her reason for coming was surely to ask for an accounting from her flock who lived at the high end of town. One of us had doubtless broken one of God's Ten Commandments or of the Church's six commandments. Or of Sister Bazilize's own special commandments, which were the small change left over from the former. Yet we always hoped she had come merely to give additional lessons on the Christian life to the little girls from the convent school who had taken their mothers' place against the slope protected from the seven winds. Far away from us. Girls and boys were not supposed to play together in enclosed fields. Since the girls never wore panties, the boys would have been able to see how they were made if they happened to fall. And boys are very clever at tripping little girls in meadows.

Old Sister Bazilize used to teach us the rudiments of the catechism in a small room located in the center of town, between the church and the square. For us little boys from the high end of town, it was the entrance hall to the sanctuary. The room was in a private house which belonged to the mayor's secretary, an important person who was willing to lend it for a good cause. A rather dark cubicle, furnished with a few wooden benches, it had a door that was always open and a window that wouldn't open, which gave onto a wall close by. Thus the light was pitiful in that Purgatory where the catechism was explained to us every Thursday by a nun who had promised Saint Faron and Saint Fiacre to lead us to Paradise—with blows from a rod, if need be. She did her best, poor woman.

The catechism was in Breton, as were the explanations. However, the religious vocabulary lent itself to certain misunderstandings. Even when the words seemed to be those we used normally every day, they hid unexpected treacheries. We discovered that fact several times at our own expense. Once the victim was a good boy, whose only failing was that he answered too often, swallowing his saliva, and occasionally before he had even heard the question. That day the nun was brandishing a long reed, which was her usual weapon for calling us to order. She was brandishing it as Joan of Arc had brandished her standard at the siege of Orléans, or so I imagine, not having been there.

"Pay attention, children! Joseph is going to tell us which are the oldest of all creatures. Come now! Be quiet! Let Joseph answer."

In spite of those strict orders, her pupils kept muttering from one bench to another: "Adam and Eve. Adam and Eve." But Joseph had hopped up, beaming with knowledge and bursting with good will.

"The oldest of all the creatures are Jean-Marie Le Goff and myself."

He had barely finished speaking when a small group of pupils began to scream with laughter. The rest of them, who were in the majority, sat tight, awaiting help from the Holy Ghost! I should explain that in the catechism, the Breton word *Krouaduriou* refers to all beings created by the Lord God, but that in everyday language it is used only in the sense of "children." And among the children in our town, the two oldest were indeed Jean-Marie Le Goff and Joseph himself. But Joseph—I guarantee—didn't stick around very long. Vaguely uneasy about his success, he leapt to the door, leaving nothing behind but a gust of wind. At that point, one of the Corentins, nicknamed "Fat Boy," had contracted his body to such a degree in his desire to understand what was happening that he finally broke the bench he was sitting on. Therefore half a dozen children (or creatures, if you prefer) on the same bench began toppling over each other. Given the terrorized silence that suddenly fell upon the room, we could hear the clatter of Joseph's sabots in the distance as he ran away to hide his shame, though he didn't know the extent of it. Every member of the class was stooped over, expecting the long reed to fall on his shoulders. But by then the old nun was merely a black shadow turned toward the window and rocking with laughter.

Thus provided, somehow or other, with Sister Bazilize's elementary catechism, and having learned enough to be able to make out the question-and-answer pamphlet in Breton, which was to assure our being full Christians, we were allowed to go to the church, where two priests would teach us at the highest level. The rector, Monsieur Pelleter, was a fat, red-faced man, with a double chin, who liked snuff and would blow his nose into a huge red handkerchief. He wouldn't stand for any loss of time in the classroom and had no qualms about wringing the ear of anyone who happened to make noise with his sabots. His vicar was gentler and somewhat sanctimonious—not to be trusted altogether. But if we failed to give the right answers, neither one of them had any qualms about sending us, as a punishment, to stand under the statue of Saint Herbot, offering his dish of butter. (Herbot, of course, is the patron saint of horned animals.) Sometimes Monsieur Pelleter would forget we were standing in that corner once the catechism lesson was over. On the other hand, the grown-ups had told us, assured us, even sworn to us that the arm with which Saint Herbot offered his dish of butter, and which hovered directly over our heads, was completely rotted. Indeed, it wouldn't have been at all surprising if it fell off one day and knocked one of us out on its way down. So the penitent would look up from time to time, keeping an eye on that arm. But if the priest noticed him doing so, the poor little boy was brought to order by a voice raised in anger; for standing with one's nose in the air is by no means a position that shows humility or repentance.

On Sundays we all had to go to High Mass and, after that, to Vespers. Without fail. The bells were rung three times to call out the faithful. On the second ring we were supposed to have taken our places for a detailed inspection—first by the verger, and then by whichever of the priests was not officiating. The women would line up in front of the chairs on the Epistle, or south, side of the altar; and the men, on the Gospel, or north, side. The big shots were already in the chancel, armed with their thick, red-edged prayer books. Under the large statue of Christ, the harmonium, tuning up, would groan two or three times. After some creaking of ropes at the back of the church, the third peal of bells would clang out from above. They were still ringing when the priest would appear, flanked by his altar boys. Then we would have to keep absolutely quiet for an hour and a half, trying to control those feet, knees, elbows, and hands which refused to obey us.

What helped a lot to ensure our continued good behavior was the spectacle that unfolded before us and during which we'd try our best to get our bearings. In our catechism class the vicar wanted to teach us the meaning of the various colors worn by the priests for Mass. White stood for joy and purity; red, for fire and love of the Creator; green, for confidence; purple, for sadness and penitence; black, for mourning. The first three colors could be replaced by gold. All well and good. But I really don't think any of us ever managed to recall the precise Sundays on which they were to be worn. Even the altar boys, before entering the vestry, would discreetly consult a small pamphlet on the subject which was kept permanently behind the altar. All the same, we had to know what the colors were for Advent, Pentecost, Lent, the Rogation Days, and all the "-gesimas." What curious words!

When it came to the language of the Mass, we were divided between astonishment and respect. Actually, it was pure luck that not a word of French was involved, since we had enough trouble with Breton and Latin. The oldest among us had already become accustomed to our "priests' Breton" because of their catechism book, which was written in the dialect of the Léon region. Our priests themselves generally came from that region, from the seminaries of Saint-Pol and Lesneven. They carefully articulated every word, never omitting a syllable, whereas we and our parents, as people from the south, tended to stress our vowels rhythmically at the expense of our consonants. Especially the women, who spoke to everyone at large. In ordinary circumstances it had no great importance, since the words we used in common were almost always the same. But the "Church words" were strange to us and rarely used—the word *priedelez* (marriage), for example, and about a dozen others scattered throughout the hymns and which no doubt concealed some of the mysteries of faith. Certain of them (*induljansou*, *ofis*, *sakramant*), as we learned later on, were borrowed from the French—from that French language about which we knew almost as little as we did about Latin. To us, Latin, which prevailed from one end of the Mass to the other, was "Sunday Breton"—a language we never heard during the week or from the lips of anyone other than priests. Even our teachers, who spoke French so fluently, never used it. Yet the faithful who attended Mass—the verger heading the list—appeared to be familiar with the language, since they replied to the officiating priest in chorus, without ever missing a word. So we tried to make connections between that Breton of the Mass and our everyday Breton, thanks to a few words that stood out in the Latin and which seemed to be our own.

That was why we gave our total consent to the *Dies irae, dies illa*. In Breton *dîez* means "difficult," and we couldn't have agreed more: all that surely wasn't easy; they were right to repeat the word. But alas! The rest of it completely eluded us. From the catechism and the Stations of the Cross, we knew what a sad character Pilate was. Therefore, when singing the *Credo*, we'd strain our voices when we got to *Pontio Pilato* in order to show clearly our disapproval of his behavior. The adults did the same. Why was it that the name Pontius Pilate always had a strange ring to it in our ears, whereas the name Jesus Christ sounded quite normal, just as if it were Breton? Perhaps because of *Kristen* (Christian), which we heard throughout all the sermons, the prayers, and the hymns. But *pilad* in Breton means "to knock over." And that damn Pilate was the one who threw Jesus to the ground. As for Judas, he was a traitor. Now *that* was one of our words. When anyone said "Judas weather," he was warning us that the weather was not to be trusted.

Yet there were so many problems to be solved, as we realized, taking note of our scant knowledge. For example, we sang the *Kyrie eleison* fervently; we modulated the sounds with such delicate compressions of the throat that they seemed to waft down upon our faces from on high instead of coming out of our mouths. And yet we wondered what all those wagons had to do with celebrating Mass. That was because what we heard in our ears was the Breton *Kirri eleiz 'so* ("there are lots of wagons"), but never did we see even one of them. Either outside or in. I mean, after all!

The hardest thing to bear without misbehaving was the sermon. We had a feeling, each time, that it would never end. The priest got angry rather often, especially Monsieur Broc'h, the rector, who was true to his unpleasant name, which means "badger." Indeed, he never let us off, no matter what. Not one of our failings ever eluded him. He must have had informers in every corner, and assured us that we were destined for Hell and Purgatory. Not only us, but the whole congregation, each of whom got his just deserts. We'd bend our heads so low that our noses were virtually buried in our vests. From where he stood—in the pulpit joined to the first pillar, on the north side—he could see everything. So it was a bad time to move either our feet or our hands, or to whisper to our neighbors; for that terrifying priest was perfectly capable of taking us to task, and by name.

When the preacher came down from his pulpit and returned to the chancel, we'd discreetly give a great sigh of relief. Then the harmonium would start up again, along with the hymns. And the six churchwardens would solemnly rise from their high-backed chairs, go and fetch the collection plates from the vestry, and pass among the faithful. After the harvest, all six of them would also go out into the countryside, in three horse-charabancs, to collect gifts in kind from the farmers. They were followed by the verger, who made his rounds, then the vicar, and finally the rector. At which point it was considered that the tithe had been duly paid. Everybody was let off for a year, unless they wished to procure special indulgences.

The last hymn of the High Mass—the one that preceded our departure—we sang with such enthusiasm that the mistrustful eyes of the servants of the Church would all turn in our direction. The verger, Jean-Marie Plouhinec, attentively followed the movement of our lips to be sure we weren't parodying the respectable words, which the seminarians, reportedly, did very well. And who among us hadn't at least once replaced the last line, "Jezuz hag et vadelez" ("Jesus Christ and his blessings") with "Gwelom piou ar henta 'r mêz" ("Let's see who'll be the first one out!"). In fact, when the bells started to ring, and as soon as the priest had disappeared through the vestry door, all the children would rush out into the narrow corridor that led to the cemetery. The reproaches of Sister Bazilize had absolutely no effect. We were in a hurry to spend our one or two copper sous in a candy store.

Although I was pledged to attend High Mass every Sunday, once in a while I'd feel like going to six o'clock Mass instead. Not because it was shorter, but to get an idea of what the town was like between ten in the morning and noon. Probably the picture of a desert. For it was understood that anyone who didn't attend High Mass was not to go out into the streets unless absolutely necessary. There was no question of men taking off to have a drink, since most of the cafés or bars wouldn't have dared to serve anarchists of that type for fear of bringing the rector's wrath down upon them and of being named from the pulpit, which was the shame of shames. Of course, there were always a few young men—sailors on leave or sworn objectors—who managed to play cards during High Mass in some remote little bars, but on condition that they remained in the back room. For woe to that man by whom the offence cometh! As for the six o'clock Mass, it was reserved for those who were unable to attend High Mass, particularly farm people, who had to care for their animals.

The rector of our parish truly deserved being so-named. He led us with rectitude and resolution. In certain towns of the county there were tradesmen so forgetful of their duty that they organized dances for occasions other than weddings. But not in our town. Dances were forbidden under penalty of being refused the sacraments. And when, by way of an exception, the priests would authorize one, they didn't loosen their control for all that. In fact, they would issue strict warnings against immodest, or "belly to belly," dancing. Young men who wished to go to a dance elsewhere had to hide in order to leave the region. There was always someone on the lookout to proclaim their licentiousness. Girls, of course, were more strictly held in tow than young men. That's why they were almost unable to follow the modern dance steps, which made them the laughing stock of the "smart crowd" when they happened to be in a position to set foot in a real dance-hall. If one of them took it upon herself to shyly follow the fashion by lowering the back of her velvet bodice or pulling a few curls out from under her coiffe, she was directly, from the height of the pulpit, threatened with downfall because of some sort of moral decadence of which she was completely unaware, poor little thing. If certain girls fell prey to the Devil, it certainly wasn't their clergymen's fault. When we were twenty-year-old students and, as such, public dangers insofar as morality was concerned, we were watched more closely than ever by a person we called the "prefect." He'd know, far better than we did, at what time of night we had returned from a dance at Plonéour or Plozévet. One had to believe that he never slept. And to get to a dance, we'd have to push a motor bike down back roads, and didn't dare ever start the motor for fear of getting caught. The "prefect" had sharp ears. And the rector would have known all.

On Sundays nobody worked except to prepare meals and to care for animals. The rector strictly forbade it. And since the women couldn't even crochet, they'd slide their hands into their wide sleeves to show clearly that they respected the day of the Lord. By way of exception, when the harvest happened to be endangered by constant rain, the rector—out of the goodness of his heart—allowed the farmers to work on Sundays and even on August 15, the Feast of the Assumption, if the rain had stopped. But that was a special favor to the farmers, which they had to acknowledge later on by being doubly devout.

Until their first communion, and even afterward, at three o'clock the children had to attend Vespers along with the women. All the children and all the women who valued their reputations. Almost every man got out of it, except for those who sang in the choir or were pillars of the church. That almost no men were present made us feel somewhat humiliated. And besides, the older adolescents couldn't resist rubbing in the fact that we were still in our childhood. "You're going to Vespers with the women!" So we hoped that period would come to an end as soon as possible. But curiously enough—perhaps because our fathers weren't there or because out of the whole congregation we were almost the only ones in trousers—we didn't really dislike going to Vespers. We even showed off a little, testing our voices and our memories when it came to the five psalms, the hymn, the Magnificat, and the "Oremus." Actually, we felt good among all those women and little girls. The atmosphere was gentler and more serene than at Mass. And the priest didn't climb up into the pulpit to thunder out his sermons.

Once Vespers were over, we had a holiday from religion until the evening prayer. I would pray aloud behind the closed door of my box-bed so that my mother could hear my paternosters. On the important feast days, wearing a scapular round my neck, I had to cross myself with a lighted wax taper that had previously been blessed. As for my morning prayers, I can't truly swear that, until the age of ten, I said them every day. For lack of time, you understand, and because of the school work I had to remember. But I did just about carry out my duties as a Christian. How could I forget them when the house was filled with crucifixes and pious images? Every time my mother opened her wardrobe, on the left door I saw rosaries hanging next to my father's military lanyards, and, nailed to the right door, a picture of Saint Teresa of Jesus. On the back of the bench on which my grandfather sat, the carpenter had sculpted the blessed sacrament exposed. On each of the panels that closed in my box-bed, the three holy letters IHS (*Jesus Hominum Salvator*) had been cut straight out. I was protected on all sides. My father and grandfather apparently counted on me to protect them in turn, for they never seemed to be overly concerned about religion. They merely attended Sunday Mass—my father some of the time, my grandfather without fail.

In the house, aside from my mother's prayer books and a few collections of hymns, there were only two large volumes. One of them, which was kept permanently on the window sill, was Monsieur Larousse's French dictionary. I shall speak of that later. The other was closed into the cupboard that my mother had received as a wedding gift. It was *The Lives of the Saints*, written in Breton by Monsieur Morvan, canon of the cathedral-church in Quimper and published for the fifth time in 1913, revised and enlarged by the rector of Taulé, Jean-Marie le Gall. That was the book in which Alain Le Goff showed me the alphabet for the first time, because the letters were larger than in Monsieur Larousse's, which, to complicate matters, contained nothing but French. When I began to learn how to read fluently in school, my greatest pleasure was to try and make out *The Lives of the Saints*, for it was a book of incomparable stories. It related the miraculous adventures of people who, because of their virtues, deserved to be represented by statues in the churches. All of our own saints were in it, along with lots of others who must have been godfathers to the parishes around us. There was even the great Saint Corentin of Quimper, after whom not only two of my uncles were named, but also many men and children I knew. Moreover, one of those saints is invoked for every day in the year. But since they're too numerous, a few of them had to be sacrificed and are entitled only to a brief mention in the tale of one of the others' lives. That's why Saint Faron, even though he was a bishop, is discussed only in connection with the hermit Saint Fiacre. In our church he's portrayed with his miter, whereas Saint Fiacre has no right to anything more than a frock and a spade. That clearly shows, according to our rector, that grandeur in this world is of no importance. Everyone serves in the station to which he was assigned by the Lord.

It was I, however unworthy, who read *The Lives of the Saints* to the rest of the family; for if I wanted to be head of the catechism class in Breton, just as in school I was head of the class in French, I needed practice. Besides, my mother was flattered by the compliments she received about me from people who had merely heard that I could read well. Sometimes she'd invite some neighbors in for the ceremony. And the women would cry out in admiration, predicting that I would at least receive my elementary-school certificate the first time round; for there was no question of my going to the seminary. My father wouldn't hear of it.

One day in 1923, if I remember rightly, two or three monks arrived in our parish, dressed in their roped-in frocks. Full were their beards, from cheekbones to chin; huge were their bare feet, strapped to soles of thick leather. They had come on a mission—to infuse new life into the roots of faith, which, as the rector declared from his pulpit, was withering away in our souls. One of the monks was called Barnabé. His voice resounded prophetically in the chancel, where our wooden saints began to look stern—even good old Saint Fiacre, whose eyes always seemed to forgive us beforehand. They were very angry at us; that was clear. But after all! It's better to have dissatisfied saints than satisfied swine. And all of us were swine.

Father Barnabé concentrated, above all, on winning back the men—those who scorned Vespers, those card-players, those blasphemers, those laughing fools who reeked of red wine, those profligates who sneered at their wives' piety and shamelessly corrupted the pure souls of their babes. The terrifying monk never ceased thundering out against them, his voice bellowing like an organ. And the men who were there foundered and trembled with contrition. Even the rector no longer dared to pull his big red handkerchief out from under his cassock for fear of letting the monk see traces of his pet sin: snuff. He would even forget to straighten his biretta. As for the vicar, he was no more than a pale shadow, hugging the walls in hopes of being forgotten.

We children sought refuge in the Rector's Field. The mysterious spot under our three favorite elms quieted our palpitating hearts. We felt altogether unworthy, of course, but the four slopes protected us momentarily from any sort of punishment, and something in the air—a kind of natural incense—led us to hope that we'd be forgiven. Yet it wasn't Father Barnabé who frightened us, despite his quivering beard and torrential sermons, rolling out stones of Breton words that were unknown to us. The adults sitting behind us probably had good reason to lower their heads and scratch the tile floor with their newly shined shoes and clear their throats when the monk's voice stopped between two sentences. For once they were getting their due. For once our parents weren't our judges anymore. They had found their master. The most dissipated members of our group would have felt like sneering, had they not known that one day our own turns would come. For even then, hung on a rope across the chancel like stiff and multicolored laundry, were Father Maunoir's twelve Tablets, swinging gently.

We didn't yet know who Father Maunoir was. We imagined that he had the features of a monk like Father Barnabé, but with black hair and burning eyes. Later on, we learned that he was a seventeenth-century missionary—a fiery soul if ever there was one—who had forcefully led our fathers back to the strait way. Not without great trouble, nor without imperiling his mortal body. Indeed, in Plonéour the people had wanted to shoot him down. That was about the time of the well-known rebellion of the "Bonnets Rouges," following which two of my peasant ancestors had been hung by the Duc de Chaulnes, the "cursed duke." One of the two was a fourteen-year-old boy whom we knew only by the name of Pôtre Tin. May that fourteenth Louis be damned! Precisely what Father Maunoir had to do with all that, we didn't know, but we had to admit that he was an admirable painter.

His Tablets were large pieces of cardboard, or so it seemed to us (none of us had the courage to go up and look at them closely). On each of them was the drawing of a large heart, on top of which sat a head with long curly hair—the head of a musketeer or of some king out of a deck of cards. And the expression on each of the heads varied according to the contents of the heart. In the first painting the heart was filled with the peacock of pride, the he-goat of lust (what could lust be, I wondered), the pig of gluttony, the turtle of sloth, the tiger of wrath, the viper of envy, and the toad of greed—all seven beasts surrounding a Devil that was winged, horned, bearded, clawed, and shamefaced, carrying a pitchfork in place of a scepter. The spectacle was harrowing. But one star and one eye implied that the Lord God was watching over the whole of it. The paintings that followed showed man as repentant, casting the Devil's henchmen out of his heart that he might welcome the dove of the Holy Ghost. And there were also struggles, penitence, the instruments of the Passion, worldly temptations, seats won and lost (*et fiunt novissime pejora prioribus*), fire and swords, the Ankou* and the Guardian Angel. I could hear Father Barnabé's voice singing the opening lines of the initiatory hymn:

Sellit piz ouz an taolennou
A zo melezour on eneou.

*A symbol of death. (Trans.)

Look closely at the pictures
Which are the mirrors of our souls.

The Tablets hymn was not the only one we sang with Father Barnabé. Indeed, while he was with us, we went through a fair number of hymns from our own repertoire. And that church music both quieted our bodies and exalted our souls. I'd noticed that it had the same effect on adults. Could it have been an illusion? The voices of the sternest matrons became angelical, whereas those of even the toughest men seemed imbued with some emotion. Besides, Father Barnabé and his acolyte intoned them so much better than our own celebrants that the meanings of our ordinary hymns were suddenly revealed to us: we had never known how powerful they were. Although the hymn about the "Mute Devil" is one of the best known in Lower Brittany, I can testify to the fact that the one we sang most resolutely in the church of Saint-Faron et Saint-Fiacre was the hymn "Da Feiz on Tadou Koz" ("To Our Ancestors' Faith"), during which the entire congregation, at the end of the Mass, would promise to remain faithful to their fathers' religion, swearing that they would rather die than forsake it.

Now in Father Maunoir's Tablets it wasn't the horned devils or the winged dragons spitting fire or poison that terrified us the most. Nor even the caldrons in which the damned were boiled. It was rather a character who appeared in the center of the eighth painting, which portrays the wretched state of a sinner at the hour of his death—a character who appears in the space between the bed and the wall, a character whose name one never pronounced without shuddering. It was "the Ankou," a skeleton with a scythe—Death itself, the harvester of bodies. Everyone preferred to call it "Him," and this "Him" was always, sooner or later, the victor. In the tales we were told, there were no doubt frightful dragons, but after all the hero finally managed to cut off their heads seven times. There was also the Devil, but he invariably lost the match, being held up to ridicule by the first wily creature who came along. However, there was, and is, no question of ever having done with the Ankou. All one can do is to try and elude him, to outwit him through every sort of guile. But one cannot do more than put him off for the time being.

Monsieur Pelleter didn't much like to talk about the Ankou. One day, during our catechism lesson, we had asked him what exactly it was. He had replied that the Ankou was the one who came to fetch you and lead you to the next world. Then he immediately returned to the catechism. Perhaps he too was afraid of him. Yet he alluded to him from the pulpit whenever he got himself into a state about our salvation. Father Barnabé spoke harshly when he made us take stock of "the Ankou" in the eighth painting. He ordered us not to close our eyes. "The day he comes," said Father Barnabé, "your eyelids will be of no use to you. You'll see him right through them." Luckily, next to the skull and the bare rib-cage was an angel with large wings on which we could focus our eyes without blinking. But we had great trouble keeping them on it; for they would be irresistibly attracted from the wings to the bones.

However, the formidable name was rarely heard. Some very thin person, being eaten away by an invisible disease, might be called an "ankou." And that terribly emaciated person was never long in dying. Yet Alain Le Goff, who knew so many things, claimed that he knew nothing about the Ankou; whereas my grandfather the sabot-maker confirmed the notion that he had had two servants—one of them thin, the other fat. The former died of poverty; the latter, of overabundance. "That's why, my son, one has to keep to the middle road in order to stay alive." The sabot-maker had never seen the Ankou, but he had heard the axle of a wagon screech in the night. "A noise," he said, "that was enough to dissolve your guts." And the next day there had been a death in the neighborhood. He also showed me, somewhere between Kerveillant and Plozévet, one end of an old and very deep path that suddenly hollowed out at the bottom of a moor and then, for no reason, disappeared fifty feet from there. The path was completely overgrown with weeds. There were even trees growing right in the middle of it. However, it would seem that every time somebody died, you could easily detect fresh tracks made by a heavily laden wagon. But whoever dared to look at them would end up in the next wagon.

It was in a bar-grocery-bakery and general store at the so-called Ti-Lonk crossroads, not far from the sabot-maker's new house (he had just left Kerveillant), that I heard the story of Corentin

Calvez's deathlike state. I had gone to fetch a package of Leroux chicory for my grandmother Katrina. When I walked in, I found six men and women there, one of whom was my grandfather, looking very attentive. All of their attention was riveted upon a seventh person with a large moustache who was speaking in a muffled voice. And the story he told is the following.

It hadn't happened to him but to one of his cousins who was killed in the First World War. His cousin was still a child when, on the evening before All Souls' Day, he saw a ploughman he knew come into the house. It was Corentin Calvez, a small tenant farmer who lived nearby. His face was very pale and drawn, and at first he was unable to talk. Somebody rushed off to get him a strong drink. He refused it with a wave of the hand. Then he was made to sit down on the bench. When he found his tongue, it was to say that he had seen the Ankou while he'd been up on his pile of straw, busily covering it with wire that was weighted by stones to keep it from being scattered by the wind. And the Ankou, through his empty sockets, had looked him right in the eye. He didn't recall how he had managed to flee, but he was sure that the Ankou was still searching for him. He kept on saying how cold he was. There was only one easy way, he said, to escape from Death's procurer and that was to hold the warm hand of a person who was very much alive. And indeed, he seized the head of the household's hand and wouldn't let go. After some time, the others tried to reassure the poor man, but nothing worked; even they themselves were beginning to feel strangely anguished. Suddenly, Corentin Calvez started to shout: "There he is! He's come! Do you hear the wagon creaking? Do you hear those countless voices around him singing the hymn of Hell? Why Hell? Purgatory's one thing, but Hell! I don't want to go there. Hold on to my hand, tightly!"

The others had a hard time keeping him under control, for he thrashed about with the strength of two or three men. They themselves were sweating with apprehension, yet they didn't hear a thing, not the slightest sound of a voice or of a wagon. The struggle lasted so long that their arms were at the breaking point. All of a sudden the man relaxed and breathed a sigh of relief: "They're gone," he said, and agreed to drink down a good shot of *lambig*. He then thanked everyone and went home.

Now here's the best part. The following day they learned that Corentin Calvez had fallen down from his pile of straw shortly before dusk. He had been carried to his bed. He could hardly breathe and didn't move at all. He had remained in that state all through the night, watched over by his family. At sunrise he came to his senses again and went back to work as usual. But how could it be that an entire family had actually seen him at some distance from his home and had taken part in the scene described above? How could it be that he had squeezed the head of the household's hand so tightly that his nails had been driven into his palm? There is no explanation.

The man with the large moustache had told that story in 1925, between Christmas and the New Year. I had then just entered the lycée in Quimper. During the holidays my mother had sent me on a visit to my grandparents to show them my school cap, its peak stamped with the gilded insignia of the Ministry of Education. I wouldn't have remembered that story so well had the sabot-maker not repeated it time and again over the next few years, not only for my benefit but to entertain others. I got the impression, however, that he told it far better and with many more details than the man who had known the man who had taken part in it when he was just a child. The sabot-maker had a talent for bringing such things back to life. The other man had merely a talent for remembering them.

The deathlike state of Corentin Calvez was the only really terrifying story my grandfather knew or cared to tell. Fantastic tales of that sort were not suited to his nature. Of course, he didn't believe them; nor did he ask me to believe them once they'd been told. After all, he was a Republican. But he did believe his tales the entire time he was telling them. That was one characteristic of a good storyteller which I often had the opportunity to note later on in life. But don't ask me whether, or to what extent, the people who listened to that legend about death had actually credited what they'd heard. I only know that the theme of death has always impressed my close friends and relatives. Probably because of a vestige of paganism which must be acknowledged and which colors their obsessions and enriches their powers of imagination. The seasons also play a part. For example, if the sabot-maker had been asked to tell the story of Corentin Calvez during the month of

April, he would have been not only insulted but dumbfounded. There's a time and a place for everything, as we all know. So don't be surprised that the "portents"—those notifications of recent or imminent deaths—almost always occur during the "black months." If by chance they occur during the summer, it's because the rain or the winds have been excessive. And people who work the land are very sensitive to the weather, since both their work and their subsistence depend on it in great measure, but also because they have a kind of sympathy with nature that transcends its more obvious manifestations. There are certain regions in which the people experience joy more profoundly than mourning. In my own, the climate is such that at times it favors an obsession with death and consequently the Cult of the Dead.

There can be little doubt that we are indeed the heirs of the Celts, those whom Yeats called the "twilight people." For us death is a funereal feast on the occasion of someone's departure for another world that is on an equal footing with this one. And the stage for that feast used to be, quite naturally, within the enclosed parish land at the center of town, which was the realm of the living, yet separated from it only by the wall of the cemetery, where the dead lay at rest. One had therefore to walk among the graves and to tread on the relics to reach the House of God—that is to say, Eternity. The dead were thus in constant contact with the living, who were unable to forget them. When a new cemetery was built just outside of town, I heard complaints from old people nearing death who were distressed by the idea of being relegated to a place far from the houses and far from the steeple, far from the living and far from God—a double misfortune.

During the week there were almost always people in the cemetery. Women most of the time. In white coiffes, they would move about among the graves, kneel down here and there, and earn the right to indulgences for saying paters and aves for dead people other than their own. Country women who had come into town to do their errands rarely failed to climb over the low wall and turn their thoughts to God as they stood facing the crosses of their deceased, a shopping bag on one arm and a loaf of bread under the other. But on Sundays, at the end of each Mass and even after Vespers, there were more of the livng than the dead in the cemetery, all of whom were bent on greeting their own deceased before taking off to listen to a public announcement of the news or to savor some coffee, bread, and butter. And during burials, what better way is there to honor the newly dead than to meditate on the rectangle of land that covers your own and that will cover you yourself when the time comes? Besides, saying prayers for the dead never stopped the people from talking about one thing or another, spreading a little gossip or moaning about the decline in the price of pigs—all subjects that would have greatly interested the buried, had they been able to hear.

The flowers you used to see on graves were either bunches from the fields, which varied according to the season, or potted plants that had first thrived on window sills or in cottage gardens. No one would have dreamed of buying flowers, assuming they had ever heard of a florist. It was not until after the new cemetery had been completed that people began putting up stone or cement monuments to the dead as an excuse for not going to see them as often. Thus, at the time of All Saints' Day, heaps of chrysanthemums covered all the graves. And it was the chrysanthemums that people came to visit, not the dead. Everybody was interested in knowing if so and so hadn't balked at the price of them or if someone else hadn't spent more on them than he could afford. On Saturdays the women would get busy with pitchers, shovels, and knives in order to clean up the plot, afraid of what the gossips would say if, the next day, after High Mass, they noticed that you'd been neglecting your duties to the dead. Why you'd be covered with shame! And as people grew richer, they were to replace the old gravestones with finer ones. Indeed, the new cemetery was to become visible proof of a family's prosperity or of its degradation. And in all that, you took the dead less to heart than you did the monument you had paid good money for and which was a sign of your station in the parish. "Status" was to replace faith just as the wallet was to replace religion. But isn't that sort of competition, which was flaunted precisely in the form of tombs, significant of the latent permanence of worship? And isn't endowing the dead with signs of their family's prestige a way of continuing to associate them with their living descendants, a way of paying them homage? That's what we had come to in 1974!

Fifty years earlier, while I was still in school, death itself was accepted with a kind of fatalism that was not resignation but rather a simple submission to what everyone called his "star." Religion was a consolation previous to death, and it inspired the hope of posthumous rewards that the Lord couldn't haggle over if one were among those who had obeyed His and the Church's Commandments. Death was easier to take if it occurred at some distance, outside the parish community, which was the fate of sailors and soldiers. We fully experience only the death struggles that we witness ourselves or the accidents that brutally eliminate a member of the family when we aren't prepared for it. An accident disturbs the normal progress of oncoming death, which is well expressed in the following remark: "He was in good health when he got sick and was sick when he died. There's nothing more to say."

But to go back in time: The dying used to give a performance before the whole community. They and their families knew that they were playing their last roles. No matter how poverty-stricken, for once in their lives they were stars. They were anxious to depart according to rule, without offending anyone, without being unworthy. They were concerned about leaving their affairs in order—meaning not necessarily their possessions, but their former tasks: Had the laundry that was put out to dry on the upper meadow been taken in? Had the bay been reshod? In those days, when a horse was about to die, in many places its owner removed its horseshoes. Which accounts for the last words of a peasant who was convinced he was about to depart this life: "Well, here I am, unshod once and for all." Most especially, every debt had to be paid, even social debts. "We owe a meal to those cousins in X. Be sure and invite them once you've finished with me." And so they died in peace: their work was done—work that had in fact amounted to bondage and exile.

The performance would begin with extreme unction. People died in public, somewhat like the kings of old, said Uncle Piron. (Where in the world had he dug that one up? He couldn't even read!) The priest, wearing his surplice and carrying his "black bag," would come out of the presbytery, preceded by an altar boy shaking a small bell. Then they were on their way. As they passed, people would kneel down and cross themselves.

At the dying man's house everything was ready; the family was there; the neighbors were drawing near for the ceremony, holding their rosaries. And from that moment on, the entire region was on the qui vive. The people would go on with their usual occupations as they awaited the death of a man (or a woman) from whom they could hardly dissociate themselves since he was a member of the parish, which was in the process of saying farewell. They were all preparing to pay their last tribute to him, even if he had been an enemy of theirs at election time, even if they had quarreled with him. When there's a death in the family, the members always become reconciled. Death wipes out grievances and settles all scores.

As soon as the man died, his neighbors would take off for the church to fetch the crosses they planned to set around the bed on which the body was lying in state, and the church bells would toll the knell. The people working in the fields on their knees would stand up and listen. They'd hear seven strokes for a woman, nine strokes for a man. At that point, just about everything fell into place to form a replica of Millet's painting *The Angelus*, which could just as well be called "The Knell." The peasants would turn their thoughts to God and recite, as they stood, a pater and an ave before returning to their tasks. On several occasions, when those prayers were being said, I had been present as a third party, along with my mother and my grandfather, in the Méot field. In our house, as in many others, there was a fireplace closed off by a wooden frame to which was glued a reproduction of Millet's painting. All ploughmen recognize themselves in the characters. Millet is perhaps not considered one of the great painters by those who have a taste for genius, but his truth is unquestionably ours, both on the surface and in depth. As a matter of fact, not one of us used even to know his name.

In the dead man's room the clock had already been stopped, and if there happened to be any mirrors around, they had been covered. All glittering objects had been removed; the "pardon balls"* and framed photographs, hidden; the useless knickknacks, picked up. Nothing was left but the crucifixes and pious images that had been gathered up from the rest of the house. The people whose

*Toys one bought at those religious festivals. (Trans.)

job it was to dress the dead man would silently bustle about the corpse. They were specialists and known as such. Women or men, but never the two together, never women for a dead man, never men for a dead woman. Then the bed was fixed up for the lying in state. If it was a box-bed, sheets and cloths were hung on the inside of the enclosures, or if not, on the walls around it. It had become what we call a "white chapel." The poorest among us would borrow anything they needed. On the bed seat or bed table a blessed palm would be soaking in a white dish of holy water. The dead man could thus receive people respectably. He was completely dressed in his best clothes from top to bottom, including his socks, but not his hat, although some would ask that their hat be buried with them. As for a woman's coiffe, not a pin was ever missing.

The family was left to their grief. Neighboring women would take over the house. For two or three days they'd do everything that was appropriate and even more, occasionally scolding the deceased's close family when they were looking worried about this or that: "Aren't you ashamed, thinking about your house when your father's dead?" A few men from the same "group" would put on their best mourning clothes, take their sticks, and go out to walk through the county to inform all the members of the family, not to mention all those related by marriage. No matter if they had already heard the news from someone who had been roaming through the region on business of his own—a ragpicker, a peddler, a horse dealer, a chance vagrant. One had to await the special messenger, duly commissioned, who never failed to come. If he didn't, it meant that you had been "dropped from the family," and how humiliating for you! By no means could you attend the funeral, since no one remembered your name. On the other hand, you did have the option of rushing off, without having been invited, to keep vigil over the deceased for one whole night. That was the best means of becoming reinscribed in the others' memories as a cousin, no matter how many times removed. And you would even be entitled to special consideration, because they'd feel guilty about having forgotten you. But it was rare that a relative be forgotten, especially if he lived in poverty. It wasn't too terrible to neglect rich relatives; they'd come in any case, if only to show off. They couldn't do otherwise. But the poor would not come if the messenger hadn't crossed their thresholds to make his announcement in accordance with the rules. After all, it's hard enough to be poor. If, in addition, you had to renounce your honor, you would soon come to the point of losing your name.

The news of death was always brought by men, either two, three, or four of them, depending on how large and how scattered the family was. Each man had to organize his rounds in such a way as to be able not only to inform everyone but to return and attend the funeral himself. At a time when walking for hours didn't put people off, there was nothing exceptional about having to cover miles and miles of bad roads. But upon entering a house, it was only courteous to stay until you had had something to drink or even to eat. Under such conditions you might well have lost your way before nightfall or dragged your legs to such a point that you were unable to resist taking a short nap behind some slope. Above all, of course, you weren't to stop. But people were well aware of the fact that mourning fosters weakness. When you had just sat down on their bench and they realized that you could barely stay awake, they would leave you in peace, put on their leather shoes, and go to inform the next cousin themselves. It did happen, however, that one such harbinger of death was so tired out by his journey and his libations that the funeral took place without him. The poor man was still out there somewhere, digesting his wretchedness. Everyone had come but him. May God forgive him!

As for relatives who lived some distance away, there was the post office and its telegrams, which were sent only to the brothers, sisters, and children who were clearly able to afford the trip. What good would it have done to humiliate those who hadn't enough money to come! You would write them a letter sometime later.

From my earliest childhood I have been brought face to face with the dead. It was always the custom that at least one representative of every house go without fail to pay a call on the corpses of the parish before they were put into the "ark." When the deceased was a member of the family or a close neighbor, no one—not even a child—was relieved of that duty. One fulfilled it just as one fulfilled the others, and even more easily in that the rite which prevailed from the death throes to the funeral service satisfied some instinct in all the members of the community—an instinct that came from one's very depths.

The first corpse I ever saw was that of an adolescent girl named Françoise, one of our neighbor's daughters. She used to take good care of me, dear Françoise. Since she wasn't very strong, she would often stay at home. We used to see her sitting on the doorstep doing fine needlework and coughing so much as to spit her heart out, yet constantly smiling at the children around her. She was afflicted with decline, with the "wasting disease." At the end, one could almost see her soul through her body. Then suddenly she departed for the next world. I was dressed by my mother in something between my Sunday best and my everyday clothes. I hung onto her skirts as we went through the door, above which there was a large white cloth marked with a black cross. Even out in the hall one could hear the murmur of prayers. Françoise was stretched out in the middle of the "white chapel," between two candles, only just a bit thinner than when alive, but blind forevermore. Her eyes had sunk into her head; nothing was left of them but two frightful shadows. Behind her, shining softly, were two silver crosses, taken down from their brackets, and which would precede her at the cemetery.

My mother pushed me toward the bed. Then Françoise's father, who was sitting on the fireplace bench, rose and came to me. He took me in his arms, lifted me up, and had me kiss the dead girl. It will be a long time before I forget the feel of her stony brow or the indefinable smell that came to me through my lips, not my nose. I was set down on the mud floor, my knees shaking. I had a terrible time finding my mother's skirts again as she was telling her beads along with the other women against the façade of cupboards. She was pleased with me. Soon, on our way home, she would tell me that I had behaved well. Then, hidden under the table, I would have the right to cry my eyes out because there was no more Françoise.

One would keep vigil over the dead for two nights. During the day, on the benches and chairs that were lined up against the walls and partitions, people came and people went: some had nothing else to do; others lived at the opposite end of the parish; still others had only a minute to spare. And there was also the coming and going of good friends and relatives who were bent on being there to greet any and everybody, and to make note of those who came, for in that way they would know how to behave with them on similar occasions. But at nightfall, after the family had had their soup, the house would fill up with their intimate friends who had come to spend at least half the night. The mistress of the house had made sure that there would be enough food and drink for everyone. A state of recollection prevailed in the "white chapel" room. But all around it, in the hall and in the other rooms, the pitch of the conversations would rise higher and higher as the night went on. The talk was at first centered on the deceased, and people would reel off all the commonplaces on the shortness of life. Then they'd chat about the weather. They would go and sit at the table to have a drink and a bite to eat before returning to join in the prayers for an hour, a half-hour, a quarter of an hour. Once, twice, three times. Some of them finally just stayed at the other end of the house, commenting on the latest news and even talking politics in louder and louder voices, especially when one or another of them, or both at the same time, had had a bit too much to drink; that did happen. Sometimes there was such a racket that, in the end, a woman—generally the wife of the man making the racket—would emerge from the "white chapel," her rosary in hand, to give those who were behaving disgracefully a good talking to. "Aren't you ashamed of yourselves?" Then the most sensible among them would take hold of those who didn't know how to honor the dead properly, and lead them out into the night—after which they themselves sat down and played a nice game of cards.

But when the *diseur de Grâces* (or "offerer of Prayers") arrived, and during the whole time he was there, any activity other than praying was out of the question. The *diseur de Grâces* was one of the most important figures involved in the funeral rites. He was more impressive than the priest himself, perhaps because he was an ordinary man, a peasant or an artisan, who had never gone to any school and was therefore, like the poorer classes of the parish, still imbued with a faith that wasn't altogether Catholic. Indeed, the priests never seemed to be wholeheartedly in favor of the *diseur de Grâces*, although for the most part he stuck to the usual prayers. But didn't he in fact usurp the privileges conferred by ordination? And sometimes, carried away by emotion, he did go astray, using words that repudiated the Commandments and offended the Trinity. I heard of one of them, for example, who had violently reproached the Lord for the death of a gentle young girl because she hadn't deserved such a fate—after which he threw himself down on his knees, beat his breast, asked for forgiveness, and wept over what he had done, while the congregation witnessed his psychodrama. In some places that offering up of prayers was performed by a woman, which meant that superstition wasn't far behind. The Church must have had good reasons for refusing to ordain women; no doubt of that! Sorcery, perhaps. But how was it possible to allow someone to depart this life without intoning prayers in accordance with the custom of our ancestors? And the *diseur* was often more eloquent than the priest, and sang more in tune, and found words that were more within our possibilities because they were his very own. So why not? And after all, anybody—needless to say—could offer up prayers; but as it happened, it wasn't just anybody who did.

Our very own *diseur de Grâces* used to be Jean-Marie Plouhinec, the verger of our church. Since he was perfectly versed in the forms of religion, he could hardly fail to convey its essence. So our minds were at ease. He abominated heretics, schismatics, and pagans. When he took over, he would stand in front of the "white chapel," open his book, and sharply clear his throat. It was an old book with a broken binding and a black cloth cover. "In the name of the Father, the Son, and the Holy Ghost . . . *Pater, ave, de profundis* . . ." We even heard passages of the Gospels that, in church, were read only in Latin. And then Jean-Marie would conjure up visions of the Apocalypse for us, including the opening of the seals and the four horsemen on their mounts—one white, one red, one black, and one pale. And "lo, there was a great earthquake; and the sun became black as sackcloth of hair, and the moon became as blood; And the stars of heaven fell unto the earth, even as a fig tree casteth her untimely figs, when she is shaken of a mighty wind. And the heaven departed as a scroll when it is rolled together; and every mountain and island were moved out of their places."

Jean-Marie Plouhinec's voice would become terrifying and his eyes would flash. No one moved. From time to time a woman would choke down some sobs, making a strange noise in her throat. Given the presence of a dead body, we were all more overcome by fear than when Father Barnabé explained Father Maunoir's Tablets. And yet I'd stay right there, motionless, with all the others, convinced that the end of the world was at hand and that nothing could be done about it. Really nothing. I was then seven years old, or nine, or twelve. When I heard those prayers offered up for the last time, I was fifteen.

I may be wrong, but I have the impression that once the ceremony was over, no one had the heart to go back through the kitchen to get a drink or a bite to eat. And yet Jean-Marie also managed to speak in loving tones when he mentioned the triumph that awaited us after the trial of death.

The next day, when the carpenter and his helper appeared with the coffin, the rites reached another peak, after which everything started to calm down. The members of the family walked up to the dead man in accordance with the degree of relationship and gave him one last kiss, holding back their sobs. The carpenter gestured to his helper. They lifted up the body and placed it in the "ark." After taking a last look, the women would finally break down and begin to sob, scream, and wail, louder and louder, each one outdoing the other. Outbursts of true and infectious grief, but also the people's own rendering of both the *Dies Irae* and the *Libera*, which still linked us to the terrors of the millennium. And perhaps, too, a vestige of the rite of paid weepers, since I myself have seen and heard the loud lamentations of old women who had no special ties to the deceased. Then the priest came, his biretta in hand, under his open missal. Prayers. The tears would subside. The pallbearers entered.

Outside there was a horse-charabanc waiting. Its owner had cleaned it up as well as he could without making it shine; otherwise people would have said: "That one seems to think he's taking somebody to a wedding!" The coffin would be placed inside and covered with the black cloth from the catafalque, decorated with silver teardrops. And the procession would get underway, each one in his place according to some subtle hierarchy. Accompanying a dead man on his last journey was a moral obligation that took precedence over all the others. Youenn, for example, passed away. The news had been brought to his cousin Louis, who was about to be operated on for a hernia. "But I can't go to the hospital," said Louis. "Tell the doctor to wait. I must lead Youenn to his grave. I'll take my hernia with me." At any rate, with or without their hernias, everyone who should have and could have been behind the coffin was there without fail.

Once they reached the church (sometimes it was a two- or three-mile walk over country roads), the funeral service would take place in all its magnificence in both Latin and Breton. The congregation was inevitably moved by the *Dies Irae* and the *Libera*—in other words, the next world as experienced within oneself. But the people would then wait for the moment when one of the priests announced the list of requested services and Masses for the deceased—in other words, this world here below, as one must adapt to it. How many Masses had he said there would be? More than for So-and-So, who had a higher standing, or so he thought. Less than for my father when he died. Well, well! The young cousins from Paris had arranged for a Mass to be said, but his sister in Toulon hadn't given any sign of life. Shameful.

The coffin was carried out of the church. Just a few steps and there was the grave, newly dug. An aspergillum was lying in a basin of holy water. Everyone would make the sign of the cross on the box and go over to his own family's tomb. There were no condolences. Condolences were for the city bourgeoisie. Here people weren't even quite sure of how to shake hands. Nor had they any idea of what to say. They had done what they had to do.

Funerals were a godsend to the tradesmen in town, who served as much to drink as they did during high festivals. Gathered round the women in their mourning capes, the only cloaks they ever wore, the members of the family would slowly return to the dead man's house. His widow or daughter was already worrying about whether she would be able to provide a decent enough feast for everybody, or whether she hadn't forgotten someone, or whether anything in the house might possibly shock her relatives' eyes. The others had done their duty; it was now up to her to do hers, which meant sending everybody home pleased and filled to the teeth, with a nice warm feeling around the ears, even if, at the end, funeral meals tended to be disrupted by quarrels and old grudges. Life had begun again.

On Christmas Eve, when I was about five or six, my grandfather Alain Le Goff, usually such a quiet man, was rushing back and forth between the house and the courtyard, making a great racket, reprimanding his daughter because nothing was where he had expected to find it, and announcing to one and all that on the following night the family's honor would be unpleasantly put to the test, if indeed we hadn't died by then in utter disgrace, which would have been less than what we deserved, given all our blunders. My mother was choking with laughter as she set about looking for her scrubbing brush. I myself was outraged. How could it be that, in a house so well run on the whole, nothing was ready, especially given the fact that in a few hours we were expecting a guest who was entitled to our greatest consideration. For that night the Infant Jesus himself was to come down my chimney to bring me my reward for having been so well behaved that whole year, despite a few venial sins, each of which I had paid for with the skin of my behind.

I knew nothing about Santa Claus. Nor did my parents. And my grandfather even less. The Infant Jesus had not delegated his powers to that bearded figure in a greatcoat who was later to become a caricature of all grandfathers once they'd been relieved of their grandchildren's education. No one would have dreamed of uprooting a pine tree in some wood or other and setting it up in state right in the middle of the house. Has anybody ever seen a pine tree take root in a mud floor? Whereas the Christmas log has a favored spot in the fireplace, and rightly so! It's a log that feeds the fire, warms up the house, and also protects one from storms, not counting its other virtues, of which one isn't necessarily aware. But that log was already prepared at the back of our hearth. The Infant Jesus could come in his white gown and bare feet. He would not be cold.

He never entered through the door, which let just anybody in. And that "anybody," even Grandfather, was always burdened with some sins. The Infant came down the chimney. No matter how black it was, the chimney was pure because of the fire, which purifies everything. And that was why Grandfather was raging around, trying to prepare our best ladder in honor of the Son. The Son had wanted to be a man. Therefore he doesn't have wings, like angels do. That was easy to understand. And that was why my mother allowed her best scrubbing brush to be used for cleaning the ladder, helped along with a pail of water. What a hullabaloo! Finally, there it was in the fireplace, clean and dry. The Infant Jesus could climb down at his own convenience. I was wild with expectation.

"He'll come around midnight," said Grandfather. "If you can stay awake until then, you'll see him through the hole in your box-bed door." I should have liked to see the Infant Jesus, who must have been about my age, right?—and who surely knew how to play marbles. But the excitement of that day had been too much for me. And besides, Grandfather never stopped sending me here and there, without allowing me a minute's rest. At seven in the evening, I was already falling asleep over my soup. At eight, after a heroic struggle to keep my eyes open, I could just barely climb up onto my straw mattress by myself. Then I succumbed, body and soul, to a far-off squeaking sound of bed-doors, which were closing me in.

A thunderous noise woke me up. Could it be that the end of the world was upon us? But the Archangel's trumpet happened to be a drum I knew well, since I had beaten it myself. The one my uncle Jean Le Goff had brought me from some city before he'd got himself killed in the war. But it was booming out so loudly! Who would dare . . . I sat up in my hemp nightshirt, stuck my eye into one of the letters that had been cut out of my box-bed door, and I saw. I saw Grandfather, also in his nightshirt, his bare feet in a pair of sabots, standing on the mud floor and banging away for all he was worth. He had guessed that my eye was behind one of the holes, and he could see my fingers clutching the bed rail. He stopped and in a disconsolate voice said: "I was caught unprepared. I woke you up just as soon as I could, but even so, it was too late. He just came down and went right up again. Even I never got to see more than the tail end of his gown. He has so much work to do tonight, the poor Infant Jesus! But he left something behind for you. Come on now and take a look!"

In my right sabot there was an orange; in the left one, a sugar Jesus. I had been told that I couldn't eat either one of them before they had been exhibited on top of the kitchen cupboard for days and days. "Look more carefully," said Grandfather. At the bottom of my left sabot there was a cornet filled with just ordinary red candies; and at the bottom of my right sabot, a chocolate bar. I sat down on the hearthstone to taste them right away. They were destined to console the poor budding Christian who had missed his rendezvous with the Saviour.

But I was promised that the next year I'd be taken to Midnight Mass. Of course, the next year was not precisely the following year. It finally did come, however. In the church, filled to overflowing with the faithful, I was still obliged to sit with the women, jammed in between heavy dresses that gave out the smell of velvet mixed with other indefinable musty scents. From time to time, over the sea of coiffes I could just barely see the altar, which appeared to be lurching in the flickering light of the candles and, to the right of it, another burning bush, which in fact was the manger set up under Saint Herbot's dish of butter. It also seemed to me that the singing was better than usual. I don't recall what time I got home, but the little Infant Jesus had already come and gone.

A week later came New Year's Day—not, strictly speaking, a religious feast, but somehow at one with the Christmas season. New Year's Eve was something else again, and a "feast" that the clergy of our parish found hard to tolerate. The night is a bad counselor—the Devil's favorite time for holding his sabbath. The priest, from his pulpit, would tell edifying stories about "night cats" who were found dead the next day in some ditch and in a state of mortal sin, of course. But on New Year's Day itself, the big meal was served at noon. And, in anticipation, I, like the other children, would go to bed earlier than usual.

The smell of fresh coffee woke me up. And the hanging clock had waited just for that smell to strike seven. My mother, who had been bustling about in the other room so that I could sleep, went into the kitchen with her portable kerosene lamp. My eye was already looking out of my box-bed door, right through the hole at the top of the letter *S*, the last one on the left. It was through the

Salvator that I always watched what was going on. I caught Grandfather's eye as he sat on the bench across the room, meditating. "I see something blue," he said. That something blue was my eye. Then I heard my father pull out the piece of wood that barred the door. And my mother took her very own bottle of brandy—a three-star cognac called "Fidelig"—out of the four-door cupboard.

It was at that point that the sound of galloping sabots echoed outside: the first group of children were on their way to our doorstep to collect their treat. A moment of silence. They were kneeling on the stone; then, all at once, piercing voices—altogether out of tune—began to screech out the New Year's litany: "I wish you a happy New Year, all good things, a long life, and Paradise at the end of your days!" "I must go," said my mother. I could hear her bunch of keys jingling. She went into the bedroom to open her very own cupboard, where she had prepared some piles of copper change and a few silver coins. She distributed them to the children according to the relationship she had with their parents. The one-sou coins were for children we didn't know, once they had introduced themselves. Now it was done. Another litany of thanks, and the little devils flew off toward somebody else's doorway.

I got dressed in a hurry, standing on my bed between the three wooden partitions. My bowl of coffee was already steaming on the table. I gulped it down so that I too could make the rounds of the houses we knew and which were authorized by my mother. I wasn't supposed to forget anyone. Nor was I supposed to call on people who were too poor even to give me a sou. I wasn't supposed to take any chances of delivering my good wishes to those who wouldn't be able to tell, from my face, whose son I was. I wasn't supposed to stop short in the middle of my litany. I wasn't supposed to . . .   I wish you a happy New Year . . .

The whole year was punctuated, divided, and rhythmically measured out by religious feasts, some of which were dazzling, whereas others came and went without my even noticing. But all of them served as guidelines for the adults. There were even certain old people who paid little mind to dates as such and who figured out what day it was depending on its relation to Sundays and Feast Days. "I'll come to your house the day after Michaelmas," or "on the Thursday before the 'Seven Weeks' [Septuagesima] Sunday," or "on the eve of Trinity Sunday." They knew which days were favorable and which were not. They had a certain number of proverbs that fit those Feast Days so that they could plan the work that had to be done in the countryside—sowing, weeding, the care of animals, harvesting. Their religious calendars were absolutely precise and accurate. As for me, I used to get awfully confused, especially when it came to celebrating the Virgin: "Mary in December" (the Immaculate Conception), "Mary full of light" (Candlemas), "Mary in March" (the Annunciation), "Mary in July" (the Visitation), "Mary in mid-August" (the Assumption), "Mary in the black month" (the Presentation), and so on. But all that my mother managed to make out perfectly well.

Palm Sunday—which we called "Flower" or "Laurel" or "Boxwood" Sunday—marked the beginning of the Easter Season. Everyone would bring home a bunch of laurel or a clump of boxwood that had been blessed at Mass, and distributed them behind the crucifixes, where they were to remain and dry out properly. They were also put in stables and on the gates to the fields. Nothing that would place the men, animals, and plantlife under the protection of the Trinity could possibly be disregarded. Easter Sunday was the one on which new clothes, new coiffes, and new shoes were worn for the first time. A Sunday of pride, awaited all the year through.

On the Feast of the Sacrament (Corpus Christi) the streets of the town through which the procession wended its way to the new calvary on the road to Penhors, at a place called Locmaria, would be adorned with especially well-kept flower beds. The evening before, the women would bustle about decorating the section of the street in front of their houses with large, radiating patterns made of reeds, rushes, and whole basketfuls of white, red, yellow, and blue petals. Each group would pride itself on its work, return to make it all the more beautiful, and then go to visit the others' in order that they might rejoice or feel mortified by the comparison. And we children were forbidden, on pain of the usual punishments, to set foot on those carpets out of *The Arabian Nights* with our unworthy sabots. So we'd hug the walls of the houses, which were hung with sheets enhanced by bunches of flowers. The next day, bawling out hymns, we would devoutly tramp down the way of glory, behind crosses, banners, and the gilded canopy under which a priest in a golden chasuble carried the monstrance, amidst acolytes who were almost as golden as he himself.

There was also Midsummer Day, which we call "the Feast of Saint John," and which, despite the apostle's name, led us to wonder whether it didn't reek somewhat of the Devil. In fact, we had the distinct impression that the clergy looked upon it with disapproval. It was not actually a parish feast but rather a neighborhood festival. And the various neighborhoods were even in competition, each doing its best to build the most beautiful and long-lasting bonfire. At nightfall on Midsummer's Eve, we had only to climb up one of the elm trees in the Rector's Field to discover that a good dozen of them were flaming across the countryside. Each family would contribute something to its neighborhood bonfire—a log, a bundle of firewood, a barrowful of bark, or, from the poorest among us, a few branches of dead wood. For it was understood that each one gave according to his means, neither more nor less.

The Midsummer's Eve bonfires were lit by recognized specialists who refused to allow anyone else to do the job. Once the roaring flames had died down, the most daring of the boys would jump over the bed of glowing embers. Some of them would get slight burns on the soles of their feet, but that made them show off even more. By then, the girls were beginning to hide behind their mothers, for in a short while the boys would grab hold of them either under their arms or under their knees and swing them over the embers nine times (we called that *ober ar wakel*), while they shrieked at the top of their lungs. But in fact they were delighted. And those who pretended to flee did it only to make sure they were caught in an even stronger grip. If some of them, by accident, escaped the proceedings, they remained embittered for a long time to come. Or at least disappointed and full of regrets. Besides, the mothers couldn't resist urging their daughters upon the young men. So they too were peeved if their offspring happened to be ignored.

Now, of all the "Faith Days," we are fondest of those called "pardons." A pardon is the annual festival held for the patron saint of a church or a chapel, some of which are most especially revered because of the indulgences granted and the cures that take place. Those may even have two pardons a year, a large and a small one. The small one is about limited to the population in the area and is more truly religious in nature. The large one gathers together the faithful of one or several counties, not to mention the pilgrims who come from afar owing to the very special reputation of the Virgin, Saint Anne, or whichever saint reigns supreme in a specific place. We ourselves had no qualms about leaving the Bigouden region to attend the large pardon of Sainte-Anne de la Palud (it was the least we could do) or the one at Notre-Dame du Folgoët, all the way to the north, in the Léon region.

As for the Bigouden pardons, there were so many of them that it was impossible to attend them all. But they were an occasion for family reunions, for inviting each other from one parish to another, for laying out a great spread and having a "square meal." Our own family was scattered throughout Pouldreuzic, Plozévet, Landudec, and Pouldergat, which made for at least a dozen pardons, if you included the chapels.

Some of our pardons were very well attended, though they took place in small hamlets or even in the wilderness. And they had reputations that went far back in time. That was true of the chapels of Saint-Germain and Tréminou, which are famous in the history of our region because of the brigand La Fontenelle and the revolt of the "Bonnets Rouges," rebels who left us with some obscure but deeply rooted memories. Near the chapel at Tronoen there is the oldest calvary in Brittany—an object of everlasting devotion. The chapel overlooks the rough Bay of Audierne, separated from it by marshlands and a long row of resonant stones against which huge rolling waves crash down. Farther down, toward Penmarc'h Point, the chapel Notre-Dame de la Joie, imperiled by the sea, attracts many pilgrims. And finally, there is our own chapel, Notre-Dame de Penhors, whose pardon was the high point of our religious life. It was also our pride, for it brought such a crowd of outsiders into the region, one could only believe that our Virgin was among the most powerful of the ladies of Heaven.

Now before the pardons season began, I used to hear talk, every year, of the phantom chapel—the chapel at Loc. "Loc" was once within the territory of our parish, toward the northeast. Nothing is left of it. Long ago, our ancestors would crowd in there for the first pardon—the first fair after the afflictions of winter. A livestock market was set up around the chapel; tents were scattered about to satisfy people's hunger and thirst; and a selection of sweets were sold from handcarts. There were also wrestling matches between the young men—matches so rough that, in the end, blood would flow onto the yellow flowers which covered the slopes and spread all the way to the chapel: the most sumptuous carpet of Corpus Christi. Flowers which, in French, are called "primavères," or primroses. Every woman and child would pick huge bunches of them which were blessed at Mass and then brought back to the house, where they gently withered away during the following week. Eating them was forbidden. When the pardon-fair at Loc was over, men covered with blood would take the sunken roads that led home, savoring their triumphs or pondering their defeats, and surrounded by their families carrying armfuls of the yellow flowers. All the gentleness and violence of springtime together in one place. For us primroses have only one name: "bouquets from the fair at Loc."

They say that the pardon was abolished because of drunkenness and pitched battles. And from that time on, the chapel was abandoned. It fell into ruins and was finally used as a stone quarry, as was the large metalled road which led to it—a work of the Romans, perhaps; a giant's causeway, said Grandfather, who had seen the remains of it. The last stones had been carted away to the churchyard of the Penhors chapel. Nothing was left but what amounted to two cartfuls. No one even knows the name of the patron saint anymore. Grandfather always said that, roaming through the happy meadows of Paradise, there's an old Breton saint, with a mournful smile, whose name Saint Peter doesn't know unless he looks it up in his book. My own books were to teach me that he was none other than the great Saint Guénolé himself. I should have preferred not to know.

Notre-Dame de Penhors thus collected what remained of the chapel at Loc, the sanctuary of Guénolé, its cousin "à la mode de Bretagne"—in other words, several times removed. Penhors had every right to do so, since its chapel, facing the sea, is anything but abandoned. There is good reason to believe that its first pardon took place shortly after the Pope had granted plenary indulgences, in 1482, for the Great Pardon at Reims. As early as the thirteenth century there had been a chapel at Penhors which, time and again, had been altered, enlarged, and struck by lightning; but the Virgin had stood fast. In 1970 the roof of the building had been in danger of crumbling. Yet despite hard times and rather apathetic faith, a means was found to remedy the situation. How was it possible to allow a building to collapse when, over a period of five to six hundred years, floods of people had come there to sing Mary's praises and to beg for her protection! Floods of the faithful who had poured so many liards and écus into the collection plates that a roof of gold could have been built for the Virgin! There are certain places of worship which generate such fervor that even atheists cannot help but be impressed. That's why, of all the pardons in Breton-speaking Brittany, Penhors' is still one of the most important.

On September 8, 1919 or 1920, when I was still a child in skirts, wearing a tasseled cap, I was sitting in the doorway of my house at dawn, watching long lines of horse-charabancs bringing the faithful from far out in the country to the shores of Penhors. Even horse-drawn omnibuses came by, overflowing with dozens of *petit bourgeois* from Quimper. And crowds of people would come on foot, some strangely rigged out, others who had run two leagues and who, for once, were going to wash their feet in salt water. And all the beggars from South Cornouaille, with begging bowls in their hands and paternosters on their lips—the cripples leading the blind—were rushing to grab the best spots along the narrow, sunken road to await the procession.

My mother was on the lookout for the Pouzéog farm's charabanc, which would soon pass our house. She had been promised a seat for me. I was still pretty young to face such a long, hard day in the midst of a crowd. I had first to travel one league to Penhors, then remain standing for two hours during High Mass, plus another good hour during Vespers, and then follow the procession all the way without weakening so as not to bring dishonor upon my family.

The charabancs filed by. They were filled with old people and children for the most part, the adults walking and chatting behind. When the one from Pouzéog arrived, I was held at arm's length and shoved into the back between shy little boys in their Sunday best who didn't say a word because they were so busy straining their eyes in order to take in every bit of the spectacle. My parents joined up with the people walking behind. After a long and rather eventful ride, I suddenly heard shouts and saw arms stretched out, pointing. Behind the motionless cross of a windmill, we caught a glimpse of the Penhors chapel, perched on the shoulder of one of the last hills facing the sea. All the land around it was already black with people. From every side, those on foot, as well as streams of carts, were leaving the main road and converging on it by every possible approach. And finally, there we were ourselves. The sea suddenly came into sight, calm and sparkling, at the end of a huge expanse of beach, in back of which, on the land side, was a coastline of reefs. Piles of seaweed, gathered up by the fishermen, were drying on the cropped grass of the cliffs. There was no port. Only a narrow drain that descended toward the stones, and a small slip through which a half-dozen boats could be pulled by hand. They were there, on a dry shelf, their cheek blocks in the grass. The little peasants were already walking round them. We ourselves could go no farther with the wagon.

However, crowds of "pardoners" were still arriving, group by group, spreading out all over the cliff or reaching the chapel itself by walking through fields of stubble. Pulled by my mother—half-walking, half-running, and complaining to boot—I got to the last cliff on the south side, beyond which began the long row of stones (*ar vilienn vraz*) that protected the marshlands from the sea. To my left there was the *loc'h* of Penhors, a pond of brackish water. To my right the rising tide was already swelling into rollers. Two leagues farther out, stretched between the two and facing me, was a huge shoreline blocked by a large hollow rock called "the Torch," the one I could hear roaring wildly at night when the wind was a southwester. And beyond the rock itself, rising up like a high taper at the end of a long violet streak, just barely outlining the surface of the water, was the big lighthouse of Eckmûhl, the good angel of ships.

On the shore the groups fell into a series of lines. At the head of the first one, which was rather near us, walked three bare-headed, barefoot men, their trousers tucked up to their knees. The man in the middle raised the large processional banner of his parish high into the sky. It had been brought from the church to the shore, rolled up under somebody's arm, and had, just a short while before, been attached to the top of its pole. Behind the three men walked a priest in his cassock and surplice. The pilgrims were moving ahead at a steady pace, and to their left, the sea continued to rise. A few minutes later a second banner went up, then a third. All around us people were coming down the cliff to the stones, behind the small slip that had been built by my grandfather the roadmender. Despite the unsteady wind and the muffled sound of the rising tide, one could hear snatches of the hymn to Saint Vio, sung by the group from Tréguennec. On a level with the *loc'h*, they were silently moving across the stones and getting back into line before starting their walk along the pebbly road that led to the chapel. And then they began chanting (to give the Lady her due) the hymn to Notre-Dame de Penhors. We followed them. I would really have liked to wait for the Penmarc'h group, who were drawing near, but my mother pulled me along with a firm hand. It was for me that she had sacrificed her seat inside the chapel, and she wanted at least to be able to get into the churchyard.

All the doors to the sanctuary were open. Inside, you could see candles burning above all the motionless coiffes. It was impossible to get in, except for those carrying banners and the priests, who seemed to have their own door. We walked around the dry-stone wall that encircled the churchyard and, near the triumphal arch, managed to slip into the crowd pressed against the south wall, very near the porch. It was from there that we heard the Mass. All the people around me were singing, praying, reeling off their beads, and even going so far as to chat a little about this or that. After all, they had to give each other the news.

Two hours later, when the Mass was over, some of the faithful dispersed and ate in the fields, in the shelter of walls or slopes, since they had brought their food along with them in baskets or bags. The young people without families and those who hadn't wanted to load themselves down with provisions went to take refreshment in the long, arched tents that had been set up by the innkeepers of the region, who served not only drinks but food all through the day. As soon as all four of us had finished eating, my grandfather took to the road and made for home. For him the pardon was over; he had to care for his cow. My father had met some of his wartime buddies and went along with them to a tent nearby. Since he had brought his watch with him, my mother knew that he'd be at the Pouzéog charabanc at five-thirty without fail. She herself had met some women friends and relatives, and we all walked along the reef. Then the women sat down on the stones once they had lifted up their dresses in order not to ruin the velvet. And we children, our shoes left behind, took off for the rocks in search of green crabs and small fish with big heads swarming in the water holes. But we had been warned that every time we turned over a stone, we were to put it back in place; otherwise the people from Penhors would be displeased with us. In any case, we brought nothing back from that fishing trip. We had only gone to look and to enjoy ourselves. When we'd had enough, we walked over to the sand, for by then the sea was starting to recede. And it was there that I saw coming toward me a half-dozen horses led by the same number of peasants, dressed in old trousers and old shirts—a strange sight on the day of a big pardon.

But it was the custom, after the great labors of August, to bathe one's horses. And not only to wash their hides. According to the old men, that ritual bath brought them as much luck and health as a priest's blessing. It was also an opportunity for the owners and the important foremen to show their skill and their daring; for the horses were anything but amenable to the idea. Soon, however, the bells summoned us to Vespers. Not a soul was left on the beach. It would have made a bad impression if one were seen there once Vespers had begun.

There were even more people than there had been for the Mass. Since it was a weekday, many of them couldn't give all their time to Penhors. So they chose the afternoon and Vespers because of the procession, one of the most beautiful in all of Cornouaille. Out of the church they filed, the cross and the banners leading the way. Directly behind were a great number of the clergy in surplices, amices, and chasubles, standing around a gilded canopy under which walked a mitered bishop leaning on his crook. And bearded missionaries in white robes, and discalced friars in russet sackcloth. On a litter shouldered by sailors of the Navy was an ex-voto sailboat. Then more litters, more statues, and still more crosses and banners. How could all that have fit into the chapel? Finally, Notre-Dame herself left her home, carried by the brides of that year in their wedding dresses. That very old statue of painted wood was clothed in a veil and a new cloak. The procession fell into place, again according to some mysterious hierarchy which everyone knew. Then the priest chanted the first couplet of the hymn and off they went. I was quite ready to follow on the heels of the clergy, but my mother held me back. First we had to let the "big shots" go by, then the men, with whom I would walk later on. My place was still in the rear, with that lesser class—the women.

To the solemn swell of the hymn sung by all the faithful (even, according to my mother, those who sang so off-key that it was enough to make the frogs climb to the top of the pine trees), we started, from every direction, down the hollow road, on which the beggars had taken their places. A crowd right out of a "Beggar's Opera"—the blind, cripples exhibiting their wounds, their ulcers, and their stumps, and others who had no visible disabilities. Most of their begging bowls were in fact mugs that dated back to the First World War. Sous clinked around in them more effectively. Ever since morning, the "expensive poor," as they were called, had been ceaselessly reeling off, in head voices, the couplets of the Penhors hymn, never dropping even half a one. Now, as the singing crowds passed by, they remained mute and motionless, but their begging bowls were still clinking.

At the end of the sunken road the procession moved toward a cliff on which there was an "image" of Notre-Dame set up at the very top of a square gray granite column. The tide had already ebbed, exposing a vast wet beach. Everyone stopped singing the hymn while the clergy proceeded to bless the sea. Then they started up again, their banners flying high in the wind. The procession's return to the chapel meant that the faithful were about to disperse. The women who, between Mass and Vespers, had not lit candles directly in front of Notre-Dame waited until she was back in her place to offer up their own prayers to her on behalf of their households. The men slowly went about harnessing their horses to the charabancs. They had managed to fit in a few drinks under the tents and in the taverns. Now they knew it was the women and children's turn to go, wide-eyed, from shop to shop. It was the custom that "pardoners" bring a gift back to those who hadn't been able to come—a gift that was called their "share of the pardon." It could be some pious object—a likeness of Notre-Dame de Penhors—which one bought in the stalls around the chapel. Or some strange toy that one couldn't make oneself—a jack-in-the-box, for example. (The spring would always come in handy.) Or a big shiny ball—red, yellow, blue, or green—to hang on the rafters, but they were expensive. The well-known "pardon ball." Or some walnuts, just some walnuts, which a well-brought-up young man might give to a girl who pleased him, without in any way committing himself—merely to ask her out and take his chances.

While the venders of pious objects were allowed around the churchyard of Notre-Dame, the others were kept at a distance and had set up their wares here and there along the road that led to the slip—the site of the profane festival. Gypsies, whom we call "filthy asses" (*toullou louz*), owing probably to the color of their skin and their questionable get-ups, would offer lottery tickets to women, urge men to take part in shows of strength in which tricksters were used as bait for simpletons, hold shooting matches that were no small attraction for hunters and war veterans, and suggest visits to certain phenomena hidden behind gaudy curtains and which were always disappointing. (But, after all! You had to go and see.) Between their booths the card sharps and venders of all types of quack medicines and items that performed miracles spent their time making their usual spiels. All those people could speak French, which at once intimidated and captivated the customers. But the Breton-speaking Breton shopkeepers were not deserted for all that. From them you always got more or less what you paid for. And besides, they were better informed about the tastes of serious-minded people, being part of the family. Yet there was also a rather fat woman wearing a coiffe from another region who sold sheet music—those popular songs which, in endless couplets, tell the story of infanticides, shipwrecks, soldiers back from the wars, the misfortunes of drunkards, and unrequited love. I never saw her in action, but I've heard tell that she did a good business. Yet no one was ever to see her more than once or twice again. The young people were beginning to prefer French songs.

At the time, however, those young people were making an assault on the merry-go-rounds set up in a field of cropped grass enclosed within dry-stone walls. One of them, which was always full up, had wooden horses that moved to the accompaniment of a wheezy barrel organ. Children in beaded caps, little girls in coiffes, and adolescent boys in hats with velvet ribbons went round and round on it looking earnest or apprehensive. My mother put me on it too, but only for one round, just to see. Some day perhaps we might be richer. Anyway, I preferred to stand gaping in front of the other merry-go-round—the favorite of the young men and girls—called the "break-neck." On that one, which turned very fast and had seats attached to the top by chains, the passengers were swung high in the air, holding on as best they could with only one hand, for the other was needed to keep their coiffes or hats from flying off. The "break-neck" was an instrument of perdition, said the rector, who, from his pulpit, never failed to warn the young people against it. It was especially dangerous for the girls, because in spite of all the precautions they took, the whirlwind would lift their velvet dresses and reveal the white lace on their petticoats, which was indecent. Some of them even lost their coiffes as they swung around. And what good did it do them to weep for shame when they got off? The harm was done.

The priests did everything in their power to keep the fair activities from encroaching upon the pardon grounds. They relegated them to spots far from the sacred chapel and from the route taken by the procession. As for the itinerant merchants and entertainers, they did their best to be agreeable, making a point of not running the merry-go-rounds during the services. But that concession did not mollify the clergy. The town council was at a loss as to what to do. The religious were acting in their own interests and everyone else in theirs. And those everyone elses were fairly often the very people who supported the Church. Not to mention the fact that the Penhors fishermen, owners of the land on which the fair people set up their profane festival, were Republicans and thus made light of prohibitions. The Devil was abroad.

When I climbed into the Pouzéog charabanc to get back to town amidst a flood of people who seemed to be beating a joyfully chaotic retreat, the shore—free of the sea once again—was dotted with countless black specks. The people from the coast, their banners furled, were making their way home to Penmarc'h with their indulgences, battling against a southwester. The pardon was over.

Hélias in front of the sacred fountain in which he was dipped as a child—as protection against bellyache

4 Children of the Republic

> They are a people with latent treasures which have never been able to emerge. French culture does not suit them; their own cannot develop; therefore they have necessarily remained at the very bottom of the lower social orders.
>
> Simone Weil, *L'Enracinement*

One summer afternoon, all alone in the house, I was sitting on the first step of our stairway, busy with bits of string, trying to tie knots. Suddenly, just as I had started making some headway, a huge shadow completely blocked the open door, closing out the sun. What a way to behave! No one in our "group" would ever have come in like that, without introducing himself from outside, without asking in a loud voice whether anyone was at home. It was some stranger, obviously—which meant I was in danger. What if he had been planning to take me away in his shirt pocket, as the gypsies or all kinds of tramps often did, or so people said. I had learned to beware of women without coiffes and men who didn't at least wear a cap, for lack of a hat with ribbons. But what was I to do with my bits of string? I remained motionless on the step, my whole body stiff with anguish.

The stranger walked calmly into the hallway, like a man returning home. He was leaning on a thin and shiny stick which would have broken, I thought, under Grandfather's hands. Without giv-

Above: A family wedding. The bride and groom are in bigouden *costume. The little girl is too young to wear a coiffe.*
Below: A funeral by the sea

ing me so much as a glance, he went into the kitchen. Then I could see him clearly. On his head he wore a hat shaped like an upside-down stewpot. He was dressed in a long black coat with a fur collar. In the middle of summer! When he turned around, I saw that he had long sideburns, like my grandfather the sabot-maker. Under his chin he wore a large white wing-collar and a knotted black tie with something shining on it. He was a gentleman.

He came back toward me, knocked at the bedroom door (why in the world do that?), opened it, looked about, and closed it gently. Then, between his thumb and his index finger, he took hold of my cheek, and I heard his grating voice. I heard, but I didn't understand. He must have been speaking French, I thought. I had already heard some French words, of course, but not those. Suddenly, I burst into tears. And he got angry. He didn't look easy, that man. A moment later he asked me (this time in Breton): "Are you the only one in the house? Where is your father?" But I was too upset to answer. He struck the floor nervously several times with his stick, shrugged his shoulders, walked toward the door, came back, and crouched down in front of me.

"You will tell your father that Monsieur Le Bail came to see him. Monsieur Le Bail from Plozévet. Will you remember? Monsieur Le Bail."

And off he went. As soon as I had choked down my sobs, I ventured out onto the doorstep. Near the square, in front of Alain Le Reste's house, the gentleman was climbing into a kind of barouche which a horse that wasn't exactly made for ploughing pulled right off, under the smack of a whip, in the direction of Plozévet. The horse and carriage had just barely disappeared when most of the doorways were filled with men, women, and children who had waited for the gentleman to depart before making their appearance. What had happened? Who was Monsieur . . . what was that name again?

It wasn't long before I found out. An hour later, since my parents had not yet returned, I went out to join a few of my little friends who were playing at knocking marbles against the wooden door of Jean Kerdouz's house. The minute I got there, they stopped short and, without saying a word, gathered up their marbles before I'd had the time to get my own out of the bag. And they withdrew, never taking their eyes off me. I stood there motionless, amazed. Then one of them pointed his finger at me and blurted out in rage: "Red head!" And the others followed the lead, making up a dissonant chorus: "Red head! Red head! Red head! Red from top to toe!" What was eating them? After all, I didn't have red hair! One thing was clear: that day I couldn't seem to understand anything about anything. All of a sudden, from behind, I heard the voice of the kid from Pouloupri, the one who had no known father: "You've got white asses! Damn white asses! You and your white shit!"—as well as further insults implying that the people on the other side had crotches—and, most especially, two balls—that were repulsively white. Behind the kid from Pouloupri were two or three others, equally unrestrained. The Whites didn't feel they stood a chance, and disappeared after the boldest among them had called us "Red pricks" and "Le Bail's dogs." What? That Monsieur Le Bail again? Still, he hadn't looked any more like a redhead than I. When I asked the kid from Pouloupri and the others to explain the reason for that sudden outburst against the kids from the high end of town, who were our neighbors and usually our good friends, he made me promise never to forget that we were Reds and that the others were Whites, that there were a lot of Whites around us and very few Reds, and that the big leader of the Reds was Monsieur Le Bail. At which point, before returning to Pouloupri, he stood squarely in the middle of the street, his legs apart, put his hands around his mouth like a megaphone, and shouted in the direction of the town: "Long live the Republic!"

That evening I told my parents all about my adventures of the afternoon. Alain Le Goff and my father looked flattered at having been visited by Monsieur Le Bail and were terribly sorry not to have been there when he arrived; on the other hand, everyone had surely noticed that he'd come into our house. Our house in particular. Who was Monsieur Le Bail? He was the Mayor of Plozévet. He was also a "deputy." He defended our region in the "Chamber." The "Chamber" was in Paris, not far from where my Uncle Corentin lived. The "Chamber" was divided between the Whites and the Reds, who fought each other year in, year out—the Whites being pro Church, and the Reds, pro Republic. Monsieur Le Bail was Red. Therefore we were Red, since for two generations my father's family had been related to the Le Bail clan. What everyone hoped was that I hadn't acted too simpleminded in front of Monsieur Le Bail. I admitted that he had spoken to me in French and that I hadn't been able to answer him. "That's why you have to go to school," they told me. Monsieur Le Bail apparently never tired of repeating that the Reds had to be better educated than the Whites. Education was the only possession that fathers did not bequeath to their sons. The Republic offered it to everybody. Anyone could take as much of it as he pleased. And the more he took, the more he could free himself from the Whites, who were in possession of nearly everything else. Take my uncle Jean Le Goff, for example, who had left the region knowing barely how to read and write, and who, by educating himself, had become an officer. If he hadn't been killed in the war, he would have risen to the rank of captain, perhaps major. Not colonel, though—not yet; all the colonels my father had known for seven years had been Whites and the sons of Whites, sometimes even of the aristocracy. But all that was to change because the teachers had become Reds. And it was the teachers who would soon educate the colonels. If only I could become a teacher, Monsieur Le Bail would be pleased.

That, in sum, is what my parents told me. Of course, if I hadn't had all that French to learn, I could have started right away. But the school, which belonged to the Republic, spoke French, whereas the Church, which was White, spoke Breton. You see the problem. What more is there to say? "Besides," said Grandfather, "when you go to see your Uncle Corentin in Paris, boulevard Voltaire, you'll be as embarrassed as Madame Poirier, the tobacconist in front of the church, who just about understands Breton but doesn't know how to use it at all. If she weren't the only one who sold tobacco, she'd never see anybody, poor woman. That's what it's like to live in a region where you can't visit with people."

"But all I ask is to stay here, Grandfather."

"Exactly. Because you still don't know any French. The day you speak it as well as Monsieur Le Bail, you'll want to go somewhere else."

"Then why does Monsieur Le Bail stay in Plozévet?"

"He doesn't always stay in Plozévet. He goes to Paris to make speeches in the 'Chamber.' He goes to defend people in the law court at Quimper. With French, you can go everywhere. With only Breton, you're tied on a short rope, like a cow to his post. You have to graze around your tether. And the meadow grass is never plentiful."

It was all very difficult. The Church—well and good. I knew what it was. But the Whites were on that side, and I was a Red. Then why did my mother make me go to Mass and to Vespers every Sunday, not counting the nightly prayers? Why did she drum Sister Bazilize's shorter catechism into my head?

"The Whites certainly don't know the catechism any better than I do."

"Luckily," said my mother. "Otherwise, God knows what they'd dream up to say against you. Would you want to make me ashamed of you?"

"Of course not. But what in the world can the Republic be, with a name like that, which makes such a funny noise in your mouth? And why isn't there a Republic with a tower and bells, like a church?"

"In school they'll explain everything to you, from beginning to end," said Alain Le Goff. "That's the real seat of the Republic. At the town hall it isn't always honored as it should be."

All right, then, I'd wait until I went to school to become acquainted with the Red Republic. What a pity that it spoke French. Another problem was that its schools were located right at the center of the low end of town, wedged into a White neighborhood. I would therefore have to cross the square, walk all the way to the church, and then venture into enemy territory—the hangout of a gang of boys my own age who, even then, used to taunt us from time to time as they skirted the fields. There would be a daily war. Grandfather reassured me. "The schoolmasters will keep order among you. You'll be able to fight anywhere else if you like, but not there," he said. One other thing bothered me. The street in front of the big school was called "Shit Street," probably because it was covered with mud and filth. It wasn't nice. But

Grandfather had an answer for everything. "Exactly," he said. "At school you'll be cleaned up in every way possible. Besides, the town hall itself is down there too."

The town hall was a *penn-ti*,* or private house, consisting of just one room, a corridor, a door, and a window, which was built onto the house of the "headmaster," who was in charge of the boys. The classrooms were behind it and could not be seen from the street. Both schools, the boys' and the girls', were said to be *communales*—that is, elementary schools which belong to the commune. Another queer word, *communal*, but we knew it was Red and that it made the Whites fume with rage. One had to be a professed Red—and a very vivid Red at that—to dare to send one's daughter to the *communale* school. For there was another school run by the nuns and under the patronage of the rector and his vicar. It was located below the level of the road that ran along the south end of the church. There, the daughters of the Whites received a religious and tasteful education which was suitable to making them into good lambs of the Lord. Those whose parents lived under the domination of the Whites—in other words, who depended upon them for their jobs and their daily bread—were obliged to go there as well. More especially, if you sweated over a farm that belonged to a city White, from Quimper or Paris, or if you were forced to shelter your family under some White's roof, there was no question of having your daughters educated anywhere but at the Nuns' School, under penalty of being requested to clear out by the next Michaelmas Day and to hang yourself somewhere very far away—as far away as possible—for you would be pursued by a curse. "Red head, wrong-headed, Revolutionary!" Even those who were known to be Red and who worked for Reds, and therefore owed absolutely nothing to the Whites, were exposed to constant harassment. But there weren't many true Reds, particularly in the town and in the well-to-do countryside. The majority of them came from the village of Penhors on the sea, which was inhabited by fishermen who loudly extolled the name of the Republic; but that didn't hinder them from honoring their

*The Breton term *penn-ti* has two meanings: "farmhouse," as previously used, and "private house," when in town. (Trans.)

chapel's Virgin in private, while at the same time taunting the clergy with sarcastic remarks about all the gold and silver they derived from the pardons. The great concern of the state teachers was to convince the tenant farmers who weren't under the thumb of any White and who claimed to be sympathetic to the Reds, yet didn't profess their allegiance to them. That was also the case of tradespeople whose customers were divided between the two clans. Bringing all such people to a decision was a matter of skillful calculation. The most important consideration in favor of the *communale* school was a parent's ambition to see his or her daughter rise to the rank of a teacher or a postal clerk, since the Nuns' School trained girls mainly to be good Catholic housewives who would remain at home, unless they entered the Church. The priests and their allies counterattacked by loudly proclaiming that a state school was "the Devil's school," that one never learned any prayers there (and what, then, about eternal salvation?), that Christ on his cross was not admitted, and that the Red teachers corrupted youth and undermined the very foundations of society. The nuns' girls, who were both curious and frightened, would ask the Red children whether it was true that the Devil sometimes came in person to dance on the tables, with his horns and his horse's hooves. And the Red children never failed to reply that it was indeed true, adding that when Satan appeared, he was completely naked, from top to bottom, including the middle. Horrors!

On certain Sundays, especially during the month of September, before the schools had opened, the rector would thunder out from his pulpit against "the Devil's school." From my bench I could see my father and a few others cringe under the curses raining down upon them from nine feet above, whereas the Whites, as they were leaving, would shoot them glances filled with disapproval. And before coming down to the altar again, the terrifying rector or his insipid vicar would lift his eyes to heaven and call upon the Lord: "Deliver us, O Lord, from Godless schools and faithless teachers!" The entire congregation, including the Reds, would reply as one man: "So be it!" One memorable day a preacher even more violent than the rector launched into a historic diatribe against the incarnate devils who wrote bad books. And we were to beg the Lord to deliver us from somebody called Voltaire and another called Renan. Who in the world were those two? If anyone knew, he kept it to himself.

However, while those scathing sermons, which the Reds always dreaded before Mass, were forgotten by them (and apparently by most of the Whites as well) as soon as they had left church, the same was not true of the sanctions imposed by certain militant rectors on parishioners who were so forgetful of their Christian duty as to entrust their daughters to the ruffians of the Devil's schools. The most terrifying of those sanctions was to be forbidden to take communion and, most especially, the sacrament at Easter.

Once they had recovered from their shame, the men adapted to the situation rather well. And I noticed, quite early on, that they were generally very careful not to gibe at the clergy, whereas their counterparts among the Whites didn't hesitate to sneer at or complain about the rector's stinginess and the vicar's tendency to be sanctimonious. Odd, wasn't it? Could the anticlericals have been the Whites? For the women, however, being deprived of the sacraments was a nasty business. No one would have dared swear to the fact that the most pious of the White husbands all believed in God. It was clear that, for some of them, religion was, above all, the guarantee of a social status which satisfied them and which was a threat to the evil forces embodied in the Reds. For the Whites in the region were obviously rich; it was flagrant. As for the wives, whatever reasons they had for being practicing Catholics, there was nothing to justify the opinion that they had no deep-rooted faith. The highest honor to which they aspired was having a priest for a son or a nun for a daughter. To have had three, four, or five children who had entered the holy orders was a crown of glory for which they were ready to make any sacrifice imaginable. But I am almost of the opinion that the wives of the Reds were even more devout than they. First of all, because they had nothing to gain from the Church and merely suffered affronts at the hands of certain intolerant rectors. Also, because their husbands readily accused them of bigotry and of going to church just to sniff the priest's ass, as they put it. And finally, because they suffered at seeing their children relegated to the back of the church, especially their daughters, who, like themselves, were doomed to remain in the dark aisles or under the bell-rope while the nuns' little ewe-lambs glorified the Lord in the gallery. If the daughters of the Reds didn't find some way to make do (the best of all was to leave), most of them would become servants to the Whites' daughters, and even so, on condition that they whitened themselves.

My mother, Marie-Jeanne Le Goff, was certainly one of the best Catholics in the parish flock. And everybody knew it. Yet once my little sister was old enough to go to school, every pressure possible was brought upon the family so that she would go to the nuns. But she would not go; good Red blood doesn't lie. And Marie-Jeanne Le Goff, who was therefore deprived of taking the sacrament at Easter and humiliated from the pulpit, was to walk in the wilderness the entire time her little girl attended the Devil's school. Six years of tears and prayers to the Penhors Virgin. I will bear witness to that. No White, to my knowledge, ever intervened in her behalf, not even those who were fond of her, and there were a lot of them. No one ever took a stand against the rector. Actually, she was so unhappy that, one year at Easter time, my father was quite ready to drag the rector out of his lair, take his trousers off in front of the war memorial, and spank him with a fistful of nettles. Even though it would have meant having to leave and earn his living elsewhere. And I myself had decided to lend him a hand. Altogether disconsolate, Alain Le Goff tried to calm us down, repeating in a hollow voice: "That man will not last as long as any of us." But in vain. For it was in fact my mother's despair that revived our more Christian feelings. When my sister finally left the Devil's school, Marie-Jeanne Le Goff rejoined the Easter communicants, joyful as could be! And all will be forgotten until the day the poor woman's God recognizes her as his own.

When I myself left for the state school, no one made any great fuss for the simple reason that no other school existed for boys. Plans were in the works for building a school run by priests, and it was indeed built later on. But for the time being, the sons of the Whites had to attend the Devil's school and submit to Republican teachers. As a matter of fact, they didn't seem to suffer much. They gallantly received their elementary-school diplomas, which were not reputed to be diabolical: what luck! Even their parents didn't find it hard to admit that our school was well run and that our teachers were equal to the task. Obviously, the Devil was as partial to the Whites as he was to the Reds. So there was no question of the rector's penalizing the Reds or their mothers.

When school opened in October, since the weather hadn't yet turned cold, my mother had my Uncle Jean's khaki uniform recut for me. There was another one as well, almost brand new, in the uniform chest. I thus had enough to wear for quite a long time. Only the buttons on the jacket were changed. It hung somewhat loosely over my shirt, but that was because I was to wear a woolen vest which my mother had knitted me for the winter. It was also a little too long and too wide all over because I would soon grow bigger. Well, at least that war had served some purpose: it had provided us with a bit of clothing. Thus many of my little friends strutted about, as I did, in army surplus. We owed yet another debt to the war, but that one we could have done without. It was the lice which the soldiers were said to have brought back from the trenches. Day after day we had to fight a merciless battle against them. It wasn't all that bad for the boys, who as a rule had close-cropped heads. But the poor little girls wept every morning while their mothers combed their hair, energetically, over a white plate. When the black lice fell into it, the girls would crush them one by one under their thumbnails, "the little lice-hammers." We thus inherited our fathers' woes.

On the other hand, since my father had been in the artillery, my cap had red braid on it, in contrast to the yellow braid of the infantry, which adorned those of the other boys. And given the fact that in our region red is always preferred to yellow (it's more pleasing to the eye), they were jealous. So to avoid scraps, as soon as I arrived in the schoolyard, I'd fold it up and hide it in my pocket, even though it meant remaining bareheaded for a few minutes before entering the classroom. And—would you believe it?—in the classroom all of us had to take off our caps, as we did in church. But that didn't bother us nearly so much as leaving our sabots at the door. They would stay there in a pile, all mixed up, tossed one on top of another. The families of some of the little boys weren't rich enough to provide them with slippers, which were replaced by inner soles and straw or hay pads. When the time came to put their sabots on again, they weren't always able to find the insides. Also, there were sometimes bitter disputes over the sabots, for the stronger boys would try to take the best ones if they happened to be the right size. But things never got too out of hand because the schoolmasters kept order.

At any rate, the rich and the poor were dressed almost alike, with nearly the same number of patches on their clothes.* And what all the kids gloried in was sometimes wearing their new Easter suits, made entirely of striped plush velvet, which left a very strong smell in the room—the smell of wealth. But the new trousers were often provided with extra bottoms, since schoolchildren work sitting down. When the extra bottom wore out, the child's mother would rip it off. Meanwhile, however, the trousers had changed color because of the salty rain, so that the little boy would be called a "faded ass." The elbows, too, got terribly worn out on the tables, as did the knees on the schoolyard ground and on the road when we played marbles. In that case, some dressmaker, for a few sous, would sew on patches that invariably clashed with all the rest. But if you think that bothered anyone . . .

Since I was an only child at the time and the son of a mother who was fiercely determined to keep her good reputation, I was among those who were the least badly dressed. I even had a good pair of drawers under my trousers, which was not true of everyone—far from it. Underwear was rare. And none of us, of course, had a coat for the rainy season any more than our fathers or our mothers did. The worst off were those who came from some distance—from Penhors, for example—who had to jog for two and a half miles in all kinds of weather. When they got wet, they would stay wet for the whole day, even though the classroom stove—if there was one—did its best. Then, on the way home, they'd get soaked again. Their old clothes, all covered with mud, would be spread out to dry in front of the fire. The next day they'd wear them again, still stiff with dirt, dry or not. Many of the children didn't have an extra pair of trousers or slippers. When

*See explanation below, chap. 8. (Trans.)

there was a real downpour, the parents, as a last resort, would cover themselves with potato sacks, but their children would stay at home—never mind about their studies.

Thanks to the First World War, we had also inherited haversacks, which we used instead of briefcases. The children from far out in the countryside and from the coast would put not only their books and notebooks in them but also hearty snacks to last them through the day. Butter, lard, or molasses sometimes contaminated their history or grammar books, but it couldn't be helped. There was no cafeteria or lunchroom. As I mentioned before, a saving grace was to be invited at noon, now and then, to the home of some little friend, but that didn't happen often. Life was hard for everyone, and parents would refuse any invitations to their offspring that could not be reciprocated. The poor are even prouder than the rich.

Classes would begin at eight in the morning and end at four in the afternoon. There was a break from eleven to one. At eleven o'clock some of the children would rush over to the church for a catechism lesson. When they were late, the priest would storm around and fulminate against the teacher, who had kept his pupils overtime on the pretext of preparing them to win scholarships. The teacher would retort that all of Thursday* was reserved for catechism lessons. And the kids would do their best to avoid being punished by both sides. It wasn't easy.

Since winter was meant to make us cold and to force us to protect ourselves from the cold, we learned how to shiver properly and even how to make our teeth chatter to digest the cold. But there was a teacher—luckily, only one—who, in his moments of rage, would let his temper get the better of him and strike you on the knuckles with a steel ruler if your work was bad. Your chilblains would burst and ooze. Discomfort and pain. He was also the one who, with two fingers, would grab you roughly by the hair on your temples and at the same time call you every unpleasant name he could dig out of his vocabulary. That one really went too far. On two or three occasions the strongest boys fought with him. And people say that one day a farmer whose son he had badly

*In France, until very recently, schools were closed on Thursdays, not Saturdays. In some regions they are now closed on Wednesdays. (Trans.)

mistreated arrived in the schoolyard with whip in hand to thrash the torturer. We were all rushed back into the classroom, and apparently the matter was finally settled.

But anyway, it's true! We knew perfectly well that we were always on the lookout for an opportunity to do something foolish, being free little scoundrels. We also knew that our ears were made to be tweaked, that from time to time the blackboard pointer would be cracked down on our backsides. We knew that it was for our own good, or at least what others considered to be our own good. When we were very young, we had been given a few spankings on our naked asses and had got rid of the burning sensation by sitting on the cool stone of our front steps. Some of the kids had even been spanked with a handful of nettles on great occasions. Then, to cool down, they had had to keep their behinds in water for a long time or apply a poultice of herbs to them. For two pins they would have gloried in it. Most mothers would slap a naughty or rebellious child across the face with a dishcloth. Even my own, the best of women, did not refrain from doing that when I provoked her. As for my father, he whipped me twice or three times on the back with his belt, but surely I deserved it. What terrified me was his cap, which he would slap over my face to keep me quiet when I exceeded the bounds of being objectionable. Since he was then working in a sawmill, his cap was filled with sawdust, and it would take me a good hour of rubbing my eyes to get the bits out. Yet none of us would have ever thought of holding such minor occurrences against our parents or schoolmasters; they were merely penalties for our failings. We paid the price and that was that. Obviously, one of our rectors, who used to freely slap our faces with his big red handkerchief after he had blown his nose in it, would have done well to stop taking snuff. For getting snuff in our eyes made us cry without repenting. But that rector was a good sort, all things considered, whereas we knew instinctively that the teacher with the steel ruler didn't very much like the children of mankind.

The first day of school was, of course, always approached with apprehension. We would have barely crossed the threshold and there we were, in another world. It was a little like going to church, but far more disconcerting. In church our parents were with us, but in school they didn't come in. In church we talked and sang in Breton; the catechism was in Breton. Even though the priest reeled off a lot of Latin, he at least didn't ask us to learn it. At school we heard nothing but French; and we had to answer with whatever French words we had picked up. Otherwise, we'd keep silent. We read and wrote in French. If at home we hadn't had our missals, our catechism book, and our hymnals—all in Breton—in addition to *The Lives of the Saints,* we would have had good reasons for believing that no one ever wrote or read Breton. The schoolmistresses didn't wear nuns' coiffes, but dressed in fashionable city clothes and even wore leather shoes during the week. The schoolmasters might have looked quite like ordinary men had it not been for their collars and ties hanging over ridiculous little single-breasted vests. (Rather often we saw them walking on wooden soles, which made them less intimidating.) And those men and women normally went about bareheaded, a thing our parents would never have dared to do, nor would we. As I said, we were told to remove our caps when we entered the classroom. Just as in church. But the lessons we had to learn were harder than the catechism lessons, and there were more of them. And we had to write all the time, wasting expensive paper. In the end, we would receive our elementary-school diplomas, which were much harder to earn than the first-communion certificates.

Thus the servants of God and of the Republic were our masters—the only people to whom we had to take off our hats wherever we met them. The Whites acknowledged the former without any objections. We, the Reds, were supposed to be the faithful disciples of the latter. It wasn't easy. God seemed to us more powerful than the Republic, and the priests closer to us than the teachers. The rector and the vicar always spoke to us in Breton, even though it was said that they were just as capable of expatiating in French as the lawyers in Quimper. The teachers spoke nothing but French, even though most of them had spoken Breton when they were our age and still did when they returned home. According to my parents, they were working under orders. Orders from whom? From the "Government Boys." Who were they? The men who headed the Republic. But really! Was it the

Republic that wanted nothing to do with Breton? Apparently, they wanted nothing to do with it for our own good.

"But you, my own parents, never speak French. Nobody in town or in the country speaks French, except for poor Madame Poirier."

"We don't need to," said my parents, "but *you* will need to. There are still some old people who don't know how to read or write. They didn't need to. But we ourselves did. And we also had to speak French once in a while. Only once in a while. *You* will need to speak French all the time."

"But whatever happened?"

"It's the world that has changed, from one generation to another."

"And what will I do with my Breton?"

"Just what you're doing right now, with people who know Breton, but there will be less and less of them."

"But why . . .?"

My father put an end to my questions with a blow from his cap filled with sawdust. Exactly what I deserved. What business was it of mine?

In any case, at school we were soon put to torture when, overflowing with good will, we had to make up short sentences in French. Was it our fault if some Breton words slipped in? Anyway, the schoolmaster was the only one to notice. Whenever he'd strike the table with his ruler, we knew that we had failed. He would go over the sentence, inserting the French word. "I saw *eur c'hwede* this morning," one of us said. The schoolmaster wrote on the blackboard: "une alouette"—a lark. "Repeat after me: 'I saw a lark this morning.' " But sometimes he himself, all tangled up in his own definitions, and realizing that he hadn't been understood, would finally resort to a Breton word when he had no picture to draw on. With pictures, there wasn't any problem. He showed us one of a château; we thought "*maner*"; he said: "This is a château." All right, then: a *maner* and a château were the same thing. Then we found the word *manoir* in our book. He explained that it was a small château. Fine. A château was therefore a *maner braz.* We had understood. We even enjoyed that game. But some words couldn't always be conveyed by pictures. Our strict schoolteacher, with a slight gleam in his eye, would have to whisper the Breton word. The entire class would smile, breathe more easily, and feel relieved. "Ah! So that was the one!" But we had noticed that he always resorted to "our" words reluctantly. So, being mischievous, we'd get together and decide that on certain days we would pretend not to understand anything he said. However much he would knock himself out trying thirty-six ways of explaining what he meant, we kept straight faces. He'd go on to something else. Fifteen minutes later, someone would raise his hand and, looking perfectly innocent, ask: "Sir, how do you say *firbouchal* [to ferret] in French?" Now that was an exact equivalent of the word the schoolmaster had been trying to explain. He had even done his best to get it across through gestures. But in vain. The class was choking with joy. He rapped his ruler on the table. Everyone was to be punished. We were terrible little hoodlums and would end up as slaves, doing penal servitude.

For the time being, however, we hoodlums were slaves to French. Especially when we had to tell a story in writing. There was only one way of doing it: First, tell ourselves the story in Breton, sentence by sentence, and translate it into French as we went along. Sometimes that didn't work too badly. At other times the schoolmistress (who told about this later on) would be amazed when she read, for example: "A flock of three houses flew over my village." She, of course, surmised that something in the translation had gone wrong. The author of that surrealist poem was asked to explain. He couldn't manage to without giving the original. The story was about a flock of starlings—*tridi,* in Breton. But *tri di,* in two words, means "three houses." And how was one to know whether it was written as one word or two? Once the whole matter was clarified, the class burst out laughing, and so did the schoolmistress. No punishment. Clearly, there were joyful moments in the lives of slaves. On the other hand, it took a long time for anyone to get us to understand why such sentences as the following were incorrect: "Coffee there will be at my house tomorrow"; "I sent the apples with me"; "I haven't seen that one for a long time which it is."

Blurting out a few Breton words in the classroom didn't have any great consequences. It was in the schoolyard, during our supervised recreation, that we were in danger of being caught using full sentences in Breton while chatting in a covered corner of the yard. Once, at the height of a passionate discussion among the boys, one of the schoolmasters—who was in the habit of pacing up and down between the back of the town hall and the fence around the headmaster's garden—had walked stealthily up behind them. In the lower grades we would, in such cases, get off with a slap, a bruised ear, and our promise never to do it again. But the older we grew, the more frequently punishment rained down upon us. And still for our own good. For example, the year we were competing for scholarships, I was penalized by having to conjugate the verb *dactylographier* (to type)—that horror—in every tense and in every mood. That I *dactylographiasse*; that we *dactylographiassions*! I don't know what was wrong with me that year, but it was the third or fourth time that the headmaster, Monsieur Gourmelon, had taken me by surprise when I was in the process of discussing things in Breton with Alain Mazo or Alain Le Gall, two of the other candidates. How could we speak French to describe what was happening in our town, where no one spoke anything but Breton? And anyway, French really lacks vigor. Take insults as an example. Calling someone an idiot or an imbecile is pretty innocuous. In Breton we have at our disposal a whole stock of terms, each of which is related to some anatomical deficiency that represents the adversary's intellectual inadequacy and strikes him like a rock. It didn't take us long to learn the French word *merde* (shit),* without even knowing to which language it belonged, since our schoolmasters never used it, whereas the veterans of World War I would use it freely in conversation. But *merde* in Breton, *kaoc'h*, is far more positive, especially when accompanied by *ki* (dog) and reinforced by *du* (black). As everyone knows, a black dog is an incarnation of the Devil; therefore his excrement is the most loathesome rot in the world. "Black-dog shit to you!" Isn't that the most insulting way of sending someone to the Devil? When that phrase—or something even worse—burst

*Perhaps because the word *merde* is so commonly used in France, it is a shade less vulgar than its English equivalent. (Trans.)

out in the schoolyard, it was impossible not to hear it. And the punishment was double—first of all, because the insult was in Breton, and also because, when translated into French, apparently it was considered offensively vulgar.

Although I was at the head of my class, I had terrible trouble conjugating the verb *dactylographier* in writing. A word like that doesn't resemble any other; it has a disagreeable sound to it; it seems to be made up of bits and pieces; it never even appeared in our books. Indeed, I wondered what use I could ever make of it. What good did it do me to learn from Monsieur Larousse's book that it meant to write by striking the keys of a machine with one's fingers, when—writing with my steel nib and my violet ink—I was inscribing its incredible litanies on graph paper? In our region there was nothing that remotely resembled a typewriter. But no matter, since it was a question of punishment, pure and simple. Monsieur Gourmelon had told me: "It's a word that comes from the Greek. That will teach you not to speak Breton when you are supposed to be improving your French." In any case, having sweated over the verb *dactylographier,* I had been forced to pay closer attention not only to my conjugations but to my articulation, for I conjugated aloud as I wrote. And I almost managed to do it without making a mistake—word of honor.

When one of us was punished for having allowed his mother tongue to be heard in the enclosure reserved for speaking French, he either got it in the neck with a peculiar or an irregular verb, or he had to stand in a corner behind the blackboard after his friends had left, and could count on another punishment awaiting him at home. His father and mother, who probably didn't understand a word of French, after having given him a good thrashing, would reproach him bitterly for being the disgrace of the family, assuring him that he would never be good for anything other than tending the cows, which—even in those days—was considered dishonorable by the very people whose work, in part, consisted in tending the cows. Moreover, the word *cow* (*buoc'h,* in Breton) was used for insulting the dim-witted, the hopeless imbeciles, those who never learned anything about anything and whose daily life was a succession of idiocies. Since there were no asses in the region, people had to fall back on a familiar animal that was hardly known for its intelligence. Its long horns were a worthy equivalent of the asses' long ears. Could that have been why, throughout Breton-speaking Brittany, the punishment inflicted on schoolchildren who were caught speaking their native language was called *la vache,* "the cow"?

As for the schoolmasters, ever since the creation of the Ecoles Normales (teachers' training colleges), many of them had been the sons of peasants, so they often acted like one of my friends' fathers. In other words, during the day they severely punished any pupil they caught speaking Breton. But after class, their greatest pleasure was to speak that very same Breton with their families and the townspeople. Inconsistent? Not at all. Once they had finished being hussars of the Republic, they became men again.

Nor was our parents' behavior inconsistent. They had made sacrifices to send their children to school to learn spoken or written French, however much they needed them at home to tend the cows or to care for their brothers and sisters. Therefore the children's work was to apply themselves to French. Speaking Breton meant that they were shirking their work; they were balking at the labor involved; they were having fun. And what, if you please, does someone deserve who has fun instead of working? A good thrashing to teach him how to live. Consequently, the child who was punished in school had to expect that when he returned home, he would receive a hiding, together with a severe reprimand in Breton. Whether his parents were Whites or Reds, he was in for it. In spite of the Whites claiming, along with the priests, that "in Brittany, Breton and faith are brother and sister," it in no way excused their offspring from learning French, even though they didn't have to use it in everyday life. When they had arguments with the Reds, the Whites were quick to assert that the "Government Boys" made the children from Lower Brittany learn French because they needed servants to empty the Parisian bourgeoisie's chamber pots; thus it was indispensable for those servants to understand the language of their future masters. That was quite possible. But the Reds vigorously retorted that a sound knowledge of French would allow their children to rise above the rank of servants, and all things considered, if indeed they had to work under others, they would be less miserable serving the bourgeoisie than slaving away in fields that didn't belong to them, and they would earn more money to boot.

"So you want them to go and sniff the Parisians' urine," replied the Whites derisively. "Here everyone goes outside to pee."

"You say that because you want to keep them around your cows and your horses," charged the Reds. "A man's piss isn't any worse than mud and dung."

And so the debate went on. But neither the Reds nor the Whites ever argued about the fact that it was necessary to learn French then and there.

That was because they had fought together in the First World War. At the start, they hadn't known what it was all about. Certain big shots fancied that the war was a way to shut up the poorer classes, who were becoming demanding and listening to such voices as that of Jaurès, who, as it happened, didn't want any battlefields, the bastard! People were still talking about the rich White in the parish who had left for the front, shouting:

"This time we'll get them!"

"Who do you mean?"

"The poor!"

And then for four years all of them had led the lives of martyrs. For four years they had given up the clothing that symbolized their roles as masters and servants to become brothers in arms, floundering about in the same muddy ground which didn't belong to any of them. They had learned a few verses of "The Marseillaise" and other songs in French. They had beaten the Krauts, or so they had thought, which amounted to the same thing. And then they found themselves together in front of the war memorial, on which no distinction was made between the names of the Reds and the Whites. They had all saved France; France was theirs; it had become part of their heritage; so why not the French language as well? And the state teachers, however Red, taught their children patriotic songs. Our fathers, the veterans, were flattered. They had not suffered in vain, had not lost an eye or a leg so that an epic four years would be passed over in silence. Of course, it was the last war forever more; that was understood. But that was also the point: they were more than a little proud of having been the ones who had put a full stop to so many centuries of sound and fury.

Indeed, tears came to their eyes when they heard the word *country,* which the teachers used constantly in school. No doubt about it: those teachers weren't bad at all. And mainly because many of them had fallen gloriously at the front. You could count on people like that to bring up your children properly, however Red they happened to be.

When the kids came back from school with their books in military haversacks, their fathers (and sometimes their mothers) would take fifteen minutes off to flip through, as best they could, the amazing tools which, as they well knew, were used to discover the world. Most of them—not all—had learned to read, but many had forgotten; they hadn't had any need or opportunity to develop their small skill, and so could barely make out the words. Every man to his trade, as they say. But all of them aspired to having their children sanctified by the elementary-school diploma, which would be framed and hung nobly on the front of the cupboards, between the pious images and the photographs of family weddings. We called it *ar zantifikad,* a name that endowed it with a sacred quality because of its obscure reference to the Creed: "*sanctificetur* nomen tuum." And that celebrated diploma was in French from top to bottom.

There was another reason for our parents' resolute desire to have us learn the language of the bourgeoisie, even if it meant being humiliated by "la vache" and, to a certain extent, repudiating our mother tongue. It was that they themselves were humiliated because they knew nothing but their mother tongue. Every time they had to deal with a city civil-servant and every time they ventured into a city, they were exposed to sly smiles and to jeers of all kinds. They were called "straw-choppers," for example, or "gorse-grinders," since their language seemed uncouth to those who didn't understand it. Or else they had to put up with charity in the form of pity, which was still more insulting; or they were simply told to go to the devil until they could talk like Christians. Because of that incapacity, the Breton-speaking Bretons were considered simpletons or retarded by tough guys whose intelligence quotient was lower than their own. But what could they do about it? Later on, after four years of fighting and of associating with all sorts of people who used a kind of bastardized French either well or badly, they were able, in some measure, to defend themselves. However, they had either picked up elegant expressions from the officers, which would virtually astound the tax collectors, or they had been contaminated by the lower-class Parisian accent and slang. To complicate the situation even more, the children of the region who, since World War I, had gone to Paris to earn a living soon began to hate their own language, which to them was not only synonymous with poverty, but a symbol of ignorance and an assurance that they would be mocked. Indeed, they were within an inch of cursing their parents for that patrimony, which they found more deplorable than a hereditary physical disability. After having spent a year at the most in some lowly job in the capital, they would return to the region to swagger about in front of those "worm-cutters," their poor relations. And never ever would they utter a word of Breton, except when they'd inadvertently step on the prongs of a rake, the handle of which would snap back and hit them in the face: "*gast a rastell*!"—"whore of a rake!"

Though our Breton-speaking parents never made fun of French—you can be sure of that—they did make fun of those who were pretentious about it or who spoke a neo-bastardized French, especially when they had picked up a fake Parisian accent. Like all populations who never express themselves other than orally, they were very sensitive to language, very heedful of it. They could easily detect a mixture of tongues and could recognize what was wrong with it. And they themselves were doing their best to learn the proper French of the teachers, not that of the "Parisians."

At the lycée in Quimper we little Breton-speaking students were made fun of by the day students from the city, who spoke a frightful "Quimperian" and transformed all their *r*'s into *a*'s. In addition, I was so mortified by the mockery of the bourgeoisie that I promised myself I would win, unequivocally, the prize for French. And I received it, on my honor as a Bigouden, with the other Breton-speaking students as runners-up, leaving far behind the dead-beat gang of those who had spoken a bastardized French since birth and who never recovered from the shock.

Another latent humiliation that obsessed our parents when they were outside their own region (and only when they were outside it) was their status as peasants. Those who work the land have never, over the centuries, gained the recognition that should naturally have been their due as providers of food. They had always been relegated to the lowest levels of the Third Estate. They constituted a crowd, nothing more. History books hardly ever mention them—a fact that struck me early on. Undervalued (even when they were rich) by the so-called higher classes, starting with those pathetic little employees who wore celluloid collars, and even repudiated by the merest tradesman who had moved up one rung on the social ladder, the "worm-cutters," the "sabot-wearing lugs," the "dung-covered nitwits" were never at ease outside their clans. And they preferred to remain in their clans so as not to be embarrassed or to embarrass others. As an example, take one of the lycée of Quimper's award-giving ceremonies. The municipal theatre, green plants, "The Marseillaise," the prefect and the colonel, professors in their gowns, the orchestra and balconies packed with parents dressed in their Sunday-best city fashions, speeches, and gilt-edged books as prizes. And I was about to carry off a good-sized pile of those books. Outside, however, on the steps of that bourgeois palace, was my mother, sitting with other country women in their gala coiffes and dressed in velvet right down to their ankles. They were telling each other their life stories, as they had done at the pardon of Sainte-Anne la Palud; and each one, in turn, sang the praises of her children. A supervisor rushed out, as he was told to, and asked them to come in. But to no avail. The vice-principal himself went out to urge them. Among those women were mothers whose sons were about to receive first prizes.

"Do come in, ladies. There are seats for you. Don't be afraid."

"We are not afraid," they replied serenely. And they thanked the gentleman, but didn't move a hand or a foot. They would quite simply have felt out of place in the municipal theater. Their sons were to become teachers, inspectors, doctors, professors, naval officers, or engineers. But the women themselves were "housewives," and their husbands weren't there. A short while later, when I came out, Marie-Jeanne Le Goff stuffed my prize-books into her shopping bag, which for once had no food in it. On that day of glory we were not to eat on a bench. We went to the Sauveur Restaurant, on the Place Saint-Mathieu, where everyone spoke Breton and was at ease with everyone else. Like traveling salesmen. We didn't order the whole meal; it was too expensive, and we had to have enough money left to pay for the bus. But we each had a big portion of stew for a few sous. And Madame Sauveur even gave us napkins. Later on, I, who by then knew French almost as well as Monsieur Le Bail, would go and eat at the Hôtel de l'Epée with the big shots. My mother would not go, wouldn't have wanted to. It was another "bourgeois palace."

I have recalled all that to explain why our parents, especially the Reds, added their own punishments to the teacher's when he caught us speaking Breton in a place where it was forbidden. Why, too, when someone who spoke only French came to the house, they did their very best to understand him and to answer him. Breton was their personal property—meager property, like their *penn-ti,* their cow, their pig, their two fields, and their bit of a meadow. We, their children, had to climb over the barrier of French to gain access to other riches; that was all. It was French that conferred the honors. And it was the honors they liked. But they would go on speaking Breton to the end of their days, never wondering about what might happen to their language once they were gone. It was none of their business. Breton was the only language they had been granted for their everyday lives; French, given the circumstances, wasn't worth a row of beans, and they knew it. Only Breton could represent them, body and soul; they knew that too. For them it was far too late to borrow a tool they would never be able to handle properly among themselves. And as for the city people, who thought they were so clever (indeed, the lower their rank, the cleverer they thought themselves), why didn't they learn Breton? After all, the notary public and the doctor spoke it very well.

Learning French at school did not turn out to be all that difficult. But arithmetic was something else again—from the four operations to sums about filling a bathtub, via surfaces and volumes. And there was another problem. Frenchmen didn't calculate the way Bretons did, which complicated life, to say the least. Our lessons began with a thick cord stretched across the classroom, in front of the teacher's desk, and on which empty spools were threaded, every tenth one painted red. With the tip of a long reed, the schoolmistress would separate them from each other, and we had to count them aloud, one by one or by groups. Those who made mistakes or who just stood there gaping were called to order by the tip of the reed, which was imperatively brought down on their heads. We then progressed to little sticks, those twig-fingers of which we had a good supply in our tables' compartments—packets of ten, tied together with bits of woolen yarn. They were very important to us, those sticks. Some of them were bent, so it was hard to line them up with the others and not at all surprising that *they* made the mistakes. Others were straight and smooth, covered with polished bark. They were the easiest to manipulate; you could count more quickly with them; and you were almost never wrong. Therefore the pupils with whom arithmetic didn't agree (I was among them) would try to get those sticks by bartering or stealing. But generally we considered ourselves honor bound to whittle them ourselves. Several of us were known for making them so straight that they were practically infallible. In the countryside there were some trees from which you could make good ones, and others that were worthless. We heard tell that in the cities one could buy the sticks readymade. What cheats those people were! But the schoolmistress assured us that the city children were no better at arithmetic than we.

Actually, we made out rather well, perhaps because our parents were remarkably good at calculating in their heads, without resorting to any pencil at all. Alain Le Goff was a past master at it. When I asked him how he did it, he wasn't able to explain, but he looked at me with sparkling eyes and said: "We in our family have always been very poor. If we had been stupid as well, we would have starved to death. So we were condemned to using our minds in order to have some chance of staying alive. Now it's up to you to use yours." I wanted to stay alive, no doubt of that.

However, my friends and I had some trouble with the number eighteen, which in Breton is called "three sixes" (*tri c'hweh*). We were somewhat surprised to discover that what the French called "forty" was our "two twenties" (*daou ugent*) and that their sixty was our "three twenties" (*tri ugent*), and yet they said eighty, *quatre-vingts* ("four twenties"), just as we did. But by that time the four operations had become gratuitous exercises in which Breton played no part.

What really riled us were coins. Since we had already been sent out to do small errands, we were accustomed to calculating everything on the basis of the real, which is worth five sous. We didn't know, of course—nor did our parents—that the real is a Castilian coin which our ancestors had adopted centuries ago, when the Spaniards had more or less controlled the region, and which we had kept on using. Four reals made a *livre.* To the French, that meant one franc or twenty sous. Yet our mothers, some of whom didn't know a word of French, and our grandmothers, some of whom hadn't even gone to school, counted very well in terms of reals and écus, and could do it for very large sums. One had only to see them at the market or at the fair when they were buying or selling eggs, butter, pigs, and cows. However, since they were women of good standing, what they received was always a bit heavier than what they had asked for, and a dozen always meant thirteen. But in school we had to arrive at precisely the right figure. We had to work out grams and milligrams like the apothecaries. That system was invented by a miser or a hypocrite, take your choice. People who deal like that are capable of skinning lice and selling their hides at the price of leather.

The same was true for measures of length, surface, and volume. How petty can you get? You don't need more than your fingernails, fingers (especially your thumb), and palm to gauge nails when you know what you want them for. You can take other measurements with two closed fists. Your arms are rather good for estimating a cord of wood. Have you ever seen anyone weigh stone before building a house? Stone is sold at a quarry by the wagonload. True, but a carpenter cannot do without his folding rule, nor can a cloth merchant or a tailor do without his yardstick. And even our grocer has copper weights so small that they'd fly away if you happened to breathe hard right next to them. So we had to go through with it, and go through with it we did. It hardly mattered. When we spoke of a "hectare" of land to our farmer parents, they would translate it into Breton as "about two days of ploughing." There was no "about" in school. Only a measuring chain.

I was not very good at problems. In the evening, under the kerosene lamp—my mother raising the wick as high as it would go so that I could see better—I made myself dizzy and sweated blood trying to solve those arithmetical traps in which time and distances play blind-man's buff. I didn't always succeed, especially the year I had put in for a scholarship. And when my tears began to drip down on the paper, smearing the violet ink, the arithmetic would become more and more resistant; my calculations, aberrant; my decimal points would shoot out right and left; and the sum totals were flabbergasting. No one around me could help. While my father swore into his moustache, my mother would accuse the teachers of cruelty, dropping a stitch in her knitting. And my grandfather Alain Le Goff would wipe his eyes with the back of his hand. He was even unhappier than I. "Put down something for them anyway," he'd say. "Maybe it will turn out to be right." It never turned out to be right except when I hadn't been weeping.

At school we also had to learn new names for the animals and plants we knew well, after all!—having marched up and down the paths and inspected the slopes while tending the cows. And the French names for them didn't make much sense to us, whereas their names in Breton were often more clearly meaningful. To take one example, the French word for pig, *cochon,* isn't nearly so evocative as the Breton word for the same animal, *oc'h,* which is actually the noise a pig makes, isn't it? However, it was lucky for the schoolmaster that he had pinned up cardboard pictures of the animals of our countryside, for we could thus unmistakenly identify them, and we knew about their eggs, their nests, and their habits. So we had merely to replace the Breton names with French names. I, for one, never quite managed to get them all straight. You might think that we found it easier when it came to fish and shellfish, since their names are often quite similar in the two languages. For instance, we say *sardined* for sardines; *birinig* for *berniques,* or limpets (in that case, it would seem that the French took over our word); and *bigornigou* for *bigorneaux,* or periwinkles. But for all the rest of them, there are few, if any, equivalents. Still, Breton words said more to us than French words, and that, combined with our ignorance when it came to the latter, perhaps explains why our spoken and written sentences were shot through with the local vocabulary. At the same time, our parents were increasingly mixing French words into their Breton sentences. All of us, then, fell between two stools—and often right on our asses.

As for the names of plants, I believe we, in fact, knew more than some of our schoolmasters because of having run through the fields and filled our bellies with everything that was edible, even though we got diarrhea from time to time. Besides, botany in school was always rather limited. Did our schoolmaster know about nothing but medicinal herbs? Would he have been able to find mouse-peas, silver-drops, snapdragons, Virgin-eyes, devil-bells, dog-tails, crow-leeks, larkspur, groundnuts, and catnip? There were many other things he didn't know and about which even his books said nothing. But the very worst thing that could happen to country children was being closed in behind a door for five days a week in order to learn things which had nothing to do with their everyday lives, whereas man's real work, we thought, was outside. It was particularly unpleasant to remain seated on benches for hours while the springtime sun shed its light, ironically, on spelling mistakes and turned our nine-times-seven-equals-fifty-six into smoke. That was perhaps good for city kids, who were to earn their livings in offices, if they could. But they didn't know about ungrafted bushes and had never had a fox among their acquaintances. What in our schoolbook they called "l'école buissonnière" (playing hooky), we called "l'école du renard" (playing fox). Was that because "playing fox" implied learning from a fox instead of a teacher or because one had to be sly so as not to get caught?

Playing fox meant the violent smell of freedom which suddenly got you by the throat in the month of April or May, to the sound of the scratching of steel-nibbed pens. The sad violet liquid stagnating in our inkwells made us feel like vomiting. Meanwhile, the French language went on setting traps for us. One of my friends wrote that things outside were blue. What he meant was that nature was turning green. In Breton there is only one word to designate blue, green, and a few other colors—*glaz.* It is used, for example, to describe blue thistles and green clover. The boy who made the mistake reworded his sentence, which he had translated from the Breton: "*An traou zo glaz er-mêz*"—"Things are green outside." Outside there were bird traps, slingshots, willow whistles, elderberry guns, and all the sunken paths, and all the old wild stones that were awaiting us in vain on the arid hills to the southwest, those which, as it happened, were nearest to the schoolhouse. So do you find it surprising that from time to time there was a Pierre, or a Louis, or a Jacques, a Corentin, a Demêtre, a Gourgon, or a Joachim who didn't answer the afternoon roll call? Generally, they would disappear in twos or threes. "Where are they?" questioned the schoolmaster, who knew perfectly well where they were. And the whole class would answer in unison: "They are sick, sir." The class wasn't lying. The absentees were purging their minds and their spirits once and for all, and how right they were!

The fox's favorite school was on a hill that rose up behind the village of Ménez-Fuez, in the direction of Peumerit. Since the Republic's school was right at the edge of town, you merely needed enough courage to walk right past its door, the point at which "Shit Street" ends and becomes a small dirt road that penetrates deep into the countryside before breaking up into a series of very narrow and almost impenetrable sunken paths, mysterious and fearsome, therefore more attractive then most. If merely a cow happened to be taking its horns and its udders for a nonchalant walk down one of them, we had to scramble up a slope to the right or to the left to let it pass. Because of the branches that met above our heads, we could never see the sky. What an adventure it was every time! We had to cross a small stream on a culvert made of a long, blue flagstone, and we thought we had reached the center of the world. Then the idea was to find the kingdom of Kodelig, the holy man who had become a hermit in those parts countless ages ago. We weren't quite sure of his name; the priests never spoke of him, and our teachers had no notion of who he was; but we knew what he had left behind: his bed, his wardrobe, and a huge dish of butter which he had left virtually untouched. People even said that he returned from time to time. There was always someone who had seen him and who, as it happened, had just died, right before he could give any information—bad luck! But our idea was to find his moor and his wood, which wasn't easy. All the pinewoods looked alike; the moors were taller than we; there were paths all over which led nowhere or, worse yet, turned back on themselves to jeer at us. Apparently, the holy man's retreat was defended by lots of witchcraft and illusions. We were serving our apprenticeship as Knights of the Round Table. Once one of the boys suddenly screamed with joy and gathered all the others round him. The Dish of Butter was there. It was a block of stone, evenly striated, sunk into the ground, and a bit lopsided. It was as high as the shortest boy among us, but so much thicker! It really did look like a huge mound of butter which you could make in a day with the milk of all the cows in the parish. Since it was there, the saint's wood had to be the nearest of those whose tops we could see. We walked straight to it, pushing our way through the gorse, which got caught on our clothes and stung us all over. One more slope to cross, and the Stone Wardrobe rose up before us in the middle of the pinetrees. It was actually shaped like a wardrobe, but our walking around it looking for doors proved useless. At least we were able to climb on top of it. From up there we got a bird's-eye view of a massive rock that had a deep hollow resembling a man lying on his side, all curled up. It was Saint Kodelig's bed. We climbed down the wardrobe and, one by one, up to the bed to lie in the imprint of the body. And that was the end of our expedition. For the next one, we made up our minds to go still farther, in search of a stone table on stone legs in a thickly wooded copse surrounding a very old manor house and which was called the "Great Altar." Our teachers called it a "dolmen," but they were the only ones who did.

The better behaved children made those expeditions on Thursdays. But Saint Kodelig's kingdom, right in the middle of its wooded wilderness, was so attractive that the others "played fox" while their friends were doing dubious battle with dictation and problems. So one day the school's headmaster decided to take us all there to exorcise both the saint and the fox. I no longer recall the explanations he gave us on the spot, but the Dish of Butter became a *lec'h* (or megalith), and the wardrobe, a menhir. As for the bed, our pedagogue got somewhat muddled in his stories about erosion, but in any case, at the end of that expert's appraisal, the "playing fox" enthusiasts were so disgusted that they resigned themselves to putting up with classes and to not missing one day of school. If only for reasons of nostalgia. When they were not present, it was because their parents needed them for work that couldn't wait. At such times, what could the teacher say?

I might add that, to our minds, the most interesting events outside took place during the hours we were closed into the school. Word of everything that happened in town got around very fast, since people were in the habit of communicating all the news to each other by shouting from house to house. We knew, for example, that on a certain morning L's bull, whom nobody but its master could handle—and even he had a hard time of it—was finally taken to the butcher's after a rather harrowing escape. Another time we learned that the cartwright Jean-Marie Guichaoua was going to put iron bands on two wheels for a new wagon on the following day. As it turned out, none of us had ever seen that work done from beginning to end. Usually children were not allowed into a forge because there was always some risk involved due to their careless blunders. How, then, would it be possible for a whole gang of us to get into Jean-Marie Guichaoua's yard, especially on a school day? There was only one way: to ask our headmaster to take us. Since I was at the head of the class (except in arithmetic, alas), I was entrusted with the job of going to see him about it. Monsieur Gourmelon—at first, completely nonplussed and even enraged by our strange request—chased me out with his bowler hat. Then he thought better of it, perhaps because he had realized we might learn something about the expansion of metals. So the next day we were all to go and see the binding of the wheels if Jean-Marie Guichaoua was willing and if we promised to give up our dissipated ways. We swore on our honor that we would be angels and gluttons for work. After class, Monsieur Gourmelon walked out in the direction of the forge. It was in the bag. On the other hand, we had to pay for that bit of entertainment by submitting to a lesson on metals and on the problems of the circle. We did our best and sweated over the work, since we had been paid in advance. We even reread, for the pure pleasure of it, the passages on the work of an ironsmith, which can be found in any textbook-anthology worthy of respect.

In our textbook-anthology there was also a section on circuses. Almost every year one of them came through our town. Luckily, they arrived during the summer or all of us would have been perfectly capable of forsaking school in order to watch the shabby parade which marched up and down the streets, announcing the evening's show. Those circuses were made up of only two or three caravans—four at the most—which, as we gazed at them with our eyes popping out, would disgorge a brood of creatures of all ages, dressed in dazzling rags and tatters. The night of the performance all of us would sit on the benches around the pole and be far better behaved than we ever were during our catechism lessons under the old nun's iron rod. Some of the boys had wheedled a five- or a ten-sou coin out of their parents; others earned their seats by doing a bit of work for the circus people; and two or three adventurers, not the poorest among us, would slide inside the tent under the canvas. The tightrope walker, corseted with tinsel, sparkled under all the lamplight. The horses with their combed tails would brusquely circle round at the lash of a whip; the clowns made such coarse jokes that you had to be an utter fool not to understand them, even though they were in French. And you were almost deafened by the drums, while the brasses sounded like trumpets straight out of the Last Judgment every time the acrobat let go of his trapeze. There were also strong men who lifted weights and broke chains—especially one tough specimen, an Italian giant who arrived at my father's workshop one day to get sawdust for the ring in an open wagon he had borrowed. When it was full to overflowing, that Hercules pulled it behind him with only one hand. His name was Primo Carnera, and shortly afterward he became a well-known boxer.

All types of tumblers would also come through the region. In Breton we called them *termajis* in memory of their predecessors, who used to work the *lanternes magiques.* Alain Le Goff had actually seen one of those magic lanterns. In still pictures it showed how the inside of a man was made. The showman explained the pictures as they were projected. He had a strange name, preceded by "Professor." Apparently, from those anatomical pictures and his accompanying speeches, one got the feeling that he was a sorcerer. But then he'd show others that were related to history—especially one of a balloon used by a man named Gambetta and which impressed the spectators to such an extent that they did not regret having spent their money.

The more modern *termajis* were "dirty asses" who worked a new invention called "the cinema," in which the magic-lantern pictures were made to move. You could see people walking, working, and arguing with reproving eyes and open mouths, but you couldn't hear them. All you heard was the noise of the machine that projected the pictures onto a sheet hung on the wall of Alain Trellu's bicycle-repair garage. Sometimes, too, there was a man, a kind of street hawker, who explained what was happening on the sheet. In addition, to help you understand more clearly, there were sentences in fancy handwriting which appeared between the pictures. And the people who knew how to read French would do so aloud, translating them for the others. Those movies often told stories about women and children who were being persecuted by bad men. You could hear the people commiserating with the victims: "It's just shameful, seeing all that." Or they would vent their anger every time the persecutor made an appearance: "It's high time *that* one got a punch in the nose." Alain Trellu told me that one day a woman in the front row kept spitting at the villain. Another time somebody who couldn't bear watching him make the poor wretches miserable grabbed hold of the sheet and tore it off the wall. I hadn't been there and was sorry to have missed it. But the performance always ended with the comical adventures of a little man in a bowler hat, dressed in a jacket that was too short and a pair of trousers that were twice too big for him. His name was "Charlot"—Charlie Chaplin—a man who delighted everyone and made them forget all the rest. Whenever the *termajis* arrived, people would rub their hands together and say: "We're going to see Charlot." And the *termajis* beat their drums through the streets and never failed, in their speeches, to make it clear that he'd be there.

We had another show as well—one that didn't cost anything and which we never tired of seeing. It was the train. Yes, we had a train that came into a real station, with a stationmaster who spoke French, whereas at the county seat they had nothing at all. We called it the "carrot-train" because it also transported loads of vegetables of all kinds. It would come from Audierne and go as far as Pont l'Abbé. There, at the station, it would meet the "limpet-train," which was so called because it came from Penmarc'h, the fishermen's capital. The limpet-train went all the way to the large station in Quimper, if you please. Both of them bore the name "trans-Bigouden."

Our carrot-train had an adventurous life, chugging along the slopes of valleys and through the pinewoods. To us its locomotive was a "black horse," and no one ever called it anything else except in school. It was a living, damp animal with a paunch, and it sweated, breathed, spit, and had nothing in common with an "iron horse"—that is, a bike, a dry machine that we didn't treat with much consideration because it moved ahead solely at the expense of our calves. From time to time, airplanes would mistakenly wander into the sky above us, but they did not yet have any right to our respect. We found that birds were more skillful, faster, quieter, and—all things considered—better made. For, if I may say so, we knew quite a lot about birds! Those airplanes were merely "flying wagons" and good only as models for making modern weathervanes out of bits of wood. The absurd name we gave them put them in their place. A wagon was never worth a horse. And what dealings could we have had with machines we couldn't even get close to?

The "black horse" had its moods, its bad days, when it got tired and moped because its cars were overloaded with potatoes. We heard that sometimes it broke down at the bottom of a hill, and people would worry about its health. They'd blame such breakdowns on the weather, which was either freezing or too hot. "It has a cold," they'd say, when its whistle began to wheeze. If it came in late, they would ask its servant, the "coal-man," about its state of mind:

"What's wrong with it today?"

"It's angry."

"Then feed it, for heaven's sake!"

The train cut through roads and paths without further ceremony.

It wobbled at the edge of the fields. It whistled not only to warn I don't know whom about I don't know what, but to please young people in the pastures. And its whistle gave comfort to the travelers, who got the feeling that all was working admirably, that they would arrive soon, if not before. Of course, it didn't always climb the Plonéour hill the first time round, even when it mustered up a tremendous burst of energy before tackling it. People from the neighboring farms would stop work and, with a twinge of anguish, keep their ears open for the noise it made as it climbed. Finally, when they heard a strong and staccato blow of the whistle, they'd think: "Ah, that good old black horse. It sure is worth stuffing its belly with food." And they would use it as an example to their children. "Work! Don't spare yourselves!" But who would have believed that that conscientious, that very courageous "black horse" was also a first-class joker? Do you know what it said, in its puffs of steam, when it labored at climbing a steep rise separating two parishes?

Merhed Plonenvel, gisti toud!
Merhed Plonenvel, gisti toud!

Meaning, in Breton: "The Plonenvel girls are all whores!" And thus it belched forth, over and again, that deplorable opinion of the women from Plonenvel (the place-name changed, of course, each time), held by the men of the parish it was leaving. And when it went gaily down the hill on the other side, it measured out—in a quick succession of puffs—the tantalizing reply of the women from Plonenvel or whatever the place:

E-giz emaint emaint (They *are* what they are.)
E-giz emaint emaint (They *are* what they are.)

On Sundays, after Vespers, people liked to go to the railway station to watch the "black horse" pass by with its two or three carloads of travelers. It was mainly the old women and the young men and girls who actually went through the gate. For old women, curiosity is one of the best consolations in life. And what's the point of shame after a certain age? The spectacle of a train would keep their tongues wagging for hours. The young men were always in hopes of seeing some sailor on leave, his bulging gray bag over his shoulder and his pockets ringing with écus—his pay. And the girls, flaunting their lace and velvets, would strut about in front of two or three unknown gentlemen who, from their boater hats to their watch chains, were framed by the windows. As for us, being the town hoodlums, we didn't have the right to go through the gate. The stationmaster always kept an eye out for us, because we had a bone to pick with him. What bone?

Well, about thirty feet from the station the train crossed a road that led to a canning factory, and it was there that we used to place long nails on the rails, wedging them in with pebbles from the tracks. Each nail was cleverly placed so that the end of it would be flattened by the "black horse's" wheels. Sometimes a handle had been attached to it beforehand. Once the train had passed by, we had a tool which we then sharpened on an ordinary stone or a grindstone. What a godsend, especially for those of us who didn't yet have knives!

Once the nails were in place, we'd go and take cover behind the slopes or the wash-trough below. Now sometimes the engineer would catch a glimpse of our little setup just as the train was moving out. If so, he would give two or three short toots on the whistle to warn the stationmaster that, yet again, we had cluttered the tracks. Straightaway, the latter would dash over to us. He had learned to run at the same school that we had, the brute. Our group would scatter like a bunch of sparrows, pursued by countless curses and threats, mostly to the effect that our ears would be cut off. None of us ever did lose our ears, but some were taken back to their parents by the railwayman, who held them dangling from that small piece of flesh, just as one holds a rebellious piglet. While the boy's father gave his offspring a thrashing with a dry stick of wood, the stationmaster, with tragic eyes, would assure him that some day the train would jump the rails because of us. Occasionally the picture of that catastrophe almost kept me from sleeping. Or I'd dream that the "black horse" reared high up over our nails and fell head over heels into the wash-trough, greeted by our mothers' piercing wails.

That wash-trough was one of our most constant worries. It was there that the women held their own county-council, and the business of the day was often ourselves—either an enumeration of our good qualities (some of the time) or a discussion of our depraved behavior (most of the time). The place was called *ar prad* (the meadow), and the verb *prada* meant both paddling the laundry and giving spankings. The "meadow" was a waterhole surrounded by a clump of willow trees and was reserved for women. Never would a man dare to show his face there for fear of hearing some home truths about himself or, at the very least, of providing the gossips with a lot to talk about behind his back. It's so difficult to sing anyone's praises at a wash-trough. Vigorously paddling their laundry prompted women to strip the trappings of innocence from their fellow beings. Even the angels would have had trouble safeguarding their halos. Sometimes two of the women, each trying to monopolize the conversation, would start making nasty remarks, reviving old grudges, and all the catcalling necessarily ended with one or two coiffes being torn off and the town divided into two clans.

One day the excitement reached such a pitch that you would have thought we were back at war or in the midst of the Revolution. When school was over, a few of the boys, with uneasy consciences, were on the watch behind a slope. They heard the women groaning—their voices raised in anger—about the modern children's lack of respect for their headmaster, the most important local figure after the rector. Each one in turn promised to chastise that potential jailbird, her offspring. And as they were progressing from groans to threats, one of them happened to accuse another woman's son of being the leader of the gang: her own son, of course, being one of the Good Lord's little lambs. And war broke out at the wash-trough: revolution in the midst of soaked laundry. It wouldn't have taken much for the most inflamed of them to throw each other into the water. What, then, was the reason for all that uproar?

The school's headmaster was an old man with a black beard all spread out under his chin. He liked to fondle it with his white fingers, which ran through the hair like a living, long-toothed comb. On his bald head he wore a black bowler, which would move from one side to the other, according to his mood. That was why, among ourselves, we had nicknamed him "Wobbly Caldron." In secret and with all due respect. Now the old gentleman (who, by the way, was much younger than we thought) was very good at his job. He trained us to put ink on paper without diverting most of it to our fingers. Indeed, that particular caldron distilled sustenance for us that was both rich and plentiful. Finally, he managed to make men of us. He really hustled us on, I can tell you. His voice would boom out like thunder when one or another of us would go so far as to "play fox." And it was pointless to try lying to him, I can assure you.

At the very back of the schoolyard there was an orchard in which all sorts of fruits were ripening: gooseberries and pears, but especially black currants. The children, quite naturally, felt like tasting them. Anyone who has not gone out and filched some apples or peas in his early youth would reproach them for that, but he wouldn't be right, because fruit was obviously created by the Lord God to be eaten, above all, by children, wasn't it? And Satan whispered into the little kids' ears: "Go and eat the gooseberries, enjoy the black currants. Go and pull some pears off the trees to lighten the heavily laden branches. No one will ever find out. Wobbly Caldron doesn't see well through his tinted spectacles. Go ahead!" How could they have resisted Satan's whisperings? Most of them didn't have either gardens or orchards.

Now, occasionally, the master would take his disciples into the enclosure to show them how you graft trees, how you dig up potatoes, or for some lesson on horticultural work. But we were forbidden to touch the fruit, no matter how our mouths watered at the sight of so many good things. One day Wobbly Caldron was sent for urgently right in the middle of teaching us about black currants. We were left to our own devices in the midst of the Garden of Eden. What a temptation! And what did we see but one of our Jean-Maries stretching his hand out and picking one currant and then another and still another and yet another. Having lost their heads, or so one must believe, the others followed suit. Soon they were picking whole bunches of them. Before the master had returned, each and every one of the black currants in his orchard had been blown away by a thousand-fingered hurricane. Once the crime had been committed, the children got frightened and, in a great rush, started swallowing down the fruit, at the risk of choking. The Jean-Marie who had started it all had not, in his haste to strip the tree, taken the time to eat his stolen goods. So when he saw the headmaster's bowler hat, he was reduced to hiding the berries in his pockets. Wobbly Caldron flew into a rage. "Who stole the black currants?" Not a word. Every one of us was cringing, ready for a storm of blows. "Line up," howled the master, "so I can tell who the criminal is!" When the children were all standing in a row in front of him, the gentleman with the long beard examined us one after another, slapping each of our pockets with his big hand. The strongest blow fell on Jean-Marie's pockets. A reddish stain began to spread over the material and denounced the thief. Ow! The Caldron started to boil with anger, his black beard quivering to the point of getting tangled up in wrath. A second later, Jean-Marie's ears were redder than his jacket. "How many of you others ate my black currants?" shouted the master. All of us, lined up on the garden path, raised our hands at the same time. And there stood the headmaster, starting to laugh silently, but laughing so hard that his large belly jumped about under his short vest. Laughing just like Sister Bazilize when she had heard a pupil say that the two oldest of God's creatures were in the catechism class. We didn't quite understand. Were we supposed to laugh too? But a moment later Wobbly Caldron left, furious. For at least two weeks he gave us such a hard time that merely recalling the black currants made us sick to our stomachs.

I don't think the good man ever breathed a word about our shameful pilfering, but the wash-trough women knew all about it that very afternoon. And that evening we paid for our misconduct, each in his own way. The following day two unlucky boys had to admit that they were beaten by their mothers with laundry paddles.

There was one last figure who belonged to our personal universe. He had nothing to do with our "playing fox" or with the *termajis,* but he had one thing in common with our teachers and the stationmaster: he spoke French like a book. And he had a considerable advantage over them: he preferred Breton; and besides, he wore the dress of a Bigouden peasant, like our fathers. Yet it was he who linked us to the rest of the world and who faithfully kept us up on the news. The wash-trough women were highly capable of reporting, orally, all that went on in the town and the parish. But to learn what was happening elsewhere, to read it in black and white handwriting, we counted on the "letter-man," the pedestrian-postman whom some of the old country people still called the "postilion."

He came to us every day, on his leather-and-wooden shoes, from Plogastel-Saint-Germain. Since Plogastel was seven kilometers inland, the man's rounds amounted to seven leagues on foot, if you counted his walking down to the port of Penhors and also down the dirt roads that led to isolated farms. Ever since, many long-distance walkers have seen his name in the gazettes and realized that they were covering a thousand times less ground than that poor postilion. True, he always tramped through the same region. And many others also had to go out and earn their living at the expense of the soles of their shoes. But he, from early dawn to dusk, never stopped placing one foot in front of the other.

The pedestrian-postman was not talkative. Yet he knew a thing or two. He would even read letters to the people who had never learned to make out handwriting. He was generally fed at one farm or another, depending on the value of what he was delivering—somebody's old-age pension, a money order, an important parcel, or the news of someone's long-awaited return. When he sensed that a letter brought bad news, he would refuse to go in, no matter how much the recipient insisted. I used to see him placing his bag on the table, uncorking his bottle of ink, and holding out his penholder for a signature. He didn't seem to be of this world. Whatever one said to him, he'd reply: "Yes, indeed." "Alas, no." "Probably." "Of course." "Maybe." "That's good." "It's only fair." He had a kind of hem inside his upper lip, like a scar.

It was always late when he came past the house again on his way back to Plogastel. He often had to fight against the rain and the wind with an empty mailbag on his belly. And because of fatigue, he would relax from time to time at the edge of the road. It was not long before our pedestrian-postman, who was about the same age as my grandfather, had to retire. Since he almost never again left his *penn-ti* in Plogastel, he could feel his old, doomed legs itching to walk again for quite a while before they finally left him in peace. He was replaced by a civil-servant cyclist in a blue suit and a peaked cap whom we found as intimidating as a rural policeman. And that postman spoke almost nothing but French. Was he afraid of being punished? Was he afraid of *la vache*?

Before we knew it, everyone was again talking about the elections. The Whites and the Reds, who, in general, lived on relatively good terms with each other, gradually grew belligerent. Except for the notables, who were more or less electioneers, many of them had nearly forgotten what color they were; but no sooner had the campaign begun than passions started running high, people looked at one another less candidly, and conversations between neighbors and relatives were shorter than usual. There even came a time when men would pass one another on the road without a word of greeting, each one pretending to look at something over the slope on his side of the road. Moreover, they would make detours so as to avoid walking in front of the enemy's house or property. They would give up drinking in taverns whose proprietors were not of the same color. Our mothers, who were less interested in politics, never ceased indulging their bad moods in preparation for the difficult weeks ahead. At the wash-trough the only noise you heard was that of the paddles, as the women hurried to get their laundry clean; because one wrong word, one misunderstanding, even a hint or an allusion, might well have provoked a battle among them and brought out the men on both sides. It was they themselves who decided to be silent, but at home the clouts would rain down more profusely than ever, so that their children were careful not to make a false move.

At school, however, our teacher's duty was to explain to us the mechanism of the elections, and the voting process was to be carried out in the classroom. That we might understand more clearly, he asked us to nominate candidates from among ourselves, after which, in a cardboard box set up on the desk, we would each place a piece of paper that we had folded in four behind the corner blackboard, which was to serve as a voting booth. We didn't have any envelopes either, but never mind. I was one of the two candidates chosen by the class. Of course, all my friends knew that I was a Red and my opponent a White. That was probably why we had to confront each other—to make it seem realistic. Since the Reds were a weak minority in the commune, I expected to be beaten. But to the amazement of the schoolmaster himself, I won hands down. What had happened? Had they voted for me because I was at the head of the class, the boy who did the best homework and who recited better than the others, hence the one best qualified to defend my constituents in the Paris Chamber and in front of the "Government Boys?" Had there been some obscure reasons for the fact that my opponent hadn't managed to rally the Whites around him for a unanimous vote? Be that as it may, I was nicknamed "deputy," and some of my schoolmates have been calling me that all my life. But the recreation period following the election was very stormy indeed. Single combats took place under the covered corner of the yard and also around the lavatory, which resulted in one of the doors being torn off. Soon the schoolmaster didn't know whom to slap first. The rest of the day was a waste of time for everybody. At four in the afternoon the Whites rushed out of school. The deputy was the last to leave, surrounded by a few Reds from the high end of town. No one was in the street. But when we reached Pierre Cardou's bakery, a commando of Whites leapt out of a dark alley and jumped on us, fuming with rage. Among them were a few of the boys who had voted for me but who now wanted to redeem themselves in the eyes of their clan. I was separated from my protectors, took the worst beating I'd ever had, and returned home in a pitiful state, swearing that I would never again stand for any election, even to please Monsieur Le Bail. And I have kept my word.

That very night everyone in town and in the countryside, all the way to the commune boundaries, had heard about the foray. The Republican boys from Penhors swore that they'd get even with those damn Whites and would refuse them access to the coast. The Whites were also in trouble with their own families, who found it impossible to understand how they could have allowed a Red to "get on the inside," even for laughs. The Reds couldn't resist insinuating that the White boys were not as stupid as their parents. The Whites' response was to accuse the teachers of corrupting their offspring. And on they went, provoking each other. I myself was dressing my wounds.

Since the real elections were imminent, the mutually offensive remarks were reinforced by action. Whereas the Whites had several heroes, the Reds had only one—old Le Bail (*ar Baill koz*), who was called *ar baill kaoh* (pail of shit) by his adversaries. Lots of epic stories about him—in fact, two versions of each—were going the rounds. One day, campaigning around Tréguennec, on the coast, he was said to have been attacked by a gang of unrestrained Whites who wanted to pull out his sideburns, hair by hair. Then the women, who were real furies, had armed themselves with their kitchen utensils and kicked up a frightful row. Not only was old Le Bail's barouche stopped, but his horses were unhitched and bludgeoned until they fled miles away. His Red guardsmen protected him as best they could, massed around his carriage, where he sat with his arms crossed, unperturbed. It was said that the jeers and insults made more noise than the waves crashing down on the Torch Rock at Penmarc'h during the height of a storm. But one Red managed to escape by way of the beach and ran, barefoot, to Plozévet, where he gave the alarm. A rescue party, made up of the strongest and most determined of Le Bail's followers, was immediately organized. They charged down upon Tréguennec, brandishing pitchforks and cudgels, and extricated their hero, but not easily and not without getting knocked about. Then the men picked up the shafts of the carriage. It was an unforgettable spectacle, that withdrawal of the parliamentarian with sideburns, down the beach and along the small coastal roads, swaying to and fro on his button-covered cushions, pulled by his barefoot Reds and inveighing in Latin against the White commandos who were hurling rocks and stones at his Republican and radical-socialist guardsmen, armed with fire-hardened sticks. The Whites, of course, considered that escorted return of the Antichrist to his lair a brilliant victory against the Red Devils. They had done in the old Satan in spite of all the Latin he had poured down upon them and which would have been enough to terrify Christians far more apathetic than they.

During the war, as I said, the Whites and the Reds had met as brothers in the trenches, cursing their foolishness or making fun of it, but swearing never to act like that again. Yet when peace was restored, they did act like that again. Not as fervently, as stubbornly, or as violently, but they did act like that again. They were still intravenously Whites or Reds. And each side, without really thinking it possible, tried to indoctrinate the other. One day, as my father and I were on our way to see my grandfather the sabot-maker, we found the miller from Brenizennec awaiting us on a bridge. He no sooner saw us than he set out to convert my father, promising him the earth if he could bring himself to vote for the Whites. My father held his own like the very devil of a man, whereupon his opponent raised his voice, began to swear and threaten, and predicted that we would die of starvation and bare-assed to boot.

"What's happened to him, Father? He's not usually like that."

"Let him rage and fume. He'll be more relaxed starting next Monday."

The electoral campaign was in full swing. The candidates themselves and their devoted followers preferred to canvass the region and to work the back rooms of cafés than to make a big show of confronting each other, as they did in the cities. Each one also paid for rounds of drinks, which, after all, was only polite! Nevertheless, they both held public meetings to work up their partisans' enthusiasm and perhaps win over a few uncommitted citizens who were still wavering. When opponents came to have their say, they were generally strangers to the commune. People knew beforehand that they'd be there and went to see them do their act. No one had yet learned to clap properly, but they shouted with all their might, not to intimidate the speaker, but to provoke those in the region who belonged to another party. They knew the word *radical*—a panacea to the Reds and an abomination to the Whites. As for the word *socialist,* it was equally worrisome to both camps.

On election day that good man Alain Le Goff put on his new hat, his best velvet waistcoast, and his striped trousers to go and throw his voting paper into the box. My mother had polished his new pair of shoes, made entirely of leather, which he had bought in anticipation of a trip to Paris to see his other children. He took me by the hand, and the two of us walked down toward the town hall and the school. The polls had just about opened, but there were already lots of people outside and in. When we got there, I recognized the Reds by their smiles and the Whites by their frozen faces, even those of Alain Le Goff's friends. I felt less and less like being a deputy. Grandfather did what had to be done and we rushed away, without even saying a word to my father, who was already there, in the midst of a small detachment of Reds, to be on the lookout for squalls. Grandfather had only one desire—to take his cow out of the stable and go to the Méot field with it, far from the vanities of this world.

There was at least one other philosopher in the town—the man who always put two ballots in his envelope, one for each candidate. Perhaps he had drunk to the health of them both! Perhaps he had sworn to one group that he would vote for them, and to the other, that he would vote for them, and didn't want to go back on either promise! Or perhaps he wanted nothing to do with the whole business! I shan't give his name.

Once the elections were over, life went back to normal, and it appeared to me that people came to terms with each other like the yoke and white of an egg. But it was all an illusion. For example, the time for first communion was drawing near. Now, as it happened, I was also the head of the catechism class, and so far ahead of the others that if I had been relegated to second place, the statue of Christ, nailed to the column over the benches on which we studied his law, would have bled. But it was customary for the head of the catechism class to be entrusted with "reading the book"—the Gospel—in the choir, in front of the whole congregation of Christians, during the High Mass for First Communion. Was it possible, I ask you, to grant that honor to a Red's son? The answer was no. Therefore the reading was done by the boy who came in second, a good friend of mine, but White as a lily. Not a single soul protested, most especially not my parents or myself. But the other children, the Whites more than the Reds—and, above all, the boy who had replaced me at the esteemed lectern—were shocked by that injustice. They never ceased commenting on it, at the risk of getting thrashed. Following heaven knows what consultation between the big shots and the clergy, I was surprised, one Sunday at Mass, to hear the rector himself announce that since little N would be unable, for some reason, to fulfill his duties as an altar boy, he was to be replaced by Perig Hélias, who had his catechism at his fingertips and was better than anyone at reading and singing Latin. What the rector did not know (for he would have choked with exasperation) was that my first—and my only—lesson in Latin had been given me by Monsieur Le Bail himself, the Antichrist, while I was visiting my great-uncle Michel Hélias, who worked for the radical deputy.

My father did not want me to become an altar boy. It wasn't

suitable for a young Red. My grandfather didn't want me to either, but merely because it meant getting up too early. Yet my mother, who—deep down—was pleased, pointed out that if we refused, we would be put in an awkward position with regard to the others. And so it was that for a few weeks, dressed in red and white, I carried the great book from the Epistle side of the altar to the Gospel side, handled the cruets without ever tasting what was in them (I swear it), and sang as beautifully as I could during High Mass. Right in front of me, among the faithful, was my mother, who had great trouble concealing her pride in me. My father, who sat in the most humble spot, directly behind the pulpit, couldn't see me. But he was trembling at the idea that I might fail to respond properly or miss a note, which would have been humiliating for the Reds in general and for him in particular.

Meanwhile, I was slaving away for the scholarship examinations. Not long before I was to take them, the rector came to see my mother at a quiet hour in the afternoon, taking advantage of the fact that my father was at work. He spent his time complimenting her on her son, who was so good in school that he would do brilliantly at a Christian college such as Saint-Gabriel in Pont l'Abbé or at the seminary. She was not to worry about the expenses involved, which were not within her means, because he himself and other generous patrons would see to them. My mother, as a good Christian, could not say no. She got out of it by saying that she would discuss it with her husband, who was the master. That was what all Bigouden women answered when they were in trouble. But it meant no. When my father was informed, he settled the matter, saying he had not brought up his son to be a priest; that was fine for the Whites. The only proper ambition for a Red was to be a teacher. "Anyway," my father added, "he'll go to the lycée in Quimper for nothing. Monsieur Gourmelon said that he'd have no trouble getting a scholarship if he would be a little careful with his arithmetic."

I personally should have really liked to become a carpenter or, if not that, a quartermaster in the Navy.

And to remain a Red, of course.

Long live the Republic!

Les Sonneurs: a monument to Breton musicians at Plozévet

5 Learning by Experience

> One cannot know a country through geographical science alone . . . I don't believe that one can know anything through science alone. As an instrument, it is both too precise and too harsh. The world is filled with so many sorts of tenderness. To understand them, and before knowing what they represent as a whole, one must yield to them.
>
> Jean Giono, *L'Eau vive*

We live in a region where the wind is master and prevails wherever it so desires. The sea and the land are both subject to it; the men owe it all that is best in themselves. I don't think there is one single inhabitant of this vicinity, either man or woman, who is not indebted to the wind—a west-northwester or a southwester—for that physical and moral exuberance which, in Breton, we call *startijenn*. Without it, many of us would probably listen to the persistent voices of fate whispering to us, suggesting that we forsake all endeavors and sit under the gable of the house waiting for what may come. But the wind keeps us joyful and anxious. It gives us a good shove in the back to force us into our adventure of the day. It slaps us in the face to make us flex our muscles and swear like blazes. It rains salt down upon us just as one salts the flesh of pure-bred pigs to keep it from rotting. It shakes, manhandles, jostles, and maintains our bodies with its blows, and our minds are kept alert, constantly aggressive,

The news of the day

and watchful for hard knocks and ways of getting one's own back on life. How it does harden us, the brute! No, that invisible lord is not indifferent to the human grit that litters its eye. Perhaps it even loves us, given the resolve it puts into thrashing us. Besides, it's alive—what more can one say?—and an unrestrained lunatic, which suits us perfectly. What would we have become without it?

As far back as I can remember, I have heard it rushing throughout the region—roaring, whistling, hissing, whining, sobbing, choking with laughter, singing through the walls of stone and flat rocks. And as it passed through, everything would rattle—the windmill vanes, the sheets and clothes drying on lines, the women's heavy dresses, the ribbons on their coiffes, the processional banners, the loose slate on the roofs, and Marie-Jeanne Kerveillant's pail on the lip of her well. Any worn-out sabots left on doorsteps would knock against each other, sounding like empty walnut shells before they went wandering idly through the neighborhood. In the fields the cows would take a firm stand on their four legs and offer their hindquarters to the wind, as if wanting it to impregnate them. The young shepherds had, by then, hidden themselves in the hollows of trees, if there happened to be any, or had stretched flat out in the grass. Their only reason for standing up was to play at being pushed by the wind, their short coats flying, and letting themselves go except for working their legs in such a way as to keep their balance. The Icarian intoxication they felt on such occasions I leave to your imagination. The following day the newspapers would note that at Penmarc'h Point there had been a veritable gale—winds up to 120 kilometers an hour. And Alain Le Goff would tell me that, this time, "the master-wind himself" had come.

Indeed, you had just to look about! The clumps of trees around the farms were bent backward toward the east, curried again and again by a formidable comb. You would have thought they were stacked, judging from the side struck by the squall. Except for the blue thistles in the dunes, there wasn't a plant that had not bowed to the master-wind. And while it was there, it thorough-cleaned the sky. The sun would never have done that, lazy as it is! Shadows of storm clouds drifted across the land to the barking of dogs.

People had to shout so that they'd be heard six feet away. Once the turbulence had ceased, they would clean out their ears and give their heads a good shake in order to come to their senses again. It was then that they felt recharged with *startijenn* and would have a sudden urge to laugh. To them the sun seemed old and insipid.

Our wind is capable of blowing without stop. That it didn't was because it enjoyed contemplating the results of its work. It had cleansed the coast and the countryside. Colors were more vivid; lines, sharper; volumes, more solid. The light was as fresh as on the first morning of Creation. And all the Bigoudens were moving about in that atmosphere like fish in an aquarium filled with clean water. Corentin's voice was deeper, and tall Anne's burst forth like a flourish of trumpets. Their insides had been washed out from head to toe.

One evening the sky over the sea was red—an uneven, spotty red—but strangely motionless, which meant that if the moon helped out, we could expect a wild wind the next day. The housewives were already calling to each other from doorstep to doorstep, for the next day was pine-needle day. The time had come to prepare the ropes. And to rejoice.

It was the custom that all the pine needles and cones blown down by the wind in the parish woods be left to the poor people so that they might light their fires and keep them going. No landowner, not even the stingiest of them, ever dared to object lest he lose his reputation. And the next day we children would see huge piles of dry needles emerge from the Ménez-Fuez woods, held together by some miracle, and moving ahead along the road at the steady pace of an old woman bent in two, very like an ant bringing back loot that is bigger than itself.

The next day we could expect a wild wind. The kid from Pouloupri, the oldest of the scamps from the high end of town, had heard the news—that is, unless he himself had been able to predict the wind, for that devil of a kid knew all the things that are never taught in school. We were in the process of playing leapfrog or blind-man's buff when he arrived, looking sterner than our teacher announcing a test. "Little Pierre," he said, addressing me.

"Tomorrow morning in the Rector's Field. And if you don't show up, you'd better watch out!" Whereupon he took off, whistling, his mouth all crooked.

I knew what he meant. An ordeal was awaiting me, and if I came through it successfully, I would go up one degree in the hierarchy of children. If I botched it, I would be humiliated, excluded from their important expeditions, and perhaps even relegated to the group of little brats two or three years younger than I. I had no idea what the ordeal was to be, but I was sure that the wind would be more of a hindrance than a help. How in the world would I manage to sleep that night? I thought of the previous winter, when that kid had already begun to put us through our paces and had given us a hard time.

But the next day we could expect a wild wind. One night to go and my second ordeal would be awaiting me in the Rector's Field. I was awakened by a rapid banging of shutters. And I remembered: the next day was in fact that day. What had the kid dreamed up this time to see if I could make it with the big boys? Well, up and at 'em. It was time to go.

All the children from the high end of town were already in the Rector's Field as I approached. From some distance I could see them huddled against the slope to protect themselves from the wild wind. The kid from Pouloupri was right in the middle, lording it over them. They had taken their places to the left and to the right of him, each according to his age and his acknowledged rank. In all humility I confronted that court of law. Not even bothering to honor me with a glance, the kid turned his head in the direction of three tall elm trees planted on a level with the slope and stripped bare by the winter.

"Climb up there," he said, "and bring down that nest!" It was a dried-up magpie's nest at the very top of the highest elm. And the top was moving back and forth in the sky, blown by the seven winds of the compass, like a scale that seemed to be weighted by the nest in question. I cursed the pride of magpies. The first one I caught perched on a pile of droppings would be turned into carrion by my slingshot.

"He's got a bellyful of fear," said the smallest boy, playing up to the kid from Pouloupri.

Some member of the general staff added: "He's gonna empty it all in his breeches."

"By golly, we'll see about that," Grandfather would have said. I buttoned my jacket right up to the collar and hugged the trunk. It seemed pretty think, given the size of my arms, but I nevertheless managed, by fits and starts, to hoist myself up to the first large branch, helped along by my plush trousers, which were as rough as the bark. After that, it would have been easy for me to climb from branch to branch had it not been for that damn wind, which grew stronger the higher I went—which grew so strong that I had to make absolutely sure of my holds and my supports in order not to be thrown to the ground like a ripe fruit. My heart was pounding against my ribs for all it was worth when I reached the level of the tree at which the twigs were so thin that there was no way of knowing whether they could bear my weight. I returned to the bole and clasped it with all my might. Then I felt the swaying of the tree throughout my whole body. I began to get dizzy. I was under the nest, which seemed huge to me, but it was still nearly six feet away on its single bough. Swinging like a censer, I glanced down and, beneath me, turning vertiginously, were a lot of gaping faces following my ascent. My innards were feeling sort of queasy. To hell with the kid from Pouloupri and his general staff! Let them go and crap all over the nettles!

I managed to climb down because I was quickened by a violent rage. As I jumped to the ground from the last branch, and addressing the kid, I yelled something like, "Go and get it yourself and swallow it down without salt or pepper." He gave me a sickly smile and said: "Good for you. Come with us!" And he chased the other little boys away with a few strong curses. That was so I would understand that I had been made a member of the general staff. He was clever, that kid. He knew perfectly well that had he sent me away with the other brats, my father's son would have challenged him in public, ten times a day, to go and bring down that nest. And he wouldn't have managed to do it either.

One day my grandfather said: "It's time I taught you how to push the wheelbarrow in front of you. Then I'll show you how to pull it behind you. That's harder, my boy." Actually, I had already practiced doing it, secretly, in the farmyard. I had first spit into my hands a lot so that they wouldn't slip on the handles, which were smooth from constant use. But the shafts of a wheelbarrow are made for grown-ups. My arms were too short; the barrow was heavier than I had thought; and that damn iron-bound wheel had surely struck roots in the soil, for some invisible force would weigh it down to the right or to the left as soon as I'd lift the two wooden legs from the ground; in sum, the best I'd been able to do, having given my all to the task, was to push the contrivance a few yards, at which point it had gotten so stuck between the wall of the house and a pile of straw that I couldn't extricate it. When my grandfather returned from the fields, he merely smiled, and said: "Well, well! Just look: a wheelbarrow that takes off all by itself."

But this time Grandfather had rolled the wheelbarrow all the way to a sunken and flat road between two high slopes. There was no one in the vicinity. There wouldn't be anybody to make fun of me if that devil of a wheelbarrow dragged me, in spite of myself, into the brambles and nettles. My throat refused to yield enough saliva to wet my hands. Well, tough luck. I grabbed hold of the handles.

"Pull it toward you," Grandfather told me, "as if you were trying to put your hands in your pockets. Don't look at the wheelbarrow; look at the path in front of the wheel. Lean forward a little bit and push down with your heels. Go on, try it!"

He told me lots of other things and—miracle of miracles!—the wheelbarrow finally obeyed me, after having refused two or three times.

On our way back to the house I do believe I had looked contemptuously at the other children my own age that we'd met. For I had heard Grandfather mumble: "Arrogant little boy." To a Bigouden, that was both a reprimand and a compliment. Grandfather had been delighted. As for me, I had walked behind him while he pulled his wheelbarrow at his own pace and I'd wondered how, without being able to see it, he had managed to keep it upright.

From then one, every time I could get my hands on the wheelbarrow, I never failed to push it in increasingly difficult places. I'd get out of breath making it climb small rises, and then dirty the seat of my trousers getting it to roll down the other side, for the weight of it would drag me along so fast that I had to curb it by flopping down on my backside. At the same time, the other children were also in the process of learning. We would compare the progress we'd made; we would challenge each other to do such things as getting the wheel to roll along a narrow board or to cross a stream on stepping stones. But we had a lot of trouble pulling the wheelbarrow behind us. Our grandfathers had told us: "Wait until next year!" But no. We paid them no mind. We didn't have the time to wait.

Meanwhile, we were growing. The most gifted among us were already rolling our wheelbarrows along the main road. There were even some who, between Easter and Pentecost, would push them, running barefoot. It was then that the grown-ups took them sternly to task: "What's the use of your wheelbarrow, my boy? If you at least put the snot from your nose into it!" We were offended. Since we didn't want to hear that reproach twice, we began loading the wheelbarrows. First, with stones; then with ourselves. Each one in turn would sit in the barrow, trying to throw the puller off balance by making the most chaotic movements possible. It was a game; it was also a test we wanted to pass with honors. Indeed, we refused to stop grappling with wheelbarrows until we were capable of filling them with bales of hay from the meadow or a load of cabbages from the field, and of bringing our goods back to the house without being responsible for them kissing the road. There were so many things to learn and so many compliments to earn. For the whole region was watching us grow. And the whole region was judging our growth in accordance with a certain number of tests, the most conclusive of which was that of the wheelbarrow. Still, in a short while (which in fact amounted to ten years) I was strong enough to use my back instead.

We never had either a horse or a carriage or even a handcart.

One of the great days in my life was when I went to the shoemaker's to buy a new pair of wooden sabots. The ones I was wearing that morning were so worn out that nails could no longer be hammered into the soles. And actually, for some time, the left one had been split at the top, even though it had been bound with wire like the other. What I had not confessed to my parents was the fact that we had been using the Ménez-Poullou pinewoods as a boxing ring ever since one of us had found a picture portraying a boxer taking cover behind huge gloves. Those gloves had fired our imaginations. A sabot is a kind of glove for your foot, isn't it? Then why not use it for your hand? And that was why we indulged in boxing matches, two by two, with a referee, if you please, to make sure that we respected the rules, although he knew no more about them than we did. But hitting your opponent in the face or on the body was forbidden. We were only allowed to strike the sabots that covered his fists.

At Guillaume the shoemaker's a pile of impressive sabots were awaiting us. There were so many that it wasn't easy to choose the best pair, but everyone happily put their minds to it. My mother began by buying me padded slippers, which, from then on, would go inside the new sabots and wear out along with them. Then came the great problem of whether this pair would suit me better than that pair, and which fit me the best. For if you're uncomfortable in your sabots, you start walking crookedly, and you're also in danger of scraping your ankles. Indeed, we chose my new pair of sabots with as much care as a man of the world trying on patent-leather pumps. Once the choice was made, the two objects were held up to the light and examined from every angle, one after the other. The insides of them were closely scrutinized to be sure that the sabot-maker hadn't hollowed them out too much and that the sides weren't too thin in certain fragile spots. Finally, the purchase was made. That evening my father studded the soles with hobnails, which were to make sparks on the cobblestone roads until those roads wore them down to nothing.

Of course, on the roads we used to lose some nails here and there. But those nails were not a loss to everyone, though they were the despair of cyclists, whose tires would be punctured too often because of the nails' tiresome tendency to lie with their pointed tips in the air. Even we ourselves, when walking barefoot in good weather, would get them in the flesh of our heels or our toes. On the other hand, we liked to pry them out from between the stones, for they proved to be very useful. To begin with, they could serve as replacements for those that were missing from our own sabots. That was a good way of gaining our fathers' respect. They also had an exchange value when we traded with other children. Or else, and at the very least, they could be used as tops—a nice game to play when you're all alone.

As small change, however, buttons were far more precious than nails. A lost button was always found. The first one who saw it would pick it up and bury it deep down in his jacket pocket, like a gold coin. That was a good way of gaining our mothers' respect. The number of jackets we used to see with unmatched buttons! But it didn't matter. However, there were buttons and buttons. There were the small ordinary buttons that didn't have a very high rate of exchange on our market, the least valuable of which were white shirt-buttons. Then there were the thick horn buttons, which were worth far more. Best of all—but hard to come by and a real godsend—were those metal buttons that had been sewn on hunters' jackets, and which had the head of a dog or a wild boar on them. It was a pity, truly a pity, that we had so few hunters in the region. Finally, there were the Breton buttons, those that would fall off old-fashioned *chupennou*, or cloaks—brass-bound buttons which, under the glass center, had strange multicolored drawings on them, symbols of a secret kaleidoscope.

In any case, one Breton button was worth at least two French buttons. When you owned a real beauty, you could sometimes cash it in for eight or ten others. For there was a button market that was especially active on Thursdays, our day off from school. There were button-changers and button-lenders—I give you my word!—sly little boys who were lucky at games and combined their luck with skill. It was when we played games—any games, including cards—that we lost and won buttons. And we used that small change—for lack of silver coins and bronze sous, which we rarely had at our disposal—to buy and sell all sorts of services and objects among ourselves. But only among ourselves, for—would you believe it?—the shopkeepers who sold candies and cakes never accepted buttons.

There were tragic days when we had no buttons at all; in other words, we were broke, unable to keep up our position in our own society, avoided, humiliated, insulted. So what choice did we have?

We were obliged to tear one or two of them off our own jackets, at the price of incurring our mothers' wrath that very evening. Or else we'd go through their sewing baskets in search of some "button-money," swearing to ourselves that we'd return it after we had made our fortunes. Generally, we were merely postponing the well-deserved punishment for pilfering. The shrewdest of us had one last resource: little girls, with whom we bartered. Girls were always short two or three pins. They simply adored safety pins and long pins with big heads for their coiffes. Pines get lost too; therefore they can be found. We'd have a few of them in our jacket lapels, and the girls would have buttons in the pockets of their dresses. We used to find some corner so as not to be seen; for a young female who associated with boys that were not her brothers or cousins was called a tomboy; and a boy who had dealings with girls had to be prepared to put up with a fair amount of affronts from his friends. But when in need, what was there to do?

Besides, it was better not to be on bad terms with the girls. They were capable of playing the kind of tricks on you that boys would never dream of. For example, going around telling everyone the last piece of mischief you'd been up to, and which they knew about almost before you did, because they always kept their eyes and ears open. Also, they wept so easily and so noisily that if someone merely pulled their hair a bit, they would immediately stir up the whole town. It was not at all surprising that they were generally in sympathy with parents. But they were quite ready to admire you if you gave them the slightest opportunity. And when they really liked you, you could expect lots of little presents. Of course, in spite of the reserve we maintained when it came to girls, it goes without saying that each of us always defended those who were related to us. With our feet, our fists, our nails, and our teeth.

Sometimes the little girls offered us empty spools, which we made into teetotums, or "drunken cats," as we called them. But when we grew older, we gave them up in favor of tops. Ah, those tops! That's a serious game for you, and it isn't everyone who can excel at it. First, you would practice with other children's tops, usually those they didn't want anymore bacause they were half-broken or didn't spin properly. Then you made your own, as any son of a good mother learns to do who would have, one day, to live by his wits. Since I must tell the truth, my first top had been hewn with an ax out of soft wood by my grandfather Alain Le Goff. But it was I who finished it off, for better or for worse, with the small knife I'd been given when I cast off my skirts and began to wear breeches. It was quite an endeavor. A top must be perfectly pear-shaped, as smooth as possible, and well balanced if you want it to "sleep" and seem motionless while it spins. A top that acts like a "drunken cat" is enough to bring dishonor upon its maker. The same may be said for a top that can't stand upright. You must polish it carefully and choose a very special nail which you stick into the stalk-end of the pear. Finally, you have to find a first-class piece of string, both strong and supple, not woolly, and you're ready to take part in the top competitions, the winner of which became cock of the walk until he met his master.

Then, there was the *galoche*, a piece of wood sculpted or carved with a knife, and which, as a rule, had the diameter of a two-sou bronze coin and was long enough for a man to clasp between his thumb and his index finger when he spread them as wide as possible. The *galoche* was the goal of a local game of quoits, which, at the time, was all the rage in our region. There wasn't an innkeeper in the town or, above all, at any county crossroads who didn't have one or several sets at his customers' disposal. But a lot of people had their own sets. *Galoche* was played preferably on the road, not far from an inn, at a spot where a section of the roadway was almost flat and which the regular players kept in good repair, having made it perfectly clear that others could use it by invitation only. The game involved three iron quoits, eight to ten centimeters in diameter, which had been made by some blacksmith. The point of it was to use those quoits to knock over the *galoche*, which had been set up about ten to twelve yards from the thrower. At least those were the rules and measurements I had learned from the Cariou brothers, who were the champions of the high end of town. We ourselves were greatly honored when the men, having lost or broken their *galoche*, would borrow one of ours. As a reward, we'd have the right to practice with their iron quoits while they were at the inn. Those iron quoits made men of us, or almost.

You had to be even older to play ninepins. The pins we had were wide wooden cylinders, almost tree trunks, carved to a point at the top. To begin with, you drew a square, and at each corner of it you set up four middle-sized pins, which were worth five points each. Between them you placed four small ones, which were worth only one point each. We called them "les bidouches," or "the last-born." And in the middle of the square, in the place of honor, stood the largest pin, the "Grandmother" or the "Old Nine." No need to say how much that one was worth. In short, our game of ninepins was the very image of the family as we knew it—that is, three generations living together. Ruling over the tribe and deserving of honor and respect was the Old Nine, which in itself represented all grandparents. Then came the parents in the form of the five-point pins, and finally, the children, only one point each, and which generally acted foolishly. Rather than use wooden balls to knock the pins down, as people often did elsewhere, we used big round stones, a supply of which was always in the corner, but each player could also go and choose his own on some beach nearby. Between Penhors and the Penmarc'h Torch there were millions of them.

While waiting to play ninepins with the men, I got my eyes and hands into practice with other contrivances and with other goals in mind. In the copses I had learned to choose forked branches which you rounded off by sticking them into a fire. With two elastic bands and a piece of leather for the pocket, you could make slingshots and aim the stones at tin cans, which would noisily roll down the road. I must confess that we also aimed at other objects which were not meant to be broken, thus creating minor crises that filled the town with outcries and disputes. Whenever the swallows would fly low, heralding a southwester rain, they were in danger of being killed by slingshots armed with old nails. What could you expect? We had to get our training at the expense of whatever came to hand, so long as it didn't belong to anyone. If you happened to shoot a stone at a chicken or a duck, which was a constant temptation, you had to beware! For it wasn't long before the animal's master boxed your ears or dealt you a blow with his whip. There was no excuse for it. Absolutely none.

Another thing we did was to construct large turning slings out of string. Only the most skillful of us knew how to weave the central pocket, which had to be very flat, otherwise the stone might have got entangled in it or would have shot out in the wrong direction, knocking you senseless or doing damage in the vicinity. Therefore it was prudent to manipulate the large sling in the middle of some field, and even so!—only on condition that it was empty. If any ploughman saw one in the hands of a young scamp, his blood would boil at the thought of the harm it could do. Throughout the region there remained a vague recollection that it had formerly been used as a military weapon. And the story of David in the Old Testament didn't help any. Of course, all of us tried to use it at one point or another. One December morning the best slinger in our gang shot down a large sea-bird that was flying very high. But his glory was tarnished by the gull's death throes, which made even the worst pupil in the catechism class sick to his stomach. So we went back to bows and arrows, with a preference for crossbows. Using such weapons, you could aim at precise targets—a beet placed on top of a slope, for example, or stuck on a pike. The game would go on until the beet, shot through all over, fell to pieces. Then we would carefully pick up those pieces and throw them into a bramble bush before anybody could see them. We had destroyed a beet, which was food for animals. We had done wrong and we knew it well. We also knew that we'd start all over again, for what other way was there to become a man? Once we were men, we would never again do anything wrong; that was understood.

One of our blessings was the elderbush—a shrub that wasn't all that rare in the region, but you had to know where to look in order to find one. You also had to take care not to cut one on a slope that clearly belonged to another neighborhood, for that led to war. No one outside your family or your group of accomplices would ever tell you where to find an elder. The type we were interested in had the thickest stems. You'd cut off a section of one at the bottom end, between two nodes, and then carefully empty it of all its pith. With a knife, you'd thin down a hard and very straight branch of wood until it could be easily manipulated inside the tube. That kind of piston measured about one centimeter less than the elder gun and had a handle at one end so that you could operate it. The missiles were made of short hemp strings that had been chewed for a long time and softened into a ball by saliva. The first one was forced into the gun and remained stuck at the tip. Then you inserted a second one, pressed the piston's handle against your hip bone, and drove it in with one shove, at which point the first missile shot out, and the tighter it had been stuck in, the louder the report. Once you retrieved it, you put it back into the tube, and it, in turn, made the other one explode. That sort of pistol was called a popgun. The noise it made simply delighted us.

To transform a popgun into a water pistol, you had merely to take the tip where the ball of hemp had been stuck and shove a one-centimeter wooden plug into it that was perforated by a pinhole in the middle. As for the end of the piston, you wound as much black thread around it as necessary so that it would completely fill the part of the tube that had to be watertight. On the other hand, the best water pistols were made not out of elder stems but out of a special type of bamboo that grew only in very rare spots, especially around the dams of the many mills in the region. Now the owners always kept an eye on us. They were willing to cut a section of bamboo from time to time for their friends' and their customers' children to make a good impression on parents, but that was all. Those who had no relatives or no grain to be ground were forced to put their ears or the skin of their backsides in danger in order to provide for their needs. That was how I happened to take part in a reed-operation organized by the kid from Pouloupri with as much care as gangsters take in robbing a bank without leaving a trace. It was a complete success.

All the tubes we had at our disposal, including popguns and pistols, either began or ended as musical instruments. We used to make recorders, flutes, and fifes out of them. But I can hardly say that the music we made on them was at all in tune. Whistles were something else again. All of us knew the precise time of year when the branches of the willow trees were ready for use. There was a certain color and a certain feel to the bark that never fooled country-scouts like us. First you cut the branch at a spot where the bark was at its most even. You fixed up one end as a mouthpiece, cut the bark in circles six or eight centimeters below it, moistened the bark, hit it with a knife handle or a piece of hard wood, and moistened it again as often as necessary (saliva was said to be better than well water). Then the bark came beautifully unstuck from the wood, which you had merely to turn a bit so that you could pull it out without breaking it. And the bare wood was carved in such a way that air could pass through it, after which you covered it again with the bark. Your whistle was ready for use.

What else could we do? Make sounds with certain high grasses that grew during the spring by running a moistened thumb and index finger down one of the long stalks. Blow on another type of grass wedged between our hands like a striking reed to make it sing. Or get a laurel leaf to hum in our mouths. There was no better pastime while tending the cows.

It was a little girl from the heights (that was what we called the remote, inland farms toward the east) who taught me to make a mirror out of a stem and saliva. Not an easy thing to do. Here's how you went about it: You took a well-rounded stem, folded it in two to make a closed loop that would serve as a frame, put it in your mouth, and strongly salivated. Then, as you removed it, you were careful to moisten it profusely between your lips, which were not too tightly closed. When it came out, if you had proceeded properly, there was a glassy film of saliva in the oval space. You could bring it up close to your eye and the world immediately became more beautiful. You had to begin with very small loops and then enlarge them until they completely filled your mouth. But, my God, those mirrors were fragile, and how quickly they burst! It was clearly a game for little girls.

That girl was at the Nuns' School. People said that she had once been punished because of having whistled in the schoolyard to the great stupefaction of everyone around her. A girl who whistled like a boy—what a scandal! I can testify to the fact that she did, and very well indeed. But the little girl who made the saliva mirrors knew how to drive horses. She was of the same breed as a farmer's wife, in the vicinity of Plozévet, who was apparently the last woman who ever whistled into a seashell in order to summon her men to their soup when they were delayed in the fields after the

Angelus. The sound that boomed out of her shell could be heard throughout half the parish. And one of the men would reply with a whistle, meaning that they were on their way.

All the men whistled. Anyone who didn't was not a man; that went without saying. As soon as you were in trousers, you had to whistle as you walked, with supercilious eyes and your hands deep in your pockets, so that everyone would know who you were. My grandfather had taught me how to whistle in the Méot field very early on, and though I wasn't especially gifted, I did manage to keep up an honorable position among my little friends for some time. But then one had to climb a step higher and whistle through one's fingers. Of course, none of the finger-whistlers would ever show us how. They'd say: "Look at me!" And they'd whistle loud enough to make the windows shake. But how was one to know what went on inside their mouths? I tried for quite a long while without managing to do more than drool all over my hands. I would have willingly asked my grandfather, but by then I was a little too old to go to him for help. And anyway, the good man would have felt badly had he learned that I was lagging behind the others. One day, on our way back from the fields, we met a friend of his.

"Does your grandson know how to whistle through his fingers by now?" the man asked.

"He knows lots of things," Alain Le Goff replied. And he dragged me along with him for fear that the intruder would corner me. But I had realized that he was ill at ease. He was waiting for me to make out on my own, since the family's honor was at stake. So I spent hours wasting my energy, until one day I managed to make a sound. Not a very loud one, to be sure, but it was a whistle. I failed to repeat that successful attempt several times, then did it once again, and worked on it in secret. When I got it exactly right, I went to try it out in the Ménez-Fuez woods, where there was an obliging echo. And the echo ansered me very clearly. I quivered with joy, as I suppose Christopher Columbus did when he saw Colombia. And then, at the next meeting of our gang, at Poull-Bodig, I took the first opportunity to show off my know-how. The gang looked at me and said nothing. Whistling was not an authorized test. But my grandfather soon knew that I had finally caught up.

There was no end to it, however. A few of the others were already able to whistle using only one finger. And back I was with the youngest boys, the cowards, and the sissies. I made every effort again, working at it as hard as I could. Finally, I made it. That time I waited for somebody to make fun of me, and then, straight into his ear, hit out with a monodigital whistle that left him deaf for three-quarters of an hour. From that point on, I was allowed to converse with the birds. For the ultimate was being able to imitate blackbirds, nightingales, wrens, thrushes, and larks in such a way that the winged whistler would answer you three times before flying from his branch the minute he'd hear one false note out of you.

We were also able to distinguish one bird from another—first, by its chirp, which could be translated into good Breton. The lark emitted a series of *toui rin* ("I'll swear") in quick succession, since Saint Peter didn't want to open his gates to it precisely because it was swearing. So it went furiously on and on. *Gwag, gwag* ("soft, soft") cawed the crow pecking about in a dung heap, except when it, too, was furious—about the bad quality of that godsend: *brein, brein* ("rotten, rotten"). They all held an incessant conversation, complete with disputes, choruses, duets, and solos. Grandfather said that each bird's song harmonized with its feathers and its weight. I never tried to find out if that was true because it *was* certainly true, but I got as close as possible to the singers in order to confront the actual fact. And I also tried to find out where their nests were. When I'd see a blackbird somewhere, I knew its mate wasn't far behind. And wherever its mate was, so was its nest.

At the first signs of spring, even before the cuckoo had sung in the woods, we'd search the underbrush, the thickets, the slopes, and the moors, looking for nests. We would then keep watch over them, because it was understood that they belonged to the first boy who discovered them, and who made it a point to tip off the others: "I have two nests on *X* path!" You were allowed to keep them unless the path happened to be on someone else's territory. There were also nests which belonged to the two or three boys who had discovered them together. Actually, it was preferable that such expeditions be made up of several boys. While one of them would search nearby, the others would keep watch on the birds from a distance to spot their hiding place. Once the nest was found, you would go and look at it regularly, taking care not to touch it; otherwise, the birds would abandon it before laying their eggs and it would dry up. To us, that was considered a defeat.

When the birds had finished making their nests, we were always amazed at the delicacy with which they had been put together and, above all, at how carefully the spot for them had been chosen; it would have made a fully qualified architect green with envy. Actually, the very best nest-seekers had merely to observe a copse or a slope to cry out: "There must be one right over there!" They were rarely mistaken. They had calculated just like a bird.

But the booty we hankered after were the eggs. What good were they to us? First of all, we liked showing them to each other—one way of making the unlucky boys dumb with admiration. Or to swallow them raw after having made a hole at either end. Or to string them like rosaries, which we hung in the house or the shed, just as hunters display their wild trophies. Or to trade them with the little girls, who were fond of such delicacies, for a bale of embroidered chiffon. We also bartered the eggs among ourselves. The most valuable were the titmouse and turtledove eggs. The blues were worth more than the whites, and the spotted ones worth more than the blues. As for magpies' or crows' eggs, they were not within everyone's reach. It was a real feat not only to go and seek them out in the treetops, exposed to the screeching and to being attacked by furious birds, but especially to get them down under your shirt without making an omelet out of them. Still, it was worth considering. For in addition to the magpies' nests themselves, you'd sometimes bring back the strangest objects: combs, snuff boxes, safety pins, and one day even a touchwood lighter that had been lost by the postman.

One of my friends once wanted to have a caged squirrel. We began by building a cage out of stripped osier, using the bark to link the bars together and to hinge the door. We had carefully observed our fathers weaving baskets for potatoes. We ourselves knew how to weave baskets out of rush for various, unexpected uses. But a cage is harder to make properly. When ours was completed, for better or for worse, we went out hunting in the pinewoods around the town with an eye to capturing one of those animals that shade themselves with their tails. My friend had already hoisted himself up several trees in which there were nests containing baby squirrels all ready to take off on their own. It was one of those that he had to have. Once it had got used to the cage, he said, we would construct an osier wheel that it could turn the whole time. I myself had never seen a captive squirrel. I let my friend climb up toward one of the nests he had spotted, while I waited at the foot of the tree with the cage.

Suddenly I heard a frightful scream, then a few wails. Shortly afterward, the boy climbed down in tears. He showed me a bleeding finger. What had happened? The father squirrel had been in the nest. When my friend thrust his hand in, the animal had bitten down hard on his index finger and had refused to let go, so that the nester had had to start his emergency climb down with the squirrel clutching at his finger. Finally, the nutcracker had decided to let go and return to its nest. Absolutely furious, the wounded boy grabbed the cage from me, threw it on the ground, stamped on it, and destroyed the patient work of our hands. He was still gasping as he wound his dirty handkerchief around his deeply punctured finger.

On our way back, we met an older boy of fifteen who was tending his cows in a pasture. "It serves you right," he told us sternly. "You oughtn't to do things until you've learned how. If you plan to take a chance and approach a squirrel's nest, you first hit the tree trunk with a stick and you'll see the animal rush out. Then you can go up to the nest; but even so, the squirrel might very well come back to its young. The best thing to do is to take a stick in your hand and thrust it into the nest. The squirrel bites into it instinctively. The minute it does, you throw the stick, with the animal at one end of it, as far away as possible. But you kids don't know anything. You're just a couple of jerks."

That night, in my box-bed, I rubbed the index finger of my left hand (I'm left-handed), thinking that the squirrel might have stuck its teeth into it. And I said farewell to hunting of any sort. I realized that I was not at all cut out for that kind of sport. I was truly the grandson of Alain Le Goff, who always wandered out into the countryside as far as he could go on the day our pig was to be killed at home, because he could not be present at the death of an animal he had fed with his own hands. But there wasn't much Grandfather was afraid of, and I took after him. I was neither big nor strong. And once in a while, when I got caught picking flowers in the countryside so that I could put bunches of them into tin cans, I'd hear people call me a girl. But every time that happened, it led to a fight, and I didn't always come out the loser, even when I fought the older boys, because I was determined to let them cripple me rather than surrender. Getting hurt was one thing, but yielding was out of the question! And I continued to pick flowers. May the Devil take all the boors to whom I gave stomach aches!

Rather than get my index finger bitten by a squirrel, I preferred to slip my fingers into foxglove. You sometimes had to go quite a distance to find your size. Whenever I saw a bunch of foxglove up on the slope of some sunken road, I'd insert my fingers, one by one, into the small bellflowers and detach those that fit me like a glove. In our region foxglove is called "Our Lady's Thimble." Therefore, when I had one flower on each finger, I was not only protected from snake venom, but the Devil himself couldn't get the better of me.

In March, when the hazel-tree catkins were out, very long and still weeping, you knew that spring was on its way. And at the same time as the first primroses were beginning to bloom, the willow-tree catkins, those tender flakes made to smile by the morning sun, were lighting up the half-bare branches. You may think I'm trying to be poetic. You may think that country children aren't sensitive to things like that. Well then, tell me why Alain Le Goff, upon his return from the meadow, used to tell me that the willows were shaking themselves like colts, and why little boys couldn't refrain from picking the willow catkins and filling their pockets with them to no purpose, well aware that when they took them out the next morning, they'd be merely a handful of dust. But during the night the cuckoo had sung while they were asleep, and soon they'd be able to pick that curious plant which, in Breton, is called *skrap-d'al-laez* ("high-climber"), though I don't know its name in French or in Latin. It's a plant that you surreptitiously slip under somebody's jacket from behind, and every time he makes a move, the plant climbs up his back, until finally it pops out from under his collar. Among ourselves, it was understood that an experienced boy would let the plant make its way up and not try to tear it away from his backbone; for it is a "patience plant" which teaches you not to scratch the itchy spots too soon.

In the month of May, cockchafers abound in the oaks and in the elm trees. Every evening they make a loud noise with their buzzing, but they don't fly very far and they alight all over the place to catch their breath. So we could gather them up without any trouble. We used to draw a thread through their short tails with a needle, and holding the thread in our hands, make them spin around at the end of it until we heard the sound of their elytra. Then we'd keep them hanging, and they'd go on vibrating, upside down. If we let go of them, they'd fly straight up and disappear into the sky, dragging their thread behind them. There was clearly no lack of those maybugs, but we used to wish that we had the thread back, since it was hard to come by and we were forced to pinch it from our mothers at the risk of being smacked on the ears with a dishrag.

When the time came for haying, the edges of the fields were covered with large daisies, and the "Virgin's eyes" (forget-me-nots) would open. Later on, red poppies blazed out in the fields of wheat, barley, and oats, along with cornflowers, the plant that cures fever. The little girls used to come and gather bunches of them, while we ruffians would throw the fruits or flowers—or whatever they were—of a kind of scratchy thistle over the hedges and slopes and into their hair, where it stuck and was the very devil to get rid of. But the girls had a tiresome tendency to tell all when they got home, and that led to small civil wars between their parents and ours, the burden of which inevitably fell upon us. We would try hard to butter up the incensed little lambs by offering them a cricket in a rush cage. We knew how to make the crickets come out of their holes by tickling them with a stem. When they were rebellious, we'd piss on the stem in question. Sometimes, when all else failed, we'd be reduced to soaking the soil with our piddle. Then the crickets would surrender unconditionally to escape from that mud which—to an insect that lives in uncultivated ground—stank. But that was a last resort, and none of us would have ever dared to boast about it to his best friend. Even when there were no witnesses, taking out one's natural squirt to break down the resistance of a cricket meant losing face. God forbid!

When springtime comes, I'm not quite sure what the little boys of today do or by way of what ceremonial they are received into the garden. To us, spring was very like an open-air church where we would go to frolic about barefoot and to pick primroses—not to make bunches of them but to eat them. To be sure, we didn't find that the food had much taste; but unleavened bread isn't very savory either. I think that, to us, primroses were the communion of springtime, pending the arrival of Easter. Of course, to me and the others, the greatest pleasure of spring was walking barefoot. All through the winter we had dragged about our heavy and bulky wooden sabots. Once we had repaired them with a copious supply of brass or tin wire, those martyrized sabots became instruments on which their owners had learned to play barbaric music as best they could, and each one according to his own sensibility. With my eyes closed, I used to be able to recognize every one of my friends from the sound of his sabots. But, alas, the more they pleased the ear, the more uncomfortable they were on your feet. So all that mattered to us was the blessed season during which we'd be able to harden our bare heels on the ground. And that season was the time of the primroses.

We never knew when spring began officially, according to the calendar. Ours was proclaimed by the smell of the wind and the colors of the earth, especially at the break of day. There was also a subtle and quivering echo of every noise and of every voice. At school a secret restiveness would annoy the teachers and cause showers of punishment to rain down upon us. And then, one day, a splendid piece of news would leap from one tongue to another: on Thursday next, we were to follow the cyclists along the Waremm-Wiz circuit with our hoops. It was the great chaotic moment of springtime.

The Waremm-Wiz circuit! That was the event for which the big boys had been toiling away since the age of ten or twelve so that, later on, they might win the Tour de France, our national bicycle race. The circuit was two and a half miles long or almost, just think! The road was stony, bumpy, and full of holes and ruts, with short rises that were hard to climb. It circled round the town toward the south and the east, crossing through moors, rabbit warrens, and pinewoods. A wilderness in which mythological wild beasts were said to wander. You had to have courage to venture into it, even astride a bicycle. All of Judas's treachery was lying in wait for you there, and it was still more fearsome when you lost sight of the parish-church belltower. Moreover, all winter long, the nails from horseshoes and men's sabots had been scattered between the rolling stones. True, some of the budding cyclists couldn't have cared less. Their tires were not filled with air; they were actually ropes of hay. And those cyclists were like the nobility of the Crusades. For we little ones, the poorest of all, had been chosen by them, our captains, to run behind them on our bare feet, pushing small iron hoops in front of us. The nails on the roads went right into our flesh, as did the splinters of glass and the sharp pieces of flint. But none of us would ever have dared to leave for the Waremm-Wiz circuit in our wooden sabots. It was a question of honor, which is important, and a question of pleasure, which is even more so.

When the month of the "White Straw"—in other words, September—rolled around, the winds began to get into position for winter. The harvested fields out on the *trestou*, or plains, which were not bounded by slopes, were spread over a large area in the direction of Peumerit, bare and treeless. That was where we used to fly our kites. What a serious undertaking it was, making those contrivances! Apart from the sticks of wood, which one could find anywhere, we had to manage somehow for all the rest. Several balls of string were necessary if you wanted your kite to rise high enough to reach the best air currents. Our small savings went into the enterprise. There was no possibility of obtaining any cloth, for the merest fragment of a worn-out shirt was kept for the family's needs. What about strong paper? But strong paper was very scarce. Only the tradesmen in town received it. Each of us used to go to the ones with whom our parents dealt and beg for some. Then you had to sew the paper onto the frame. But a needle and heavy black thread don't grow on trees. Rather often, the little girls would supply us with some if we promised them that they could hold the string once the serpent was up in the air. For the frills on the tail, you had to get hold of a few old newspapers, which was no small matter, believe me! But how glorious we felt when the contrivance rose up as we ran barefoot through the stubble, feeding it string! And what pleasure we took in controlling it way up there, and keeping it in the wind's eye, and making it toss about like a sailboat on the high seas!

Then the rains came more and more frequently. The streams swelled. And we returned to the pinewoods. We would crack off big sheets of bark which, with a knife, we carved and hollowed out into boats, and provided them with masts and old handkerchiefs for sails. Under the keel we'd put a large bent pin or a row of nails to ballast the romantic boat. And downstream it would drift. As soon as it began to rush along with the current, we'd jump from one bank to the other, watching carefully in order to extricate our little skiff from all the pebbles and branches. After an hour or two of navigating, our slippers and stockings would be wet up to our ankles if we hadn't taken the precaution of removing them and going barefoot. Since we had noticed that a wooden sabot coasted along very well without either a mast or a sail, we occasionally put one of them into the water. But it takes a high stream to hold up a sabot. And the high streams sometimes ended at a millcourse or at some chasm or other. So any reckless sabót-navigator would return home hopping on one foot, and the gruel stick would do its job.

Children always enter into the activities of grown-ups by stages. Since we lived in a region of windmills and watermills, we became millers on our own small scale. Almost all of us, somewhere around our houses or our enclosures, had a crossed-vane pinwheel which revolved at the end of a stick. But we preferred diverting the watercourses that meandered through our meadows and at the bottom of our fields. We would build dams and waterfalls just made for Tom Thumb. And those new canals of running water were our own way of getting our little mills to turn. Generally, we'd stick a wooden fork on each bank, and on those stays we would prop a spindle provided with four vanes which dipped into the current. The trouble was that the vanes had to be properly directed or the current would carry them off and we'd have to start all over again. The most skillful boys would fit a cogged wheel onto the end of the spindle, and by means of a whole transmission system, contrived to get a mini-thresher of their own invention to turn.

There were winters when the water froze in a string of ponds that sparkled throughout the Ménez-Poullou pines. We were apprised of them beforehand by the icicles ("January's teeth") which hung down from the edge of certain roofs. The first of us to see them spread the news to the others. Then we'd rush to our sheds to fetch the pair of worn-out sabots we had set aside in anticipation of that godsend. Nothing better for sliding on ice. And we competed to see who could slide the farthest. Of course, the surface would cave in occasionally because we had arrrived there too soon or too late, but the ponds weren't deep. On the other hand, those who were afraid of such accidents could slide on sections of the roads where the ruts made by wagons were always filled with a little water—enough to make fine icy patches. Strictly speaking, they were only good for beginners who were learning to keep their balance but were nevertheless called "little kids" until they tackled the Ménez-Poullou ponds.

We also competed on stilts. I don't know the reason for our great desire to walk on them. Was that the way our ancestors had crossed the brackish swamps which ran all along the coast, behind the belt of stones? People still point out two tumbledown thatched cottages in the middle of the Plovan marsh, with no roads leading to them and no discernible path. Or perhaps it was because we didn't think we were growing fast enough; perhaps we wanted to look at the world from the vantage point of adults just to see if it were different from our own. The fact remains that we couldn't rest easy until we were perched up on something so that we might walk high above the ground. And what helped us, to begin with, were empty tin cans.

Those cans were truly a blessing. We used tin for a variety of things, and fountains was one of them. Here's how we went about making them. We'd pile a half-dozen cans one on top of the other after having punched holes in the bottoms of them and on the cylinders. With an old pail, we would then pour water into the top can, and if we went about it properly, the water would squirt out of the holes of that column of cans in all directions. Of course, we didn't always succeed. It depended on the number of holes, on their size, and on how they were arranged along the cylinder walls. Anyone who succeeded in making a fountain, and it was most often by accident, would take his cans with him to preserve the model, which—no matter what his calculations—could never have been reproduced without it.

Now with two of those same cans we used to make stilts. Two holes punched at the bottom edge of each, one across from the other; a thick string drawn through them; and you were all set. Then you had merely to climb up on the cans and to knot each piece of string at a level suitable for controlling the cans under your feet, the way one controls a horse with reins. And off you went!

But they weren't real stilts. A time came when you were no longer satisfied with them. At that point, you tried to get your hands on two broomsticks or, failing that, any two sticks that were very straight. Using a big supply of old pins, you'd nail onto each of them—six inches from the bottom—a right-angled triangle made out of a thick board that the carpenter was generous enough to give you. Those triangles, the right side of which held our feet, were nailed on higher and higher as we became gradually more adept at handling our sticks. After we had got into training on flat ground, we tried to climb up and down and were finally good enough to jump on both stilts at once. Soon we'd be ready to pit ourselves against others in races. It was generally then that we began to lose interest in our sticks. What more could we get out of them? And could one afford to waste time in this world here below?

One year, however, all of them were rounded up for a production that nearly made the high end of town shiver at the thought that the Millennium had come. Just before All Saints' Day, we were in the habit of hollowing out huge beets, cutting holes in them in the shape of eyes, noses, and mouths, putting a candle inside each one, and closing them up. A human-head lantern like that, placed at night on a slope or concealed in the underbrush along a sunken road, always terrified a few night owls. From time to time, we also set a beet-head on the windowsill of some old maid—one who was known for being timorous and credulous. Somebody would tap on the window and then crouch down nearby. The old maid, warming her limbs at the fire in her hearth, would turn her head toward the window and think she was seeing the Ankou, in flesh and in flames. She'd let out a frightful scream. She'd call upon the Holy Virgin. Then, in a state of panic, she would rush out and run to find whatever help she could. At that point the little scoundrels would take back the death's-head beet and disappear. When the old maid returned with her closest neighbor, there was nothing left to see. And the whole town would have a good laugh. For several days the poor woman's latest vision would provide food for wagging tongues, at least for all but a few of them: What, after all, if it had really been the Ankou?

That particular year we had decided to enliven the spectacle. Each of us attached the beet-head to his flesh-and-blood head and climbed onto his pair of stilts. Some Timen or Le Galle or Le Corre got the idea of lining us up in single file. And that was how, in the dark of night, we walked down the path that ran along the Rector's Field. Suddenly, someone started intoning the *Libera*, and the others joined in as best they could. That chanted dirge attracted many puzzled women to their doorsteps, letting their gruel burn out of curiosity: Who could have been being buried at that hour of night? When they saw the procession of fiery eyes and hellish mouths seven feet above the ground, they made such an uproar that we ourselves were overwhelmed. We got down from our stilts and at the same time our beet-heads fell off like an avalanche straight out of the Last Judgment. None of us ever admitted that we had taken part in that little drama. The *Libera* had been just too much. One doesn't trifle with the Next World, even on stilts.

After that funeral service, we got tired of hearing ourselves called "beet-heads" and had decided to fight the "dogs from the low end of town" at the first opportunity. We eventually took them by surprise at the small railway station at Plovan, which was merely an open shelter in the middle of the countryside where the carrot-train stopped by request only. Since the others had not been on their guard, they were outnumbered, and our surprise attack gave us the advantage. Our leader, the kid from Pouloupri, had had us stuff our pockets full of stones we had picked up on the beach, extra supplies of which had been stored in the holes of the old walls. No sharp rocks, though; no blood was to be shed. "If you hurt my son, I'll kill you," all fathers used to say. And since the culprit would be killed a second time by his own father, or so his father had given him to believe, it was only sensible to obey the laws of our own warfare insofar as possible.

As soon as the kid from Pouloupri gave a shrill whistle, we began firing stones, from a distance, to the right and to the left of the railway line, to keep the other gang from fleeing. However, our advance guard, under cover of the slopes and copses, was making its way up to the small station, where the enemy was entrenched, obviously not knowing where to turn next.

The "dogs from the low end of town" were wavering. Ought they to counterattack, drawing their supplies from the bed of stones that propped up the railroad tracks? But if they did, blood would be shed and the grown-ups would kill us all. So they decided to wait. We closed in on them. And then there began an exchange of insults, the mildest of which I shall spare you, because your eyes are perhaps more sensitive than were our ears. They had no connection with Caesar's exhortations to his soldiers during the Gallic Wars. But then Caesar was only a Roman. In short, it all ended in a series of fist fights, one boy pitted against another, in which Breton wrestling worked wonders.

We had been trained in that form of wrestling very early on, in the fields. We knew nothing about the titles bestowed upon it over the centuries, since it was hardly a noble art; nor did we know the precise rules of the game; but our bodies reacted to it instinctively, for we had been born to it. So each of us went right in there kicking with his big toe, which threw his opponent off balance, and then butted him hard, which floored him properly; that is, both of his shoulders were flat on the field at the same time. He had to fall. And it had to be a clean fall! Around the small Plovan railway station there was no ram to be awarded the victor, as in the real matches, but we went at it with all our might. That I got beaten, as was generally the case, didn't matter very much, puny kid that I was; but this time the beet-heads won. The gang from the low end of town made a disorderly retreat down the railway line, protecting themselves from a distance by rolling the stones from under the tracks at our legs. Revenge was in the air—and to a high degree, since that very evening the whole town knew all about it, so that the losers' families had trouble digesting their shame, whereas our own merely pretended to tweak our ears.

The next to the last ordeal was that of conquering the ocean waves at Penhors. We had learned to sort of swim about in the "Grand Canal" stream, which was barely eight or nine feet wide. The sea was two and a half miles away. For small children, just getting there was a real expedition. Our parents, peasants that they were, disliked the sea for lots of reasons, the first being that they generally didn't know how to swim and had no desire to learn. Secondly, they loathed having to take their clothes off; the Garden of Eden had existed too far back in time. And thirdly, there was little or no connection between their work and the sea; besides, they preferred meat to fish, that Lenten and Friday fare. Some of them would go down to fetch wagonloads of sand and even seaweed for their fields, but it ended there. They were in no way inspired by salt water or by water that moved in two directions. That was treachery. The sea at Penhors was the site of the great pardon of Madame Mary, whose chapel had been built on the coast specifically to exorcise that particular treachery. They therefore did everything in their power to dissuade us from going. However, we had but one desire: to confront the ninth wave, the hardest one. Nothing less would do if we were to become men.

One day our little gang met together on the slip that had been constructed by my grandfather Alain Le Goff. Since each of us had brought a makeshift pair of bathing trunks, we went and undressed in a hole in the cliff. It was cold; the heavy sea was rising; and we walked along the beach, our teeth chattering, and preceded by the biggest boys, for whom the waves held no secrets, not even the ninth. In front of me I saw huge, foaming rollers, crested with very long beards, terraced one behind the other, and the farthest one spewing straight down from the sluice-gates of heaven. The whole spectacle was accompanied by the roaring of countless beasts. I was in the water up to the middle of my thighs when the big boys dove into the first roller. As I was waiting to see them rise up from behind it, I was knocked down head over heels, quartered, dragged, choked, and God knows what else! The end of the world had come. But—not so! I managed to pick myself up, half-blind, and discharging water from every hole in my body. Somebody shouted to me: "Watch out! Go straight into it! Head first!" It was too late. By then the second roller was on top of me, and I was again being swept about so forcefully that I ended up almost aground, against part of a bare reef—not a limpet on it—and with good reason! While I was trying to catch my breath, a few arms lifted me up. Then somebody was slapping my back and another was rubbing my ears. The big boys had come to my rescue. Two of them took me by the hands and pulled me along with them—not toward the beach, but toward the walls of waves. Those bastards! Absolutely terrified, I was about to resist when I recognized them. Both were from the low end of town. By golly, we'd see about that! At a distance a wave was forming and rising, ready to crash down. A mass of foam loomed up to attack. The others let go of me, shouting: "Do what we're doing!" I flung myself into the roller like a madman. And miracle of miracles! I never knew I was that supple. I came up to the surface on the other side of the wave with the two accomplices, all three of us squatting in the water, making our way to the beach. However, we didn't have much breathing space. Before we had time to turn around, another roller was behind us. But I heard a voice say: "Ass up, head down!" I obeyed to the best of my ability; the wave knocked me over gently; and I found myself doing my breast stroke as calmly as in the "Grand Canal." Let the ninth wave come, thought I, unless it already had.

Getting back to town proved to be rather difficult. I had the feeling that I'd been soundly thrashed. I was bleeding from long gashes made by the reef and streaked across my ribs. But I was happier than I had been the month before, when I'd received my scholarship.

Henceforth, all I had to do to be a man was to learn to smoke. On the edge of the Méot field there was a lane of chestnut trees which we called "the Barrier." We would wait until the male catkins had fallen under the trees and had dried out a bit in the grass, and then we'd make "monkey tobacco" out of them. The idea was to show that we were capable of really smoking without fouling our breeches and, above all, of rolling the "monkey tobacco" into a piece of newspaper, which required great skill and even more saliva. Indeed, once the cigarette was made, you had to be able to smoke it without its falling apart, otherwise jeers would rain down upon the clumsy boy, whose only recourse was to bow his head and secretly dream up startling ways of getting his own back.

But first we each had to make a pipe in order to get ourselves used to the smoke. Yet again, the elderbush came to our rescue. For the bowl, you'd cut a section five or six centimeters above a node, which made the bottom. If there was a bough attached to the node, all the better, for it could serve as the stem once the pith had been removed, as it had to be from the bowl as well. Or you could use a section of bamboo. When the pipe was completed, you stuffed the bowl with male catkins, having chosen the driest of them. One of you had always managed to filch some matches. You placed the light on the pipe, breathed in, swallowed a choking amount of smoke instead of exhaling it, coughed, got your eyes full of tears, and admitted that that masculine pleasure was an awful punishment, but you had to persevere, put a gluttonous expression on your face with each puff, and look about you arrogantly. When you started to get dizzy, the color would leave your face, so you'd pass on the calumet to the next boy, and lie down in the grass looking altogether delighted. One bit of luck was that you had to relight the monkey tobacco ten times, because it kept going out. That gave you long enough breathers to come to your senses again.

I have described, above, how I began my earliest education—by learning to use all the resources of the countryside: the trees, the plants, the stones, the birds, the winds, and water in all its guises; by learning not to waste the slightest thing—for example, not to cut two branches from the same copse to make only one stick. I described how I, like the others, took the steps necessary for becoming proficient at doing a peasant's job, which would have been my fate were I not to become a teacher, a postman, a railway employee, or a petty officer second class in the Navy. A peasant's job consisted, above all, in knowing everything about the surroundings, including all the traps that were set, and into which you were bound to fall if you were a novice. It was thus that you adapted yourself to nature and occasionally held it in check at the same time as it satisfied your basic needs.

Now in those days, to live in the country and to work the land meant that you had to learn a number of bodily gestures which were means of saving your energy and which had to be acquired early on so that you wouldn't tire yourself out to no purpose. Moreover, a certain manual dexterity was essential to a peasant, since he had to be prepared to make minor repairs himself—repairs that would normally have been made by harness-makers, carpenters, roofers, masons, and weavers—for in emergencies he had no time to call in those artisans, even if he had the means to. In short, he was doomed to doing odd jobs. The manger, the stable, the open shed, and the cart shed were also workshops. At school I had seen one of my friends carve a peg out of a piece of hard boxwood in order to hold up his trousers, which had two buttonholes, one facing the other, but no buttons. That didn't surprise anyone. We were all in the same boat and were accustomed to making, by hand, all those objects that people call toys and which were not. A country child had no toys. You can't even say that he had fun playing. He had fun while he learned, that was all. But first and foremost he was an apprentice. And his share of the work was awaiting him even before he had reached the age of ten.

That was why the grown-ups, and especially his parents, would keep careful track of his progress, but from something of a distance and, above all, without helping him any more than was necessary. They let him confront his own ordeals; they took pride when he succeeded; they were more mortified when he failed or was behind in his work than when he was not promoted in school. In the country all the bodily skills, whether at work or at play, provoked everyone's admiration, whereas all of them clearly distrusted philosophizers and those people who were too clever for their station in life. I'm not sure whether any of that has changed. As for the children, they knew how to size each other up. For example, it didn't take long for the braggarts to be put into the category of those about whom mothers used to say: "Talk he does; do he doesn't." But those who went through their ordeals with good grace and without false pride were always paid the honor that was due them as lords, which they were.

As for those toys we never had, when we were schoolboys we hardly ever hankered after things like rubber balls, if I remember rightly, because it was impossible for us to make them ourselves. And since they were beyond our means, well, that was that! Now the last time I bent down, with the other little kids, to look into the Saint-Fiacre fountain, I was an old boy of nine or ten. At the bottom of the water was a metal toy, a small yellow and red automobile, the type that has a spring inside which you wind up with a key to make it run. The key had sunk along with it. Something strange had just taken place.

Gathered round the fountain were the Queffelecs, the Carious, the Bossers, the Guichaouas, the Le Galls, the Le Goffs, the Le Cozes, the Le Corres, a few Timens in their patched-up plush clothes—and a little boy in short pants and a sailor collar whose family name nobody could recall. He had been baptized Paul, but he was the only one to bear that curious name in a parish full of Gourgons, Alains, Corentins, and Clets. As a crowning disgrace, he was not able to express himself very well in Breton, although he had a grandmother in the region. He wasn't exactly a tourist, but almost. In spite of his walking about every day in his polished leather shoes, we all really pitied him, once we had stopped making fun of that girl in disguise.

Poor little Paul was not able to do much with his hands. He didn't know how one prepared traps in the ground to catch birds. He was incapable of making a water pump out of a reed or a blowgun out of an elderbush stem. He couldn't even whistle with two fingers in his mouth. And he was afraid of cows, pigs, and chickens. A good little guy, but brought up in another civilization.

When he had first arrived, he thought he could get his own back one day, on the square, by flaunting his small yellow and red automobile, a toy that was frightfully expensive and the likes of which we had never seen. But what was a small automobile—even one with a spring and a key—to children who, all by themselves, were able to build four-wheeled wooden carts in which they could pull each other around? We had always refused to play with his ridiculous contrivance.

And then, the day I was speaking of, the poor forsaken child had decided to throw his precious and useless toy into the Saint-Fiacre fountain. We weren't a bunch of barbarians. We had clearly understood that he was giving proof of bondage in order to be received into our brotherhood.

Before nightfall, the boy had torn off his sailor collar and had scraped his bare knees learning to climb trees, with our encouragement. He was on his way to becoming a man. Glory be to Saint Fiacre!

6 A Hard Life

> It is in the poor nations that the lower classes feel comfortable; it is in the rich nations that, as a rule, they feel poor.
>
> Destutt de Tracy

One winter's day, around three in the afternoon, the light seemed to come straight out of Purgatory, and my mother had lit a big fire in the hearth in an attempt to dry some clothes that were still wet because of the very damp wind outside. I was sitting on a small bench right next to the fire, wallowing in the warmth. With an old knife blade, I was scraping the bottom of my trousers, which I had soiled that very morning as I'd scouted the countryside, heaven knows where. Suddenly, to her mute son, my mother said: "Be quiet!" Despite the crackling of the flames, she had somehow managed to hear a rumor that was spreading throughout the neighborhood. I wondered how. A second later she rushed to the doorstep and then back inside, all red and fussing about.

"What's wrong, Mother?"

"Stay right where you are! One oughtn't to make people feel ashamed."

And she ran over to the drawer of the large cupboard. She took something out of it and clutched it in her hand. She hesitated for a moment before hiding that hand under her apron and going back to the doorway. I climbed up on the window ledge in order to look over the curtains.

Outside, walking slowly toward the house, was a big fellow, very thin and strangely dressed in government-issue sailor pants and a woolen cloak that must have been blue before he was born but was so worn out that nothing was left of it but a grayish woof. On his feet he wore brand-new sabots lined with thick straw, and on his head, a huge Bigouden hat without the usual ribbons. He probably had a face, but—though I don't know why or how—it was so blotted out that he looked like a walking scarecrow. Behind him, moving even more slowly, as if frightened or ashamed, were a woman and three little girls, the tallest of whom must have been about seven. The smallest one was still wearing a bonnet, and the other two were clothed like their mother, in heavy, patched-up dresses that hung down over their sabots, with colorless bodices minus the velvet trim, and low, cloth coiffes that had turned brown. The mother gave one hand to each of her eldest daughters, while the youngest clung desperately to her cotton apron. They were relatively clean, given their rags and tatters, but had clearly fallen under an unlucky star. They stopped in the middle of the road and, motionless, without saying a word, looked at the door of our house. And there was the father, who had almost reached the doorway, taking off his hat. I knew that men never took their hats off except in church and in the presence of the dead. Only beggars took them off outside.

This one had dust-colored hair. He was so gray that I couldn't make out his features in the gray of winter. I squashed my nose against the windowpane to find out what was happening. And I saw my mother's arm held out, her palm open, while the woman and the three little girls bowed their heads and made the sign of the cross. Then the father covered his head again as he moved on, with his family six steps behind him. At that point, my very own mother, who had, without making a sound, come back inside, grabbed me around the waist, dragged me away from the window, and gave me a good talking to, asking if I were not ashamed of myself. I rushed outside, behind the house, to choke down my tears. What wrong had I done, dear Jesus?

That evening, sitting around the pot of gruel, my parents talked about the beggars toward whom I had apparently behaved so badly. I learned that they were people from another county, to the south of us. The father and mother were day laborers. A month ago, their house had caught fire and everything had burned up, including the cupboard in which they'd kept the little paper money they had earned. Even their cow had perished in the manger. Luckily, they had only five children. Their two sons, aged nine and eleven, had been taken on as shepherds in exchange for food. The rest of the family had left and gone begging along the roads of the Bigouden region, counting on the charity of well-meaning folk to stay alive until, once again, they had a roof over their heads. It's very hard to ask for handouts, even in the name of the Trinity, when one has always lived honorably, doing an honest day's work. And that was why I ought to have refrained from looking out while my mother was giving them what she could. The hardest thing to bear when you've become destitute is having people watch you. I should not have climbed up on the window ledge and shown my nose, however squashed it was against the pane. My father thought I had gotten off easy, that I deserved a good thrashing. Alain Le Goff sighed. "The boy couldn't have known," he said. "It's the first time he ever saw that."

Unfortunately, we had no lack of professional beggars, although people said there were not nearly so many as before. For the most part, they were blind men and women or cripples who went about in pairs or were led by a woman or a child. Of course, every parish had its beggars and took charge of them, which was a good excuse for not helping others except in emergencies. We had one by the name of Marie Gouret, who was known as "Blind Marie" and was the scapegoat of a few big kids who found it impossible to believe that the poor woman couldn't see a thing. From time to time one of them, a sworn skeptic, would go and stretch himself out flat on his stomach right in Marie's path as she'd be groping about with her stick, her head to one side, holding a dialogue with herself in two different voices which didn't seem to come from the same person. Marie would stumble over him and fall down, scrape her forehead or her chin—what difference did it make?—sit on the ground, and say: "I hope I didn't hurt you, my boy." The boy would then return to his friends, rubbing his body. "She fell right on top of me, and on purpose, the bitch! And before she fell, she hit me across the ribs with her stick." No one will ever know whether Blind Marie saw a half, a quarter, or merely a shadow of her misery.

She would come to eat at our house twice a year, on specific days that were known to my mother. And a third time during the week we had killed our pig. She was a wily creature. She knew that she'd have fresh meat. The other houses in town and the country women also knew that she would appear on certain given days which never changed. How did she ever keep count of the seven or eight hundred meals of the year (there were days, they said, when she had lunch and dinner twice) without ever mistaking the place or the day? She must have had a calendar in her head or in her belly. And she calculated the number of meals she invited herself to according to people's means, for she knew each one's financial situation better than anybody else. Whoever didn't feed Marie at least once a year was necessarily a poor wretch of the lowest rank.

On the other hand, Blind Marie could never manage to satisfy her appetite. There must have been several generations of starving people in her family whom, although dead, she would try to satiate by filling herself. After she had noisily wolfed down a bowlful of soup, she'd keep her head bowed so that everyone would know she hadn't yet finished. Moreover, she was always the first to arrive at a wedding feast and the last to leave. When the others had gone off to church, to dance in the square, to chat, and to sing—a waste of time—Marie was emptying all the plates. And when anyone asked her if she'd had enough, she would reply, sadly: "Almost." Though her coiffe was always beautifully arranged, she didn't have a house. Perhaps she ended her days like another poor woman who, during a dreadfully cold winter, had found that the best place to sleep was in a bread oven in some farmhouse. At dawn the farmer's wife had heated her oven and the beggar was roasted. May God forgive them both!

Also living among us were a few creatures who, as we say in Brittany, had "fallen off the back of the cart too late." In other words, they were simpletons. One of them, Lan-Maria, who had long since reached manhood, was still dressed in skirts, like a girl, to indicate that he had not yet emerged from childhood and would therefore no doubt have made a mess in his breeches. Another one was Jakig, who drooled all over his smock, his head hanging to one side. Yet another was a huge hulk of a man called Big Pierre.

People said that that hulk was led by a hollow nut that rang out in Pierre's head whenever it moved. Each time I happened to be near him, I would strain my ears to hear the noise made by the nut. But I never did, nor did anyone else. There were others whose heads were sound but whose bodies were martyrized by all the miseries of weak legs. They worked hard at walking; they even found it a chore trying to stand upright. And more women than men were afflicted by that hereditary disease of the Bigoudens. Swinging to the left, then to the right, they went about their business all the same, as if nothing were wrong, bowing to the ground on either side. Everyone has to adapt to his fate, and so they did! One of them told me, bursting with laughter, that he was drunk every day without having had a drop to drink or having had to pay a red cent. What a godsend for a broken-down cripple!

After all, he was a happy man. Not nearly so happy were two simpletons who worked as beasts of burden in a certain mill, and to make them move faster when they were laden down, their boss used to stick a large hatpin into their rear ends. And to boot, they would bawl out their apologies, to their torturer's delight.

The poorest and most deprived of them did everything in their power to be able to eat once a day, thanks to small jobs that were perfectly honorable, though not good enough to fatten them up. Indeed, the only way they managed to save a few coins was at the expense of their innards, which fairly often growled with hunger. There was one woman named Del who had served time in jail for petty crimes which no one remembered, and who had kept, from that period of retirement, a kind of uniform made of sackcloth and a penitentiary cap. She lived on nothing but the two sous she earned by selling things like pins and barrettes throughout the region, hawking her wares in a shrill voice. She also sold letter paper and envelopes, pronouncing the latter—a French word—as *blopou*. Everyone understood it, even those who never wrote because they could barely manage to draw an *X*.

"Del ar Blopou" was not the only one to deal in those articles. The town and countryside were tirelessly scoured by peddlers who walked about with an entire shop fit into a wooden box or a wicker basket, not to mention the day laborers, who went wherever they were needed, or the tailors and dressmakers, who would park themselves on straw in the barns for a few years and then disappear, or the gelders, the pig butchers, the marriage brokers, the distillery guys, the one-eyed ragman from the Monts D'Arée, and the Planter from Haifa, who gave the impression of being a great lord, with his fragrant three-wheeled chest. There were also other characters one saw for only half a second. The small paths of the parish were kept in good condition by all those feet.

Women from another county, who would change from one horse-charabanc to another in the hopes of meeting prospective buyers, also came through to sell coiffes and needlework which they themselves had edged with picot in the Irish manner. Ever since the beginning of the century, picot had saved many a woman from destitution. Almost all of them, and little girls as well, crocheted constantly when they had nothing better to do with their hands. And around Penmarc'h even young boys were said to crochet out of need, which meant they were often humiliated.

Some people actually had to go without matches in order to save a few sous. Old women used to cross the road and go into some house facing theirs if the chimney was smoking. When they'd come out, their own middles would be smoking because each of them had an old sabot filled with glowing embers given her by a neighbor and which she'd carry under her cotton apron as if it were the Holy Grail. It was called the fire-sabot. But the best embers apparently came from the baker, a very generous man who willingly helped out. Often, he had barely taken his batch of loaves out of the oven when two or three little "sabot-bearers" from the vicinity would arrive. They always left with their embers, manipulating them in such a way that the wind wouldn't get at them, while at the same time keeping them feebly alive by blowing on them. In any case, no one would have dared ask to be paid for embers, any more than they would have for yeast. Matches were something else again. People kept precise accounts so far as they were concerned. I once heard somebody complain: "That woman owes me four matches and she's never said a word about giving them back to me."

The large and small coins in poor people's houses used to pass from one pocket to another, thus keeping alive a whole group of little hucksters who knew exactly the right time and the right place to get those people to open their purses. And the man who had nothing but an apple tree would load his apples into a cart and walk barefoot for five leagues to find a taker. And the man who had no apples at all would sell pinecones to those who were too rich to go out and gather them up for themselves, or to people he knew and who bought them because they knew him. Or he'd give them away for nothing, assured that he'd be paid back somehow for his generosity. As a result of all such exchanges, the poorest people managed to live at the expense of those who weren't that poor. And not a fig, not a medlar, was ever wasted.

After the needy footsloggers came the tenant farmers, whose work was almost guaranteed. They had yearly contracts with the big farmers or, at the very least, were sure to be employed whenever anyone needed them, and they were needed often enough so that they never were short of food. They would live in tiny houses which some of them owned but most of them rented. (Those tiny houses generally consisted of one room with a mud floor, a corridor at the side, and an attic under the roof. But not even an inch of ground on which they could lower their trousers. They managed somehow.) Happy were those who had a real house, like ours, at their disposal. Little lords they were, so long as they remained healthy and were not dogged by bad luck or, even worse, born under an unlucky star. Faced with that misfortune, they were disarmed. What could they do about consumption, decline, emaciation? And what could they do about a cow that died, pigs that weren't profitable, harvests that rotted? It was enough to drive them to drink, and then, before they knew it, the poor wretches were gazing into a yawning chasm. Or else the owner took back your land or your house for reasons of his own, because he was a White and he suspected you of being a Red. And that was that!

There used to be one day during the year that made the tenant farmers toss and turn all night on their oat-filled pads. It was Michaelmas, which came at the end of September. On that day or the next, they had to come up with enough écus to pay their debts—their house rent and their share rent. If there was nothing left in the cupboard, they had to leave. They would load all their household goods on a wagon with a rack—their beds, tables, benches, utensils, and their meager wardrobe wrapped in a thick sheet of sacking. They would perch the children on top, tie the cow (if it hadn't been sold) to the rear, and silently leave for new and even more wretched lodgings. They'd take off very early in the morning, between night and day, so as to meet as few people as possible. You considered yourself lucky if you didn't pass another wagonload belonging to the people who were to replace you and who were gathering together everyone they met along the way—the bastards—to make it clear that they were climbing the ladder, whereas you were on your way down.

Around 1925 you'd see innumerable processions of that type filing by on the road from Quimper or Pont l'Abbé. They were poor sharecroppers or small farmers seeking a better life in the Dordogne.

"Where *is* that Dordogne, Grandfather?" (I was old enough to know that it was a place and not, as the little boys still in skirts believed, a witch.)

"It's farther than Nantes," said Alain Le Goff.

"But why go way out there?"

"Because there's more room."

We had enough room so far as I could see. But I never managed to find out if going to the Dordogne was a good or a bad thing, for you got the impression that some of them were going to a wedding feast, and others to a funeral. What was I to think? We never heard a word from many of those who left. But thirty years later I went to the Dordogne and met several of them who had become mayors of their communes. It was due to their "star." I should have liked to know where one of them went—a man who passed in front of our house one day pulling all his worldly goods in a handcart. He was walking barefoot down to that terrific Dordogne as others walked to Lourdes.

What more could a poor man burdened with small children do when he didn't have a cent to his name and had never learned to do anything but work the land? The region was unable to employ all the day laborers; there were too many hands as it was, and the new machines were already arriving. Luckily, some of the laborers had learned to speak fluent French in the trenches during the war. So off they went to the Dordogne! Besides, it was the clergy who were organizing the exodus and who were very good at reassuring people. Out of strangely distorted mouths, the people would hear odd names of regions, which they had their children verify in their schoolbooks: Lot-et-Garonne, Tarn-et-Garonne, Gironde. But the only name that stuck was Dordogne. And those who were too old to uproot themselves went about sighing and saying how the Dordogne was "the Isle of Hope."

The new exiles were neither the first nor the only ones to go off and roam around the world in order to make a living. Quite a few young men were already in uniform, though their only vocation was to eat every day. Some of them became soldiers to make a pile of money in the colonies—mostly in Indochina, where my uncle Jean had earned enough to keep his family from poverty. Others joined the Navy, or "La Royale," as it was still called. On the kitchen cupboards in most of the houses, photographs of young men with red pompoms and blue collars occupied a place of honor. Some of them even had gold stripes on their sleeves. When they happened to be in the region, they'd spend their time drinking in taverns, where they'd squabble endlessly with the old sailors or the new tradesmen. The few who had gone to work for the railroads would come back to show off their city suits and straw hats to their elder brothers, all of whom had remained "worm-cutters." The most elegant of all was a gay blade who had become a butler at the home of a great lord in Paris. He even had a gold tooth in his mug.

As for the girls, no one liked to let them leave. Whenever possible, they were kept at home. There were so many dangers awaiting them in the big cities, said the rector from the height of his pulpit. Besides, there was still a need for servant girls in the farms and the shops in town, where they were treated almost as members of the family; no one would have dared to do otherwise. Their yearly contract, like that of the farmhands, brought them in a few large bills plus a few pieces of clothing and one or two pairs of sabots. They also found employment in the bourgeois houses of Quimper and Brest—well-known, respectable houses whose owners had farms in the country. When the girls had to go down to Paris (everyone said "go down," or *diskenn* in Breton), it was because their brothers were already there. One word we often heard was "Montparnasse," a district in Paris where the Bretons lived as a group, much as they had at home.

Nine of my uncles and three of my aunts had left.

Among those who were forced to go off were men who had spent years learning a trade. Why would they stay around thrusting their fists through their pockets on the square while awaiting a godsend in the form of some improbable job? There were enough masons, carpenters, roofers, cartwrights, and blacksmiths; enough shoemakers, tailors, bakers, and butchers; even enough well-sinkers, although the poor devils too often ended up buried at the bottom of the wells they were digging. In order to get work, it was necessary to take it away from those who already owned shops or had hung signs on their doors. Neither the Reds nor the Whites would have dreamt of doing any such thing. It would have meant running the risk of upsetting a society in which everyone had his place and all the places were occupied. If one was seeking his fortune, it had to be sought elsewhere. So farewell!

Luckily, there was Jean Hénaff's canning factory, whose steam whistle had been measuring out the days in the commune ever since 1907. It was a "White" factory, of course, but the Reds themselves were proud of its cans of peas and beans, decorated with a picture of Notre-Dame de Penhors, and of its pâté, into which thousands of pigs went each year, including their own. That factory provided jobs for lots of humble workmen who were thus able to make out and live nice little lives in their small houses, free from the dread of having to take the train to Paris. During the stringbean season there was even employment for women who had time on their hands, as well as for the elderly and the adolescents. And there was night work, which was said to be better than day work. You were sheltered from the mud and the rain. Reason enough for thanking the Lord (the same for both the Reds and the Whites) if you were healthy and if the worm of ambition wasn't preying on your mind.

Thus the poor people of the region managed to keep the World Bitch at arm's length by dint of hard work, thrift, ingenuity, and the many sacrifices they made, but which didn't seem like sacrifices so long as, five times out of ten, the meager compensations derived from them were enjoyable. Of course, the dealers in hair suffered, since poor women were no longer reduced to selling their mops for a few silver coins, a scarf, a fake satin apron, or a watch chain without any watch at the end of it. The last woman who, out of need, had had her hair cropped was said to have died during the Battle of the Marne. Why, then, did that dealer persist in coming back to the region? Probably because, as we later discovered, he had been merely cropping the top of a woman's head, leaving her with a full crown of hair on which to arrange her coiffe and to hide her shame. When, soon afterward, city women decided to have their hair cut, the hairdressers took over from the traveling dealers. But I have been assured that one of them had nevertheless been seen in Quimper, on the Place des Chevaux Gras, during World War II.

The worst off among the women were those who had had a roll in the hay (or "in the strawberries," as we say in Brittany); in other words, the unwed mothers. A moment of weakness because one is too hot-blooded, a sympathetic ear because one is too tenderhearted, a naïve faith in vain promises, or merely a fatalistic surrender to a tyrannical master, and the poor girl was rejected by a society which denounced all women by whom the offence cometh. A long life of humiliation awaited the unfortunate creature, who was doomed to a solitary struggle every minute of the day in order to subsist along with the child she had conceived accidentally or unavoidably. She could also look forward to the most arduous and thankless work possible, as well as disdainful condescension, the most hypocritical aspect of charity. Or else it meant the train to Paris. If she remained in the region, the only way she could gain respect was by taunting people with her courage and with an imperious manner, as well as by stating certain truths that were not easy to tell. The others would then admit defeat with sickly smiles, for none of them were altogether beyond reproach. There were thus a few tough-minded girls who had decided to hush up the scandal by freeing themselves of all the taboos which too often took the place of morality or civility. And long live life when it's alive!

Other tough-minded girls, as well as overworked women, would periodically cheer themselves up by swigging down some red wine or a bit of *lambig*, our local cider-brandy. One would see them stealthily stealing out of the grocer's with a bottle under their aprons. And since a bit of alcohol helps you to weep your troubles away, which is the only way to get some pleasure out of them, why not? For a woman drinking at bars with men was out of the question. The men wouldn't have stood for it. She'd have kept them from exulting over their great feats, whether real or imaginary, after their second drink. So from time to time she would close herself up in the house, double-lock the door, and treat herself with red-wine balm. Sometimes her husband, who had returned by climbing in through the window, would finish off the treatment by beating her with a stick.

As for the men, if they succumbed to that same temptation ten times more often than the women, it was because of the three pinecones that were hung outside the taverns, which would lead one to believe that the dryness of the sign itself, as it crackled in the wind, made them thirsty even before they went in. Some, however, preferred to drink alone and, like the women, would lock themselves into a room. A man's house in his castle, at least when his wife isn't firmly holding the reins and doesn't treat her drunken husband in the manner suggested by a certain jingle which children were delighted to recite when they saw confirmed drunkards at their worst:

> When Yann is full of wine, beware!
> First catch him by his mop of hair.
> Then tie him to the nearest bench
> And work him over with a wrench.
> Next, tie him to the foot of the table
> And beat him with a stick from his stable.
> Then toss him into the nearest cot,
> His ass on the pillow, the poor old sot.

On the other side of the main road, and right across from our house, was a dry-masonry cottage called, by its occupant himself, "The Three-Holes Manor"; in other words, it had a chimney, a door, and a window. The chimney smoked only two or three times a week, when things were going well. The door was closed all the time, even in the middle of the day, which would have been worrisome had we not known that it was a question of bad grace on the part of the fierce old man, who wanted to relegate us to the outer darkness. It was opened only when the owner came and went. But often, at dawn, we could hear the shutters banging against the wall, and a square head covered with gray hair would lean out of the window to cast an arrogant glance to the right and the left. Then, to clear his throat of phlegm, he'd make a variety of successive noises which at first recalled a pig's grunting and inevitably ended like the crowing of a hoarse cock. A few more gobs of spit, and what was intended to be his washing-up ceremony was over. Directly after it, a cork would noisily pop out of a bottle. The breakfast of red wine was all ready, and a magnificent baritone voice would start to sing the *Gloria in excelsis*.

Other explosive noises would then punctuate the hours of the day. Your ear could actually follow the progress of his increasing intoxication. Sometimes the frenzied man would leap out into the road with a shotgun in his hands, heap insults on the townspeople, one after the other, and threaten to kill all of Christendom. Yet the old devil was shrewd enough to do his clown act when the men were busy elsewhere. The great bully preferred to terrorize women and children. However drunk he was, he delighted in hearing them call upon the Virgin Mary for help. At the end of the day, when he'd uncork his last bottle, his baritone voice was not up to more than blabbering out the Vespers. After that, the drunkard would snore until the following day, dreaming of his former glory as choirmaster of his church.

There were two or three men who weren't used to drinking in the ordinary course of life, but who enjoyed going out on a spree once or twice a year, just as a cow takes off like mad when it's goaded by an invisible gadfly. For five or six days you would see them making their pilgrimage throughout the county, each station of which was a house with three pinecones hung above the door. As long as the sun was still in the sky, they would hold court standing at some bar, gulping down drink after drink, and offering them to anyone who happened to come in, until they ran out of the écus they had put aside for their little escapade. At nightfall, if they hadn't found a good samaritan to drag them into his grange, some ditch or other would serve as their bed. Then suddenly, just like that, they'd stop drinking and return to their homes and their work as respectable members of the middle class and irreproachable heads of the family, until their next fling. They thus managed to take a holiday at a time when paid vacations were unheard of. And they probably did the right thing, clearing their heads by way of their stomachs. We knew of others who, one fine day, would just up and leave home without warning, having allowed themselves to be carried away by some fit of nostalgia or of latent despair which was in no way helped by their utter sobriety. Men like that never came back.

The owner of "The Three-Holes Manor" did not belong to that brotherhood of holiday drinkers. He died all alone amidst his empty bottles, after having sung his *Libera*. A few days later, when his neighbors broke down the door because of the smell, they found the rats already feasting on his remains. And the holiday drinkers spent all of the following month doing everything in their power to find some thirst-quenching virtues in well water.

The trade of the town was in the hands of just a few families, who shared the 2,324 consumers in 1921. Give or take a certain amount of competitive buying, they saw to it that their shops were stocked with everything their customers were in the habit of purchasing, as well as some few novelties that were apt to please them in the long run, for it took them time to examine goods they had never seen before and also to save enough money to buy them. Of course, they had to know that fabrics were sold at the wine merchant's, and candies at the watchmaker's, but everyone did know that. The tradesmen used every means at their disposal to increase their assets, but most of them also farmed a bit of land and walked a cow or two between the town and the fields. They didn't think they were rich enough, and they were not so foolhardy as to forgo producing their own food. Besides, the people wouldn't have had confidence in them otherwise. The truth of the matter was that they needed both a spade and a shop to make out, due to the fact that their customers were, for the most part, penniless. And I'm not talking of the little two-bit hucksters. If *they* ever saw two customers in a day, they would have sung the Magnificat.

Aside from Jean Hénaff of the canning factory and three or four dealers in agricultural machines, wood, and fertilizer, the real big shots were the big farmers. They were called big farmers, though many of them were mere tenants who paid rent for their tracts of land. They were rarely seen except on Sundays at High Mass when they'd arrive in horse-charabancs with some of the family, decked out in all their finery. Now we knew, since we had paid calls on them, that they lived in much the same way as we did; they, however, had acres of land around them, herds of cattle, mangers filled with pigs, fowl in the farmyard, and money with the notary public, a mysterious character we knew nothing about except that he kept official papers and guaranteed large sums of money.* During the week the big farmers' clothes were as patched up as their servants' and often filthier, because they were in charge of the work and didn't spare themselves. We also knew that, on Michaelmas Day, one or another of them would have a lot of trouble paying the bourgeois from Quimper or Paris who actually possessed the land, the name of which had been borne by the farmer for generations. Bigwigs, perhaps, but way back, their ancestors had been the sons of boorish peasants. At any rate, every one of them was always ready to buy land, but they would have let themselves be skinned alive rather than sell the merest patch of it unless it were absolutely necessary. And in that case, it was another bigwig who took possession of the lot, even if some poor devil had saved up for years in order to have the privilege of standing up and peeing against a slope of his very own. His fate was to remain a renter. That was the way things were.

Not that the bigwigs were bad people. Some of them were even rather nice, should charity be mistaken for niceness. But they were always intransigent when it came to property. What belonged to them could not belong to others, even if it were merely a dead branch of wood. They were obsessed with the fear of running through their possessions or of having them nibbled away by the proletarians. They were perfectly willing to give, but not to have anything taken. And when they gave, the person on the receiving

*See below, chap. 7. (Trans.)

end was in their debt. Both parties were well aware of that. And the poor were always grateful so long as they were not insulted because of their poverty.

My grandfather the sabot-maker, after having taken the many necessary steps, had rented a piece of land that was a dependency of the big farm on which he was then living, in a rented *penn-ti*. He had cleared and worked the land, and had sown it with buckwheat, from which he hoped to make bread. His field was an open *ménez*, or mount; it had no boundaries—no slopes or fencing of any kind. It was right next to a meadow where the owner's cows grazed, so that my aunt Marie-Jeanne, a little girl at the time, had to keep those cows out of her father's unripened buckwheat. You see the situation! Now one day my grandfather's two cows, at some distance from there, had had the nerve to browse on young shoots of pruned trees planted on a slope belonging to the owner. Crazed with anger, she had the bailiff come to ascertain the ten or twenty sous of damage that had been done, which, for my grandfather, almost meant ruination. The ogress must have felt that the sabot-maker's children were too well fed and that they were inclined to look her straight in the eye.

Give us this day our daily bread! For many poor wretches that was a prayer which came from the heart, for bread was by no means guaranteed. There were still households of children who fought over the slices or the crusty chunks. I used to see little girls aged eight or nine caring for babies who were their uncles or their aunts. There might have been as many as seven, nine, twelve, or even more of them, all ravenously hungry. And cooked flour was at the base of their food, with little to supplement it. True, since World War I, families were smaller. The fathers had been gone for so long. They had seen a great deal of misery that they'd not been accustomed to. But when they came home, they found the World Bitch right in front of their houses, sitting on its hindquarters. And they had to go back to making bread or providing it, as before.

Those who made their own bread were well aware of the price involved. Sweat and anxiety. And a kind of religion as well. They would always make the sign of the cross on the bottom of each round loaf. Some of the old people would still cross themselves before cutting into it. And you'd have had to watch them eat it to realize that they were observing a rite. They would sniff it, chew it slowly, then savor it, deep in thought. The crumbs that fell on the table were carefully gathered up into their palms, and every last one of them was gobbled up. To them bread was their body. Otherwise, they weren't hard to please. The sabot-maker would tell anybody who'd listen that there were only three things in the world he was unable to eat: soot, chicken droppings, and granite. But bread was everyone's Garden of Eden.

The children knew that as well, and very early on. When one of them went to the baker's for ten pounds of bread, he would keep an eye on the scale, young as he was. Ten pounds meant ten pounds, not one ounce less. The baker would weigh the loaf and, with his large knife, cut off a piece from another one and add it as a makeweight. He'd delicately place that piece on top of the loaf and immediately remove his hands to show that he wasn't touching the pan, that he was giving him what he'd asked for, even a bit more. So the child would place the loaf on his head, hold the extra piece in his hand, and go on his way. Sometimes his home was far from the bakery. He'd get hunger pangs. He would start eating into the piece in his hand—first one mouthful, then another. Suddenly he'd realize to his surprise that his hand was empty. Anguish. When he finally put the loaf on the table, his mother would ask: "Wasn't there an extra piece to make the ten pounds?" He didn't answer. His mother went on: "And what about your brothers? And your sisters? Aren't you ashamed of yourself?" Or he'd get a slap or two. The worst of it was when the loaf weighed exactly ten pounds. Sometimes that happened, and it was a frightful temptation. With the unwrapped loaf on his head, the child would struggle all the way home. In the end, he'd lift his hand up to the soft kissing crust on the side. He'd pull out a bit of crumb, just a tiny bit. Then his hand would somehow rise up all by itself. Before he knew it, there was a hole in the bread. His cheeks, ears, and backside would pay for it. It would have been useless to blame it on a mouse.

Do you know the story of the little boy, a bit of whose gut was always partially empty? He thought that if, one day, he could manage to fill it up, he would never want anything ever again. The problem was that there were three little things which went into meatless soup—bread, salt, and water—and the former was often lacking at his parents'. Once he was invited to a rich house where there was a profusion of food on the table. He worked so hard at eating steadily that you would have thought he was bottomless. At one point, having lost his breath, he stopped dead and began to weep bitterly.

"Why are you crying, little boy?"

"Because I'm full—from top to bottom—and yet I'm still hungry."

What accounts for the fact that the best-fed people among us were always hungry? "It's an inherited trait," said Alain Le Goff, "which comes to us through our navels. We must accept it like all the others." I didn't quite understand, but no matter. One thing was sure: when we scouted the countryside, we knew instinctively which plants were edible and which were not. None of us would have ever taken the risk of picking or eating mushrooms: they were toads' food (*boued touseg*). And we had been taught to distrust red berries. But for all the rest, it was our business to experiment, even if we had to spit things out that had a horrible taste to them. "Eat the springtime, children," said old Marie-Jeanne Bourdon, "while waiting for the winter to eat you." Along with the sweet milk from the honeysuckle, there were the pinecone seeds that served as a dessert, all types of wild peas, and primroses, which were sheer delight; wild sorrel was our real treat, though, as were the young bramble shoots. We'd get home with trickles of green saliva around our mouths. And we would eat less bread. Which was so much to the good.

Around the countryside every tree belonged to someone or other, but its fruit was up for grabs if the owner was good-natured. And we knew those owners, as did our parents. To begin with, there were wild blackthorns which bore tart, astringent fruit, much of which made you wince and wasn't worth anything. But some of those sloes were almost like plums. We would take a good supply of them home under our shirts, after having gorged ourselves while up in the tree. When it came to chestnuts, however, we were in competition with the grown-ups. That was because they could make entire meals out of them, and in certain houses they were really needed to save on flour.

Looking for food truly became an adventure when we had to sneak into cottage gardens, orchards, and fields of turnips, carrots, onions, and green peas—delectable food for little Yanns who had no land of their own. A good turnip would calm your innards for a few hours. Red carrots tasted better than the big white carrots eaten by cows, but they were planted very near farms, and there was always somebody in the field who saw you coming and knew what you were up to. Green peas were another real treat, but a careful watch was kept over them because they were sold to the factory for crisp new bills. We were well aware of that; our own parents wouldn't stand for a single one of them going to waste. We ourselves ate not only the peas but also the pods, after having delicately removed the inner pellicle. Actually, it wasn't easy to resist the temptation of slipping into the furrows, although we'd leave someone to keep an eye out and give a sharp whistle if the owner happened to appear unexpectedly on the scene. I personally didn't filch food very often, being a well-brought-up little boy and having a grandfather who would have been incapable of cheating the biggest marketeer in the world out of a red cent. Yet from time to time I had to take part in such expeditions or I would have been called a sissy. One's honor was at stake, after all. And because of that honor, we had to stay away from the fields of the poor or of anyone in our "group," and play at being pirates, preferably on land that belonged to those big shots who were thought to be misers.

The temptation to filch food was greatest if you were a kid whose job was tending the cows. The first and even the second hours weren't so hard to live with, especially if you had a knife. There were so many resources on the four slopes. But sometimes, if a few of your little pals happened to be scouting about or if another shepherd called you to join him three fields away, the Devil would win out.

Tending the cows. Do we really know what that means? You often hear: "He's good for nothing but tending the cows," applied to a child who does badly in school. And yet when you think of what it takes to make a good cowhand, how many bookworms could carry out that task with honors? How many would qualify? You have to have a sharp eye and choose games that leave you with a free mind, even if you're in charge of just one animal tied to a post by its rope. The post must be moved when the cow has cropped all the grass within the circle drawn by that rope. The cultivated fields in the area are a temptation that the cow finds hard to resist. In addition, it might choke on a cider apple, die from a bellyful of damp clover, get caught in its tether and break a leg trying stubbornly to extricate itself. A big car passing on the road behind the slope might cause it to flee across the fields and vales, urged on by the terrifying, wildly excited barking of a dog overflowing with good will. A gadfly might slip under its tail, and that would mean panic—blind and desperate—with the rope between its legs and the post battering its flanks and its spine as the beast shakes its horns in vain. So many things may happen! Catastrophes lie in wait everywhere. Watch out, my boy! If the cow has to be slaughtered, it could mean ruination for your family and shame for you.

In 1966 I recall having read in the newspapers that a young boy from the commune of Issac, in the Corrèze, had just been killed by a freight train. He had tried to save one of his cows which had got caught in the gate of a grade crossing. Of course, there was talk of his having been foolhardy. People even said that a cow wasn't worth risking one's life for. Perhaps. I should merely like to pay homage to the conscience of a little cowhand who was at most twelve, in remembrance of my own adolescence, when a cow—just one single cow—was our most valuable possession. None of us had had to sacrifice ourselves for our cow. Moreover, the small train that used to cross our region was too humble and too lazy to require a grade crossing. But I'm prepared to swear that more than one of us, at age twelve, would have been perfectly capable of facing death to save his one and only cow.

When my friends and I were twelve, we were impatiently waiting to be old enough to string the beans at Jean Hénaff's factory. You had to be thirteen—and no cheating, for it was apparently a law. Now stringing beans during those weeks when the yield was at its height gave poor children, along with a few old women, the opportunity to pile up a big nest egg at a time when money was not only hard but impossible to come by. If they went at it all day long and then part of the night, when the beans were canned, they might well have earned more than their parents if they were at all hard-working, and nearly every one of them was, innately.

We were carefully trained to do that sort of work. The older boys taught us how to set up two crates, one across from the other—the first to be used as a seat, and the second, for throwing in the heap of vegetables. We neatly shaped the heap itself in such a way that one end of every stringbean was visible. We would straddle the first crate, which had been picked according to our height, and we'd tackle the heap with our two thumbs and our two index fingers, rocking our bodies back and forth at a steady pace to give us the right rhythm. With each movement, one bean would lose both its ends and its string. The speed that some of us achieved was absolutely staggering. But we had to watch out! The lost end couldn't be too long. The entire string had to be removed from the bean, and the supervisor could verify that by breaking the bean in two. Everything was closely examined. Then, to can the vegetables, each of us had a tin mold that we used, with great care, to prepare both the top and the bottom of the can's contents so that they'd appeal to the eye. To keep track of the amount of work we had done, we were each given slips of paper or tin tokens which we cashed in on payday.

But every night, and sometimes during the day, we would add them up and calculate how many sous the factory owed us. The best part of our yearly income came from those five or six weeks of working with beans. Apart from that, we used to find people who would buy our snails, which we had picked off the old walls, and also our moleskin. But when it came to moles, you had to invest money in iron traps, keep a close watch on the molehills, skin the moles, and then dry the skins on slabs of wood. Only the most skillful made out in that trade. The oldest boys went and broke rocks on the roads, kneeling on an old bag and wearing eye-screens made of wire netting. They were proud of doing that sort of manual labor. You should have seen how they preened themselves when the road-surveyor calculated the cubical content of their work in a wooden measuring box. They were children no longer. And just to prove it, they'd go on striking at their rocks even in the pouring rain, having, like their fathers, covered themselves with a large hemp bag, whose two bottom corners they had tucked into each other to make a hood. Umbrellas were fine for Sundays.

It was around 1925, if I remember rightly, that my grandfather gave me a flail of my very own, a flail that was just my size. And that gesture gave me to understand that I was authorized to participate in men's work. Not yet working with them, but working beside them, so as to learn all that I still didn't know, which amounted to about three-quarters of what was essential. Grandfather, who guessed everything without having to be told, had carefully chosen two very dry sticks—one for the handle, and the other, which was shorter, for the thresher. He had tied them together with two leather straps in such a way that the thresher would swing freely; then he greased the straps with a rind of salt pork to make them even more supple. And there I was, the owner of a tool which had no connection with the child I'd been the day before. The next day we were to go out threshing with our flails in the farmyard of a sort of lady we called Aunt Jeanne. We were going to thresh the wheat, barley, and oats of the small farmers who owned one cow and two pigs but no farm and therefore no farmyard, and who would rent a field or two, along with a small meadow, in order to supplement their salaries as day laborers and be a little better off. There were a lot of us.

The sun had hardly risen when Aunt Jeanne's farmyard was echoing with shouts and laughter. The women, barefoot, were carefully cleaning the ground with brooms. They had left their coiffes at home, but their hair was tightly piled up on top of their heads and held in place with a curved comb and a black velvet ribbon. The men, holding flails, stood grouped in a corner, wearing their hemp shirts, their patched-up trousers, and their work hats. They were deciding on which place would be assigned to whom. Once the farmyard was clean, the first wagonload, which had been waiting in the street, was brought in. The horse was unhitched, and the shafts were lifted as high into the sky as possible to tip the wagon all the way down. Then the men got busy unloading the sheaves, unbinding them, and spreading them out on the threshing floor, with all the stalks placed next to each other at the same level. Soon the courtyard was covered, except for a narrow passageway on either side. All the men stopped for a moment to inspect the site and to be sure everything was in order. One last glance at the sky to be certain the weather wouldn't turn nasty. "Let's go!" said the owner of the harvest. He removed his sabots and, barefoot, took first place, to which he was entitled. The others did the same and took their places, each according to his rank in a rigorous hierarchy determined by his strength, his reputation, his relatives, his regular acquaintances, his obligations, and the question of one man's doing justice to another.

At that point, there were two rows of men facing one another, spitting into their hands, horsing around, and slyly challenging their friends. "Ready, boys?" asked the first thresher. "Follow me! One!" He raised his flail and every man in his row did the same. "Two!" The flails were brought down and, all together, struck the stalks, while the flails across the way were raised. The work was off to a good start. Of course, the first blows were not very steady, since the threshers hadn't yet caught the rhythm. But in no time they did, and about ten thousand blows were said to have been struck that morning, and the same number that afternoon.

The women had the hard job of turning over the shelled husks with wooden pitchforks and raking up the grain, which was to be put in bags, after which they would again begin to sweep the threshing floor so that a new layer could be placed on it. Meanwhile, the men gulped down lots of cider to quench their thirst. The children over ten had permission—and were sometimes ordered—to manipulate their flails in a corner of the threshing ground so as not to get in the way of the men but, at the same time, to learn by imitating them. The worst humiliation was to have the threshers dash over to us, their blows raining down on the site reserved for us. It was proof that our work was worthless, and we were more ashamed of ourselves than dogs that stray into a church. But we finally cheered up: perhaps next year we'd be allowed to do our best behind the last man. And a few among us, from one harvest to another, would gradually move ahead until they were promoted to the rank of leading threshers if they showed any possibilities of becoming foremen.

Unfortunately, the time of flail threshers was almost over. A year or two later, Aunt Jeanne's farmyard was empty in August. Once and for all. Well, the work was too hard. A few meager little bags of grain weren't worth breaking one's back over from early dawn to nightfall. Of course, there was always the pleasure of being among other poor devils—not a big shot in the lot—and of helping each other, but not out of charity, since everyone had the same status; there was pride involved also—once your harvest was threshed by hand, and especially when you were down and out—the pride you took in treating your people to a feast and savoring their joy, which was always expressed spontaneously; there was that strict equality among flail threshers, which meant no pretenses, for you were among people of the same good stock; finally, there was your own performance, which was a way of sizing up your own stamina. I am repeating what the flail threshers told me later on. And they are people who don't mince words.

Now on the farms, harvests had, for a good long time, been threshed by four horses which, turning round and round, drove a mechanical thresher that worked by means of a whole system of drums, spindles, cogwheels, and straps. But in our region there weren't any farms that had four horses, not one. Therefore the farmers had to lend horses to each other. And since the thresher worked much faster than the flails, a lot of people were needed to assist in the process. So the farmer would go out in search of those to whom he had agreed to rent a few pieces of land, the little people I mentioned above, who were hardly in a position to refuse. Who, in any case, didn't want to refuse. Who would have been hurt to the quick if they hadn't been asked. Who would have lost their reputations to boot. And perhaps, a year later, the land they had been renting as well. Besides, they were paid for their help. But not in money. While he was at it, the farmer would thresh their harvests by machine, once his own was done. He would even lend them a horse and wagon to take theirs home. Flails were no longer used for anything but threshing dry peas so as to obtain the seeds.

During the entire day of those machine threshings, everyone—the men, women, and children—would eat properly and well. Drinks were also available: wine in the house and cider outside. But during the threshing season the last hours of the day were arduous and very painful. For example, fatigue alone was responsible for certain accidents which took place every summer: some carter would be pushed against a wall by the shafts of his wagon, having all his ribs crushed; some exhausted carrier would fall off a pile of husks and break his neck; if somebody happened to be reckless, he'd get trampled by the horses driving the thresher; and if the chap at the wooden slab, on which the sheaves were unbound, put his hand out too far, it would get caught in the drum. Also, it was important that men who had certain specific functions not drink too much. It was the farmer's job to keep an eye on them and to replace those who got tipsy before it was too late. They were easy to pick out. Being drunk from fatigue is not at all the same as being drunk from alcohol. Fatigue slows down your movements; drink makes them hasty and uncoordinated. But in order to avoid violence, quarrels, and blows, the big farmer had to be tactful and not hurt people's feelings.

At one point somebody would say: "It's time to finish up now," which was the signal for the mistress of the house and her helpers to get busy preparing for the *pleurzorn*, the meal that traditionally followed the threshing.

One of the first times I had taken part in the work myself (I had been put in charge of unbinding the sheaves), I was placed at the foot of the table, completely bewildered at finding myself in the midst of all those magnificent workers. I was then twelve or fourteen and had my very own knife, which I had already opened and wiped on my trousers. All around me were faces gray from the dust, with two black circles between their cheekbones and the curve of their eyebrows—a spot that was hard to clean. A great weariness weighed upon all those living creatures. The men were sitting with their backs bent, round-shouldered. The women hadn't had the strength to pin up their bodices. The wretched clothes all of them were wearing had been transformed into rags. Few words were exchanged until—after a gulp of wine that was needed to relax the stomach—the first mouthful of food had been swallowed. Then, and every time afterward, I was amazed to note how quickly those people drew themselves up, both physically and morally. Not even fifteen minutes had gone by before everybody started making conversation, interrupting each other, raising their voices, throwing compliments back and forth, making jokes, each one passing the ball to another and making sure that no one was left out: well-tilled land produces good seeds; it's only normal.

"You do pretty well in the kitchen, Marianne; your roast is so good I'd sell my soul for it right here at the table, and my conscience too."

"Stop talking rubbish. I do my best, but you deserve better."

" . . . the heaps of husks are as straight as Maï B's coiffe when she goes to High Mass."

"Thanks to the women's know-how when they shook the husks with those pitchforks, we had an easy time of it."

"I'd say it was thanks to the guys who were so good at feeding the threshers."

"No, it wasn't me. It was the fella who drove the horses and kept 'em going around at a steady pace."

"If you want my opinion, everybody did a good job—the carriers too, even the men in the fields, who loaded their wagons before you could blink."

"Marianne, Del, Corentine, Lise, put some more food on the table! The people are going to leave here hungry. And their empty stomachs'll growl so loud that the whole county will know of our shame."

And everyone's eyes were beaming with pleasure behind their dusty eye-shadow, and they had such broad, moist grins on their faces that you could see their gums as well as their teeth—never mind if some of them were missing! Their bodies were blooming again under their wretched clothing. If the Lord God hadn't divided the light from the darkness and seen it was good, we would have been ready to go on until we heard the trumpets of Judgment Day. And everyone ate a bit more and drank a bit more. And no one dared to say a cross word, no one dared be offensive. The meal that followed the threshing was almost sacred. The next day, of course, everybody was again rubbing people the wrong way and telling a few home truths, to them in person or behind their backs; there are very few saints in this life. But during the evening they would celebrate the joys of joint labor, which sprang up like flowers to grace their joint sufferings. There was no effort involved because they formed a "group," a "coterie" (as they still say), and that word, derived from the French, means something midway between friendship and brotherhood. No undesirables were there; no sworn enemies either; they wouldn't have dared to come. They had kept their distance and had joined other groups; they had chosen to go elsewhere or had resigned themselves to pretending they had taken part in the proceedings. For if somebody happened to ask: "Where did you work during the harvesting this year?" one felt deeply ashamed at having to answer: "Nowhere."

Among those men and women sitting at table, after having sweated the same sweat together for two or three days, were the rich, the poor, and the indigent, who were in constant contact with mendicity, yet had never been reduced to it. There were some who had their own horses and others who owned nothing but their own bag of bones. Tenant farmers, workers, artisans, and even tradesmen, all were associated with the large farm; they constituted a sort of following. But all of them knew how to work the land; almost all of them owned a cow or two. Every household had delegated a representative, as it did for weddings or funerals. That labor-day celebration of the harvesting was so important that a deputy, whom I knew later on in life, would attract voters to him by lending a hand on that occasion. He never failed to be elected. Was it really possible not to give one's vote to someone in the "coterie"?—in other words, to someone who's your equal? For around that table each and every one was equal, and they were all mixed together, since no distinctions had been made. Except for the master of the house, who could not be removed from his rightful place, there was, strictly speaking, no head and no foot to the table. And any shows of courtesy were absolutely gratuitous. As for politics and religion, everyone took care not to bring them up at all; they could be discussed elsewhere and at a later date. The Reds and the Whites were all of the same dust-color and partook of the sacrament during the feast of our daily bread.

When the threshing meal was over, they all returned home by way of dimly lit roads, and fatigue leapt on them like a wild beast. My father walked in front, my mother in his shadow, and I, behind them, constantly fumbling in my pocket, fingering the pay I had earned. But I was half-asleep, and every three steps I'd stumble over some damn rut or some bloody rolling stone. The next day, I would have to get up early to go off and start all over again on another farm—Pouzeog, Penkleuziou, le Sent, perhaps Gouridou, I couldn't remember which.

My hands were burning hot. I hoped I hadn't got myself a felon. It would have been easy to spread the rumor that since I had been at the lycée, I no longer knew what the real smell of bread was like before it was baked. I would have been accused of treason, and the world was already full of Judases, as Uncle Piron, the roof-thatcher, used to say. "All those Judases," he'd mutter between his sideburns, "and you'll be even worse than the others, my boy, because your mind is rotting away in all those schools."

It was not long before an act of treason was indeed committed. The horses that drove the thresher were replaced by an engine called Bernard. It would be a blatant lie to say that the engine was received with anything like enthusiasm. It had to be nailed to the ground with iron spikes to keep it from moving off into the distance, trembling like a sick dog. It kept knocking off the thresher's strap despite all the resin that had been rubbed on the pulley. The sparks that came out of it might well have set fire to the harvest and burned down the buildings. That was why, at the beginning, all the available pails of water had been set down quite near it. And most especially, it had a master who came along with it, the "engine guy," the only one who knew how to get it to run, which was somewhat humiliating for the others. It had arrived together with a huge machine for shaking the husks, which at first had to be worked by hand and was then hitched onto the contrivance as soon as it was running full speed. That meant the end of the ballet of the pitchforks and the women's loss of pride. Obviously, the work load of the people in the group was considerably lightened. I myself was freed from arduous tasks by the Bernard engine. Since I was then attending a university, I was promoted to the rank of "engine guy" when the latter happened not to be there and because I was assumed to be knowledgeable, which forced me to cram in order to learn everything there was to know about an internal combustion engine. From then on, I'd strut around it with a greasy rag in my hand. I must admit that, from time to time, so as to seem important, I'd jam the jet, looking worried. The engine would cough, choke, and threaten to stop. The whole group would watch me anxiously. Then I'd release it and Bernard would begin to run smoothly again. I wasn't the only one to play that little trick.

After the threshing, there was one last step: the grain had to be winnowed. I can still see the poor women, at a time before the flails had been replaced, winnowing with a sieve or a sifter—women whose entire harvest fit into a few small sacks. On a windy day they would put their harvest into a wheelbarrow, carry it to an open meadow, choose the place that had the best breeze, and manipulate the sifter with their arms for hours on end. When the chaff was finally separated from the grain, it would fly off and fall onto a cloth some distance away. Afterward, it would be used to fill mattresses and pillows. To the very end of their lives those women claimed that the grain they had winnowed by hand was much cleaner than that which went through the vanning machine. And perhaps they were right. After the winnowing, the grain would be carried up to the loft, where little by little it dried out completely. Finally, but not until then, had the women dared to breathe deeply. The miller boy could come and fetch it. They were assured of having flour and bran. "Give us this day our daily bread," says the prayer. It had been done—for a whole year.

The buckwheat harvest took place in September. The weather had to be fine for the harvest to be adequate. All the tenant farmers, even the poorest of them, like us, had a field of that type of wheat. Generally, it took no more than a sickle to cut it down. People were still using that tool even after the reaping machine had come into the region, because with a sickle there was less danger of the grain falling from the spikes into the field, especially when it was a bit too ripe. Once the reaper had cut enough to make up a good-sized sheaf, he would press it against his knee, holding the spikes in one hand and spreading the stems with the other in order to make a sort of cone that would stand up without having to be tied. That's why fields of reaped buckwheat look very like military campgrounds covered with tents, the touches of red in them glimmering as they sway in the wind.

Buckwheat was still being threshed with flails, whereas the white variety had long been threshed by machine. Apparently that was the better process, since it prepared the wheat for the following step—the pressing, which consisted in removing the hard pellicle covering the grain. Once the grain was absolutely dry, it was gathered up into a pile. The pressers would take off their shoes and walk around it, stamping their bare feet down on the grain around the edges and, with a rubbing motion, bursting the pellicles. As they circled round, the grain would tumble down from the sides of the pile, so that at the end of the process it was again spread out very flat, but with the pellicles three-quarters removed. Then it was shoveled up into a pile again, and the pressers would go on stamping until the grain was considered "undressed" and ready for the winnowing machine.

The windmill and watermill carriers would make their rounds in the region, picking up the sacks of grain and bringing back the flour and bran. They were great strapping men, with strong backbones, who seemed always to be in good spirits, for they almost never stopped whistling. That was perhaps because they were dealing with food for men as well as for animals, and because food was the main concern of most of the poor people. If there happened to be a surplus, it was always welcome. The buckwheat awn not only served to thatch roofs; it was also used for making cider. In the orchards the apples, turning yellow and red, had already been piled up under the bare trees. The cider presses had been cleaned. Soon they would be filled with the apples and the awn, placed in alternating layers. Then the screw was manipulated and the juice passed through the awn: it was said to give a special flavor to the cider. As for buckwheat flour, that was used to make "black" bread, which many preferred to white bread because it tasted better with salt pork and because every farm had its own oven, and every housewife who possessed a kneading trough had her own recipe for the dough and for kneading it.

The bees had already gorged themselves on the buckwheat flowers, which they preferred to heather and white clover. And my grandfather the sabot-maker's bees produced a rich, reddish-brown honey which was the ultimate cure for every sort of weakness. The flour from that same buckwheat gave us something to hope for: piles and piles of crêpes and pancakes. And since we did, after all, have a small amount of ordinary wheat, there was still more to look forward to. What else could you ask for? Behind the house there was a pile of straw on which to bed down our animals. And for our very own beds, there were enough bales of oats in the shed. So what was there to worry about? We had done very well again that year. So had the cow and the two pigs. Ours was a beautiful life!

Everything that didn't go down our stomachs was used for something above or below them. The big shots, who, of course, owned horses, complained that their animals refused to eat the buckwheat pellicles. Noble horses are hard to please. But pigs never balk at anything. You could add ferns to their broth or, with all due respect, horse dung: they ate everything and thrived on it; those bristly gentlemen never protested when it came to food. Nevertheless, for them—as for us—potatoes were the real treat.

The time was long past when the "Government Boys" had had to pay rhapsodist-beggars to sing "The Potato Song" throughout the countryside. Over a century ago, only a rare few were willing to eat those frightful "toads' mothers," full of navels and spots and which turned into diarrhea as they rotted. People used to say that they gave men and animals leprosy, and that the rich had found them a means of getting rid of the poor, killing them by inches. In point of fact, potatoes had kept us alive lots of times in the past. Without them, a good many Bigoudens would have gone to their graves prematurely. They were the last good turn done us by Saint Fiacre, protector of the peasants.

For my parents and myself, the hoe was an indispensable tool in every way. We even used it to dig up our potatoes. I had learned to stick it into a furrow between two haulms, at a spot where there was little danger of cutting a tuber—a shameful thing to do. Not *very* shameful, but shameful all the same. I had learned to strike deep down in order to get everything out, and to scatter the soil properly so that all the potatoes—yellow or red—could be seen; also to heap them up between a lot of dead haulms which we had first knocked against the sides of our sabots to lay bare the roots. Then, kneeling, we had to sort out the potatoes—the big ones, the small ones, and the rotten ones, which were for the animals. They were put into osier baskets which had to be shaken vigorously so that all the soil would fall out. Finally, they were stuffed into bags. That same evening or the next day, we would bring them home in a borrowed wheelbarrow.

The greatest pleasure of the children and adolescents—their best reward—was burning the dry haulms at nightfall or on the following day. Once they caught fire and a bed of embers had formed, each one would choose a few fine potatoes—long, pink sausages which can't be beat, as everyone knows—or for lack of those, the kind that are called "fin de siècle" and apparently weren't very highly thought of by the tradesmen, but which have a special smell that's pleasing to young nostrils; why, nobody knows. With a stick, each one of us would stake out his own little bed of embers into which he'd put his half-dozen potatoes to cook, turning them over from time to time. Then we'd eat them, nice and hot, at the risk of burning our tongues a bit. There is nothing better in the world to satisfy that bit of empty intestine which is always growling inside young yokels.

The smoke from the burnt patch of haulms would rise up over the whole countryside in September. But to the west, the coast was smoking as well, all along the shore of the Bay of Audierne. That was because seaweed was being burned in order to extract sodium from it, or what we called "sea bread." During the winter the women of Penhors had gone down to the water at low tide to gather that amazing crop from the fields of reefs, as far out as the waves. Two by two, weighed down by their dresses soaked with sea water, constantly stumbling over the crumbling stones, they had arduously brought their loads of algae up over the cropped grass of the cliffs. Neither the wind nor the rain had ever broken down their persistence. With the gestures of a tedder, they had spread out those strips, those corollas, those plants, those clusters of every shape and color, to get them dry. On days when it was allowed, the inland peasants had gone down to the coast and they too had skimmed off wagonfuls of that precious sea-manure. Later on, we saw the ovens, which were in fact long, narrow ditches lined with flat stones and divided into almost square compartments by slabs of stone set in edgewise. The seaweed was stuffed into them and set on fire. Heavy, pungent smoke soon seeped out and moved almost at ground level, according to the prevailing wind, while a kind of lava formed a deposit at the bottom of the ditches. The men's job was to see to the work at the ovens. Using a long stick with a metal tip called a *pifon*, each one stirred up the layers of seaweed to get them to burn faster, and at the same time they kneaded and mixed the dough, as it were, then rammed it down at the bottom. As the layers of seaweed burned, the men would continue to add one pitchforkful after another. In that way they made sodium loaves which would cool down in the compartments and finally become coarse blocks. Separated from one another by the stone slabs, those blocks were pried out with a *pifon*. Then a truck would take them to a factory, and various pharmaceutical products were extracted from them.

Once all the harvesting was over, we would prepare to settle down for the winter. Ever since Midsummer Day, we had had scarcely the time to catch our breath. It wasn't easy to be a peasant. To begin with, there were the two summer months during which you broke your back from sunrise to sunset. And even so, you were lucky if, just to complicate matters, it didn't rain day after day, spoiling everything, and if the wind didn't blow up a storm, beating down entire fields of grain, so that you had the very devil of a time cutting them properly! But when October came, it was all over; we had laid in enough supplies for a year. We would start the second season, the winter, with a sigh of relief. For us there were only two seasons. If spring and fall weren't separated by summer and winter, we would have had one more. But since they are, we considered them as merely tails tacked on to the other two.

A winter when you had everything you needed was an act of Providence. The man with the hoe would again start walking at his usual pace and breathing at his normal rate. He would live; he could feel himself living. He would think; he enjoyed thinking. From the moment he paid his respects to the dead on All Saints' Day to the birth of Christ, he would spend the days of the "Black Month" (November) and the "Very Black Month" (December) withdrawing into himself and speculating on his soul as much as on his body, his land, his houses, and his animals. And something more: there were the tales, the joyful stories, the men's going out on the town, and the big silver coins in their pockets. What did it matter if, along with the winds and the rains, came the cold? Everything within them was warm after Michaelmas. They owed nothing to anyone. They had "enough."

In November, however, the man with the hoe still had to harvest the beets, which were precious food for the animals and had to last until the end of February to ensure the great pleasure of his horse, if he had one. The horse in question would, in any case, lose its hair—that is, until the grass began to grow thickly again. Then it wouldn't take long for its coat to regain the luster it had lost during the winter, whether the horse was a chestnut or a bay. And everything would awaken yet again.

But in the depth of the black months, when the light was short-lived and cold, there was a great deal to do, even though you took your time about it: trimming the slopes, cutting firewood to feed the hearth, heating the bread oven, selling some of your bread to the town's baker; looking after the drains in the meadows, making new fencing, keeping a watch on your land, cutting and crushing gorse for the horses (if need be, in a stone trough, with the help of a wooden mallet that had a curved handle to make the task easier); weaving baskets, repairing the harnesses and the tethers, carving new posts; going to the forge when you really had something to forge; and bringing yourself to call in the veterinarian if you were unable to relieve a constipated mare. Yet that was easy enough: to clear its bowels, you had merely to slip your hand into the right place and then give it a good enema. Not so difficult that you had to trouble a gentleman trained at a university.

Nevertheless, the winter season always added to the woes of the poor, even if they had laid up enough supplies and enough small coins to enable them to await the coming springtime without too many hardships. Winter was truly black, not only because the break of day was late and the night came on too quickly, but because of the black cold, the black mud, the black rain, the black wind, and the black daily anguishes. Because of the black solitude, the black illnesses, and black death.

The old inscription that appears on the La Martyr charnel house, in the Léon region of Brittany, speaks of a cold Hell. It is more striking, and has been for a longer time, than the flames lying in wait, according to the mission preachers, for bad Christians, which we're all in danger of being at every moment. The man with the hoe was not afraid of heat, even extreme heat; but he did dread the cold hell of the world he lived in, where three noteworthy ailments were prevalent: sneezing, coughing, and diarrhea. That was why life in all the houses was organized around the hearth, where the whole family would gather, for there was no heat in the other rooms. The manger and the stable, if there was one, were also favorite spots, because the animals gave off heat which you could share. I knew of places where nothing but a door separated the animals from the people. And that door was left open when the cold was black.

Sneezing, coughing, and diarrhea. The first wasn't worth worrying about; the second was very annoying when it persisted, but not serious enough for you to stay in bed; the third was the most fearsome because it emptied you out—and farewell to your work! Cider drinkers are said to have delicate intestines. And delicate kidneys as well. What the man with the hoe martyrized all through the day and all year round was his back. No wonder so many peasants were broken down before their time, clutching sticks that they might walk and unable to look straight ahead without dislocating their necks. The poor women were no exception.

In Brittany "the Old Week" is the last week of the year. Actually, it begins precisely at Christmas and lasts until New Year's Day. Between the first Monday of that week (Saint Etienne's Day) and Saturday (Saint Sylvester's Day), the farmhands' and the servants' time used to be their own, and they were perfectly free to do with it as they pleased. It was their only holiday of the year. Those who wanted to marry would have their weddings at that time, whereas the farmers' children could lead their loves to the altar at their own convenience, unless there was urgent work to be done. However, for those who intended to keep their jobs, "the Old Week" was mostly an opportunity to live it up, whereas those who were tired of "the old soup" would go off and look for something better.

As for the big farmers, they had every inch of the work on their hands during "the Old Week," since their farmhands would spend all day in town or visiting their relatives. The boss would take care of the horses and pigs. His wife, deprived of a maid, would find plenty to do, what with the cows and the housework. Sometimes the farmhand or the maid had not yet agreed to return for the coming year. Things hadn't worked out because of, say, a blue cotton jacket or a pair of wooden sabots. It was perhaps nothing much, but it was reason enough to break a contract. There was also the possibility that during one of those days another big farmer would offer more money in order to steal a farmhand who was known to be a hard worker, or a maid who knew how to manage both in the house and in the fields. So the big farmer's wife would put herself out to prepare a feast a day for her people, if they happened to be there, while the big farmer himself would always be in good spirits and was constantly opening his tobacco pouch. All that lasted until New Year's Eve. Then, those who were still undecided would announce that they'd stick with "the old soup." The free week had expired. The next day they would all wish each other a Happy New Year and start off once again on their 358 days of joint labor, which lasted from dawn on into the night. There were no fixed hours. The farmhand's watch, or the maid's, served only as an ornament. The Angelus was enough for telling time.

Gathering seaweed

Daybreak in Brittany

7 The Book of Golden Hours

> As the background for a novel, one single day in the life of a peasant can be as effective as a century of European history.
>
> Tolstoy

Yann ar Vinell's phlegmy voice burst out into the dry morning, louder than the noise of the wooden sabots and the women's laughter. That gay blade never let a skirt go by without making some joke so that the face above it would blush. I was still in bed, curled up between my quilts like a pip in the middle of an apple. And suddenly there he was, rapping on the door as hard as he could, and shouting in that thick voice of his: "Marie-Jeanne, it's time to heat the water!" My mother rushed to the door, removed the bar, and opened it to Yann ar Vinell. He was a lord who didn't like to be kept waiting; also, a man who was quite capable of going to the Devil and staying there until Mardi Gras, especially if it was for reasons of thirst, his favorite ailment. Still, who else could have taken charge of our pig?

Any ass of a man can kill a pig. All he has to do is to stick a big knife into its throat and wait until all its blood has emptied out. But we fed our pigs for the express purpose of obtaining salt pork. And the quality of the salt pork, according to Yann ar Vinell, depended as much on the animal's death as on its life. One had to kill pigs the same way as one picked certain fruit: with countless precautions and a prayer beforehand. Otherwise, they would take their revenge by offending your eyes, nose, and tongue, and ruining your reputation to boot. Yann ar Vinell was not just any butcher; he was a certified pig-killer. The best proof of it was that he never sharpened his tools for an animal that was unknown to him, one that hadn't been introduced to him the minute it was bought at the fair in Pont-Croix. I must admit that every introduction was, out of courtesy, accompanied by a good slug of brandy. From then on, the dear little pig was Yann's godchild. Its godfather performed the operation necessary to put its body at rest so that it would desire nothing but food and thrive on it. After which, he ran a wire through its nose. And it was at the cost of that wire that the pig bought wisdom and learned not to burrow in the ground lest its salt pork be spoiled.

Once the animal weighed about two hundred pounds, Yann would come from time to time to feel its back and the folds in its thighs. During the last two or three weeks of fattening, the women would ask his advice as to the best mash to prepare for the dear pig so that it would have firm, thick skin and shining bristles—the two signs of good health that are never misleading. Yann ar Vinell would work out his recipes according to each animal's particular temperament. And it was he, of course, who chose the best day for the sacrifice of the fat prince. That was no easy task, believe me! The season and, above all, the moon had to be taken into account. I don't recall whether it was the waxing that was more favorable than the waning or vice versa, but I do know that you had to avoid salting the meat while the "wolf's sun" was shining—that is, when there was a full moon—otherwise, the brine wouldn't do its job. Where in the world had Yann learned that rule? Only from personal experience? Sometimes the scandalmongers would whisper in your ear that Yann ar Vinell's actions were governed by his thirst. If that ogre preferred to kill his godsons when the moon wasn't out, it was not at all because of the brine or because, for some reason, he was heartbroken. It was so that he could get home before midnight without anybody seeing him. For he was never alone. He was always dragging about a magnificent binge, which led him to kiss the road every fifty feet at the expense of his cheekbones or his nose. Despite his cat's eyes, he occasionally even ran smack into some wall and remained right where he was, collapsed into a heap, until dawn. The first passerby would shake that pile of snoring clothes, and straightaway our Yann would be sitting up cross-legged, grinning from ear to ear, happy as could be to have regained his thirst. And he would take off like a shot to do in another pig, his moustache still damp from the morning dew, his only toilet water.

He appeared in front of the table before I had the time to get out of my box-bed and pull on the other leg of my trousers. My mother had fled behind the house to stir up the fire under the boiler. My father had gotten the pig out of its sty and prepared the sacrificial table in the small farmyard. Grandfather had disappeared, as he generally did every time he had to part company with a domestic animal. He was soft-hearted, even though he had a great fondness for salt pork.

Yann had thrown a handful of big knives on the table, their blades gleaming in the low light of the gas lamp. It was still too early for much daylight to come shining through the window. Next to the lamp was a bottle of brandy and a glass. The master-killer winked at me. He put out the lamp before he poured himself a drink. The old fox! He came up to me and, with his big hand, began to ruffle my hair. "Should I keep the bladder for you, kid?" he asked. I was so moved that I couldn't even pronounce half of the word *yes*. To show that we were accomplices, he breathed in my face, and the smell was so strong I almost fainted. Then he took off with his clinking knives. I finally got my trousers on, grabbed my jacket from the bench, and dashed out like a colt at grips with a gadfly. The great day had come.

I had scarcely made it to the doorstep when, from behind, I heard the indignant shrieking of the pig in its death throes. Yann ar Vinell's big knife had done its job in the farmyard. The whole town already knew that fresh meat was being prepared to be put into the larder of a well-to-do mortal—no one other than myself. I held my head very high and slipped my heels slightly out of my sabots to look taller. Three women were already on the road, commenting on the event to the world at large. Then the three of them, in loud voices, began to sing my mother's praises. Behind the house the pig's lamentations were growing weaker and weaker. What a rite! Other people, both men and women, stopped to make inquiries, shooting swift glances at the bundle of pride which happened to be me. But I didn't see one single child. Maybe they were sick with jealousy. Maybe they didn't want to pay me the tribute of their respect. What pitiful Christians! They would have to hurry if they wanted to hear, in my presence, the final groans of an exceptional pig, my very own.

There they were at last, running to our place from all sides, with traces of coffee soup on their little mugs. Feeling magnanimous, I forgave them and waited.

"Is that your pig, Perig?" they asked.

"Yes, mine. And a fine specimen of a pig it is, believe me. Yann ar Vinell almost didn't manage to finish it off. So you can imagine!"

Their eyes were beaming with admiration.

"Do you think . . . could I have . . . the bladder?" stammered the youngest one.

Before I had time to answer, the poor kid nearly had his head bitten off by the others and had learned, once and for all, that no one either gives or sells a pig's bladder outside of the family because it brings bad luck. I granted him an indulgent smile. "There now," I said. "It's time I went in and gave them a hand." And I walked into the house, looking very self-important and leaving all the humble little people gaping in front of the door.

In the small farmyard behind, three shadows were rushing about in the heavy steam from the boiling water. And since the winds had shifted in the wrong direction, and the fireplace in the shed wasn't drawing too well, the smoke from the hearth was blowing all over my pig, stretched out on the table, absolutely dead from top to bottom. "Come on, let's hurry it up!" shouted Yann ar Vinell, "or else this martyr's going to turn into a sausage." His big knife, sharp as a razor blade, "shaved off the animal's beard," as we say—in other words, removed all its bristles. My father scalded the body with pailfuls of water. My mother, coughing a bit from the smoke, trimmed the ears until there wasn't a hair left on them. The entire process took very little time. The last pail of water was used to put out the fire under the boiler; the smoky steam finally evaporated; and the pig just lay there for everyone to see, completely naked, not even shivering in the west-northwest wind, its tender flesh like that of a baby monster.

Soon afterward, it was hung on a rafter in the shed, upside down. Yann stood in front of it, his legs apart, sharpening another knife. He then cut the animal open straight down the middle and began to work inside it with both arms. Once he had detached the viscera, he crammed them down to about chest-level. I saw those amazing organs shine; they were stretched to the breaking point and were a blend of pink, waxy yellow, and faded blue. "He died in good health, the old brute!" declared Yann ar Vinell. It was his usual joke. I kept wondering where the bladder was in all that.

The killer turned his head around to look at me. His moustache was steaming slightly. The bladder! Wasn't it that thick and flabby windbag he was holding in his mouth? As he blew, it started to swell up and become round, until it finally looked like a somewhat alarming balloon. It was quivering a bit, just enough to make you think it was alive. A knot at the bottom and it was done! Yann ar Vinell bent down to offer me, as a token of esteem . . . that thing. I hesitated for a moment before taking the bladder. Actually, I would much rather have had a "pardon" ball—preferably a yellow one. But after all, I had to go and show my trophy to the others. Honor makes certain demands. Besides, if the children didn't see the bladder, they would have been perfectly capable of telling everyone they knew that my pig was a pitiful animal since it hadn't had what it should have had inside. Well, then. I had to take it with some show of enthusiasm.

But out on the road there wasn't one gawking kid left to gaze with wonder upon my bladder. The children my own age had been summoned to tend the cows. The younger ones were playing watchdog in front of their own empty houses or rocking some bawling baby. Fine! It would just have to wait. Meanwhile, I hung the organic balloon on the wire that served as our clothesline. That way, it would dry faster in the wind and the air. My mother was preparing clean kitchen towels to place under the quarters of meat. And—well, well!—there was Grandfather with a supply of coarse salt and saltpeter. Yann ar Vinell was downing a glass of red wine and, between gulps, overwhelming my mother with compliments so that she'd forget to take the bottle away. The dear pig was about to be entombed in its next to last home. It was a moment of great seriousness. If the salt pork turned rancid, everyone in that room would have been covered with shame. Me too; I'd have been the first. I was somewhat relieved to see that we'd kept some brine from the previous year so that it might apprise the new brine of its duty. There's nothing like experience.

The pig was cut into pieces, and that job alone proved that Yann was a master of his craft. With his knife, he cut off portions that were precisely the right size, neither too big nor too small. Portions so flawless that they deserved to exist in their own right, quite apart from any pig. The finest of them, which had been rubbed all over with salt, were placed at the bottom of the larder, forming a perfect circle, with their thick skin against the terra cotta. Never in his life had the poor animal received that much attention. The slabs of flesh were distributed in such a way that the whole resembled a mosaic, each slab having been cut to fit into the next. The pig was recreated in its tomb so that it would last a year in the best possible condition, drowned in salt and free of all the cheap cuts as well as its natural delicacies, which would soon be made into pâté or stuffed into a sausage. The cover was cautiously placed on the sarcophagus; everyone breathed freely again; and Yann, in a faint voice, asked whether there wasn't a chance of finding something more to drink, even if it meant searching the house on all fours. Otherwise, he said, we could add his death to our list of sins. And laughed.

The following day my mother took the pâté over to the baker's oven to be cooked. She had put aside the best pieces of fresh meat, the "*freskadennou*." Some of them were to be distributed to our closest neighbors so they would know how the animal tasted. They, on the other hand, never failed, when their own pig was killed, to offer us a piece that was an exact equivalent of the one they had received from us. And they never made a mistake, nor did we. The size of the piece was in proportion to the warmth of the friendship. That was why my mother wrapped each one in a white kitchen towel and concealed the parcel under her apron before crossing the road and walking ten or fifty yards to bring it to the woman for whom it was destined. The latter, if she were polite, would never show the gift to anyone, nor would she ever make it a point to see what the others had received. That was wisdom itself, the kind of wisdom that ensured good feeling among neighbors and made it possible for you to eat fresh meat several times a year, whereas your usual meals consisted of salt pork.

But the biggest piece of the "*freskadennou*" was to be roasted for a feast that took place two days later. We would invite our close relatives and the friends we saw regularly. They would all come, unless some one of them was in bed, dying. No other excuse was valid. They would bring along with them unfailing appetites as well as a spirit of good will that always lasted right to the end—to the final drink.

The "pig feast" was one of the outstanding events of the year for those who had the means to own a pig. People who kept salt pork in their larders all the year round were considered to be well off, however modest their resources. They would always have fat on their potatoes due to their quarter of salted meat, which was at the core of the meal. That cold quarter on a plate would have a place of honor in the middle of the table every time the men's strength needed to be replenished. And what a compliment for the house it was to hear someone say: "Over there, you always have meat staring you in the face." Such houses were never at a loss for strong arms to help out with the most difficult jobs. That was because the men in the fields thought that daily food was of the greatest importance, perhaps even more important than their pay, which was always very low. A big farmer who didn't feed his household well would have trouble finding farmhands. And the ultimate in food was meat, while the ultimate in meat was pork. Of course, there was the fresh meat at the butcher's, but it was too expensive for most people, and country people didn't have the time to go into town several times a week. Besides, it was fresh—in other words, tasteless to salt-lovers. There was nothing like salt pork, especially on rye bread, which served as a plate. And who would ever dream of eating fresh meat on bread like that?

On Sundays we did eat beef or veal as a change from the weekly fare on the farms. Or, now and then, a hutch rabbit or a dung-fed cock or a farmyard fowl, if only because we saw no reason for feeding those animals for the bourgeoisie alone. But during the first ten years of my life I don't think I saw ten chickens on the table in my house. When there happened to be one, it was because the wife of a farmer, a friend of my mother's, had given it to us as a gift. Like all women, my mother did buy fresh meat as often as her pocketbook would allow. It was a matter of prestige. In town everybody knew how many times a month this or that woman went to the butcher's. It was her business to know that if she went too often, she would get the reputation of being a spendthrift or pretentious; she also knew that she had to go from time to time if she didn't want people to think she was out of cash. Moreover, it was understood that one did not receive strangers or relatives on great occasions without roasting fresh meat on the fire. For fresh meat was a part of all our ceremonial rites, whether on feast days or for very special receptions.

Because of the peasants' decided preference for meat, they usually scowled at the idea of fish, which they were doomed to eat every Friday, the day of abstinence. It was thus "Lenten and penitential fare." But also, it didn't retain the body's heat, as would a slice of salt pork. Food for the poor and the miserly. Not so very long ago, the farmhands along the banks of the Aulne stipulated in their contracts that their employers would not make them eat salmon more than twice or three times a week. There was good reason to swallow it down once, to do penance for one's sins, and a second time to show one's good will; but even three times was a bit much. In Pouldreuzig we hadn't the slightest idea of what river salmon was. But there used to be at least a half-dozen fishing boats at the port at Penhors. It would have been easy for us to stuff ourselves with mackerel and sardines, which were much cheaper than salt pork or fresh meat. And those aquatic animals are absolutely delicious sautéed in well-browned butter. We were surrounded by fishing ports, all of them crawling with boats: Douarnenez and Audierne to the north of us; Penmarc'h, Guilvinec, and Lesconcil to the south. But most of us ate fish only, and half-heartedly, on Fridays, having been ordered to do so by the rector. Since there was no fishmonger in the region, one of them from Douarnenez would come by on Fridays. However, in the twenties he began not showing up as regularly as he'd used to. The profit he made wasn't worth the journey. So we would eat eggs, pancakes, potatoes, or gruel. In the country there is always something you can find to fill your stomach. And you were a good Christian, even without fish.

Fish, as I mentioned above, was too light a food for people who did manual labor. Also, you had to empty each one of them out; and what a mess of trouble that was! Then, once they were cooked, you had to struggle with the sly bones, which made the men nervous; they didn't have that kind of patience. What they wanted was something they could eat without having to take precautions, and right down to the last bite, something they themselves had produced and knew all about.

Moreover, there was a veiled antagonism between the fishermen and the peasants, even though the former were sometimes descendants of the latter or related to them. And in our very own port at Penhors the fishermen had cows and potato fields as well. But there was nothing for it! The fishermen were apt to call the peasants louts, misers, and faint-hearted worm-cutters. And the peasants, for whom the sea was the great unknown, though they could see it from their hills and could hear it rumbling in their sleep, those peasants tended to consider the fishermen as thriftless, lacking in foresight, and even lazy—idlers who, when on land, would stick their hands deep down into their pockets and watch the waves break into foam. I might add that to the fishermen, the peasants were all reactionary White scoundrels, led by the Church. To the peasants there was not one fisherman who wasn't a Red revolutionary working incessantly to provoke a major upheaval. That was because the fishermen risked their lives for a mere pittance, perhaps not even that, whereas the peasants always had at least a bite to eat and never failed to have land under their feet. A perpetual misunderstanding among people who lived in the same county, sometimes even the same commune, and who, in any case, individually, were capable of being the best of friends, like the Reds and the Whites when no election was in the offing. But the peasants' bias against fish was, in some measure, a result of that latent antagonism between two ways of life, plus the fact that men who work the land stick resolutely to food that's tried and true, and rarely run the risk of experimenting with anything else.

As for shellfish, including crustaceans, they ranked lowest in our hierarchy of food. Lobsters, crayfish, and even prawns were almost unheard of. Although there were no oysters in the region, we did know they existed, and not too far away. Yet we had never seen any. Much later on, there was a doctor's maid who reported to her master in a rage: "What wrong did you do to Monsieur N? He sent you a package of stones to make fun of you!" The stones were oysters, and the good woman had thrown them into the manure heap. It was the doctor himself who told me the story. The strangest part of it was that, at the time, even he hadn't known what those particular stones were. One *karabasenn*, or priest's housekeeper, had been more conscientious. She had undertaken to break the stones in question in order to see what was inside. Shortly afterward, the rector saw her appear, with a disgusted look on her face, carrying a large bowl into which she had poured the slimy creatures, like so many eggs about to be beaten into an omelet. Another *karabasenn* did quite the opposite. She served the empty shells during a "pardon" meal to which a half-dozen clergymen had been invited. And when the rector glanced at her in amazement, she cried out, sorely offended: "Well, what about it? I took their bowels out, didn't I?" In any case, my own mother waited until she was seventy-five before she finally agreed to try one. "At my age," she said, "nothing can hurt me anymore."

After the meat from our own animals, it was the flour from our own grain that gratified us the most. We were very hard to please when it came to the smell, taste, and consistency of the food we made with it, starting with bread. Many of our parents found buckwheat or "black" bread the best treat of all, especially when it was stale. They found that it went supremely well with salt pork. White bread was particularly good with sauces and butter. It was rich bread, but not the best, probably not the kind we would have kept in the house if we'd had the choice. But we did enjoy eating it when it was fresh and even warm. Bread for the lower middle class, which we were fast becoming. Bread you could eat everywhere and anywhere with no problem. As for rye bread, it was eaten in the strictest privacy. If other people ever offered you some, it was proof of total confidence.

Anyone who had ever watched a Breton peasant eating his piece of bread knew what gastronomy was. A peasant would cut his chunk straight from the loaf; he did not like being served slices that had been cut in advance. He enjoyed smelling his bread between bites, chewing it slowly and peacefully, moving it from one side of his mouth to the other before swallowing. And you had to see the attentive expression on his face and the look of concentration in his eyes while he was indulging. It was almost like celebrating Mass—the Mass of our daily bread. Indeed! Who had sown, hoed, cut, and then threshed the grain that was destined for that peerless food? Who had broken his back and got dripping wet if not he? The time had come to taste the fruits of his labor.

When my mother cut bread for soup, she would line the bottom of the tureen with slices of white bread. Then she'd add a few slices of buckwheat bread before pouring in ladlefuls of potatoes. Thus the buckwheat would give the white bread some taste. But apart from the "big" Sunday soup, with meat and vegetables, which would always simmer on the fire from the end of six o'clock Mass to the end of High Mass, the best soup of all was what I ate every morning, because it was absolutely indispensable to the work that lay ahead. When I used to get up to go to school, there was never anyone in the house; by that time they had all left. My very own bowl was right next to the fire, flecked with ashes. It was smaller than the others, as was only fitting, and covered with a plate to keep the soup warm and to be sure that no soot from the fireplace would fall in. It was coffee soup—in other words, especially sumptuous. Before covering it, my mother would place two lumps of sugar at the bottom, imagine? Two! They would slowly melt and soak into the bread, which was not sliced but cubed. As I picked up my spoon, I would give thanks to the admirable man who had invented the bowl. What made the meat-based Sunday soup rather disappointing was the fact that I had to eat it ceremoniously out of a plate. Soup tastes good only when served in a bowl, like salad. Just listen to this!

In 1960 I was asked by the government to lunch with a woman doctor from Nicaragua—a very beautiful woman, and at first sight, extremely reserved and haughty. She couldn't speak much French, and I had never been able to utter the simplest word in English without making such extraordinary sounds that whatever I said was unintelligible. In short, our conversation during most of the meal was not exactly sparkling. Then we were served our salad.

The doctor's huge black eyes grew even bigger. And the lady

made it eminently clear that she was deeply offended by the look of the greens. I was covered with sweat by the time I finally came to understand that the Nicaraguan liked salad very much, but was repelled by oil. She began talking to me with great excitement, almost with passion, gesticulating with her beringed hands. And I looked at her with new interest. Was it possible that, in all that exotic chatter, there was some question of sugar? I called the head waiter and asked for granulated sugar and some salad without any seasoning whatever. Then, with a little water and a dash of vinegar, the lady and I proceeded to make ourselves a "sugar salad." I admit that I left the greater part of the preparations to her, for she was clearly better at it than I. And the salad "à la Nicaraguaise" had exactly the same taste as the salad I used to eat in Pouldreuzic (Finistère) when I was growing up.

We laughed like two babies who had just become acquainted and were playing together with their little hands. The doctor's black eyes became like velvet; she showed her irreproachable teeth; she had stopped thinking about medicine. And I would have kissed her solemnly, with all my heart, in front of three dozen people, because she demanded a bowl in which to eat her sugar salad. She was a highly civilized woman—a woman worthy of having been born in the Bigouden region. I was tempted to speak to her in Breton. From then on, to my mind, Nicaragua was a great power.

The fact was that, along with coffee soup, sugar salad had been the great joy of my childhood. As I savored each leaf, it would tell me stories about maybugs, the wild wind, playing hooky, and cows that were lost and found again. On May evenings I used to love to go and sit on my stone doorstep, holding my bowl of salad between my knees. The people who passed by on the road would smile at me and never fail to say: "The best is at the bottom, my boy!" I bloody well knew it. I'd begin by rushing through the big leaves on top, those that were less steeped in the dressing. And as I made my way down into the bowl, right to the heart of lettuce which my mother always put at the bottom, I would revel in the sugar and vinegar, enchanted—each and every time—by the thought that there were such good things on earth. When I licked the last drop, always getting a bit on the tip of my nose, I would come to despise the roasts of meat on which, according to my grandfather, the fabulous lords of this world fed twice a day. And perhaps at those very same moments, a little girl from Nicaragua was gaining the very same knowledge of higher philosophy.

But alas! I had to go to the lycée. Apparently I was too intelligent to stay in the country without either some land or a shop. I don't know whether that was true. What I do know is that at first I formed a low opinion of urban civilization when, sitting at a marble table in the dining hall, I was served a salad hideously dressed with oil. It took me a whole year to get used to that medicinal concoction. It made me so sick to my stomach that I almost quit school. However, I had to resign myself to it. And in saying farewell to sugar salad, I made my first discovery of Purgatory's homely face.

For the evening meal we usually ate *poaz-dizeh* (dry-cooked) potatoes with milk. But twice a week we had either wheaten or oatmeal gruel. I seem to remember that we all preferred the oatmeal. Once the pot was on the fire, my mother would get busy stirring vigorously with her gruel stick, which always stood in a corner of the hearth—the very same stick that our parents used to threaten to break over our backs if we refused to behave. When the gruel was ready, the pot was placed on the table. Each of us armed himself with a spoon and attacked his own section of it, starting at the edge and working toward the middle, where a lump of butter was gently melting in a hole called the "fountain." Before swallowing, we would dip the gruel-filled spoon into a bowl of milk to cool it off. But when we got to the butter, which had spread as it melted, we preferred to dispense with the milk, even if we did burn our tongues a bit. We were all forbidden to encroach upon anyone else's section. My mother was very strict about that. "Don't forget your table manners," she'd say sternly. We didn't have the right to thrust our spoons into the "fountain" either. Once the pot was empty, we would scrape off what was left on the bottom, and that too was evenly divided among us. But somehow—I don't know why—I always got the biggest portion.

At noon, several times a week, we used to eat a thick wheaten pancake. My mother would set the griddle—a very large (70 cm.)

round sheet of cast iron—on a tripod. She would first heat it on a fire made of pine needles, sawdust, dry gorse, or small kindling, and keep a close eye on that fire while, using only her hands, she made the batter in an earthenware bowl. To be sure that the griddle was hot enough, she'd spit on it (fire purifies all), then dry it, and grease it with a *lardig*, a dish towel that had been soaking in an old bowl filled with a mixture of lard and egg yokes. Everything was ready. She'd run her finger through the batter one last time to test the consistency, then dip a good-size ladle into it, and pour the batter into the middle of the large round pan. With her other hand, and a small wooden rake called a *rozell*, she'd spread it evenly over the entire griddle. As it was cooking, my mother would drop the *rozell* and grab hold of a long wooden scraper-spatula (a *spanell*) with which she'd lift the pancake, starting at the edges. That was the hardest part, for she had to turn the huge pancake over all at once and make certain that it fell directly on top of the griddle; otherwise it would break up into horrid little rolls of soft dough that turned your stomach and made the cook blush with shame. When the first pancake was finished, it was quickly lifted up with the *spanell* and thrown onto a large napkin that had previously been spread on the table. That first one was to serve as a rug, ready to receive all the others, each of them oozing with butter.

Making crêpes is both easier—because, since the batter is light and thin, you don't need as much strength—and trickier, because your every movement must be absolutely precise and you have to be quicker and more agile in maneuvering the *rozell* and the *spanell*. Whenever my mother refused to make crêpes, you could be sure she was not in good shape or was overtired that day. Or there was too much wind blowing down the chimney so that the fire wouldn't heat evenly, which meant that the crêpes would be burnt on one side and softish on the other. Now a housewife took pride, not in turning out a good stew or a fine roast, but in making flawless crêpes. To our taste, flawless crêpes had to be brown and crackling (*kraz*) around the edges and slightly softer in the middle, the "nest" where one first placed the lump of butter before spreading it over the rest. Traditionally, buckwheat crêpes were folded in half with the *spanell*, whereas the wheaten variety were folded in four. But not until they were buttered. Most of the other people didn't do that, however, for two reasons: because butter was too expensive, and because true gourmets preferred dry crêpes, with their flavor intact, unchanged by the fat.

For a whole meal of crêpes, which was served once a week, often on Fridays, we would each have a plate that was used for nothing but buttered crêpes. And the very presence of that plate indicated that it was a gala luncheon. For while you'd never ask anyone over to eat pancakes, you would willingly invite a guest to sample your crêpes if you had no doubts about your talents as a housewife. Moreover, a meal of crêpes was sufficient unto itself. It would have been an insult to the crêpe-maker if you asked for anything else.

I must say that for our ordinary everyday meals, we never had more than one course. Twice or three times a year, and always on the eve of a pardon, my mother made a bowl of an especially solid rice pudding, which she brought to the baker's to be cooked. All the other women did the same. When the whole batch was taken out of the oven, you'd see the women coming home with their bowls still hot and covered with a corner of their aprons. Then the pudding would be cut into firm thick slices. As for cakes, in most of the houses, rich or poor, they were almost never made more than once a year, on the "Fat Days"—that is, the three days preceding Ash Wednesday. And, then, what rejoicing!

On Saturday the rice was cooked and the pork sausages were soaked in water. Sunday, Monday, and Tuesday were devoted to sumptuous food and festivities. Night and day the roads were filled with families walking from house to house, visiting one another, for it was the practice to swap pieces of cake. Compliments would fly in every direction. If some woman happened to make a disastrous mess of her cake, she would never fail to put the blame squarely on the baker, who had mistaken one tag for another and had given her a monstrosity made by some other woman who didn't have any idea of how to knead her dough, poor thing. Everyone would pretend to be taken in by the lie. A week of benevolence.

Then came Wednesday, with the ashes of Lent and also the thick pancakes, the potato soup, the fish and their bones, and the coarse bread all over again. Fasts and vigils twice a week. But that wasn't enough to depress courageous people. To them gluttony meant eating one's fill, which was authorized from time to time, but which could well have degenerated into a deadly sin had it not been redeemed by periods of wholesome frugality. Yet for all that, and especially when you were crossing the arid desert of Lent, there was nothing that forbade you to keep some means of consoling yourself. And it was the cake of the "Fat Days" which served that purpose and helped you cheerfully make your way to Palm Sunday.

In point of fact, everyone had always taken great pains with their preparations and their dough, and had been extremely generous. After five days of feasting, their cupboards were generally still filled with pieces of cake—their own as well as gifts from relatives and friends. When the pieces that weren't her own had been swallowed down, each housewife would uncover an entire loaf of cake which she had hidden at the bottom of the linen cupboard. Hypocritical amazement. But everyone knew that there were reserves stored away. And they were our salvation until *Reminiscere*. Perhaps you think that was the end of the fun and games? Far from it! There were houses—my own, for example—in which each member of the family, young or old, had his own personal cake which did not have to be shared. It was up to him to make it last as long as possible, even if he had to hide it in the most unlikely places. Every day he would go to it for slice after slice of comfort. Of course, in terms of slices, it lasted two weeks at the most. Even before *Oculi* Sunday, the cake was so dry and so hard that you had to deal it a strong blow to get yourself a chunk.

Actually, it was only the younger people, boys and girls, who tried to save those terrific pastries for so long a time. First of all, to show that they were thrifty and capable of not falling into the "Sugar Devil's" traps, as they were called by the elderly. Secondly, because the act of offering a piece of cake to a girl at least two weeks after Mardi Gras had, in the past, been tantamount to a declaration of love, and traces of that custom had survived. The older the cake, the stronger the young man's feelings. Of course, when the girl accepted that symbolic gift, she had to be in a position to give him a piece of her own cake. It was her way of saying yes.

As for the women—at any rate, those who could afford it—coffee was the glory of their daily life. And they were ready to make any sacrifice in order to have the means to buy it. Tears used to come to the eyes of those who'd see the Planter from Haifa's little cart when they had nothing in their purses but the leavings of a church mouse. Coffee was expensive. Men hadn't yet attached any importance to it. They still preferred their morning soup and their four o'clock salt pork. Besides, they didn't trust that devilish temptation, that perdition of households, that woman's drug. Once one of them returned home unexpectedly in the middle of the afternoon and walked in on a half-dozen housewives gathered round a new coffee pot he had never seen before. The matrons were trying to outdo each other in tearing the trappings of innocence off their fellow creatures. The blood rushed to his head. He grabbed the coffee pot and emptied it out of the window. Then, unbuttoning the flap of his trousers, he peed into the pot. But he needn't have bothered. His wife had the last word.

Even then, however, children were given coffee in the morning more often than soup. And everything pointed to the possibility that coffee would win over those men-to-be who had become their mothers' accomplices. Four in the afternoon, in all respectable houses, was the time for coffee-bread-and-butter. The Anglo-Saxons' tea. All work would come to a stop unless it was harvest time. Full bowls of coffee were served, since cups were no better than thimbles. When you're used to picking up a bowl with both hands, how can you possibly grab hold of a ridiculous little handle with a finger or two? In any case, during the coffee ceremony it was your duty as a woman or a child not to offend anyone, even if some bourgeoise happened to hand you a cup. You would invite not only your neighbors, your friends, and the people in your "coterie," but all those to whom you wished to do honor and especially anyone to whom you owed something. And even more especially, those who had previously invited you for coffee. That was mandatory. If a woman had coffee debts, she could not die unless her daughter had promised to discharge them in her name.

Once a year every family that belonged to a "group," or "coterie," or merely a "neighborhood" had to invite all the others to the house (it being understood, of course, that each one would delegate a representative or two, the mistress of the house, necessarily, and perhaps one other) for what was called "New Year's Coffee." Those receptions took place two or three times a week, between the day after Christmas and the end of January. In any case, they had to be over before the Sunday preceding Mardi Gras. They were a combination of afternoon snack and dinner, which would begin after four o'clock and end during the evening, for it was a matter of courtesy that no one leave before the master of the house and the other working men had returned to have a last bite with them and drink the last drop before going home. At the start, then, there were only women and small children. They'd begin with a variety of cold pork meats, washed down with a mellow white wine. The aged red wine was on the table, but was uncorked only for the men, since the women never dared to drink it among themselves for fear of being called *toullou-piketez* (cheap-wine holes). They then went on to a roast of fresh meat, because salt pork was kept exclusively for the family or for guests who dropped in unexpectedly. Meanwhile, the mistress of the house was busy making fresh coffee, which would be served along with bread, butter, a platter of cold crêpes, slices of rice pudding, and—the ultimate in luxury—cookies. It was at one of those New Year's coffees that, in a well-to-do house, I first tasted long cookies called "boudoirs." Afterward, my mother, in order to keep up, bought some as well. What I did not know was that she had spent the whole autumn making frightful sacrifices in order to save up enough money to finance that feast. Of course, it was understood that each woman would keep up her position as well as she could, that she would do her very best. But if you had enough money to serve your guests cherry brandy, it did not mean they had to serve it to you in return if it cost more than they could afford. Indeed, it was considered advisable that the rich not spend too much so as not to tempt the poor into going beyond their means. One of the first presents I ever gave my mother when I had begun to earn some money was a bottle of cherry brandy, which enabled her to be as generous as she thought necessary.

At that time people still never put fruit on the table. Ever. But during those yearly coffees it was customary for the mistress of the house to show all her guests everything new she had acquired since the previous year—from faience plates to the latest in stoves.

What a shock I got the first time my mother and I entered a room that was separate from the kitchen and called a "dining room"! In it was a table with leaves (we were given a detailed explanation of how it worked), a lot of chairs, all alike (our own had been bought one by one, or at most, two by two), and a strange-looking sideboard crammed full of dishes, a dozen of each kind. That dining room wasn't to be used again until the next year, unless there happened to be some very special event. The women cried out in admiration; some of them were pale with jealousy. But it was understood that not a bitter word, not an unpleasant allusion, and no quarrels whatever were permissible during the coffee ceremony. If a woman had anything disagreeable to say, she would have the rest of the year to get her own back. The coffee ceremony was a time for compliments. "Giving leeks" was what we called paying compliments. For everybody liked leeks. And that day entire bunches of them rained down.

Out of courtesy, you also had to eat a bit of everything that was served, whether you liked it or not. On one of those coffee days, and in my very own house, I saw a plate brought to the table filled with slices of rather repulsive red vegetables that turned my stomach. They were tomatoes. Most of the women got a panic-stricken look in their eyes. But we all bravely pitched in. And they weren't as bad as you might have thought.

Once a year, generally in the winter, we also had to visit those relatives who lived in the neighboring communes, Plozévet or Landudec. We would leave very early, on foot, and come back that same night. If there happened to be too many houses to call on, we always chose the poorest of them, for the rich have their wealth, whereas the poor have nothing but their pride. In any case, we would eat all sorts of things at each of our relatives', and counted on the long walks and all the climbing of slopes to keep our digestive juices flowing.

Thus, in our society, food was clearly a matter of the greatest importance. Not only because it was of serious concern to the peasant, whose ancestors had experienced centuries of hardship, intensified from time to time by famines, which hadn't been entirely forgotten. Not only because it was the fate of our people to grow food for themselves and for many others. But also because that food, on the one hand, was responsible for everybody's health, and, on the other hand, made it possible to judge the quality of the relationships that united the various social groups. Food was considered respectable from the time it was sown to the time it was eliminated. And of the three reasons for good health—*debri mad, kaohad mad, koused mad* ("eating well, shitting well, sleeping well")—the last is dependent on the first two.

A man named Yann K never failed to walk across one or another of his fields at dawn, before the sun had completely risen. After a short while, he would suddenly feel like "undoing his breeches" or "squatting down." With the sharp edge of his spade, he'd cut a cube of earth out of the side of a slope facing away from the road. Then, with great care, he would proceed to relieve himself into the hole. When he had finished, he would consider what had come out of him. The consistency was good and the color was fine. Our man would put the cube of earth back with his spade and make his way home, whistling and light of foot. All was well: there was nothing to worry about. He would not think of death for the whole day. Yann's life was organized around the noises made by his innards. When he burped after the noon meal, he'd be beside himself with joy. But hiccups put him into a state of anxiety. And when his faeces looked and smelled unhealthy, he'd feel like going to see the priest to arrange for a Mass to be said for his dead. People laughed at him a little, but not too much. In fact, almost not at all.

Now drinking and especially eating were the true barometers of family relationships and friendships, but in the country even the most commonplace visit involved a code of behavior compared to which the bourgeoisie's manners were merely the tricks of skillful apes. The great performance would generally take place when you had to go to some farm to borrow a horse, buy a barrel of cider, bring important news, or pay your rent for a field. And, of course, on days and at times when you knew that the people were at leisure. On Sundays, for example.

You have not been invited; no one is expecting you. You begin by stopping at the farmyard gate to give the dog enough time to bark and announce your arrival. You then open the gate, enter the yard, and move slowly, but within view of the windows so that you may be recognized through the panes. Slowly, to give the mistress of the house time to tidy up the place. If she's not in, or if she needs ten minutes to get ready, the big farmer comes out and takes you to see his shed, his stables, his animals, and his orchard, while waiting for her to arrive or to make some gesture. If he isn't there either, if the door is closed, you have no choice but to go back out through the gate, without being so indiscreet as to look around you. It wasn't often that you saw a closed door. A wooden face. Even in town the doors were always open during the day. Closing them if someone were inside amounted to insulting the people passing by.

But there you are, in front of an open door. You cough twice or three times to be sure they have understood, and you ask clearly if anyone is at home. A woman's voice invites you in. You walk a few feet along the mud floor of the hallway and stop again when you reach the door to the kitchen-living-room, which is also always open. The mistress of the house, leaning her elbows on the cupboard, gives you a smile. "Well, it's Corentin!" The big farmer is sitting in his chair at the head of the table, imperturbable. "Come right in," she says. You enter slowly, reply: "Here I am," and start talking about the weather and the condition of the land. The big farmer invites you to "place your weight on the bench." You refuse twice, energetically, before obeying that order the third time round. Had you gone on refusing, it would have been insulting, especially since the mistress of the house had wiped off the bench with a clean towel. The conversation then works around to the latest news from town: first the funerals, secondly the marriages, and finally the baptisms. During that time the mistress has taken out some glasses and pointedly wiped them with a freshly ironed rag. You pretend that you've noticed nothing until the moment the bottles, as if by some miracle, appear on the table all by themselves. But you loudly voice your indignation; you half-rise up from the bench as if to leave, saying that you had not meant to bother anyone and that, besides, you never drank unless you were thirsty. Your hosts assure you that you are known for being temperate, but that conversation comes more easily if your insides aren't dry. Then you hear the squeaking of corks and you see food being placed on the table, while the delicious aroma of coffee permeates the air. A good half-hour goes by before you shyly dare to explain why you've come. Your hosts knew it the minute they recognized you at the farmyard gate. But finally your mission has been accomplished and the big farmer himself leads you out, after you have given his wife the "bunch of leeks" that her house and her food deserve. You're delighted, and so are they. You gave them what they had expected of you—that is, your time and some news they hadn't heard before. They, in turn, had received you with the consideration that was due you as a man who is more or less a cousin by the mere fact of belonging to the same parish.

Even if she had a maid or two, the mistress of the house would never sit down while she was entertaining guests or visitors. Not, as one might think, because she was a slave, but indeed because she was mistress of the house and had to keep an eye on everything that was going on. When there were only members of the family at table, she would not eat until everyone else's hunger had been satisfied. As for the big farmer, he would rise only to pour out something to drink for a particularly honored guest, and even then, he would never leave his place, which was at the head of the table, under the window to the right, facing the door. On work days he'd bang his knife shut to indicate that it was time to leave the table. But he was careful never to do that when anyone outside the family was there. Indeed, he was then courteous to the point of using a straight knife, like all the others, which was only hospitable. He had great trouble handling it, I might add.

One day the ragman from Les Monts d'Arrée passed through the region, and his horse, Isabelle, moved slowly along the bad roads with her head lowered. You would have thought that the cautious beast had no cares in the world but the wooden crate attached to the back of the wagon with four bits of rope. It was there that the ragman kept his treasures: basins, jugs, bowls, and painted faience plates, which was all he had to give in exchange for rags, animal skins, and pigs' bristles. The man was following three yards behind it. He kept his eye on his case of crockery, which was covered with thin hay and would dance *passepieds* or gavottes, depending on the whim of the ruts. Just one eye, though, for he was blind in the other.

The big news had reached town, causing great excitement. When the men got home, they found all the cupboards wide open and piles of old clothes on the floor. Or else the gruel was about to burn while Barba was busy rummaging through the attic, all red in the face. So her husband Corentin smiled and went into the shed behind the house, where his rabbit skins had been put to dry in the shade. He stroked them with a feeling of satisfaction. Top quality, he thought. The ragman from the Léon region would have to bring out his finest pottery if he wanted them. Meanwhile, in the house, the upsetting odor of burnt gruel drew Barba down from her attic by the nose. But as she rushed down the steps, she was still dreaming of a large plate with a multicolored rooster on it which would go so well on the long board above the fireplace.

The ragman was the same color as the infertile land of his region—not only his face but also his coarse reddish-brown clothes. He was respected, however, because of his "weighing hook," an amazing, magical instrument compared to which the baker's scales were nothing but dubious toys. And sometimes—just think—the man wore an animal skin over his shoulders. The ragman wasn't very talkative. After the old clothes, the skins, and the bristles had been weighed, you'd hear a number, pronounced with his regional accent. No one paid any mind to that number, since both parties were so honest. It was merely a password that meant you were to go over to the crate of pottery, nothing more. The ragman would thrust his hand deep down into the hay, under a hemp bag. He'd dig around and think so hard that his one eye would close. He had to bring up an article that had precisely the same value as the wares he'd receive in return or, even better, one that was precisely what the woman wanted. It never worked on the first try, but did on the third, after some prayers and persistency. In the end, the fox from Les Monts d'Arrée would heave a deep sigh and uncover exactly what was expected of him. With great regrets, he'd agree to part with it.

"It's my best one, woman. I won't have anything like it again for a long time."

Barba would be in raptures. A short while later, a little farther up the road, Del, in turn, would get another bowl or another plate exactly like Barba's, except that hers would be not the last but the very last—even laster than the last.

The ragman's plates, with a rooster or a rose on them, were exhibited above the large fireplace on a *mester*—a long chestnut board decorated with brass nails. They were there mostly for show. My mother used hers only for "banquets" in honor of people who deserved better than our ordinary dishes. Not necessarily the rich or the powerful. On such days there were empty spaces on the *mester*. But that didn't happen often. All the women liked to have a display on theirs, since the fireplace beneath it was central to their work and the real focal point of the house. The mantel, under the *mester*, was the shelf on which the prettiest bowls were placed—bowls that were never used. Either painted in bright colors or edged with gold, they were worth a hundred times their weight in rags. In our house, right in the middle of them, and directly beneath a crucifix, was a teapot from the Far East and, alongside it, a matching sugar bowl and pitcher (for milk? hot water? or what?). Those three receptacles had never contained sugar or milk or water or anything else. Uncle Jean had brought them back from the "yellow countries," where he had served as a soldier for so long. He had wanted not only to add some luster to his father's poor house, but also to please his four sisters, who loved fine dishes, like all girls of good stock. But when the crate arrived, it presented some problems. In it were two lacquered paintings portraying Fujiyama, and underneath, a 120-piece pink and blue tea-set. When my mother saw that, she was extremely perplexed. What was she to do with those doll-sized dishes, especially those transparent cups with handles that would have been a serious challenge to any peasant's fat fingers? Also, it would have been impossible to serve coffee in those thimbles, unless you were willing to be accused of being both miserly and pretentious. As for tea, it was almost unknown in the region. So my mother decided to honor her eldest brother by placing the teapot, the sugar bowl, and the pitcher right in the middle of the *mester*, and to distribute the other pieces among relatives and friends, one by one, or two by two, according to the degree of kinship or the extent of her obligations. For her own personal use, she kept two saucers and one cup, which she set permanently on a corner of the large kitchen-cupboard shelf. Ever since then, before going to bed, she would put the pins for her coiffe into one of the saucers, and would keep two round brooches and three safety pins in the cup. The second saucer was where my mother would leave her rosary when she returned from Mass. Probably all the Bigoudens who received them did the same, for over the years, in other houses I noticed those cups and saucers from the Far East filled with almost the very same pins and brooches.

As for tea, it was to take another few years before the women could bring themselves to touch it. Indeed, they considered that beverage suitable, in the main, for sick people or for all those weaklings who lived in cities. Some of the women never drank it at all except to be polite or to do penance; others did when they wanted to play at being ladies—a constant temptation and one that increased as peasant women began to have the "wherewithal." But the most worthy of them would have been utterly miserable sacrificing their bowls for cups that usually weren't even from the Far East. Their pins came first.

The finest dishes were exhibited on the shelf of the kitchen cupboard, just as the plates were on the *mester*. That cupboard itself was set into what I have called the "facade of cupboards." It stood against the "milk cupboard" to the left and against Alain Le Goff's "wedding cupboard" (or what he called his "four-and-two") to the right. In addition to the basins of morning and evening milk, everything that we generally used for cooking and for the table was enclosed in the milk cupboard. It had only one door. The "four-and-two," as its name indicates, had two small doors at the bottom, which was reserved for woolens, sewing equipment, and my mother's coiffes. The upper portion was strictly my grandfather's property, and the other, my parents'. The two halves of the cupboard were separated by two drawers. In the first there were family photographs, the family correspondence—letters and cards from uncles-aunts, nephews-nieces, and cousins, as well as everything one needed in order to write to them all without fail. In the other my mother stashed away her small treasures, and none of us ever ventured to open it, even though there was no key anywhere near it.

The facade of cupboards hid most of the wall, which was whitewashed. Since the pieces of furniture themselves were lined up right next to each other, you could see nothing but the facade, which meant that the carpenter hadn't had to make the sides and backs as carefully as the rest, and had even been able to use a rather indifferent wood for them. It was up to the housewife to look after all that was visible as best she could in order to dazzle her visitors. The light chestnut, verging on red, shone even more brightly because of the brass nails that had been skillfully arranged so as to light up the wood without overpowering it. My mother's facade of cupboards was her pride and joy. When she had finished polishing all the nails, she would check her work in the yellow pardon ball hanging from the ceiling, for each and every nail (and she knew precisely how many there were) had to be reflected in it. The Sunday visitors could come to the house after the morning Mass. The wood and the brass were ready to receive them.

Perpendicular to the window was the long table at which we used to eat. It was made of light wood, without any embellishments whatever—merely a board on four legs, covered with flowered oilcloth which had been nailed to the edges. That was because such tables were not intended to be distinguished pieces of furniture. The cupboards displayed against the wall were, of course; nevertheless, the box-bed was the main piece of furniture in the house. It, in itself, was a small private apartment. When you'd get into it to go to sleep and had closed its two sliding doors, you were at home. I knew one farmhouse in which three of those box-beds were lined up in the kitchen-living-room. The first belonged to the master and mistress, the second to their daughter and the maid, and in the third, somehow or other, slept three boys until the oldest of them was able to join the farmhands and the eldest son in the stable. Thus not only men and women but masters and servants could live together in the same room with a minimum of promiscuity, which is not possible if you have ordinary beds. When getting into a box-bed, on your knees—and head first—you kept your dress or trousers on. Once the doors were closed, you finished undressing inside it and then folded your clothes over the bed rail. No one, by the way, had yet heard of nightgowns or pajamas. You slept on a thick pad of broom, on top of which were mattresses filled with bales of oats. Since the box itself wasn't long enough for an adult to stretch himself out completely, he would assume a half-sitting, half-lying-down position, on hemp sheets and under a comforter filled with bales of oats, like the mattresses and pillows. But people were already talking about eiderdowns, though they waited a while before making that drastic a change. Could feathers, which are so light, possibly keep you as warm as the bales? Whether they did or not, the down won out because the big shots had adopted it.

I, who used to share my grandfather's box-bed, personally believe that there's nothing like that sleep-closet and there never will be. You felt so protected in it, which is not the case when you're in an open bed like those in the lycées, where for a very long time I felt absolutely naked and exposed to all the dangers on earth. To such an extent that I became a sleepwalker during my first year there. It's quite true that, for a long while, box-beds in farmhouses had been strongholds against all the hazards that threaten children. In the past there were wolves; and even today, some pig may devour a child's little leg (that's been known to happen), and the hens might gulp down a baby's eye while its parents are in the fields. For there are many places in which the farmyard and the manger encroach upon the house. That's why certain box-beds can be closed from the inside with a strong hook. And when the doors are hooked, the occupant has the feeling that he can hold out against a siege.

The drawback of a box-bed is that it's not easy to make or straighten up, since you can't walk around it, whether it's lined up with other furniture or standing in a corner. But it so happens that a housewife used to feel honor bound to exhibit it during the day with its doors open. If the panels had been closed, one might have supposed that the bed hadn't been made, which would have caused Corentine's or Marie-Louise's reputation to be seriously tainted. Therefore, as soon as it was empty, she'd take the time to remake it carefully with a "bed stick," which she skillfully used to beat and then to smooth out the sheets and comforters from top to bottom. When that was done, she would cover the whole bed with a crocheted spread she had made herself and would arrange it over the pile of mattresses in such a way that it took up more than half the opening between the panels. Thus the wooden frame showed the actual bed off to advantage, as it would have a painting. That was why the bed had to be tidy.

The Breton box-bed's facade was said to be the very image of man's fate. The central part of it, between the door slides, represented the World Below (*ar bed-man*), where men toiled (the bed absorbed their fatigue) and—behind the three letters IHS and the Sacred Heart carved into the doors—made sure that they would have descendants. Below, the part hidden by the box-bed bench was called Hell (*an Ivern*) because of the darkness down there, between the four wooden legs that are just barely squared off and have no ornamentation whatever. Above, the rail on a row of small columns was named Paradise (*ar Baradoz*), and had either a Quimper-faience Saint Anne or a Virgin Mary set up on an archway between two spindles. Paradise and the World Below were studded with a lot of brass nails and polished regularly with great care, as if that didn't go without saying! At night, when that room in our house used to be lighted only by the hearth fire, the nails on the cupboards, the settle, and the box-bed would twinkle in the darkness like so many stars. During the day it was mainly the chestnut wood that glowed. When my mother used to grab hold of her rags to shine up her furniture, Alain Le Goff would sometimes say, with a smile: "There goes Marie-Jeanne, cleaning the sacristy." He was right. We lived in a kind of sacristy or private chapel, not only because of Christ's monogram and the crosses, hearts, and monstrances that had been hewed out of the reddish wood, but because our carpenters had obviously learned to build seats, doors, and ornamental facades by studying church furniture.

Besides, all our valuable objects had been gathered together in that kitchen-living-room/exhibition-room, which from one minute to the next, and whenever necessary, could change from being the stage for our most humble daily tasks (making the pig's slop, for example) and become a place of such great solemnity that it would intimidate strangers. On the other hand, the rest of the rooms or cubicles hadn't one piece of furniture in them that was worth anything, except for the traditional cupboard and bed my parents had received as wedding presents, and which were of the utmost simplicity. They had been put into the room across the hall, which you couldn't even call a bedroom since it gave onto the courtyard and we all had to walk through it to get to the shed-workroom-laundry-room, which also contained a rudimentary toilet: three boards over a small vat, behind a door with an ace of clubs carved out of it. No one ever complained.

You could count on my mother for seeing to it that nobody who visited us unexpectedly would ever see the doors to the box-bed closed, concealing an unmade bed, or even one single tarnished nail, or ashes scattered over the hearthstone, or the slightest bit of dirt from our sabots on the mud floor. And she was just as demanding when it came to her own appearance. The minute she got home after a tiring day in the fields, often dripping wet from the rain and spattered with mud, she would clean herself up before you had time to blink. "As long as there's fire and water," she'd say, "I shall be properly dressed." And in fact she never stopped washing our old clothes or her own unless she was mending them or patching them up. Moreover, except during the threshing season, when it was impossible for her to keep a high tube of linen or starched muslin on her head, she would have been mortified to be seen bareheaded. Yet even then, her hair was always tightly drawn up and so neatly held in place by a curved comb that not a strand ever slipped out.

I was, and always would be, amazed every time I saw my mother without a coiffe on her head. I never caught her unawares when she was putting one on. She would get up too early, around six on winter mornings and at five during the summer. And before even lighting the fire, she would immediately go about putting on her coiffe. She had started doing that at the age of six and had never missed a day since, except for the time she fell on the griddle and burned her hand. Thus for a whole week a neighbor came in to do it for her. "I was ashamed," she said.

To begin with, every such woman would comb her hair carefully, parting it down the middle. Then she'd cover her head with a three-sided black bonnet before piling her hair up and over it, on top of her head, rolling it around a rat, and securing it with a curved comb and black-headed pins. Skillfully manipulating her two cheap mirrors, and wetting her comb from time to time, she'd make sure that her hair was very smooth at the back and that not a strand was dangling down her neck. This was the point at which, around the curved comb covered with a velvet ribbon, she would set up the first piece of her coiffe (*an daledenn*), a high trapezium which had to close the well-starched white cylinder—the actual coiffe—at the back. The cylinder itself had to be absolutely upright, and to achieve that, one needed unbelievable dexterity. A century ago, coiffes were, at the most, three to four inches high, but in the Bigouden region they gradually rose to a height of about twelve to fourteen inches. And the women had to cope somehow. (If the coiffe were slightly crooked, no man would pay any heed to it, but the women would notice it right off. Humiliation.) Once she had set the high cylinder on her head, straight as could be, she would firmly attach its corners, with white-headed pins, to the velvet on the comb. The ribbons had been pinned onto the coiffe beforehand. All she had left to do was to draw them under her chin and knot them around her left ear. One more glance in the two mirrors. It was just perfect. A half-hour had gone by. Now she was ready to go out to the fields or to the fair, to Mass or to a wedding.

When the two lower doors of the "four-and-two" cupboard were open, I used to catch a glimpse of my mother's supply of starched coiffes. There were eight or ten of them rolled together in two bundles, one consisting of her everyday coiffes, and the other, of those she wore on Sundays and feast days. The former were made of plain white linen, embroidered with stylized white flower motifs. Among them were her funeral coiffes, which, if anything, looked even plainer. The second type were made of embroidered muslin or lace, embellished with extravagant decorative designs. True masterpieces, even for a region in which all girls were said to have been born with crochet hooks in their hands. Of course, old women wore comparatively low coiffes, because after a certain age, they had stopped keeping up with the fashions of the day. But as the younger women's coiffes grew higher, the ribbons on them got wider and wider, and the designs, increasingly flamboyant. Girls found them irresistible, but their parents weren't always in a position to pay for them. Even then, many people were saying that they ought to wear "city clothes," which didn't cost nearly as much. And my mother groaned with indignation: "Really! I am *not* going to walk around in a smock, wearing a bit of a scarf on my head." We all strongly reassured her, as if taking an oath: "You will always have enough money to buy yourself coiffes."

If the women valued that headdress, it was because they knew well that it was flattering, and in more than one sense. First of all, the high white structure was a luxury and was understood as such. Also, in order to wear it properly, women had to stand up straight. And finally, it set off the hair they were so proud of, especially the blondes. One thing was sure: the few fashionable city women who occasionally made an appearance in town looked very dowdy, in their sack-dresses and stewpot-hats, compared to the elegant Bigoudens in full regalia.

For quite a long while, people retained the habit of judging a woman's social status by the amount of velvet that decorated the back of her dress, from the bottom up. When the velvet reached all the way to her waistline, you knew that you had better not invite that young lady if you were just some poor devil, because you would have been mocked for thinking that "the sun rises and sets on you." A real bundle of vanity. On the other hand, if the girl had only two hands' breadth of velvet at the bottom of her skirt, she wasn't a good match for a young man of some means. When we first went to dances, my friends and I, having been advised by our mothers, would start out by walking around the groups of Bigouden girls, appraising them according to the amount of velvet on their dresses. And some of them, arrogantly or mockingly, would grab hold of the back of their skirts and, with a movement of their hips, swish them around to the side so we could see them, as if to ask: "Are you and I of the same status?"

During my years as a schoolboy and even later, not one of the Bigouden girls or women who lived in the region had resigned herself to adopting the city fashions, even though some of them were educated and wealthy enough to do so with impunity. In fact, giving up their costume, unless out of dire need, was still considered a betrayal and almost a sign of degeneration. It was the poorest among us who were the first to change their "look," for the simple reason that it was cheaper to buy clothes in the city. As Jean Bosser, who worked with my father, used to say, one had to be rich in those days to dress like a peasant. And whereas the women were ready to sacrifice anything in order to sport their coiffes, more and more men were fast giving up their Bigouden costume. Even if they had wished to, they couldn't have done otherwise. Working conditions had changed for many of them; also, cheap ready-to-wear clothes were then being sold in town; and owing to a new sense of propriety, they could no longer spend the whole week in faded and beat-up rags. On all the town squares, peddlers were hawking striped trousers which were still very like the old ones, except for the quality, and black jackets which took the place of the tailors' short overcoats, the successors of the *chupennou*, or cloaks, which had gone out at the end of the nineteenth century. And all the men who worked in town, even the artisans, dressed in blue cotton, buttoned up to the neck, like the factory workers. Only the big farmers, the "big shots," and the head of the factory, Uncle Jean Hénaff himself, remained faithful to the men's traditional costume, which became symbolic of landowners and the custodians of authority. When there was a meeting in Quimper, most of the county councillors would sport the peasant costumes of their regions. And in comparison, the prefects were said to have looked very small indeed.

During the 1920s and '30s the poor people who had remained in the region did their very best to dress properly. They couldn't wear soft felt hats, suits, and ties, for that was the prerogative of gentlemen (*aotrounez*). Anyway, they were terrified at the idea of having to struggle with knots and with buttons that weren't sewn on. So they capitulated by stages. First the trousers and then the jacket, which they could buy readymade, although they were somewhat embarrassed at thus depriving the small local tailor of his daily bread. They did continue to wear their round hats decorated with three rows of velvet, the six ribbons of which hung down their backs, between their shoulders, unless ruffled by the wind. They also continued to wear their velvet double-breasted waistcoats, buttoned up to the neck in military fashion. That was the very last piece of the costume to disappear in favor of navy blue sweaters or ordinary vests. The fact that they held out so well and for so long was due to the two-ply material, which protected the Bigoudens' chests from a disease they dreaded. They also wore better and kept the men's bodies straight. They were a sign of dignity for those who had probably given up their hats by then and were sporting "jockey" caps or Basque berets.

A hat was the French peasant's mark of nobility. He kept it on even while eating, whether at home or in the houses of friends who belonged to his "group." There's a song in Breton which tells about Christ's climb to Golgotha. He was exhausted, battered, and covered with wounds and spittle, but the worst thing of all was that he had no hat, or any semblance of one, on his head. According to a peasant from the Léon region, even a man who wore a flat cap (which we called "cow dung") was not respected. As for me, when I grew older my mother was soon at war with me—a war that was to last for almost half a century, with a few truces—because I would walk bareheaded through the streets of my birthplace on the unconvincing pretext that I never wore a hat in the city.

When the men finally gave up wearing both hats and waistcoats, and had no silk velvet on them anywhere, it was then that they looked truly humble and pitiful compared to their wives in traditional dress. They could no longer even maintain the illusion that they were the masters of their households. It had never been true, but at least they had kept up appearances until the time came when the poor creatures, reduced to wearing caps, began to follow their wives on the road instead of preceding them. Indeed, when a couple stepped outside, traditionally the man walked ahead, his chest held high and his moustache looking lordly, while his wife followed two steps behind, giving every appearance of being obedient and submissive. But if she did not agree when her lord and master wished to turn right, she would lift her umbrella and discreetly tap him on the left arm. And he would swerve to the left at once. Naturally, there were some exceptions—a few family tyrants who had made slaves of their wives or who scorned them—but they were considered to be in the wrong, unless the wife happened to be a drunkard or simpleminded, which was rare. There were far more cases of husbands who lacked character and who would take to drink the very moment they were faced with bad luck or adversity. In such cases it was the woman who ruled with a strong hand, saving face as best she could, given her shame (*ar vez*). Bigouden women were more terrified of that sort of shame than of all the trumpet-playing archangels of the Last Judgment. That they fought it every inch of the way, anywhere, and with every means at their disposal, was beyond doubt. As a young boy, I occasionally chanced to go into a tavern, following the grown-ups in my family. When one of the men was asked what he wanted to drink, I was always surprised to hear his wife answer instead: "A small sweet vermouth." And the man, who was well known in public for preferring rum or red wine, would merely grumble: "*Memez tra!*" ("Make mine the same!") Clearly, the women lived in constant fear of seeing their husbands become alcoholics. Habitual drunkenness was one of the Bigouden's three main temptations, the other two being greed and ambition, at least if one is to believe the people from Quimper, those tight asses. To protect oneself from all three, one's best weapon was pride. Montesquieu would have said honor.

Alain Le Goff, in his gentle voice, used to tell the story of a Le Goff ancestor whose first name also was Alain, and who had been the groom, the farmhand, and the footman at the Guilguiffin château in Landudec, in the mid-nineteenth century. The château was ruled over by a marquis, a strange and whimsical character, but then people like that have the perfect right to be different from everyone else, haven't they? All the same, he was quite a good man and knew from experience how to deal with his servants. Thus, whenever he had things to attend to in Quimper or was invited to some other château, or when he himself had guests at Guilguiffin, he would politely ask his groom-farmhand to turn himself into a footman, complete with knee-breeches, stockings, a wig, and all the rest of it. Alain Le Goff the Elder was perfectly willing to help out the marquis and to do him proud. He even agreed to take his hat off to him when other people were around. The rest of the time, when they were alone, they called each other Alain and Michel. Now one day, when he happened to have a few extra écus, Alain decided to buy a standing clock as an ornament for his house and so that he might tell the time by listening to something other than the Angelus. The marquis found out about it. At the first opportunity, he overwhelmed his servant with mockery, accusing him of wanting to become a member of the bourgeoisie and of squandering his slender means just to have an altogether useless object, since neither his time nor the house he lived in were his own. Indeed, the marquis went so far as to call him vain and a "windmill peacock." All red in the face, Alain Le Goff the Elder told his master that he might be a marquis, but that the cupboard-clock was none of his business, and that if anyone else had talked to him the way the lord of Guilguiffin had just done, he would have spit at him right between the eyes. The marquis turned white; he had trouble swallowing. Finally he spoke: "Then spit at me right between the eyes, Alain Le Goff, and call me Michel as before." Sick at heart, the Elder did it as delicately as he could in order to pay back an insult that, in fact, had been merely a thoughtless blunder. After which, there was no further mention of it between the two men.

Whenever he told that family story, to serve as guidance for us all, my grandfather never failed to explain his ancestor's behavior, recalling two other uncles or cousins of old who had been hung from the Guilguiffin trees after the "Bonnets Rouges" rebellion—hung by the Duc de Chaulnes, the cursed duke, may he never cease boiling in hell-fire, even after Doomsday, the bastard! "But never forget this, my boy! A marquis is very highly placed in this world, and a poor Yann, very lowly placed. That's the way things are. But may the marquis never take it upon himself to set foot on your own territory. Do not put up with it. Ever. Smash his foot at once, even if you're dragged off to be a galley slave." And, as if to reassure me, Alain Le Goff added: "Matter of fact, there are no galleys anymore."

Fine. I would remember. At the lycée most of the punishments inflicted upon me were due to my habit of fighting boys stronger and older than myself, even several of them at once, until blood was drawn, because I would never stand for hearing them say things I considered insulting to my dignity as a Bigouden peasant. Especially when another Bigouden happened to be the offender.

That point of honor in no way precluded respect and obedience when there was good reason for obeying or for showing respect. But each of us had his own sense of duty. We used to acknowledge a few great figures upon whom we bestowed the title *aotrou* (which about corresponds to the word *lord*), the first of whom was *an aotrou Doue*, the Lord God. His representatives, ranging from the bishop to the vicar, were so called, and the title was also given to notary publics,* but never to doctors, either because health was not considered as important as property or because those qualified

*Important figures in France, who may act both as lawyers and as brokers. (Trans.)

healers had not yet completely proven themselves. Apart from such men of distinction, the only person I ever heard my family call an *aotrou* was Monsieur Le Bail, our great man, the Mayor of Plozévet. As for the population as a whole, they never seriously bestowed the honor of the word *aotrou* on anyone but those who discharged their obligations toward them and who could be relied upon to take responsibility for their well-being. It was a title that had to be earned, one that implied "vintage guaranteed," which was why most of the so-called big shots themselves would feel uncomfortable or be frightfully embarrassed if anyone took it into his head to call them *aotrou.*

The teachers were called "monsieur," "madame," or "mademoiselle," *in French.* Two or three women in town were also addressed as "madame." They were the ones who couldn't speak Breton or didn't deign to. All the other women kept their maiden names for life. For example, my mother was Marie-Jeanne Le Goff. She would never have been an Hélias in Breton. The word *itron* ("lady") before a Christian name is the feminine equivalent of *aotrou* and was then in the process of slowly degenerating into "madame." In our parish it was used even less than *aotrou*. In fact, it was almost exclusively reserved for the Holy Virgin, *an Itron Varia* ("Lady Mary") and, from time to time, for her mother, Saint Anne. But in Quimper the tradesmen (almost all of them spoke Breton) would address country women as *itron*, though it always made them blush with embarrassment, knowing perfectly well that it was too grand for them. As my mother said, "If they'd at least call you *maouez* [woman], like the tradesmen at the fairs and in the markets when they don't know your family or your Christian name, you'd feel more at ease." If absolutely necessary, they would consent to being called "madame" in French. Some of them were even flattered by it. But the flattery implied in *itron* was really a bit much. A girl was more readily disposed to being called "*dimezell*" ("young lady"), but she'd keep her distance until she was convinced that people were not making fun of her.

To children, any adult in a Bigouden costume was a *moereb* (an aunt) or an *eontr* (an uncle). Dressed in city clothes, adults were nothing at all; no communication was possible. When the children grew up, they had to be very careful about calling anyone *moereb* or *eontr* who hadn't been truly old for a long time. At the age of seventy-five, my mother still got angry if people of forty or fifty called her *moereb.* "After all," she'd grumble, "I'm not *that* old." If you called a woman in her eighties by her Christian name alone, you were in no danger. But you had to beware of calling her "grandmother" if you were not her grandson.

In Pouldreuzic we were called the *fied*—in other words, those who addressed a person as *fi* (*vous*) instead of using the familiar *té* (*tu*). We never said *té* to anyone, not even to the members of our families, not even to babies in swaddling clothes. We knew the form *té*; but when it slipped out, it meant either that we held the person in contempt or that we were really enraged: "*Té dorr din eu reor!*" ("You're a pain in the ass!") In the district to the south of us, everyone readily said *té*. They were thus called the *téed*, and we considered them shameless (*divergonted*), whereas they criticized us for always talking like snobs. Actually, the respective values of our *fi* (*vous*) and *té* (*tu*) were not the same as in French. When my mother spoke French, she had the strange habit of using *vous* as the familiar form, even when addressing me, her son; and when she wanted to be polite to strangers who came to visit, she would make every effort to use the *tu* form. The fact that they said *vous* to her in reply didn't bother her. After all, they had addressed her as "madame," when she should have been called "Marie-Jeanne Le Goff." They were wrong from beginning to end. One had to forgive them and not speak as they did.

Our great concern with giving everyone his due was responsible for the fact that conventionally polite phrases were scarcely ever used, not even "good day" or "good evening," though we were beginning to hear them, but only in French. And you would never say "I'm sorry" or "excuse me" in Breton, unless you did something frightfully offensive, in which case you were more likely to refer to yourself publicly as an animal of some sort. Nor would you ever say "thank you," because whatever you graciously received, whether a present or a good turn someone had done you, was always returned in kind. (That, of course, does not apply to beggars, who entrust their debts to the Lord God.) And when you are introduced to someone, you have no reason to say, in Breton, that you are pleased to meet him or anything of that sort, because you have no idea of how your meeting with that person will turn out. Now you know very well that every word you pronounce commits you. So you prefer to remain silent and be considered a clod. The two words that are most frequently used to approach someone or take leave of him are *salud* ("greetings") and *kenavo*, which means both "goodbye" and "farewell," and is the precise equivalent of "until then . . . ," it being understood that "until then" might mean either soon, tomorrow, some time in the future, or in Paradise. But if you do say *kenavo* to someone, it implies that you want to see him again. Otherwise, you have to keep your mouth tightly shut until he's gone.

If you're walking up the road and happen to meet someone walking down it and who is not from your region, you say: "So you're on your way down?" And if he is a well-bred man, he replies: "Yes, on my way down." If you happen to know that person, you stop when you reach him if you think you are older than he. And you exchange a few words, but neither of you would ever cross the road to meet, unless absolutely necessary. According to the rules, if one belongs to the society of Breton-speaking people, one never passes anyone in silence. There is no harm in saying: "Night's coming on!" or "The winds are changing!" or "There's a bellyful of rain up there!" Then you hear the reply: "It is coming on!" "They are changing!" "It's time to take shelter!"

I was taught very early on that when I was out on the road alone, I was to look at the grown-ups that came along and wait until they spoke to me. "Ah, so there you are, my boy!" The answer was simple: "Yes." If they didn't say anything at all, it meant they were badly brought up or that they scorned young peasants, in which case you could see it when you looked them straight in the eye. So what you did was walk on a bit, then suddenly stop, and turn around to observe them as if they were strange beasts, which indeed they were. "You have to learn, my boy. But, still, don't go so far as to spit on the ground."

Now that was our style of good breeding.

Before the First World War, members of a family almost never kissed each other, unless one of them was about to leave for distant parts and for a long time, knowing neither when he would return nor even if he would return. "In the days when compulsory military service lasted for seven years," said the sabot-maker, "our parents would kiss us when we got back, not when we left." Sailors were kissed more often than any of the other travelers because their job was known to be the most dangerous of all. Boys felt more at ease kissing their mothers than their fathers. I used to know one who refused to touch his father's cheek until his father was stretched out on his death bed. The only exceptions to that constraint were, of course, children not yet old enough to work—in other words, those who had not yet reached the age of ten.

World War I changed all that. The appalling losses during the first two years of it, which had decimated most families; the wretched life of the fighters; the newspapers, which everyone had begun to read and which had fed their anguish instead of making it easier for them to wait; the soldiers returning on leave and their departing yet again, with death in the offing—all that encouraged effusiveness. Once the heroes had returned, the people went on making shows of affection: it had become a habit. But of course there was no question of kissing one another every day.

Embracing is not the same thing as kissing. While the generation of veterans—that is to say, my father's—had learned to kiss people on their cheeks with propriety, their own fathers had great trouble getting used to it. Most often, they stuck to the old way of embracing, which consisted in each of the two parties placing his hands on the other's shoulders, and his cheek against the other's cheek; mouths never entered into it. Both of them would thus touch each other's cheekbones three times—the Whites in the name of the Trinity; the Reds in the name of Liberty-Equality-Fraternity. Some of them did it four times, as if making the sign of the cross. According to Alain Le Goff, the fourth time was called "So be it" ("*Evelse bezet grêt*") and was as common a habit among Reds as among Whites. It all took place without people coming any closer to each other than necessary.

So it was no wonder that the old people would grumble when they saw women kissing their children of school age, unless it was on some great occasion. And schoolboys who were fondled by their mothers after the age of six were the laughing-stock of their fellow pupils.

I have thus far spoken only of the most important commandments—those which forced us children to make sure that the family's reputation was upheld and that no shame was ever brought upon it. For everything about children was common knowledge, everything that concerned them was bruited about. They were the naïve facade of the family—one that had not yet become deceptive. To tell the truth, some of my little friends were not held as tightly in tow as I was. For example, they were allowed to take part in certain games that I should have liked to play, but which had the drawback of almost certainly making those who tried their hand at them look ridiculous. Adults, too, had to be cautious when it came to making exhibitions of themselves, which accounts for the end of Breton wrestling. Even in the days when I was a child, the contending wrestlers in Pouldreuzic had come from other regions. And they began to come less and less often, fighting without much conviction in front of very few spectators. Soon a new game called soccer took over, and the Breton wrestlers were put off indefinitely, awaiting a revival of their sport.

In sum, the fear of shame prevailed over any desire for popular esteem. But when there was an event that involved a sense of community, everybody pulled together, and not one individual ever failed to make the most of himself so long as all the rest of them were also players. Such was the case with work in which everyone participated—the land-clearing, the threshing, the harvesting, and the transporting of rocks. Such was also the case when a new threshing floor had to be made in someone's farmyard, bringing together large numbers of the population of a parish or a neighborhood several times a year. After the greater part of the work had been done, the floor was ready to be smoothed down and compressed by the heels of sabots to the rhythm of the local gavottes, the *jibidis* and the *jabadaos*. And the work began with merrymaking. The musicians really let themselves go. The owner had made arrangements with a few of the best dancers, who were to be in charge of leading the others—a tricky job that required great skill. Pails of water had been drawn from the wells. A few of the men would look over the mud floor, pick out the spots they didn't think had the proper consistency, and moisten them. Then they'd signal to the leader of the first dance, who would bring the couples over and have them stamp, to music, all over those spots until a well-kneaded surface had been obtained. Of course, trousers and skirts got spattered all over with clay, but that didn't matter to people who were accustomed to facing rain and mud every day of God's making. After all, the main thing was to turn out a threshing floor that was beyond reproach—nice and smooth, nice and even, and somewhat supple—in short, a kind of masterpiece about which the connoisseurs could say, referring to those who had freely given of their time and energy to perfect that "toad's clay" surface: "They worked very hard at dancing."

The girls were certainly not the last to rush over and help with a new threshing floor. Whether they were heiresses or maids, it was there that any and every body could judge their abilities. Working on a new threshing floor was not only a pleasure and a means of creating closer bonds among the members of the working community; it was also an opportunity for rich girls to show that they didn't shrink at the prospect of doing tiring and messy work, and that a husband-to-be could count on them both in the house and outside it. The girls knew that their suitors would be there, and that those suitors often needed more than a glowing heart to make up their minds. They also knew that even if they were beautiful enough to get some heir to lose his head, lurking in the background were a mother and a father who would not believe everything they were told. But the heir himself was also the object of close scrutiny from any rich peasant who had a marriageable daughter, especially if she were an only child. At times the bagpipers and oboists acted somewhat as go-betweens, in their way, since they would be rewarded for their services by playing at the wedding if they were successful. One of them told me that the owner of a threshing floor once discreetly handed him enough tobacco to fill his pipe for a month or two in return for blowing nonstop through his boxwood tube. What the owner wanted to find out was how long a certain girl could dance, how long she could hold out, for his eldest son had been courting her seriously and everyone quite honestly wondered whether she didn't have "consumption." What could you expect? One had to make sure. But skinny as the girl in question may have looked, she remained brisk and lively right to the end. From then on, her future father-in-law had nothing more to say. Nor did he say another word.

As for the farmhands and maids, they would fervently compete at dancing. Not only in order to convince each other that they'd make good husbands or wives, but because the big farmers and their spouses who were there would readily pay them higher wages, either to keep them or to steal them away from others, if it were clear, from seeing them dance, that they would not spare themselves at work. And a vigorous fellow whose legs didn't fail him and who held his back straight right up to the last blast of the oboe would be good at ploughing; whereas a girl who danced without missing a step and who was in constant control of her gestures would work quickly and not waste time or break dishes or talk too much; one could almost certainly count on that.

It was thus at the making of new threshing floors that people displayed their worth, their courage, their energy, and generally their character. On the other hand, it was at wedding dances that everyone dressed to the teeth and sought to rise in the communal hierarchy or to represent, as best they could, the family to which they belonged, even if, in order to succeed, they had to cheat from time to time. Weddings made it possible for one to act a part, because they were meant not only to celebrate the art of living but to glorify a type of society that was common to three or four parishes and acknowledged by a dozen others, with some few variations. Neither a tribe nor a clan, strictly speaking, merely an assemblage of kin, relatives by marriage, coteries, and special groups, all of whom spoke the same language—by that I mean, who obeyed the same unwritten code, with its own subtle requirements which no one would have dared to challenge if he wished to make his way in that particular society. And that is why the dancers were calculators as well—calculators in borrowed plumes.

One might have thought that poor people had more freedom when it came to marrying someone of their own choice, but that was true only for those very few who were irretrievably poverty-stricken and others who had gone off to the cities out of ambition or need. Everybody who remained had to play the game. And the game consisted in contracting a marriage with someone of the same or of slightly higher rank, but not much higher, and never lower, not even slightly. And young people had to bear in mind that they were being closely watched. As soon as they began to keep company, a good many members of the parish would observe their behavior with a curiosity that seemed to border on gluttony, but which in fact was merely an interest in a matter that more or less concerned the community to which they belonged. And tongues would start wagging reproachfully if a girl and a boy were not of the same station, whether a girl of modest rank had intentionally seduced an "heir" who should rightfully have been engaged to an "heiress" of his own station, or whether a boy who was a servant, a quartermaster, or a clerk had managed to find favor in the eyes of a foreman's daughter. And it was more than likely that a feeling of general disapproval would thwart plans which had been well on the way to fulfillment. One couldn't always withstand pressure from a society whose main ambition, in spite of its disparities and differing aspirations, was to continue precisely as it was. Anyone who didn't like it had only to leave; a train was soon to come through the town every day.

When two people in love were well suited to each other—that is, from the point of view of rank and possessions—there was no reason not to rejoice, for such a marriage reinforced the community to which they belonged, even if the merging of two wealthy families provoked a little jealousy because of the new power they would derive from each other. But being a bit jealous isn't forbidden, is it? Jealousy fosters emulation. And besides, people were beginning to see a future taking shape in which learning and the consequent job possibilities might be considered on a level with land or money. After I had received my baccalaureate and my master's degree in arts, some families deemed that I, although the son of a Red, was worthy of two or three girls who were very far above my earlier station in life, and Whites to boot. That information was given me by the girls themselves. Yet they didn't go so far as to send over the marriage broker (*le baz-valan*).

That figure, like his female counterpart, the matchmaker (*an gomer goz*), had already begun to disappear before the First World War as the official intermediary between two families. Yet the old custom was still around in the 1920s and '30s. The *baz-valan* had become the intermediary "suitor" (*ar houriter*) and was still acting as a diplomat between the two interested parties, whereas the lady matchmaker was still fulfilling her own duties. But the duties of both had become more discreet—at any rate, less conspicuous—and were carried out by the same types, most especially the tailors. They, of course, would make the wedding suits if they were successful. Or the verger, who rang the bells. And on the wedding day he would have his palm so well greased that the ropes would slide along it like eels. Or the bagpipers and oboists. Or the traveling draper. Or even the ragman from the Léon region, though he was a foreigner. Or some old "missus" desperately anxious to mate people—but first and foremost, the missus who acted as a midwife and who had hopes of bringing the couple's children into the world. Or, as a matter of fact, anyone, on condition that he or she knew everything there was to know about the hierarchies, the coteries, and the various proprieties, which had necessarily to be taken into account in order to hold the best cards and to have every chance of winning. Even today, men in the countryside are still in the habit of using an intermediary, if only to act as their spokesman on the day they propose.

Thus one winter evening a young man whom I had seen before, but couldn't place, arrived at our house. I had seen him, along with several others, conversing with my Aunt Lisette, a pleasant girl who laughed a lot and seemed to attract young men. He had come all prepared to propose to her, and had been careful to let us know he was coming a few days in advance. But ever since then, the whole family had been in a flutter, for Lisette had told us straightaway that she didn't find him suitable, that was all; she had nothing against him, except that he hadn't informed her of his intentions, in which case she would have politely discouraged him. But she now had to refuse him, taking every possible precaution so that neither he nor his family would be offended. Alain Le Goff had clearly thought out his answers, as had my mother, Lisette's eldest sister, who was to take the place of her mother; my father was to stay out of it altogether. As for me, who had been in on the secret for the most part, I had necessarily to be a witness to the whole affair since I slept in the kitchen box-bed, and it was impossible to receive my aunt's suitor anywhere else.

The large door was already closed when he arrived in the dark of night, accompanied by the man who had been entrusted with pleading his cause and who hadn't had the time to prepare his arguments. When the latter opened the door a crack and asked if anyone was at home, my father replied that he was to come right in. Both men entered slowly, apologizing for bothering everyone at that hour of the night. My mother lengthened the wick of the kerosene lamp. I was on my knees in my box-bed, behind closed doors, and was looking through the carved-out initials of "Iesus Hominum Salvator," holding my breath. Since the two visitors were asked to sit on the box-bed bench, the nape of the suitor's neck was just a few inches from my nose. He had bought a so-called "jockey" cap, the latest fashion, which smelled very new. He had probably paid a lot for it.

My Aunt Lisette wasn't there. She was in another room, sewing and waiting for the interview to come to an end. Meanwhile, conversation had begun in the kitchen, as my mother put some bottles out to quiet everyone's emotions. Unfortunately, I never did hear a thing concerning the proposal itself or the soothing phrases of refusal, for in accordance with the rites regarding visitors, they first talked about the weather, about the funeral of a man in town who had died before his time, about a new carbide lamp which the masons were then using on their bicycles, about a . . . I really couldn't say, since I had fallen fast asleep.

The next day, when I questioned my grandfather about how he had made out with the young man in the new cap and his spokesman, he merely stated that my mother and he had managed the conversation in such a way that both visitors had understood beforehand how useless it would have been to ask the question at all. They had left without ever having raised their voices and without a bitter or a spiteful word. As they went out, the *baz-valan* simply told his protégé that he would now have to look elsewhere. And the suitor replied, sighing: "I probably will. You can't win every time."

I was not yet old enough to understand the complicated wiles indulged in by young men and girls who wanted to meet or to express their feelings for each other without any go-between at all. But I did know that girls often walked together in threes, linking arms. The one in the middle was usually the most provocative because, with the two others flanking her, she felt protected. Besides, it's easier to defend yourself when there are three of you.

If one of the girls wished to flirt with some gay blade, there were still two of them to keep an eye on her. Just one wouldn't have been enough, because then she herself would have been alone and therefore unprotected.

Now girls who had been used to showing themselves off to advantage by means of their clothes, their faces, and their bearing were soon to find another way. As the years went by, the stiff band that had been wound around their chests, flattening them down to nothing, began to loosen and finally to show off their breasts, which had formerly been the privilege of nursing mothers alone. Then brassieres came into fashion, which caused one flabbergasted grandmother to say, as she waved one of her granddaughter's about: "Well, that's the first time I've ever seen milk put into baskets!"

The progress made by a young man keeping company with a girl, and his chances of sending a go-between to her father without any danger of being refused, depended upon his gradually taking more and more liberties, which were witnessed by the whole town. For example, if he asked three girls, or even two, out for a soft drink or a glass of wine, it didn't really bother anybody, but if he invited only one, that was quite another matter. And whereas tongues would begin to wag if the girl allowed her suitor to buy her some nuts at a "pardon" shop, nothing had yet been settled at that stage of the game. But surely some agreement had been reached between the two parties if you saw a young man swaggering about next to a girl and carrying her umbrella with its tip in the air. If he then managed to convince her to accept a fine scarf-pin as a gift, the die was cast. Perhaps even the date for the wedding had been set. It would not, of course, take place in the near future, because great days such as that were not arranged at a moment's notice.

Indeed, the great day actually meant a whole week of ceremonies, food, festivities, and a variety of polite gestures. In sum, a working week wasted. When the work happened to be urgent, especially during the harvesting season, there could be no question of people marrying. One of the fathers would not have wanted to give up his daughter, nor would the other have wanted to give up his boy. Of the two prospective fathers-in-law, it was the one at whose home the young couple were to live who was in the greatest rush, for he would thus have an extra worker at his disposal. He would therefore suggest that the wedding take place at Easter time, since no one got married during Lent or, if possible, before Palm Sunday. That would have made the rector angry. The other prospective father-in-law would have preferred to keep his daughter or his son with him until the end of August. Finally, they would always reach a compromise.

Marriage was an important event whether one was rich or poor, because it strengthened family bonds as much, and even more, than a funeral. For a funeral reduces the family, whereas a marriage may increase it several fold. Actually, it is hard to know where a family stops. Yet a precise inventory of it had to be made when invitations were under consideration. The mothers of both fiancés had to go out and invite everyone on their list in person, each of them accompanied by a relative. And every visit, or almost, would involve the coffee or omelet ceremony in houses that continued to respect the old customs. The expedition used to last from one to two weeks. Meanwhile, both fiancés together would visit all their close relatives in order to introduce each other to their respective families. The mails were used only to invite those who had left the region. After the relatives came the "coterie," the "group," and then other friends and acquaintances—in other words, almost the entire parish.

The parents of the engaged couple would order their bed and their cupboard. They'd go to see the carpenter, who would offer them something to drink "sitting down" and occasionally something to eat. The same was true for the tailor and the dressmaker who had received the order for the wedding clothes. There again, it was the parents who chose the fabrics. Publishing the banns was an occasion for a "gathering" of all the close relatives, as well as the bridesmaids and ushers, which meant a big meal in a carefully chosen inn so as not to hurt anyone's feelings on either side. Each of the guests paid his share to the bride or groom, depending on which of them had invited him. The main point of the gathering was to have the representatives of both families get better acquainted, and everyone knows that the best way to do that is to keep them at table for a few hours. As for the bridesmaids and the ushers, their job was to put the finishing touches to all the details of the ceremony to come. One of the trickiest problems was that of pairing off the girls and their escorts. That required the utmost in diplomacy, for it was very important that so and so's daughter, say, not be paired off with so and so's son when it was generally known that they weren't on visiting terms for a number of reasons, any one of which might have caused a deplorable incident.

The glorious day finally came. It was always on a Tuesday that weddings took place. When I say "day," I am referring only to the Christian marriage ceremony on a Tuesday morning (*an eured*), for the "feast" itself would last for three whole days, and the rest of the week the entire group would do their best to regain their senses. People never said they were going to a wedding; they spoke of going to a "feast." That again shows the importance that was attached to food and how inseparable it was from the sacraments; indeed, it was almost as necessary as the sacraments (may God forgive me!), because while religion was worthy of respect, the social rites over which it took precedence were no less so. And on the Tuesday morning, when the members of the wedding had started to go about their business in every direction, those who were staying at home would still ask them, half-joking and half-envious: "Have you taken your spoon?"

The story of the wooden spoon goes back very far in time. Only the memory of it lives on, but it is still very fresh in our minds. And although no one any longer brought his own spoon to wedding feasts, he always remembered the days when the most beautiful of them were made for such occasions. My grandfather the sabot-maker claimed that the size of each spoon he had carved corresponded to that of the owner's mouth. And when the spoons had no identifying marks on them, a person could tell which was his merely by recognizing his mouth in it. Hard to believe, but true. Moreover, some of them were very elaborate and real masterpieces. Often it was the young men who carved and decorated them for the girls of their choice. The gift of a spoon used to be one stage in the process of courting. But most of them were made by the carpenters who came to the farms with their tools to build the wedding cupboard. Heiresses and "big shots" used to have beautiful folding spoons with their own hallmarks on them! Whereas the ordinary people would go to a wedding feast wearing their spoons gloriously in their belts, in the lapel of their *chupennou*, or stuck into the velvet ribbons on their hats to let everyone know that they planned to fill their paunches right up to their Adam's apples.

The first wedding I ever went to with my mother was that of a girl from one of the big farms near Plogastel. Since shortly before, I had given up my skirts in favor of breeches, I put on my new city-style suit and was impatiently awaiting Marie-Jeanne Le Goff, who was taking forever, fussing about with her new coiffes. To kill time, I went out and sat on the doorstep, watching the horse-drawn charabancs arrive. Behind the first one, in which the bride was sitting in state, like a picture, next to her father, who was holding the reins, were others with enough distance between them so that each one could be admired individually. At least fourteen or sixteen of them filed by, followed by lots of people on foot. Most of the charabancs had been washed and repainted, and the horses had been brushed down to the hide, their hooves waxed, their headstalls decorated with pompoms and tinsel, and their manes and tails braided. The men were wearing striped trousers, black velvet waistcoats, short black coats, and round hats with six black ribbons on them. The women, except for their high coiffes, light-colored aprons with beaded designs, and the light-colored trim on their sleeves, were also in black. And in contrast to all that black were smiling faces and swaggering moustaches.

Finally, my mother was ready. We joined the group walking down to the square, where the procession was forming amidst a great deal of shouting, greetings, and laughter. The bagpipe and the oboe were being tuned and squeaking out false notes. They were about to have a hard day.

Then all the bells joined in. The procession moved slowly toward the church, led by the musicians. As for the wedding Mass, there isn't much to say about it except that, like funerals, it was an occasion on which a hierarchy based on esteem was adhered to. The average man was married at ten in the morning, without even a prie-dieu for the protagonists, only one chair, which meant that, unlike the poor, they at least didn't have a second one to turn around. The wealthy and the prominent, who were joined together at eleven in the morning, had armchairs and a carpet that was unrolled from the chancel to the entrance of the belfry, which was almost never open except for processions. Couples who had consummated their marriage and had made sure they would have descendants before ever having gone to see the mayor or the priest were quickly disposed of at nine. Those guilty creatures had the right to no more than a "minimal Mass" ("*overenn blên*"). Even so, they were lucky if some haughty rector hadn't summoned them at dawn for a "muted Mass" ("*overenn vouzar*"), without any bells, and similar to the baptism of little bastards.

When the procession filed out of the church, there were actually more spectators in the street than before. It was around noon, and even the young men and women paid by the hour were there. So were all the maids in town. For there wasn't one spectacle that people enjoyed more than that procession, which went dancing to music through the whole town after the wedding Mass.

As soon as the newlyweds stepped out of the church, they were greeted by a sort of wedding march called "The Melody for Leaving the Church." It was solemn and measured, and thus a suitable transition from the sacred to the profane. For from then on, the profane was to claim its rights. Indeed, following instructions, the bagpiper and the oboist started off, leading the procession with great ceremony toward the nearest inn. Shortly before reaching it, they changed melodies. That was the break with the sacred. Those who were a part of the procession understood it as such and began to take certain liberties which were in contrast to the pomp and discipline they had maintained up to then. They started speaking more loudly and calling to one another, whereas the cocks of the walk had a burning desire to go into their acts. The innkeeper had placed two chairs out in front of his door for the musicians, who were tuning up one last time before launching into the first piece of music (*abadenn*) for the newlyweds, which consisted in three dances: an ordinary gavotte, a special *jibidi*, and a *jabado*.

The members of the wedding party were almost the only ones to dance at that stage. The others, the onlookers, stood around the periphery of the square or on either side of the street, not missing one whit of the spectacle. And if some dancer got carried away and forgot to show his partner off to advantage, there was always someone who'd shout: "Come on now, get her to strut around!" So with a twist of the wrist, the man would twirl her out a half-step in front of him and display her properly. After all, elegance, dexterity, and gracefulness are the attributes of women, whereas boys distinguish themselves by their vigor, their spontaneity, and the heights to which they can leap. But none of them were enjoying themselves yet; they were performing.

As a matter of fact, the older people in the group rarely took part in those first dances either. Their time had not yet come. Out of courtesy, they would go into the tavern, have a drink at the bar, and offer a round, until one of the ushers appeared in the doorway and shouted: "We're now off to the front of N's place! Don't loaf about in there!"

The musicians, who had already downed a number of drinks, were fast on their way to drinking again at the next tavern, where the same performance was repeated. After they had visited four or five of them, all carefully chosen so that there would be no ill feelings among the tavern- or innkeepers, the best man would look at his watch and lead the whole party off to the farm or to some inn in town where the feast was to take place.

In those days the wedding feast was always given at the farm of the "new son" or the "new daughter," which was what the newlyweds were called. But among the rich people, that custom of receiving hundreds of guests in their own homes was fast disappearing. It meant entertaining on too large a scale and going to too much trouble for the prestige it brought them and the profit they made out of it. Moreover, it caused too much anxiety and was too tiring, especially when it took place before the harvesting. So that was that! Soon everyone was resigned to inviting fewer people and to letting an innkeeper see to it all. The last feast at a farm was to take place two or three years later, in Saoudua, quite near our town. And farewell to all the splendor!

My mother and I had left the young people, relatives, and close friends of both sides when they went off to make the rounds of the taverns and dance to the music. We had reached the farm on foot (it was barely a half-league away) and were awaiting the procession of charabancs that was soon to arrive, or so we thought. That custom, too, was beginning to disappear. Before the war, it was obligatory, but there had been too many accidents because the drivers got somewhat overexcited and always tried to pass one another on bad roads. Once they had actually lost the bride herself, who had been dumped into some field above a slope when one wheel of her carriage went into a ditch.

At any rate, on that particular day, as well as at the wedding feasts I was subsequently invited to at inns, I was dumbfounded to see the quantity of food that a man's stomach, or even a woman's, could hold. All the dishes were passed twice, perhaps even three times, and I got the impression that those who shrank at a second or a third helping were very few indeed. In spite of all their talk about eating more just to be polite, they still had to have enough room between their ribs in which to stuff the food. Soup, "head pâté" (which we called "head cheese," since cheese made of milk was completely unknown to us), pork sausages with mashed potatoes, tripe, stew, roasts, rice pudding, butter cake—all very filling and none of which went down easily—would appear, one by one, on the long tables, only to vanish shortly afterward with the help of big glassfuls of white and red wine, the latter inevitably reminding the men of the trenches.

The meal to which my mother and I were invited lasted for three or four hours: nothing serious can be done in less time than that. There was scarcely a man who, now and then, didn't feel the need to go and empty his "water tank" in the shadow of some hedge or behind a slope or a haystack—in other words, any place outside that was favorable to meditation. Inside, the bagpiper and the oboist had risen and were playing special tunes for each main dish as it arrived, generally for the sausages and the roasts, as well as for the coffee spiked with *lambig*, the cider-brandy we also called *loufog.* Inspired by the *lambig*, the oboist played a solo called "To Make the Bride Weep." While she wiped away a tear, as did her female relatives and those who had had so much to drink it had gone to their eyes, the musician, to quiet all that emotion (too much is too much!), announced a song that was meant to induce the groom to put up with his mother-in-law. At which point another hearty type took it upon himself to recite some couplets on the happiness of bachelorhood and the annoyances of marriage; but several of the couplets were so spicy that the women felt they had to shoo their children outside with napkins. During the silence that followed, since everyone was short-winded from all the laughter, the bride, on the advice of her mother or her husband, rose and sang a love song which she had carefully practiced for the occasion and for which she was repaid by an enthusiastic uproar that was far too great for her talents, such as they were. And one woman declared to everyone who was prepared to listen: "Luckily, young people are much wiser than their elders!"

By then, people had begun to appear in the farmyard and in the doorways, people who had not been to the wedding and who had finished their daily work. They were awaiting the second series of dances, in which they had the right—indeed were duty-bound—to participate. In the large farmyard the bagpiper and the oboist were playing a prelude to the first gavotte, which was about to begin. In the old days the bride used to go out and look for a beggar to dance with. But instead, any man who was there could now demand that she, or any of the other girls, dance with him. The boys in the wedding party, who had grown heavy with food and drink, were only too pleased to be replaced by the newcomers. Among them were skilled dancers, some of whom had come from quite a distance and were eager to show off their virtuosity, especially those who had taken first place in competitions for having danced the gavotte with a bottle balanced on their hats, like the "thimble boy," who was so agile that everyone called him "the flying tailor."

The elderly also took part in those dances, at least those who were still capable of controlling their limbs. And so did the children, even little boys still in skirts, who thus learned, at an early age, to celebrate the rite that was most successful at strengthening the bonds of their particular community. It consisted in doing the steps of Pouldreuzic's Bigouden gavotte, which, as everyone of good faith would admit, was more elegant than Plozévet's and more reserved than the one danced two leagues to the south of us, a place where the girls were intentionally more provocative than was fitting. (For their part, the girls in question used to call us "tight asses"—why, I'll never know. Had they ever really seen our bare asses?) At any rate, the children were thus taught to dance by their mothers or their older sisters. And with all the generations mixed together, everyone indulged in the old magic of communal dancing, it being understood that the rich, who had to keep up their standing, would dance rather solemnly and without making any unnecessary gestures, whereas the poor would let themselves go to such an extent that they seemed to be attempting the impossible, trying to take a bite out of the moon.

Speaking of the moon, it was, as a matter of fact, just about nightfall. Some chap shouted out to everyone at large: "Watch out! Here comes the rector of Landudec!" Indeed, the rector of that neighboring parish was a terrifying man who refused to put up with people dancing after nightfall, for the Devil, he said, would slip in among the dancers. Even when there was a wedding at a farm some distance from his church, he would keep an ear out for the bagpipe and the oboe, which could be heard at least a quarter of a league away. If the sound continued, he'd dash out of his presbytery, rush over to the dance floor, having tucked up his cassock, and break up the crowd of dancers in a wild rage. Our own rector didn't go so far as that, but he did forbid night dances under penalty of eternal damnation.

So there was nothing for it. But since the members of the wedding were again hungry and thirsty, we all returned to our tables and the second meal began, not quite as copious as the first, but almost. However, this time it went faster, with the women trying to get the waitresses to hurry because they had to take their children home on the roads at night. Their children and perhaps their husbands as well. By then, the children could hardly keep their eyes open. Besides, the next day it would start all over again, unless there had been some good reason, stated in advance, for limiting the feast to one day. I, however, was not to return the next day. It was too tiring for so young a boy and too costly for my parents' pocketbook; in any case, they were not close enough to either of the families to feel that they had to attend all the festivities.

Very late that night, the burlesque "milk soup" ceremony would take place, and on the third day of feasting, Thursday, only the young people and very close relatives would get together. There was just one meal that day, but the musicians would still be around and everybody would go out to the country to dance at an inn at some crossroads or occasionally join up with another wedding party in another parish. That was the moment when old antagonisms would flare up, leading to challenges, insults, and sometimes pitched battles, each one upholding the honor of his clan and thinking what a good story it would make later on.

All the young people who had their parents' permission would spend the last two days of the week recovering from the excitement and roaming about the region in small groups. They had been invited here and there, the girls to their escorts' homes and vice versa (just in case they enjoyed each other's company enough to make it lasting!). And often the innkeeper who had served the wedding feast would invite them in to eat up the leftovers that couldn't be thrown out.

On Monday morning the hard life was to begin again. No more feeding off the fat of the land; everyone would again do penance with their oatmeal gruel, their thick pancakes, their skimmed milk, and their well water, pondering the memory of all that rich food. Every day is not a feast day, and a good thing too. A person who feasted every day would no longer be able to distinguish Sunday from the other days in the week. And there's no denying that the other days in the week yielded their own satisfactions if you happened to be the son of a good mother.

8 The New Testament

> Language is the cement of actions. It not only formulates them, but it remains forever marked by them . . . Although the properties of cultural factors and the properties of language belong to different realms of scientific investigation, they in fact constitute two sides of one and the same object; it is impossible to probe either one of them without finally coming up against the other.
>
> André Leroi-Gourhan

I had received my scholarship —an event that would have sent my family into raptures had it not been accompanied by a grim feeling of anxiety. How could they ever manage to send their child to one of the "great schools"—that is, to a university that specialized in professional training? On the other hand, how could they keep him at home when he had proven himself capable of going on to higher things? The poor people were extremely troubled. In spite of my full scholarship, they would have to clothe me, pay for the bus or the carrot-train to bring me home for vacations, and provide me with some money all the rest of the year in order that I not be penniless when my schoolmates were amply provided for. My parents tended to believe that most lycée students were the sons of millionaires. At any rate, all those we knew in the region were, if not rich, at least far better off than I. Apparently, if one applied to the town hall, there were ways of obtaining assistance, but my father refused to go to the town hall. He wanted no debts, and certainly no charity from that source.

Alain Le Goff kept counting and recounting the sous he received as a pension. Perhaps they would cover everything after all. He was prepared to sacrifice his pipe tobacco, but my mother wouldn't hear of it. She had drawn up an austerity program, with herself as the one and only victim, as usual. However, the pride she would take in seeing her son wear a cap stamped with the insignia of the Ministry of Education was enough to repay her for all her sacrifices. The cap tempted me as well: it was better looking than the one worn by the sons of the Whites, who studied at the Saint-Gabriel school in Pont l'Abbé. Besides, I had already taken an exam in agriculture, and since I came in second, I received, as a prize, a bankbook with thirty francs in a savings account. Grandfather claimed that I would surely have won first prize if we had been rich enough to have a farm. And, in fact, as part of the oral exam I had been asked to tell the age of a bull by looking at its teeth. I probably missed by a few months. But that was hardly surprising. We didn't have a bull.

In any case, it was finally decided that, come what may, I was to go to the lycée in Quimper along with a good friend of mine who had just as little money as I and who also showed promise. But then an interminable list of everything I was required to bring with me arrived from the lycée, so that for a few days the family's morale could not have been lower. How could they ask a little chap to have so many shirts and handkerchiefs, all marked with his number, not to mention a uniform—a navy blue suit with a little matching vest—and a trunk in which to put it all? And what did that mean, a washcloth? And toothpaste? The entire household was in a state of dismay. Then Marie-Jeanne Le Goff dried her tears and set about making, dyeing, fixing up, or buying almost all that was needed.

Since there were at least a dozen boys and girls from the region, both Reds and Whites, going off to a variety of public or parochial schools in Quimper, our parents hired a special bus which carted us there along with our mothers. Once the formalities at the lycée had been attended to, some stern and busy gentlemen wearing hats and ties asked us to clear out until the evening meal. And there I was, leading my mother to the Place Saint-Mathieu, where she was soon to take the same bus back to Pouldreuzic. Both of us were silent, feeling uneasy in our hearts and just barely managing to exchange a few words in Breton. "Work hard," she said. "After all, it may be easier than we think." And as she climbed into the bus, she added: "Above all, do nothing that will make us ashamed of you!" Then the bus took off, leaving three or four orphans on foreign land.

For an hour or two we roamed the city streets in single file, taking note of a number of landmarks so that we'd be able to find our way back to the lycée, and whispering a few last secrets into each other's ears in the language of what, to us, meant freedom. From then on we would have to formulate sentences in French all day and every day. That evening I was closed into the Quimper lycée for seven years, condemned to speaking and listening to French without stop, except in my dreams. As far as we were concerned, the ladies and gents of the lycée were both strict and kind. They did their jobs as well as they could. The fact that they were strict didn't bother us; we had been through that before. Indeed, we were somewhat surprised at no longer being slapped or given any kind of beating. I can hardly say that we missed the physical punishment, but we would have preferred to pay for our mischief-making and our mistakes with our skin, rather than to have them all entered into an account book as reasons for being taken off the honor roll, for confinement, for warnings, or for reprimands, the worst of which was appearing before a Disciplinary Board. A few of the students contrived to accumulate so many punishments that they were sent home. But most of us slaved away and did our best to obey: "Silence!" "Line up two by two!" "Come in!" "Sit down!" "On your feet!" "Go!" All that was easy. But how could you remain unperturbed when little hoodlums from the city or elsewhere would shout out, in the schoolyard, that the crotches of Bigouden women were split horizontally, like slots in a mailbox. Honor demanded that you jump on them and give them a smack in the kisser, without paying any heed to the supervisor. And you were the one to be punished for having hit first, since blows were thought to be more serious than insults. How could you not start a fight when the lousy day-students called you "ploucs" (dumb hicks) just because they happened to live in some pompous-looking apartment on the river or in a garret near the Fairground? Humility was not one of our cardinal virtues. Nor was spite one of our worst sins—that is, if we could settle our disputes then and there, on the spot. Some of the supervisors understood that and averted their eyes until things got out of hand. For the blows that were exchanged did everyone concerned a lot of good.

Actually, our aggressive behavior was due largely to the fact that we had not yet mastered French. One could hardly say that the city students spoke good French (and we were soon to be tops in that subject ourselves), but they spoke it fluently. In order to be on an equal footing with them, we should have had to use our mother tongue, and then those "tight-asses" would have got what they deserved. But there was no question of that. We were punished for speaking Breton.

Besides, no one seemed to remember that we had been transplanted, that we were immigrants living in a civilization foreign to our own. Not only were we still translating our oral language into bookish French, but our whole way of life, our behavior all through the day, from waking to sleeping, tended to irritate the others or to make them think we were a bunch of lunks, whereas watching those city kids put on airs left us dumbfounded. I learned once and for all that the seediest bourgeois considered himself far above the most subtle peasant. A misunderstanding that hasn't yet been dispelled and is not about to be. Added to that was the fact that we were among the poorest of the students. When we'd play ball in the yard, the others wore leather shoes, whereas we wore wooden sabots tied to our ankles with a string. But sometimes the string would break and the sabot fly smack into a window, shattering the pane with a crash. We had to pay for it, of course—a great expense for us—but we were also given a good talking-to in addition to being kept in. We couldn't have cared less about being kept in on a Sunday, since no one ever came to take us out; but a document would always be sent to our parents, and it was a real event in the lives of poor people to receive a document with a letterhead, a sort of police report, sentencing their son to heaven knows what for lack of discipline. The father, humiliated and enraged, would say: "He's going to get it when he comes home." Never, ever, did the document explain that the string had broken, or that we had fought and drawn blood to defend our women, or that we had been maliciously insulted. Lack of discipline, unruly behavior, that was all.

But those children's quarrels gradually came to an end as we began to take on city ways and to learn French so well that we became a threat to the boys who had spoken it all their lives. So let us get back to the ladies and gents of the lycée—that is, the grown-ups—from the good old janitor with his wooden leg to the headmaster himself, a tall man who dressed formally, like a corseted cavalry officer in civilian clothes, and who had an astonishing three-pointed moustache. Imposing, but not at all unkind. Between the two were the school servants, the supervisor-tutors, the professors, the vice-principal (who acted like a sergeant), and the principal (who acted like an officer). The First World War was right there under our noses, with its hierarchy of sociological samplings. And given our backgrounds, we country boys still ranked with the servants.

We were fully aware of the fact that, although seriously devoted to their jobs and anxious to help us make out, those who had been entrusted with our education treated us with a touch of condescension, because we were on full scholarships and had been elevated above our station. Needless to say, we didn't hold it against them at all, but thin-skinned as we were, some of the boys I knew well found it embarrassing. Our former teachers had also been gentlemen, but there hadn't been many of them, and all had been strangers to our town. At the lycée in Quimper it was we who were the strangers, and we were in their power night and day, bound hand and foot to them and also faced with day students who were the children of ladies and gents. When I used to cross Quimper to go for a walk on Thursdays and Sundays, I noticed that the nobility and the bourgeoisie wore city clothes, the kind that were fashionable in Paris. In fact, I got the impression that I was seeing the Romans ruling rather indulgently over us, the Gauls. There are historians who have written dissertations on the subject. I was annoyed at Vercingetorix for having been beaten by

Julius Caesar at Alesia. And do you know what happened to me in the middle of my second year at the lycée? Since I was one of the best students in French, the board of professors decided that such a gifted boy ought to be promoted to the program of classical studies. I was therefore to take Latin the following year, and one of my professors offered to give me free lessons so that I could catch up. Thus the little Gaul was handed over to the Romans.

Every day, we wore our patched-up suits. It had never mattered a bit in our region, where the rich and the poor dressed alike. But at the lycée most of the day students wore complete suits, all of the same material, with no bits and pieces sewn on anywhere. Yet we knew that at least a few of them were as poor as we. They dressed in short pants, which were then the fashion, whereas we wore breeches that came down to the middle of our calves because we had grown too fast. The rest of our wardrobe was in keeping. The head laundress would complain about the bad condition of our underwear and about how few shirts we had. And whenever the vice-principal, a blustering terror, would inspect us before we went out on our walks, he'd take hold of us by the lapels of our jackets, which were of some indeterminate color, and, with a look of disgust on his face, ask: "Is that what you call a uniform?" He was right, that man. We did not do honor to the institution. But he should have known why.

During my first year, when I was desperately depressed, I should have liked to go home for the All Saints' Day vacation. I should have liked to be back in my box-bed. I should have liked to eat pancakes with apples, and crêpes and gruel and black bread, on my oilcloth-covered table under the kerosene lamp. At the lycée, during one and the same meal, I had to get used to eating several kinds of strange food. One course was called "hors-d'œuvres"; what a curious word! Ah, if only I could have returned to the fold! I hadn't spent a sou. I had enough money to pay for a bus to Pouldreuzic. Yes, but as it happened, in that season there was neither a bus nor a train that went to Pouldreuzic.

Still, after an unfortunate attempt at hitchhiking, and as time went by, I began to feel less nostalgic. We gradually got used to the place. The bourgeois education at the lycée finally overcame our native rural character. During the long vacations we would return to our regions and to our own people with the same profound pleasure, but otherwise we lived like a bunch of acculturated, almost assimilated scribblers. Once we reached the higher grades, there wasn't much difference, at least on the surface, between us and the lower-middle class. The French graft had taken on Breton-speaking wild stock, or so it seemed. A few of our boys even began to deny their origins. At the end of a long hall that gave onto our yard, there was only one window you could see through. When the face of a woman wearing a coiffe would appear in it, and a servant called out her son's name in the yard, there were some who would go and hide behind the urinals at the back because they didn't want anyone to know they were the sons of peasant women. Boys like that would never know the meaning of pride, even if they happened to be destined for high places.

During my last year I had to have an emergency operation for a bad case of appendicitis, with complications. The operation was very expensive. We had no insurance of any kind. At home there was some question of selling the cow. And then my mother worked wonders and managed to get the money together with the help of Alain Le Goff, who gave her every single one of the few écus he had saved up. My father took a job as a servant for the season, and the entire hospital bill was paid fifteen minutes before I left. I had never strung so many green beans in Jean Hénaff's factory as I did during the summer vacation that year. When the schools opened again and I left for classes in Rennes to prepare for the competitive examination to enter the Ecole Normale Supérieur,* there was electricity in the house. My mother had even bought a scalloped glass lampshade which was admired by everyone in the neighborhood. The first evening that she turned on the lamp, we could scarcely eat our soup there was so much light in the house, which seemed much bigger—indeed, far too big for the likes of us, who were used to going about our work within the circle of light shed by the kerosene lamp. We had to learn entirely different movements and to take longer steps when we walked. Actually, we were almost rich, and I had one less scruple

*The state-run, university-level school in Paris which specializes in the training of lycée and university professors, and which, not so very long ago, accepted no more than a handful of students each year. (Trans.)

weighing on my conscience. Ever since my operation, I had been feeling guilty for having almost brought the family to ruination. But the day after the electricity had been installed, Marie-Jeanne Le Goff was so excited that she awoke at four in the morning to put on and adjust her coiffe under the scalloped lampshade. And all through the day she kept telling us how much straighter her coiffe sat on her head because she could now see the whole of it in her mirror.

Eighteen months later Alain Le Goff died, after a short illness. My grandfather Alain Hélias, the sabot-maker and teller of wondrous tales, had bade us farewell a few years earlier. When his old crony had gone to visit him on his deathbed, he had said: "Alain Le Goff, I'm off to see whether the other side of the world is worth more than this one. If it is, I'll let you know that you're to come along." Whether he let him know or not, Alain Le Goff finally left to join him. And it wasn't often that one saw so many people at the funeral of that poor a man. The year he died, I found the works of the French, German, Roman, and Greek philosophers a heap of commonplaces. For me the Old Testament had come to an end with Alain Le Goff's death. For me there were very few dates in the history of the world as momentous as that one, precisely because it belonged to me alone. There wasn't even an obituary in the papers.

I was then leading a double life, and I expect I always will. I spent three-quarters of the year at the lycée—first as a student, then as a supervisor, a tutor, and a professor, or else I worked at various jobs at night so that I could get my master's degree. The last quarter of the year I spent in my village: I would go back to my mother tongue; I'd cast off the clothes I had been wearing as an intellectual and slip into my peasant surroundings as one slips into a clean shirt; I would walk my one and only cow between its shed and our two fields; I'd pick the peas and thresh the wheat, the barley, and the rye; I'd gather up the potatoes, bring bales of hay and cabbages home on my back, and string heaps of green beans; I would even break a few yards of stones on the road—that is, until my mother decided that those particular jobs were no longer suited to my station in life. "Marie-Jeanne," the good people would ask, "how come you're still sending that well-educated son of yours, with all his diplomas, out into the fields and to the factory?" It was not she who sent me, nor was it my father. I expect it was I myself who, deep down, felt the need to cling to my roots. And I finally realized that, without meaning to, but by living in schools, I had driven myself out of my natural environment. Yet I didn't feel alienated, though the others knew I was, along with my friends who had become officers, doctors, teachers, and engineers. On Sundays, at first on foot and then on bikes or by bus, we would go to the weekly dance in Plozévet, Plogastel, or Plonéour, sometimes even farther. But there again we were different from the others; indeed, we were very sweetly turned down by the girls wearing coiffes, for whom we were no longer eligible as husbands, and sent back to the girls who were studying at lycées or universities. Of course, that did not rule out friendships, but it was pointless to conceal the fact that a gulf existed between us and that peasant society which was so scrupulous about rank. No one was at fault; the world was evolving; it was due to the times we were living in. Thus, little by little, we ceased being equals and companions.

Yet no one could accuse us of having repudiated that society. Even in our own region, things and people had begun to change as life became easier and as the rest of the world gradually and peaceably invaded that cell which had formerly been so closed in on itself. Soon all the young people and many who had reached maturity were speaking French effortlessly, although Breton was still the language of everyday discourse and the only language that many of them felt comfortable with. Soon children were wearing clothes with almost no patches on them, clothes of their very own, not hand-me-downs. They could no longer play a quiet game of marbles in the middle of the streets, for too many cars came through and were driven too fast. Anyway, by then they had toys that had been bought in stores. Just a few years later they were to forsake the little Christ-Child and believe in Father Christmas (!), whom everyone had begun talking about. For quite a while they had no idea of where they were at. "The Infant Jesus was born so long ago," one of them told me, "that he's now very old and has a white beard." It was clear that he also became very rich as he grew older, for he brought them great numbers of presents instead of that untouchable golden apple of yore. As for the candy stores, they now had customers during the week, as did the butchers, who were offering fresh meat for sale almost every day. And not only were most people asking the baker for "light" bread instead of the former ten-pound loaves, but they preferred them "long" instead of round; if anyone wanted black bread, he had to find out precisely when the next batch would be baked. At home, people were eating platefuls of tomatoes, those very same tomatoes that no one would touch when I was a child, for they had been considered almost as poisonous as mushrooms. People were also opening cans of food for their own pleasure, when they weren't even expecting a guest. Another change was that the last of our beggars had died. If one or two happened to show up at the Penhors pardon, they had come from somewhere else; no one knew quite where. The wedding meals were still copious, of course, if not as well prepared, but the old waitresses told me that people were not eating as much as before and took no interest at all in finishing up the leftovers, for they had full stomachs every day. (Not everyone, to be sure; not everyone.) And there were even some men who no longer dared to use their own knives at table.

Many of the houses in town now had glass-paneled doors which were closed during the day, can you imagine? You had to knock on them with the back of your hand if you wanted someone to open them. And people didn't always open their doors. When they did, you were not always asked to come in. Why, I wonder? But if you happened to be asked in, you had to see absolutely everything, and in detail—all the new equipment, all the new furniture. The mud floors had been covered over with cement. Sometimes the rich had had a kitchen, a room that served only as a kitchen, built onto the backs of their houses. The cupboards and beds had been copied by the carpenters from pictures that people saw in catalogues. Without any brass nails on them, and no religious carvings. The first pieces of furniture to disappear from people's homes were the box-beds, which had been replaced by the ordinary variety. When I was at the lycée in Quimper and used to take walks, I often passed a shop owned by Monsieur Jacob, Max's brother.* He had piles of old things for sale and all sorts of objects, particularly box-bed facades, only the facades. It was apparently his father who had given him the idea of collecting them. Above his shop was a metal sign with the word *CURIOSITÉS* ("Curios") written on it. And I wondered what in heaven's name was curious about a box-bed, in which I still slept whenever I was at home. Then I began to understand. Something was in the process of going awry.

The Pouldreuzic masons were being asked more and more frequently to build two-story houses, both in town and in the country. The two-story house had become the sign of wealth or of social success. Its height was an indication of its owner's rise in station. As for toilets—buckets with two wooden planks set across them—the fashion was to have them in a sort of sentry box, warped by the winds, at the back of the cottage garden.

Young girls were by then wearing city clothes, though there was no question of their mothers "disguising" themselves in that way. And since coiffes continued to grow higher year after year, mature women had to stand up straighter and straighter until they reached old age. In any case, the men would have looked disapprovingly at their wives had they "been lowered to wearing sacks."

The "Old Week" of the servants and farmhands, their week of glory, had become no more than a memory of the good old days. There were hardly any young servants or foremen on the farms. The only ones left were too old and too resigned to their fates to go out in search of adventure. And even they were gradually being supplanted by the machines in which they had taken such pride. Along with the engines, the reaping machines, and the binders came the contractors, who ran the whole threshing operation. The communal bonds thus started to slacken; the "groups" gradually broke up. Even the former hierarchies, according to which everyone had had his place in our "parish" society, became blurred. The rector was no longer the master. He had to give in when it came to attending dances at night, dancing "belly to belly," wear-

*Max Jacob (1876–1944), a French writer, painter, and art critic, was born in Quimper and died in a concentration camp. One of the precursors of surrealism, he was a very close friend of Picasso's and of the cubist painters. (Trans.)

ing indecent clothes, and even the sacraments. In the late 1930s fewer and fewer people were to call the teachers by their Breton title *mestr-skol* (schoolmaster), with the result that they finally became respectable but minor civil servants, nothing more. Also, the traditional dichotomy between Whites and Reds had lost its meaning. Instead, there were socialists and communists along with the radicals; and there was a right-wing party as well as a shifting center. It wasn't easy to figure out what those people's color was! And ambiguous problems were mysteriously taking shape in the background. In 1933–34 one heard talk of the "Green Shirts," peasants led by a certain Dorgères and who finally, in Quimper, fought the horseguards gathered together on the Fairground. The poor horseguards, mere riding-school trainers, having to fight men who knew horses far better than they. That's at least how the story was told on the Square in Pouldreuzic. The cavalry had advanced upon the peasants. So the peasants advanced upon the cavalry. Resolved, fearless, and with a certain smile. They attacked the animals. Some of them grabbed hold of the horses by their bits and then smacked their fists into a precise spot at the base of their ears. Down went the horses and the horsemen. Others clutched the horses' tails and pulled. Each animal stood firmly on its four legs, stamped, and tossed its head. At that point another peasant would come to the fore and, at just the right moment, by shoving his shoulder hard into the horse's shoulder, bring the animal crashing down. And the peasants laughed like kids. The cavalry retreated, re-formed, and brought out their rifles. The peasants got ready for another and a harder battle. Whatever the result of the disorder that ensued (some say that the prefect surrendered), that epic struggle worried everybody. Except perhaps one rich woman whose chief worry in life was the leveling of people's stations, and who soon afterward said: "A lot of good it does to dress my children up to the teeth. You can't tell them apart from the poor."

There was one sure thing: the whole region was in a state of flux. And we were responsible for all the agitation, we who were studying elsewhere and would come home for our vacations behaving like strangers, bare-headed, wearing knickers, and making the kind of revolutionary remarks that bewildered our childhood friends, who were still making every effort to stick to the rules. Also at fault were the sailors, who joined up with us, completely indifferent to the "what-will-people-say?" attitude, not to mention the children of the region who had taken jobs as servants in such places as Brest, Nantes, or Paris, and whom we would see every summer, killing time like those people called "tourists," while the natives were working their hardest.

I saw the first of those tourists a long time ago, on a day when I was unbinding the sheaves for the thresher. Behind the farmyard gate was a man dressed all in white, right down to his white canvas shoes, and wearing the kind of flat straw hat made famous by a certain Maurice Chevalier. The sleeves of his shirt were cut short (what a waste!), and he was holding a black box against his stomach. "A tourist," said the owner, as he would have said "a five-footed calf." For quite a while I thought I'd been dreaming.

Before 1936 there had been very few tourists who came and spent a week or two in the region if they were able to find a room for rent. We still weren't quite sure of what a summer hotel meant. But we soon learned what real tourists were like, those we always called "Parisians" and who had two obsessions. The first was walking about with those boxes called "Kodaks" and always wanting to take your picture while you were working (after all, when you wanted a portrait of yourself, you put on your best clothes and went to a photographer). And secondly, they could never spend three days in town without rushing off to take a dip in the sea at Penhors. They not only wet their feet; they wet their whole bodies, even when they didn't know how to swim. Were their asses that dirty? If they'd gone on like that, they wouldn't have had any smell left at all. As for the women, they were shameful. Wearing nothing but a black bathing suit. Soon they were wearing nothing at all. But the Penhors fishermen watched the whole to-do with inscrutable eyes.

Little by little, on summer Sundays, you began to see peasant families coming down to sit and look at the sea, first on the grass of the cliffs, then on the beach. Shyly, they too would wash their feet, the men leading the way and their wives behind them. Soon their sons managed to get enough money out of them to buy bathing trunks. One day, when two or three of us were stretched out on the stones, drying our skin, a girl wearing a Bigouden coiffe, all in black velvet embroidered with glass beads, drove up to the slip in a car. She got out, took a good look around, watched the exceptionally calm sea for a while, and got back into her carriage. When she came out again a few minutes later, we were absolutely dumbfounded. She was wearing a black bathing suit, but had kept her coiffe on her head. Indeed, what else could she have done? She ran down to the sea, went straight in, and began to swim as well as Morgan le Fay herself. And what an amazing spectacle it was to see the girl's coiffe sailing lightly over the sparkling swell of the sea. We almost didn't believe our eyes.

I don't know why, but it was on that very day, looking at the Bay of Audierne, in a place called Penhors, that I saw the dawn of a new age.

As a matter of fact, there were many signs which gave one to believe that the Old Testament had had its day. For example, on August 22, 1937, a bronze monument depicting the two well-known Breton musicians, the man with the bagpipe and the man with the oboe, was unveiled in Plozévet. After the unveiling there was a great feast for 1,500 people to honor the guild of those musicians who had gloriously celebrated the golden hours of our lives for centuries. Men of character who had such free spirits that they had been the cause of constant concern to the religious, and sometimes the civil, authorities. Men who were the faithful custodians of the traditions of a society whose code of living sprang from itself alone. As Jean-Marie Hénaff, our bagpiper, told me repeatedly some years later, "Dear old Pierre, that day I understood that such feasts can only take place once, one last time, like funerals." However, long before that day in 1937, he had been forced, like all the others, to learn to play the accordion, while the oboist had taken up the clarinet. At the start, each of them would bring their two instruments, the old and the new. But then the young people refused anything but the accordion and the clarinet. They had wanted to dance the one-step, fox-trots, waltzes, and tangos, dances which were not in the musicians' fingers, nor in their heads, nor, above all, in their hearts. Then came the jazz band and, with it, the saxophone. Jean-Marie went to work on pâté, green peas, and stringbeans in Jean Hénaff's factory.

That was the state of affairs when the Second World War broke out.

It would be pointless, given my subject, to talk about the war and the occupation that followed, since the effect they both had on the region was to stop the evolution I've been describing, just as an image in a film is suddenly frozen and then moves on as before. But I must nevertheless draw attention to the fact that after 1942 the requisitions levied by the Germans and the many shortages in consumer goods forced the people to be frugal, as in the past. And since so many men had been taken prisoner, even the old solidarity and the communal habit of helping one another during the periods of heavy labor were again held in esteem. Out of necessity, all the people turned back in some measure to their traditional civilization, thus making it easier to bear the misfortunes of the times. The majority agreed to put their faith in the trinity of Work, Family, and Country, and in their notorious Marshal. As for the Germans in the area, apart from a few minor incidents, there weren't any bitter conflicts between the population and the occupying soldiers until the latter, realizing that defeat was inevitable, grew fearful and therefore nervous. One good woman from my neighborhood paid with her life for that nervous irritation. Shortly after their departure, in the middle of the night, a naval battle broke out across from Penhors. Dozens and dozens of survivors, many of them wounded and some of whom had gone mad, were taken prisoner on the coast by commandos consisting of members of the Resistance movement who had not yet indulged in such a feast. After which, a few scores had to be settled. But the misdemeanors in the realm of economic collaboration were relatively minor. Anyway, the Reds and the Whites had not taken advantage of the occupation to dig up the hatchet. For the most part, they let bygones be bygones.

It took a few years before pressures from the outside world brought to light the changes that had taken place in the general mentality of the people. We all know that any war is traumatizing and that whatever the outcome, it unsettles the most firmly established societies. But this time history moved so rapidly that it wiped out rural society's reluctance to go along with new customs and new inventions. It also wiped out all the barriers behind which that society had patiently formulated its art of living. And it became eminently clear that the endeavors on the part of the successive governments of France to assimilate and deculturate Breton-speaking Brittany, ever since the Revolution, had suddenly borne fruit.

After the German occupation, what the farm workers learned, above all, was that they played a role of prime importance in the nation. For four years they had been in a position to make the city bourgeoisie, many of whom had been forced to act virtually like beggars, dance to their own—the farm workers'—tune. Thus they lost their inferiority complex and became self-assured; but they made haste to take advantage of the situation, for deep down they knew that the bourgeoisie, the "Government Boys," and the civil servants of every stripe would not be long in wishing to recover their privileges. At the same time, those men who worked the land realized that the rise of industry was a growing danger to them, not only because it would progressively and fatally diminish their role, but also because it would force them to change their techniques and thus their way of life, which wouldn't be easy given the fact that their milieu was nature and that the consequences of such a transformation had scarcely entered the planners' heads. To the planners, the pride of work well done, of well-kept fields, of crops well planted according to the seasons, not to mention the very nature of the land and of the climate, were nothing compared to their one and only concern, profit, which was dependent upon quantity; the buildings and the land were no longer to be the framework of life (the quality of which is more important to the traditional peasant than to anyone else, and I know whereof I speak), but merely a working site that would become gradually more disappointing as its efficiency became more problematical. Added to that was a rapidly growing drift away from the land, the lure of cities, increasing numbers of people being forced into exile, the illusions of comfort and high wages, and industry recruiting workers from among the peasants and nowhere else, while waiting for foreign immigrants. Finally, instead of fields peopled with families at work, instead of a great many "groups" helping each other with their tasks, one now sees nothing but a few tractors, each driven by a man, a lonely man accompanied by a flight of sea birds as he ploughs his furrows. And it was a mistake to believe that machines could replace the men or even the horses. There aren't many horses left because there aren't many foremen left to care for them; there aren't many foremen left because they have become plasterers or pavers or workers on an assembly line in some city; they took those jobs because they would be paid by the hour and no longer by the year or by the sunny day; they were paid by the hour because God's creature is moving farther and farther away from Creation. There is no longer any visiting among neighbors, no longer any community. I know one man who was reduced to talking to his tractor, as he had once talked to his horse. But the tractor didn't neigh; it never brought forth a foal. And many young men, all holders of rich land, will never have children because, since the women were the first to leave, they can't find anyone to marry. A civilization is disintegrating by slow degrees in an atmosphere of general indifference. It's no longer possible to earn your living with a spade and a hoe. My parents emptied the pig's manger for the last time; they sold their cow; they returned the two fields and the scrap of meadow to their owners; and my mother became a worker in Anatole Guichaoua's canning factory. Even when she worked nights at the height of the season, she found it less tiring than tilling the soil and taking care of her animals. And she earned a lot more, in addition to having periods of leisure during the winter. True, she was approaching old age and had slaved away without stop since 1900, when other little girls her age were taking their first communion.

Meanwhile, men who claimed to be statesmen and all sorts of planning economists were gathering at round tables with the unions to try and solve a problem whose unknown quantities could not be expressed in figures. For what, by then, was quite accurately called the "peasant malaise," and which was both physical and moral, was indeed the necessary outcome of bad politics with regard to the people who worked the land. I cannot stress that fact enough: a civilization that has long been threatened is in the process of disappearing, and one ought not be surprised at the upheavals that will accompany its decline.

No one ever really knew enough about country people. Never did the members of the government bother to find out what stuff they were made of. Perhaps because they were hard to figure out and had to be observed more than once or twice. But the main reason was that they were taken for simple people; thus everyone had the impression that they understood the peasants' needs better than the peasants themselves did. Glib talkers and the most pathetic would-be writers looked down their noses at them. However, when the peasants held their heads high, they were merely keeping a watch on the clouds. They were placed at the bottom of the ladder, the very best spot for spitting when they felt like it. They were in fact what is called "le peuple," the common people. *Plebs* in Latin, *plou* in Breton. That probably accounts for their having been called *ploucs*, implying "dumb hicks." Yet they were the people who came closest to being the nobility of the land, the true gentry, who had struck roots in our country and had shaped its face. They knew that. And they also knew that a man's hut is his castle. They hadn't called the king their cousin very often. But never did they call a cabinet minister their cousin.

The borders that the peasants knew best were symbolized by, say, a Bigouden waistcoat as distinguished from a Ploaré waistcoat, although the Bigouden and Ploaré regions were merely a few leagues apart. No need for soldiers, customs officials, or watchdogs to guard that kind of a border. On the other side of it, of course, they had rivals, but never enemies. Each side tried to keep its own originality, but not to make its neighbor adapt to its own ways. It was hard enough for them to reconquer the land every year; they let the politicians handle the conquering of men. They also let them handle foreign affairs. Has anyone heard of a peasant head-of-state since Cincinnatus?

That accounts for the fact that when a peasant was taken away from the soil and, by the same token, from his sense of proportion and values, he could be made to do anything anyone wanted him to. His own deep concerns no longer counted. He was therefore greatly ill-used.

It also accounts for the fact that the peasants, thus turned in upon themselves, had never, throughout the centuries, found any adequate outlets for their virtues or their vices. They were reduced to lecturing or tyrannizing over their familiars, particularly the family unit. Seen from the outside, they were constantly either submissive and passive in relationship to their masters or would blaze out into ruthless rebellions. Everyone was always surprised by the eruptions because they never even suspected that a volcano existed.

Now from the very start, peasants have been predisposed toward independence, especially in Brittany, where thousands of their ancestors had been strung up on trees for their very love of it. The humblest of them would have liked to have his fief, even if it consisted in no more than a thatched roof and a field of gorse, some pasture for a cow and a piece of land for growing potatoes to keep the pot boiling. If he had had a pine wood and two pigs to boot, our man would have felt like a lord. Today's old generation of peasants is determined to preserve that independence, as well as the art of living that follows from it, at the price of sacrifices which seem burdensome to others but which they accept with equanimity. One of those peasants, who is getting on in years and who, I know, lives in very reduced circumstances on a farm which less than thirty years ago was well known for its prosperity, told me the following: "What did you expect? A man can't have everything. In my case, Friday is not the only day I don't eat meat; far from it. But at least I'm in my own home. And I can take my pants down in a field that belongs to me, without worrying about the smell. My son has a car and a television set, near Paris. I went to see him this year. He's fine. But there are over a hundred people living in the same building, which would easily fit into my farmyard. I can't say what I'd do if I were younger. But at my age I prefer to stay here and look at my empty farmyard, with the sky above it and the fields around it. I know perfectly well that I'm rich, with all this land just for me alone. That's why I have to live like a poor man."

A poor man and a lonely one, even if the commune did make him a fine tarred road leading directly to his farm. For there's no longer any "group" or any society. In the past a big farmer at least had the company of his poor workers. They were companions; they led the same life. Indeed, there was hardly any difference between them. The poor man didn't spend money because he had none; the rich man didn't spend it either, because money was meant to be saved to buy land. The poor man didn't have the impression of being badly off; that is to say, he wasn't. And the rich man led the life of a poor man, having put his wealth into deeds executed by the notary public. Today a minority of rich countrymen have all the comforts of modern life at their disposal. When one of them goes for a drive in his car, there's no room on the seats for the poor peasant. The inequality of circumstances has become blatant. It isn't always the rich people's fault; it is the tragedy of the new age. The lowest of the agricultural workers have clearly lost their social position, as have the farmers and their families. They know it, are annoyed by it, feel humiliated, withdraw into their bitterness, and on Sundays go from bistro to bistro drinking red wine, since people no longer visit each other as they did in the past. Every man for himself; every man in his place; and let the rest drop dead. The Breton peasants are truly going through a very bad period, which will be just time enough for the old generation to disappear.

But everything considered, it's the poor man who has made out the best because he was the first to become resigned to his fate. He lives in some isolated house with its roof crumbling down between the gables. He is now old and his children are gone. His son, who moved up in the world, is probably a civil servant or a hairdresser in New York. He has thus done honor to his father and his mother, whose one wish was just that: to see their children move up in the world. I know many of them, very many of them, who bled themselves white to keep their children in school, for they were intelligent and ambitious. The parents, I mean. Intelligent enough to understand that, the way the world was going, their children would have been far worse off than they themselves. And ambitious, not for themselves, not for their own futures, but for their progeny. Thus before disappearing, the poor tenant had made it; he had made it for his progeny. Indeed, his son may have been one of those who married the bosses' daughter.

For even directly before World War II, the peasants' lot was such that even the big farmers' children were fleeing. They had

had enough of working for their fathers, who insisted on exercising their authority until they were very old and who had no intention of paying salaries to their children who went on working for them as servants and farmhands, even after they had married. In some places they were lucky if they had a corner to themselves alone. Finally, the farm would have gone to one of them, generally to the eldest, who would then have had to spend part of his life supporting his brothers and sisters. The mirage of the cities, large and small, had a strong attraction for young people deprived of all the comforts provided by electricity, gas, and running water. How many girls with large dowries had preferred two rooms on the top floor giving onto a dark courtyard in Paris to remaining on a supposedly rich estate and leading a life of endless labor in the quadrilateral cowshed-fields-kitchen-well! How many of them escaped by marrying a sailor and settling for a rented room in Brest or Toulon! So that the farm owners were soon unable to find maids. Now they can't even find wives.

Nevertheless, despite all the change, the language of everyday life in the countryside, and even in the town where I was born, is still Breton. Almost everyone also knows how "to make do with French," some of them very well indeed. But for the most part, they speak French only to people who don't know any Breton or when they happen to be in a city. On the other hand, the country people now clearly fall between two stools. The French they had learned in school was never given a chance to improve within the family circle or in their professional lives. As for their mother tongue, they are able to speak it; nothing more. That language had been deliberately removed from the state school curricula on the pretext of national unification, which has proven to be an empty concept for so long. And we are now witnessing this somewhat laughable paradox: eminent professors of modern languages who can't even read or write their mother tongue! The peasants, however, saw the prohibition of Breton in their schools as an unqualified censure of their language—as proof that it had no validity. They developed a complex about it which has lasted to this day. One constantly meets Bretons who feel ashamed. And since French now prevails in all rural affairs and in the newspapers, with its large stock of abstract words which are not quite clear to

Breton-speaking Bretons, the latter have isolated themselves, and the others have relegated them to the background. Indeed, they have been rejected, like lepers, to the fringe of the French-speaking nation. They have been forgotten.

One last factor is the rhythm of the land, to which farm workers have yielded for centuries out of a sort of mimesis so perfect that their posture and their most innocuous gestures proclaim their occupation as one of the oldest in the world. And that curious nobility in their physical movements, the time they take to negotiate with space, that natural harmony—all that makes them appear increasingly lumpish to the average man, as he himself grows increasingly nervous. I know people who are irritated by the slow pace of the peasants walking about their cities. Perhaps they would do better to be irritated by the way they themselves rush about. We shall make it to Christmas together.

In all fairness, one cannot blame the peasants for having fallen behind either out of deliberate bad grace or narrow-mindedness or an inability to adapt. The fact is that *they* work with life. The land is alive and as fragile as a woman's belly. The animals and vegetables are alive. It is relatively easy to extract a car from a lump of metal. Metal offers no resistance to anything stronger than itself. But just try and transform a piglet into a fattened pig in less than a week! Not until it has reached its proper weight and has been killed can you have it cut up into thirty-six shapes by an assembly line using an electromechanical device. But how soon will it take for you to have factories for making pigs? How soon will you find a replacement for bread? And what will it be?

Actually, most of the techniques that constitute progress were discovered by city people for their own use. It was not so very long ago that the engineers decided to tackle the peasants' problems. The least one can say is that their achievements are not exactly dazzling. They did what they could, of course. But it is apparently easier to dig a tunnel under the English Channel than to standardize agriculture.

Yet even today—have you noticed?—the young peasants, or what's left of them, no longer walk like their fathers. That's because they wear different shoes; the roads are tarred; there are not as many slopes. Nor is their bearing like that of the old peasants. That's because they use different tools. They move faster because the tractors changed their age-old rhythm and because, for them too, time is now money. They wear wristwatches and manage to be punctual. Their fathers always arrived too early or too late.

The last trial for which the man with the spade prepared himself during his lifetime was the destruction of his garden. For the peasants were the true gardeners of the land. Their patient work resulted in most of the meticulously designed landscapes on which we rest our eyes. They, of course, were not in the least concerned with artistic effects, though they always admired the beauties of nature as much as any would-be Jean-Jacques Rousseau. Since they had no means other than their own hands and arms, a few rudimentary tools, and a few domestic animals, they had necessarily to come to terms with mountainous or hilly country, leaving the heights to grow wild or bare; and to cultivate the slopes, respecting the contours; and to utilize the valleys, taking into account the rivers and streams. In short, the land and the sky were forever their masters. They took care not to abuse the elements, knowing from experience that any abuse led to catastrophe. As a result of that wisdom, which was forced upon them, the essential qualities of the landscapes—that is, order and harmony—were maintained.

Then the gardeners went away, and with them went the hoes, the baskets, the sickles, and the peaceable horses. Giant machines sliced directly into the cake of hills and let the old roads that wound slowly through the countryside revert to grass. Entire areas became wild again, while elsewhere huge factories filled the land with concrete, electricity poles, and lots of yellow smoke. Lakes began to appear behind the dams that were built to check the flow of the mountain streams, lakes in which one was soon to hear the legendary bells of sunken villages. More and more makeup was being applied to the face of the world. Artifice gradually became obtrusive as man set himself up as master. Should we grieve over it? No; but we must hope that one day a new beauty will emerge from all that; why not? And raise our hats to the old farming community, the gardeners of the world.

During the last fifteen years we have witnessed the shattering, in all directions, of the remains of the civilization I have attempted to describe and evaluate, without taking into account any economic or political considerations except insofar as they inevitably affected the evolution in question. Like Monsieur de Montaigne, I am not teaching; I am telling a story.

And as a matter of fact, the period we have just lived through is worth telling about from my own, very special point of view, for at the same time as its emissaries managed to sell short the evidence of an art of living that has come to an end, they are now desperately seeking to recreate another based on the very same evidence, just as people go to museums and meditate on ancient remains to find inspiration that is apt to humanize the days to come. It is not the first time they have considered that as a recourse. Vanished civilizations often make a comeback in that way. But sometimes it takes centuries for the enduring aspects of their experience to reappear in the texture of the present day. This time, the revolution of the world has been so colossal and so profoundly unsettling, while the dread of the future is so great and the present so precarious, that men are clinging to the last stable values they had once lived by, understood, and sometimes repudiated, and which they have just come to acknowledge—that is, to accept as a means of taking refuge in the context of today. Fortunately, they did not delay too long, for had they remained unaware of them just a few years longer, they might well have lost everything.

But the game isn't won for all that. On the other hand, if the civilization of our countryside still has a future before it disappears completely, it also, obviously, should incorporate the positive and negative poles of the scientific and technological societies that have developed outside it and at its expense. Moreover, the cards in the game will be redistributed in some other manner, without the trumps ever changing hands. The way things are going, the king would seem to have become the 7, it being understood that, from now on, the 7 will have a higher value than the king.

I must now return to one of the most significant phenomena of modern times, the tourist trade. Wave after wave of tourists poured in everywhere and changed not only the life of the countryside but also that of the seashore, in my Bigouden region as elsewhere. After 1936 came the "congés payés"—people who, for the first time, had been given holidays with pay. And more and more of them poured in each year. Entire families would arrive and settle down for two weeks in July or August at their parents', their uncles' and aunts', or their cousins'. Some of them even rented a room from former neighbors. Moreover, they would bring friends along, either workers or clerks who were true townspeople, without any relatives in the country and who, like the others, wanted to take dips in the sea and give their children a chance to benefit from the glories and freedom of nature. But however likable and however much they distracted the inhabitants, those idle tourists invading the region at a time when the natives were working their hardest could not help but be somewhat irritating to the peasants who, whether rich or poor, were not accustomed to taking vacations and, most especially, not during the summer. Besides, their very presence made perceptible changes in the state of mind not only of the local youth, which was inevitable, but also of the older generation, who could never quite understand money that was paid to employees by paper checks or their equivalent. So they imagined that the tourists were filthy rich and that their money had been taken out of the hides of others by the "Government Boys." After all, there they were, all those chaps being paid to do nothing for two or three weeks, which gradually gave that older generation the idea that tourists were customers to be milked by just about everyone. Not dishonestly, of course, but without flinching and without according any special treatment to members of the family, who no longer belonged to the "group." And besides, why should the peasants have made allowances for those "August birds" who had an unfortunate tendency to consider themselves superior to the local people and who came there to enjoy the sea, not the countryside. They dressed like fishermen out of an operetta, wearing red canvas sailor tops in Penhors, where the fishermen never wore anything but blue canvas. But has anyone ever seen a tourist dress like a peasant?

After the Second World War there was an onrush of people who, instead of being called "tourists," went by the name of "summer vacationers." From then on, tourists were those who traveled to foreign countries, who crossed borders. The phrase *tourist trade* now referred to a new industry, and was given so much publicity and stirred up such huge and dissimilar crowds that it turned into an epidemic which, in the end, infected even the most traditional towns and the most sedentary country people. Buses from the Bigouden region, taking off from the very tip of the Old World, began to scour the roads of France and Europe, filled with adventurers, some of whom could speak nothing but Breton. "After all," said an old woman who had just toured all of Italy with a coiffe on her head and trying to make pleasant conversation in Breton with the natives of Florence, Rome, and Venice, "once you're out of France, you're in the very same position as those who speak French, since I noticed that they didn't speak Italian either." She was very flattered by the interest she had aroused just about everywhere, with her high coiffe and all the velvet on her dress. A star, in fact. The average tourist's daily bread is local color. But I admit that taking a picture of a real Bigouden woman in her best clothes in front of the Leaning Tower of Pisa must have been a rare privilege for a whole sampling of Europeans. However, just a few years earlier, that same Bigouden woman would never have agreed to let the "Kodakers" take her picture; she would have turned her face away or covered it, as most of the others still do today. Had it been a long time ago, she would perhaps have called her brothers or her husband to come to her rescue, and the tourist's Kodak would have ended up under the men's sabots; that had happened several times during the thirties. "But now, my dear Pierre," she said, "people do anything at all when they're not at home. There's no shame anymore. And what can you do to stop them?" So I told her that one of my friends had found the answer. When he'd be taking a walk in the summer with his Bigouden mother, and tourists took it into their heads to aim a camera at her, he would quickly aim his own at them. That was generally enough to dissuade them. She burst out laughing. "It's true," she said, "that most of them look like they're dressed for a costume party." Then she suddenly got angry: "We're not strange beasts, after all! People like that now take themselves for gentlemen, and they wouldn't even be able to afford to give their wives the coiffe I've got on my head. Do you know how much I paid for it, my dear Pierre? And I have almost a dozen coiffes like this one. Do their own wives have a dozen hats?" At which point she bade me good day and stalked down the street, her eyes blazing and her nostrils quivering with indignation. Anyone who will ever want to take her picture again had better beware. He'll hear litanies that have never been printed in any missal.

If I used that woman as an example, it is because the story is a rather good illustration of two facts that struck me during the 1950s: on the one hand, townspeople of almost no status were naïvely vain enough to persist in considering country people as lower class—likable, no doubt, but somewhat backward; on the other hand, country people had already gotten rid of their inferiority complex, they no longer felt in any way destined to serve the bourgeoisie, and they were even inclined to look down their noses at them because they had become aware of the values of their very special civilization and were by then speaking fluent French, while at the same time keeping up their mother tongue, which at least was useful in making fun of the others without the others realizing it. And that was a sign that a serious transformation was taking place.

As soon as World War II ended, "Celtic Clubs" were being formed almost everywhere in Brittany, but especially in the Breton-speaking regions. The members were young people whose objective was to bring the peasant tradition, with its costumes, its dances, and its games, back into esteem. Within ten years several hundred of those groups had been organized. At the same time, thanks to the persistence of a few pioneers, other young people began to take lessons from the last of the professional bagpipers and oboists, who were ending their lives in a state of melancholy. Most important of all were "The Great Fêtes of Cornouaille," founded in Quimper in 1948, and which were to take on extraordinary proportions in just a few years, with three to four thousand dancers, musicians, and singers giving regular performances and drawing crowds estimated by the police at over a hundred thousand. Somewhat later, in Brest, there was a "Bagpipe Festival" which conveyed not only the players' dynamism but a profound passion inspired by an underlying preoccupation with politics—a concern that was to grow more and more explicit as the general problems of the world, and particularly those that concerned youth, became increasingly acute. Think of thousands of young people involved in traditional art forms at a time when their traditions were both alive and threatened, perhaps even doomed, and faced with a new society which they couldn't count on in any way. How could they possibly have not protested? They knew perfectly well that they didn't agree with what was going on, that there had to be other ways of doing justice to man, other ways of changing life, and that all things considered, since the politicians took pleasure in continually referring to the past, maybe it wasn't that good an idea always to sacrifice the Gauls to the Romans, the Incas to the Spaniards, the colonized peoples to the colonizers, and the folk civilization of the Bretons to an allegedly elite culture which ensured the economic domination of those who used that civilization as a warhorse. Make no mistake about it. Politics are not limited to parties, unions, electoral campaigns, manifestos, and marchers waving signs. Politics are deeply embedded in everyone's gut and go farther back in time than any philosophy.

Politicians and their constituents know it so well that they never cease discrediting cultural events sponsored by the common people. They don't proceed by issuing edicts or prohibitions; they are still obsessed by the old fear of peasant uprisings. Their idea has been to deprive such events of any character and any meaning other than that of an agreeable and pleasantly nostalgic entertainment. And their triumph was their having taken over the word *folklore* and its derivatives, and having drained them of all revolutionary potential. They did it, I must admit, with the help of the common people themselves. Before going on, it would perhaps be well to try and understand how all that came about.

So let us talk about folklore. Given the way the world is progressing, that poor word has lost its precise meaning for most people, just as the French adjective *formidable* has come to mean "terrific." The atomic bomb, I dare say, is *formidable*, but given the word as it is currently used, so is lobster with mustard sauce or a new detergent or indeed almost anything. Literally, folklore means the civilization of a people, or peoples, taken as a whole, and including everything that sets it apart from the others; but most of our contemporaries take it to mean nothing but a number of traditional dances in local costume. To others "folklore" is synonymous with niceness, with childish naïveté, with underdeveloped art forms, with a nostalgia for things pastoral, with sitting around the fire in a thatched cottage, with innate backwardness.

I agree that such misconceptions of a rather strange word in French didn't come about by chance; ironically enough, it was criticized when it made its first appearance in England (1846) for being too scientific. It is made up of two English words: *folk* (people) and *lore* (knowledge). If you take the trouble to open a dictionary, you will find that the meaning is clear. All the specialists worthy of the name are in agreement: the word *folklore* means the comparative science which investigates everything that constitutes the civilization of a given people, or peoples, historically and socially located in a specific place, and distinguished by certain spiritual and material characteristics. The spiritual characteristics amount to a collective psychology conveyed by a language, a dialect, or a patois, an oral or written literature, music and specific instruments, dances and songs, styles of dress, games and physical exercises, traditional feasts, beliefs and customs, laws and legal practices, and social traditions. The material characteristics are conveyed by their techniques of building dwellings and ships, of making tools and instruments, of craftsmanship, of farming and the breeding of animals, of navigation and fishing, of nutrition and folk medicine. All typified by the traditional collective consciousness specific to that people or peoples.

Actually, most of our contemporaries are essentially folkloric individuals. By that I mean: they are unable to bring themselves to give up certain ways of life that correspond to their deepest inclinations. I also mean that folklore is timeless. And finally, I mean that it is a defensive reaction against a future which, despite all of its promises, cannot help but trouble the sons of man. I believe that folklore has become a process of continual protest, which it never was in the past.

In France we always celebrate the year's end with good wishes and an exchange of gifts. We celebrate Twelfth Night, Mardi Gras, Easter, Midsummer Day, and ten other days in the year that were "folklorized" well before Christianity. People everywhere went so far as to make Father Christmas, or Santa Claus, into an institution, and not only for business reasons, believe me. We put up fir trees with candles on them because of some obscure remembrance of the Celtics' Tree of Light. Just try and do away with all that! Try merely to drop the short school holidays that celebrate religious feast days! You'd be reviled by the unbelievers themselves. And I haven't mentioned events such as the Carnival of Nice or the July 14th parade or the ribbon that's cut to inaugurate just about anything at all or the bottles of champagne that are smashed against the prows of new ships. It wouldn't be easy to give all that up, would it? Yet when you come to think of it, we're right back in the Middle Ages. All that is as incongruous as a western, complete with stagecoaches and cowboys, under the presidency of Mr. Carter. In other words, all that is eternal.

Folklore continues to take on new shapes right under our very eyes. Its shapes evolve, of course, and today more quickly than ever before. It is very adaptable. But true folklore has nothing to do with fashion. It is the opposite of fashion. It takes more than a lifetime to become established. It still symbolizes the continued existence of man. Now in today's folklore festivals, what we see are images of a time when the hand prevailed over the machine, when you could drink river water, when trees were felled only to make roofs or fires, when you could be distinguished from others by your costume. Early in this century, folklore festivals were spontaneous events. Today they serve only to recall certain values that we are in the process of losing and which, as we have come to know, are essential. However much the political leaders may scorn them, they carry more weight than a good many speeches and songs. All of that, including the Celtic Clubs and the Bagpipe Festivals, is bound to disappear one day; we know it. But something else will come out of it, and historians ought to do justice to the constant protest inherent in the folklore movement since World War II, and well before all the guitars, the long hair, the beads, and the flashy shirts that have been adopted by the future Playboys of the Western World.

Today, folklore festivals are highly criticized. Some consider them entertainments of no great artistic merit and suitable only for the working classes who live in low-cost housing developments.

They wouldn't go near one for anything in the world, those same people who go to see the Béjart ballets without, of course, understanding what they're about, but so that they may rave about them over a scotch on the rocks when they get home. They are the new nobility and the new bourgeoisie, who admire themselves as reflected in their own fingernails, without ever suspecting that they're sitting on a volcano. The dormant volcano is the folklore festival. But don't trust it. The last time it became active, roads were blocked and the subprefect was thrown out of the window. Everything has its day.

Others go about proclaiming that folklore is the opium of the people: it merely shows how they amuse themselves; it doesn't touch on their problems. Some go so far as to say that the peasant civilization is prostituting itself on stages and in parades, profiting from the spectators who pay for their seats. They're right, if one judges from appearances. The folklore festival is the only theatre the people have. And theatre is essentially a protest, even when it's meant to be conservative. The more naïve it is, the more lessons it conveys. It gives the people an awareness of how the world is evolving, without there being any need for speeches. Before casting out the old man, one must know how he functions.

The truth is that in Brittany the great folklore festivals are not mere entertainments, nor do they pay servile homage to the tourists, as so many Empress Eugénies and Napoleons. Although the tourist trade is an industry and a business, it doesn't matter much to the defenders of the people's civilization except to the extent that the July and August "birds" provide them with innumerable witnesses to a peasant culture whose only means of expression is the spectacle it gives of itself; for while it constantly provides inspiration for writers and artists, that inspiration is generally attributed to their genius, even when they loudly acknowledge their borrowings. In spite of that fact, literature always prevails over what people say, as the artist prevails over the artisan. To give only one example, the Le Nain brothers and Millet will never be put into the category of great painters because they shall always suffer from the cultural disrepute that dogs their peasant origins, which they had diffidently tried to express. Bad academic painting will continue to win out until the day that intellectualism manages to win out. And the quality of the Impressionist painters will always be ascribed to their subtle artistic talents, even though the peasants, from the very start, had seen nature with the same eye as they. But it would never have occurred to the peasants to paint, except with words that are gone with the wind.

The peasant civilizations that were shattered have left material proof of their existence—fields of ruins upon which antique dealers, second-hand dealers, cobblers, and collectors of all types have swooped down. The whole of Brittany has become a huge repository of "curios," which must make Max Jacob's brother turn over in his grave. There are so many cupboards, box-beds, standing clocks, cradles, spinning wheels, settles, and horse collars—indeed, almost everything made by hand that's usable, even in unexpected ways. And if they happen to be useless, they can serve as ornaments, like the wagon wheels embedded in garden gates and which turn instead of roll. A stable lantern sits enthroned in a drawing room next to a cartwheel made into a table lamp and a Bigouden shirt-front framed against a background of black velvet, like a painting by an old master. Before sitting down on a worm-eaten charabanc seat, you can put your umbrella into a churn in the hallway and recomb your hair if you open the doors of a box-bed facade glued to the wall and which "dresses up" (dresses up?) a mirror. Ah! Those box-beds, what a blessing!

I have seen some that have been transformed into coat racks, into bookcases, into sideboards or living-room bars, and into cabinets containing a phonograph, a radio, and a television set. I even found one that had been turned into a lavatory to the great satisfaction, if not the great comfort, of those who use it. Another one serves as a dressing room in a tailor's shop. Yet another conceals a screen for showing home movies. And the one that received the greatest tribute is today the frame for a well-known masterpiece worth millions.

Now, in my view, that's just fine. Insofar as the box-bed facades are not pulled to pieces or desecrated with a saw, it's better than leaving them to rot in some barn, where they often serve as boxes for storing potatoes. Thus our ancestors' most symbolic piece of furniture is still being used, having been "converted" to meet the needs of our time. And I must admit that most of the people who own box-beds take a certain pride in them. Some go so far as to sleep in them. I give you my word!

I, however, was born in a box-bed. And when I'm sometimes asked whether I would still sleep in one, the answer is no, not on your life. Unless my youth could be given back to me, along with the complete world I was brought up in, and which time has destroyed. I wouldn't sleep in a box-bed again on any account. For the simple reason that I'm no longer in a state of grace; moreover, I would have the impression that I was offending the Manes, Lares, and Penates. That's all. Unless some old man I know suggests that I sleep in one of his box-beds, one that had never been used as anything but a bed. And even so, I should probably still say no because I'm no longer worthy of that bed or of its owner. I don't know if I'm making myself clear. It has nothing to do with regrets or nostalgia. It is merely that I've been left behind. Indeed, it was I who stayed behind, thinking I was moving ahead. And I sold my birthright for a mess of pottage.

Nothing is left of my early civilization but wreckage. There are still some trees, but no more forests. To speak only of its objects, as soon as they were dispersed, they lost almost all their meaning. Museums have been built for them; and sometimes, with touching care, the large room of some farmhouse has been reconstructed down to the last detail. But that room doesn't live anymore, doesn't work anymore. Unfortunately, some people got the bright idea of putting dummies in them to represent the inhabitants. Heartbreaking. All things considered, the objects are better off in glass cases. That at least is honest archaeology, and it interests everyone except those who see their own lives reflected in that archaeology. For it isn't the peasants who have a taste for old things; it's the bourgeoisie.

A taste for old things is one of the obsessions of our time. Due to nostalgia for a period during which the simplest objects were made by hand? Or because they compensate for a way of life that urges change upon us season after season? A reaction against synthetic materials, which are doubtless very convenient but to which we are unable to become attached, as we are to sculpted wood, wrought iron, carved stone, and woven wicker? Or against those mass-produced items that are doomed to overflow the city dumps and are made in such profusion that we're in danger of being engulfed one day in our own garbage? Or is it an admission on our parts that our predecessors, however wretchedly underdeveloped compared to us, had a certain feeling for beauty on a human scale? Or because we worship memories and have a condescending respect for the cupboard of some grandmother, not necessarily our own? Or do we wish to transform our living rooms into museums for our own satisfaction and our guests' amazement? Or are we the kind of snobs that go along with such fads as having an old-fashioned telephone installed to keep up our "status"? Or do we have some ulterior motive—speculation, for example? Or . . . ?

We know that the monuments which have come down to us through the ages are made of bits and pieces. For every period has always preferred the new to the old, at least until the nineteenth century. If a number of Breton manor houses are still standing, it is, in many cases, because the owners weren't rich enough to pull down the old dwellings and replace them with buildings that were fashionable at the time, a practice which lasted over the centuries.

What am I leading up to? Nothing. What do I want to prove? Not a thing. Which point of view do I favor? Neither one. I am merely stating facts, facts which remind me of a comment made by a notary public who had just held an auction to sell off the furnishings of a farmhouse: "It's really amazing. The gas stove and the formica tables and chairs were bought by the peasants in the area. But the old furniture studded with nails, even the worm-eaten pieces, absolutely delighted the rich bourgeoisie. When I say it's amazing, you see what I mean. Had it been the other way round, I would have been amazed."

Yes, of course. Everyone wants what he doesn't yet have or doesn't have anymore. The poor peasants are reduced to selling their family possessions because they can't remain in their homes for lack of work. And townspeople everywhere who have made a bit of money are out to buy up and restore some country house, because daily life in the cities has become unbearable. We are now at the point where, if there's no revolution, all the poor peasants will be cooped up in low-cost housing developments in the cities, whereas the bourgeoisie, the technicians and the technocrats, the heads of industry and the top executives, the tourist-trade promoters and even the politicians will be residing in the country, in the mountains, or on the sea, with all the modern conveniences. And once they have settled in, dressed in corduroy, they'll be cutting, watering, planting, and pruning gardens they have copied straight out of the plush magazines. For they are the ones who are now nostalgic and reactionary, not the peasants, who will henceforth meditate on their uprisings in concrete rabbit-warrens.

Moreover, it didn't take long for the natives who still live in the region to start imitating the townspeople. At the instigation of the tourist-trade phenomenon, they have rediscovered their origins. There's no way now to get them to give up a piece of traditional furniture which they themselves had looked down upon not so very long ago. If it's good enough for the tourists, it's good enough for them as well. And they are now rich enough to keep what they have. And their children are no longer in ignorance as to the value of their heritage. The well-to-do are building modern houses with marble floors and wrought-iron stairways to accommodate their grandfather's furniture. It's the ne plus ultra. They're dusting off the old family photographs and setting them up in their living rooms as a kind of portrait gallery of ancestors. The impoverished food they used to eat is now back in esteem, although true, it's richer. The spending, the waste, and the decadence of the Roman Empire is now all ours! We're organizing flail-threshing parties, complete with "locomobiles" and a sampling of oatmeal gruel out of wooden spoons. Craftsmanship is thriving again everywhere: the sabot-makers, harness-makers, weavers, potters, and pocket-knife sculptors are again living in a golden age. At remote crossroads, the inns that were not turned into *crêperies* or nightclubs have become artists' studios. An Armorican Park has been created, with entire farms restored, as in the good old days, which weren't good and are not all that old. Like an Indian reservation, say the gossips. *Vade retro, Satanas*!

What do I think of it all? I don't think anything. It's no longer my business. For people my own age, and with the same upbringing, who for thirty years have tried to do justice to the peasant civilization, it's a bit late; it's a craze, the background of which is very unclear; and it's perhaps a way of giving oneself a good conscience. Better late than never; better to have a temple filled with buyers and sellers than no temple at all; better to have an active good conscience than an ineffectual bad conscience. The main thing, after all, is that the value of our civilization has been acknowledged—a culture which, some thirty years ago, almost no one, not even the antique or second-hand dealers, would have dared to grace with that word.

Early in the century two aphorisms were used by a number of self-appointed, recognized upholders of the Breton-speaking society against the Jacobins and their endeavors:

Ar brezonez hag ar feiz *A zo breur ha c'choar e Breiz.*	The Breton language and faith Are brother and sister in Brittany.
Hep brezoneg, Breiz ebed.	Without Breton, Brittany doesn't exist.

The least one can say is that faith can no longer move mountains as it did in the past. To begin with, the seminaries have been put up for sale for lack of clerics. The soil in which such vocations are nurtured was washed away by too many storms. Secondly, and as I mentioned earlier, the rector has lost most of his power. In the church of Saint-Faron and Saint-Fiacre the pulpit has been detached from its pillar, leaving white scars on the granite. The big angels on the altar have taken flight to some heavenly sphere. And I truly believe that Saint Eloi finally reshod his horse and rode off to seek his fortune elsewhere. The great Penhors pardon still exists; Madame Mary's house is in good condition; but innumerable other chapels are dying from neglect and are resigned to collapsing! And the faithful are watching the disaster with indifferent eyes. As Per G told me, what good is an eggshell when there's no yoke and no white inside it? Per G's comment reminds me somewhat of a monk who leaves his precious books at the disposal of anyone who wants to look at them, even though they are the only copies extant. Rather worried, I asked: "Aren't you afraid they'll disappear one day?" "What difference does it make?" he replied. "We have photocopies of them."

It's very like the hunt for old saints that has been going on in

Brittany for some ten years now. The wooden and stone statues of them have been stolen; the calvaries have been dislodged and torn down; and all of them have ended up in game pouches—in other words, in the trunk of somebody's car. Will they serve as trophies nailed to collectors' walls or be sold on the black market? As soon as sacred symbols become mere works of art, they fall into the category of objects and end up in the hands of dealers. Similarly, pieces of carved granite and oak, which are in fact the portraits of our ancestors, have suffered the same fate as the remains of all vanished civilizations and are the pride of the great museums, which naïvely boast about such acquisitions. Does that mean that old Brittany has had its day?

With all the authority of her ninety-four years, Marie-Corentine whispered in my ear:

"And what if the saints took off all by themselves? It wouldn't surprise me. We don't even know their names. We walk past them without even greeting them. There's one of them, not far from here, who left his alcove four years ago. And no one—can you imagine?—no one ever noticed it."

"Except you yourself, Marie-Corentine."

"Oh, well. I used to bring him flowers sometimes, in a tin can. That one loosened my tongue when I was five. Without him, I would have been a mute, me who likes to talk so much."

Yet even Marie-Corentine didn't make a fuss about the wooden saints having disappeared. And Brittany, in the sense that it was once a huge outdoor religious museum, is growing poorer every day because its sacred objects are being defaced, bought up, stolen, or falling into a state of dilapidation, and the faithful as a whole merely pay lip service to the dreadful changes taking place in their daily lives. Some of the priests have even got them accustomed to seeing the old saints relegated to the sacristy, if not the belfry. And others are selling off the old statues to help get central heating into their churches. Why be more pastoral than your pastor? Perhaps the time has come when the idols ought to be burned and the healing saints replaced by the one and only Our Lady of Medicare. The people didn't have to read Paul Valéry to know that all civilizations are destined to die. Nor was it they who had the preposterous idea of building monuments. For centuries the peasant's life was so unchanged that he lived with the heritage of his fathers and transmitted it to his children. Period. When he replaced an object, it was because it had lost its usefulness. Not only was it worthless, but it got in the way. However, an object used to last for generations, sometimes for several centuries, which gave the impression of an imperturbable continuity. The same was true for the gods. Like men, they had a triumphant youth, then they grew old, and finally they died, leaving their heritage to their Divine children. The god who succeeded them merely put his coat of arms on the monument of the preceding dynasty. A cross and the instruments of the Passion on a menhir, for example. Infidelity? No. One can change kings and yet remain a royalist. And then a time comes when kings are no longer the fashion. So the dynasties change because they must.

An acquaintance of mine once asked me, bitterly: "Why don't they make new saints? The old ones don't know how to deal with our problems anymore. What's happening?" Perhaps he thought I could do something about it, given that handful of knowledge I carry around in my head. He was also convinced that opening the Bigouden region to anyone and everyone had resulted in weakening the power wielded by Our Lady of Penhors and of the countless other Our Ladys who, until recently, had guaranteed protection to a parish or a district. Now the orders come from Our Lady of Paris, Our Lady of the Government. The saints are no longer anything but little mayors and little county councillors. The sky has increasingly become an image of the earth.

Not so stupid, when you come to think of it.

The women, most especially, were upset when Mass began to be celebrated in vulgar French. The Church must have had some good reason for it, but were Breton and faith no longer brother and sister? Why were they separated from each other? Which one had been to blame? And how would God the Father be able to distinguish the Bretons' prayers from all those other prayers that wafted up to His throne? And how could you pray properly in a language you were just beginning to learn and in which you still made blunders? A language whose words were like half-empty boxes, and you weren't even quite sure what was inside them. A language that was so hard to sing that you were afraid of being off-key, ashamed of offending the Lord by croaking so badly out of tune that He would surely know it didn't come from the heart. The priest himself, the mediator, was uncomfortable with French, which the Reds knew far better than the Whites. So the Reds had won out. There were Reds in the Church, people said. Soon everyone was to go to Mass as they went to school. In other words, some were to be good pupils and others bad pupils. Not so very long ago, everyone understood everything in the same way; each one of them truly partook of the sacraments; and they all knew several dozen hymns by heart, hymns that rang out through the church. Now, the singing rings hollow; indeed, the elderly don't even dare to participate. Mass is no longer a joy; it's not even restful. Lukewarm soup without much flavor.

Today, most grandmothers know nothing but Breton; their children are fluent in both languages; and their grandchildren speak only French. That's why Mass is celebrated in French; and too bad for the grandmothers. However, under ordinary circumstances, the parishes of Plozévet and Plonéour still speak Breton. It will take a long time to die out and will last as long as the people need it to express precisely what they are and what they want. Moreover, it is such a strictly private matter that some Bretons claim that the language they speak is not the same as that spoken by the people of Plozévet or Plonéour. Indeed, you often hear them say: "That bunch doesn't speak the same Breton that we do." It's somewhat true and also completely false. But the difference between that "somewhat" and that "completely" is enough to make Breton-speaking people from two different districts speak French when they meet. "What a pity," you may say, and I quite agree. But if there were only one Breton, an official Breton, I wonder whether those who have spoken it all their lives wouldn't relinquish it more quickly than they're doing already, given the pressure put on them to speak French. For if Breton were standardized, it would no longer be their own private possession.

That's why the ardent defenders of Breton have never managed to get unqualified support from the majority of those who have always spoken it. There are other reasons, I know. It's pointless to enumerate them here; that has already been done. Clearly, there will never be a peasant uprising to demand that Breton be taught in the schools; for the Breton-speaking Bretons of today have never been aware of belonging to an entity called Brittany, assuming that such an awareness existed in the past. They call themselves Bretons when they're outside of Brittany, but they aren't quite sure where it begins or ends. What they do know is that they belong to a specific region. They are Bigoudens, say, or Glazics, Meleniks, Dardoups, Bidars. Nothing more. They behave like members of a clan or of a tribe. But to my mind, such behavior is not only the best guarantee that their particular civilization will be maintained, but the best chance that the language they speak, with all its dialectal diversity, will survive. No political or official statute would be able to ensure its survival at the present time. Indeed, such a statute might well hasten its demise. Breton, which has been ignored, scorned, repudiated, forsaken, and persecuted throughout history, nevertheless continues to ring out imperturbably at the very tip of the Old World. And the number of people who will still be speaking it in the year 2000 is of no great importance. But I should not like the last of them to be shielded like those species of animals that are becoming extinct and are put behind bars. And when there is not a single one left, should that happen, it will mean that humanity is on its way to being unworthy of its name.

Our fathers had the reputation of being blunt and straightforward, stubborn and cantankerous. They would not have liked seeing their children scattered about like small change or, for that matter, catering to the tastes of the tourists. So let there be an end to local color, when it's that and nothing more. Let it be utilized, however, when it still really exists; that's fair play. Let us take advantage of the fact that Brittany is now a fashionable brand name; in that way we can make ourselves known, and I have no objection to that. Let us become as Celtic as possible, to the sound of Scottish bagpipes and even by planting fake menhirs in front of our neo-Breton houses; it might give me cause to smile a bit, but I wouldn't disapprove. Let our poets and our singers gather together huge and fervent crowds, to the accompaniment of harps, guitars, oboes, organs, spoons, and gadgets, and with thundering amplifiers; it would delight me, and all the more so in that a few of them are poets in the true sense of the word. On the other hand, I get a little impatient when I see certain noisy types masquerading under assumed super-Breton names, whereas they are absolutely incapable of uttering one sentence in that language. We must carefully skim the beef stock if we want it to nourish the coming generations.

Today, it is the children of the peasant civilization and of those who have spoken Breton all their lives—in other words, we ourselves—who are exposed to all the dangers and all the temptations. First, the temptation of snobbery, which leads some of us to use our language for purposes which can only be described as "social." A small and exclusive caste, the ladies in mink and the gentlemen in navy blue dinner jackets, all of whom speak Breton remarkably well—the Breton of the notary publics, the doctors, and the county councillors. Who speak Breton among themselves but no longer to the country people, for whom French is good enough. Also, the temptation of intellectualism, the kind that inclines one to create a literature that has little or no connection with the old oral substance of the language, and to study Breton but with contempt for the dialectal inventions and the deviations which constitute its vital throb, its dialectic, and its poetics. Politics and pedagogy would then prevail over creativity. No deviationism would be allowed any longer. That age-old language, which is free despite the grammarians and lexicologists of the last century, would be tightly corseted, and to what purpose, I wonder. The professionals persist in wanting one single orthography and no other, which would take away what is left of its freedom and, once and for all, bridle the poets who still believe in the virtues of breaks in syntax and in the importance of having a choice between a voiced and a mute consonant. Such are the chief concerns of very good minds, who are wasting their energy instead of using it more constructively elsewhere. But since those people are well-bred Armorican Celts, they can't come to an agreement. Ought I to say how lucky that is?

The last temptation is aggressiveness. It mostly affects the new generations, who had Breton-speaking parents or ancestors and who now find themselves frustrated at not knowing their own language—a heritage that should have come straight down to them. I well understand their frustration, which takes many forms.

But a few diehards have gone so far as to forbid their families to speak a word of French in their presence. The tables have been turned.

As for me, I was convinced that the accelerated mutation of the world would shortly lead to the demise of the milieu in which that language and that civilization—in other words, traditional peasant life—had flourished. But I also know that a civilization never dies altogether and that a language, even one no longer used (and that is far from true in the case of Breton), is a concern to scholars, who are trying to unravel and clarify the characteristic features of the world of today. The triumph of Latin as literature does not console us for our almost total ignorance of Etruscan. We are reduced to digging up the soil for nearly anything that will help to reconstitute, from its remains, the life of groups of peoples who for centuries had held the fate of the world in their hands. Archaeology, how many sandcastles have been built in your name! On the other hand, a language, however humble it may appear at its moment of decadence, is a far richer ground for excavations than forsaken plateaus, with problematical and, above all, mute ghosts moving about.

I am not speculating on the fate of Breton. It is not my business, but that of the coming generations. Yet I am not resigned to the Flood for all that. And I also refuse to wash my hands of it. I believe that the generation to which I belong, by the very fact that it's located at a critical point in the history of Breton, is duty bound to draw up an inventory of the civilization conveyed by that language. To be sure, that inventory would not be a last will and testament. But my Breton-speaking contemporaries will perhaps be the very last people to have spoken Breton on their mothers' laps. They must thus assume a responsibility, and one which is not the same as that of their predecessors or that of their successors. The latter were not much concerned with the fate of their idiom, even if they did consider it inferior to the many other voices that go to make up the concert of the world. The former will always have an excuse for their future helplessness: our having been inadequate at firmly establishing their heritage. It is therefore up to us to know and to proclaim the present state of affairs.

That is what I am attempting to do here, with no vain illusions and no pretension. But it would seem that the upheavals in society, the mindless destruction of nature, the waste of raw materials, the fear of atomic weapons, and a thousand other apprehensions are forcing our contemporaries to look into various other resources so that human progress will be ensured new possibilities. And why wouldn't the Breton-speaking civilization have a chance in the transformation that is taking place? That's the reason why any and every means possible should be used to maintain it, prolong it, and even upgrade it, by being fully aware of its significance. But it's later than we think and perhaps a bit too soon as well, because the loss that would follow from its demise is not yet easy to evaluate.

One of my militant friends has calculated that in the year 2000, in 25 years, there will be 25,000 Breton-speaking people. A large number in some respects, but very small if there aren't throngs of people around them so permeated with the civilization underlying the language (though it will be lost to them) that they may rightly and loudly assert their identity as Bretons. In other words, if we manage to achieve the rite of passage which consists, for example, in harmoniously introducing radome into the fundamentally Breton village of Pleumeur-Bodou, and thus into the huge shadow cast by the château de Kerduel, an obscure witness to the Round Table, the Armorican peninsula will again, in the year 2000, deserve to be called Brittany, instead of being designated mineralogically as some QX 29, an outlying suburb of the European section F 75, formerly called Gaul.

A century ago, Emile Souvestre wrote a book on *The Last Bretons,* and how many writers since have elaborated on that theme! But they were all too quick to roll us up in a hemp sheet, like poor corpses. Others contrived to gather up, here and there, scattered fragments of our heritage in order to enrich the history of humanity, if not to soothe their own nostalgia. Their harvest was abundant, but it was scarcely a hundredth of the whole. Unfortunately, there is not much material on the peasants in the written archives. I was in fact rather flabbergasted when I thumbed through a collection of the "red" newspaper *La Dépêche de Brest* dated 1924. I came across long passages on such events as the state funeral of Anatole France and on what was currently being performed at the Paris Opéra. I also saw a great many ads. But in the commune of Pouldreuzic (district: Quimper) apparently nothing ever happened. Besides, how would one come to know that in this obscure village the inhabitants didn't speak the same language as that of the newspaper? And because of the absence of illustrations, there would be no way of knowing that they dressed very differently from the bourgeoisie in all the Quimpers of France. Or doesn't that count?

After the arrival of the "travelers," the collectors, the folklorists, and an assortment of sightseers who took an interest in our customs without looking into them too closely, we were visited by the champions of the new social sciences. Was that a portent of our imminent demise? A request to put our affairs in order before leaving room for others? Or proof that our language and our civilization were of some interest, even though we were a sickly-looking lot compared to the natives of Central Africa or of Amazonas? The new seekers of the Grail, who were of such good will and fervor that they were touching, had undertaken to travel through the region, alone or in groups, having been commissioned to write a book or working up some dissertation for their universities. Not only were they methodical and armed with research projects, questionnaires, charts, statistics, and graphs, but they came with tape recorders and cameras dangling all over them. Of course, among those fishermen's apprentices in deep water, some were not at all competent; but most of the newcomers did a good job, though they had to admit it was a huge and tricky enterprise, even for multidisciplinary teams. The essential human element forever eluded them.

We know that to learn about societies, it is not enough to count, to measure, and to fill out file cards, and that that is no way to capture more than a shadow of people who conceal the reality of their being. The point is that our peasant civilizations are more difficult to analyze than the others, probably including the primitives. Those we call "savages" don't move about much and are confined to relatively small areas, whereas rural societies in twentieth-century France, especially those who speak another language, are in contact with the larger and aggressive society around them, and are in a constant state of metamorphosis, while at the same time they react in unexpected ways, which are native to them. Now after long experience, I am convinced that the most representative figures of the Breton-speaking people since World War II are the poor peasants. But the poor peasant takes refuge behind his poverty, claiming that he is of no interest to anyone. And people believe him. He remains silent and is ignored in favor of others who are talkative. But it is often the mutes who would have the most to say.

Although I went along rather often into the rural Breton-speaking areas with researchers from all countries, and recommended a number of people to them who could provide useful information, I did tell them what a mistake it would be to underestimate the resistance they might come up against on the part of the interviewees. I also warned them against the dangers of Bigouden humor, which has confounded more people than one might believe. I suggested that they beware of taking tall stories, told with the utmost seriousness, as tribal revelations. Moreover, there were a number of people around who had recently become rich and had forgotten they had ever been poor. Indeed, they could remember nothing whatever about their former circumstances. In contrast to the Horse of Pride, they are symbolized by the Ass of Vanity.

However, the most difficult obstacle the researchers had to overcome if they were seeking the truth was that of language. I have never understood how you could venture to do research in the Bigouden region without knowing Breton. You might have an interpreter, of course. But if an interpreter is not a member of the society being studied, he is constantly in danger of making mistakes in translation; or if he is an active member, though well integrated into the interviewer's civilization, he nevertheless has the same complexes as the interviewee. I have been told that all, or almost all, Breton-speaking people now speak French, which is true. But that "almost" excludes precisely those who are the best informants. I also know from experience that even the simplest French words have one meaning for Breton-speaking people and another for native French speakers. Take my mother, for example, whose French was perfectly decent. One day I brought some friends home to eat crêpes. When they apologized for having turned up unexpectedly, my mother replied, with a charming smile: "Vous ne m'intéressez pas du tout" ("You don't interest me at all"). Of course, she had meant to say: "Vous ne me déranger pas du tout" ("It's really no bother at all"). And if, in addition to such problems of vocabulary, one thinks of the two languages in terms of structure, it is easy to imagine how the meanings of questions and answers might be misconstrued. The perfect solution would obviously be not to ask any questions and to wait for the answers to become apparent after some acute observation and a little banal conversation. But that would take too long. And according to a Breton proverb, it takes seven years, seven days, and seven weeks to know with whom you're dealing.

I seem to be saying that researchers who don't speak Breton will never be able to draw up the necessary inventories. In fact, I am not saying that at all. We are in great need of them to tell us exactly who we are and, above all, where we are. But I must emphasize yet again the difficulties involved in such an enterprise, if only to apologize for my own mistakes. I have now spent fifteen years undertaking to gather material about the civilization into which I was born. Of course, I have always lived in the vicinity of my native region and have been fortunate enough to have kept many Breton-speaking friends and relatives, all of them informants to whom I could, and still can, have recourse when my memory failed or fails me. But my greatest debt with regard to the substance of this present work is to my mother Marie-Jeanne Le Goff, who died in 1973 at the age of eighty-three, and who helped me to recall the slightest details of my childhood and adolescence, along with invaluable background material. Besides, I had only to watch her live her everyday life to find myself immersed once again in a period when the modern pace of the world had not yet affected the stability of our society. She was also a talented storyteller, like her father Alain Le Goff and her father-in-law Alain Hélias, combining good sense and humor. But since she was a woman and a Bigouden, the subtlety of her stories was a necessary counterbalance to the male point of view. Now in my region it was the women who were worthy of being in command by dint of self-sacrifice, selflessness, and indomitable pride. Without them, there would be no way of explaining more than 25 percent of what we are. They're the custodians of profundity, whereas the men, more often than not, bear witness to the surface of things, except in the case of Alain Le Goff, my first master, and his peers, who are few in number but exist nonetheless. Seek and ye shall find them.

This book, with the exception of about thirty-six pages, was first written in Armorican Breton. It had to be, since my objective was to recreate a Breton-speaking people's civilization which had almost no contact with French civilization, at least during the first twelve years of my life. Whether or not this re-creation of mine will serve some purpose, the grandson of both Alain Le Goff and the sabot-maker of Kerveillant should not like to end without dedicating two of his tales, or rather two dreams he has had, to their memory, in the hopes of cheering them in the other world. Although they may find the substance strange, I trust they shall recognize the tone.

> I'm about to tell you a pleasant tale
> And you'll understand it straight through.
> Everything is true, detail for detail
> All, perhaps, but a word or two.

One day something very surprising occurred in France: the members of the government passed a law to the effect that Breton would be taught in every school in the land and to anyone who wished to learn it. No historian has ever managed to give an adequate explanation of what happened in the Chamber of Deputies that day. Some have written that the proponent of the bill got so caught up in his own words that he suddenly lapsed into Breton. And when the people's representatives heard those resonant and noble tones, they at once gave him their support. Actually, it wasn't the first time they had voted for a law they knew nothing about. But that's another story. Whatever the reason, the law was promulgated and the teaching of Breton was organized without delay.

Now no sooner had the news been circulated throughout the country than a great number of young people enrolled at the universities. There were not enough professors to satisfy their hunger to learn. In Paris and in Rennes the huge lecture rooms in which Celtic was being taught were filled to the rafters. Even the Bretons were rushing out to buy books in their own language, six of which were being published a day. In the elementary schools the children would sing the four forms of the present tense of the verb *to be* (*beza*) for an entire week, and on Sundays the priests were again chanting the Mass in Breton. Greek was permanently done for, and Latin had dropped to the level of Sanskrit. Grammarians throughout the world were undertaking to write very scholarly theses on the subject of the infix pronouns in the subdialect of Keriblbeuz. As for the ancient civilization of the Celts, all types of evidence had been discovered which ranked it, at the very least, with Egyptian civilization. And from then on, when the subject of "Our fathers the Gauls" was brought up in school, even the dunce at the back of the class was filled with respect: he knew who those people were. His teacher had come to know it as well, once and for all.

Within a few years every one of the townspeople in Brittany had given up French in favor of Breton. The country people followed suit and caught up with them rapidly, because they had kept Breton deep down in their throats. Of course, Provençal had already conquered the southern half of France, with the exception of a rather important area, between Bayonne and Bordeaux, which had veered over to Basque. But Breton was outdoing French from Nantes all the way to Lille; indeed, it was soon to encroach upon Belgium. And although French was still putting up a good fight between Chartres and Senlis, it had become sadly debilitated: its vocabulary lacked savor and its syntax was weak. Finally, the members of the government, all of whom spoke either Breton, Provençal, or Basque, ordered that a museum of honor be devoted to that dead language in the château of the ducs de Longueil, in Maisons-Laffitte, two leagues to the west of Saint-Germain, where the Musée des Antiquités Gauloises is located. So be it!

There you have my first tale, or dream. The second is altogether immoral.

During the twenty-first century the revolution which had begun with the bomb that fell on Hiroshima was complete. In Europe the last of the peasants had long since given up living in the country and had been transformed into workers on assembly lines in three huge cities. There was no longer any need to provide food for the populations, since factories were producing enough chemical pills and synthetic gruel to keep everyone alive. A few old people in the cities still vaguely recalled the taste of apples and pears, but not their shapes. In enormous laboratories the children of the former vine-growers were bottling a drink that looked like water but which had never flowed or run anywhere. The word *grape* had disappeared from the dictionaries.

Things had been moving very fast. After the peasants had abandoned the countryside, all the villages, towns, and small cities had fallen into ruins. As for the seashores, which had been covered by cement from end to end, and transformed into marinas, only the top executives and big contractors were allowed entry. They had worked hard to gain that privilege by having built the low-cost housing developments in the cities, wherever it had been possible to reclaim the land by felling trees. There obviously wasn't one bird left in the skies over any of the metropolises, and not a fish left within a hundred miles of the coasts.

The new masters, however, were residing in the country. They had been townspeople, and as shrewd as their funds were substantial. They had begun by buying up abandoned houses and tumbledown mills, which they restored in order to have a place in the country. The wealthiest of them had acquired entire farms and villages, where they would receive their friends. But they could no longer find anyone around to keep up their large estates or to serve them. So they themselves were forced to cut their own lawns, prune their own trees, care for their animals, and fight against wild vegetation. And what happened then was bound to happen. They began to love the land. They took pride in planting, picking, harvesting, and eating what they themselves had grown. They rediscovered the taste of fruit and even the taste of bread. Since they were businessmen, they got the idea of selling their choice produce to the city people. A thousand francs an apple. Their country homes soon became their only homes. And so it was that the former bourgeoisie became professional peasants, while the descendants of the former peasants were consoling themselves with electronic toys.

Finally, in order to live peacefully in the country, the new masters had the monstrous city housing developments, which were crammed full of poor devils, surrounded with barbed wire. They built watch towers armed with machine guns to keep the occupants from getting out. And once those aristocrats were alone among themselves, protected from the common people, they founded very exclusive regional clubs, the members of which were forbidden to speak anything but Provençal, Basque, and Breton.

With warmest regards.